MINING TOWN CRISIS

Globalization, Labour, and Resistance in Sudbury

edited by David Leadbeater

Fernwood Publishing • Halifax & Winnipeg

Editing: Scott Milsom
Text design: Brenda Conroy
Cover photo: Chris Elzinga
Cover design: John van der Woude
Printed and bound in Canada

Published in Canada by Fernwood Publishing
Site 2A, Box 5, 32 Oceanvista Lane
Black Point, Nova Scotia, B0J 1B0
and #8 - 222 Osborne Street, Winnipeg, Manitoba, R3L 1Z3
www.fernwoodpublishing.ca

Fernwood Publishing Company Limited gratefully acknowledges the financial support
of the Government of Canada through the Book Publishing Industry Development
Program (BPDIP), the Canada Council for the Arts and the Nova Scotia
Department of Tourism and Culture for our publishing program.

 Canadian Patrimoine
Heritage canadien The Canada Council for the Arts
Le Conseil des Arts du Canada NOVASCOTIA
Tourism and Culture

Library and Archives Canada Cataloguing in Publication

Mining town crisis: globalization, labour and resistance in Sudbury / David Leadbeater, ed.

Includes bibliographical references.
ISBN 978-1-55266-273-1

1. Sudbury (Ont.)--Economic conditions. 2. Sudbury (Ont.)—Social conditions. 3. Public
health—Ontario—Sudbury. 4. Labor—Ontario—Sudbury. 5. Globalization. 6. Working class—
Ontario—Sudbury. 7. Corporate power--Ontario--Sudbury. 8. Resource-based communities. I.
Leadbeater, David

FC3099.S83M55 2008   971.3'133   C2008-903366-3

Contents

Sudbury in North America

Preface

David Leadbeater

Sudbury, Canada, is the largest hardrock mining centre in North America and among the largest in the world. The Sudbury Basin region contains one of the world's richest nickel reserves and biggest nickel-copper-platinum group elements mineral deposits. The region is the historical base of two of the world's leading nickel-mining corporations, Inco Ltd., formed in 1886 as the Canadian Copper Company, and Falconbridge Ltd., established in 1928. Between the early 1900s and the 1960s, Sudbury mine workers of these two companies produced well over half the capitalist world's nickel. Based on their Sudbury-generated wealth, Inco and Falconbridge expanded across the globe to become major transnational corporations. In 2006, in a merger mania lubricated by escalating metals prices and profits, both companies were taken over, Inco by Companhia do Vale Rio Doce (CVRD), a Brazilian mining transnational, and Falconbridge by Xstrata Plc, a Swiss mining transnational. (For purposes of this book, we use the names Inco and Falconbridge, which are still commonly used in the community, although their official names are now Vale Inco and Xstrata Nickel.) Sudbury continues to mine and export its non-renewable mineral resources, and rumours and proposals continue to appear about further rounds of corporate takeover and consolidation.

Given that Sudbury is such a world-level centre of mining atop such enormous mineral wealth, one might think it would exude substantial prosperity, with well-provided cultural, educational, health and social-welfare institutions, and a well-maintained and attractive physical infrastructure. But this is far from the Sudbury most people know. Despite doing a major share of the Canadian economy's heavy lifting for well over a century, the Sudbury area *as a community* has relatively little to show for it. Nor is this likely to change — at least as long as the forces of and for corporate globalization continue to direct and dominate Sudbury's economic and political development.

Concerns about community conditions, social change, and future local development motivate this book. We will explore the impact of globalization and corporate power in a hinterland mining town — particularly their effects on working people — as well as how and why resistance has emerged. We will investigate alternative visions that envision a better future. While Sudbury is the book's specific focus, many other mining and resource-dependent communities have been through similar circumstances. There is much in the economic, social, and political experience of Sudbury to learn from.

The focus of the following chapters is on the decades since the 1970s, when globalization began to emerge. This has been a period of traumatic change for many Canadian mining communities: massive job losses, increasing unemploy-

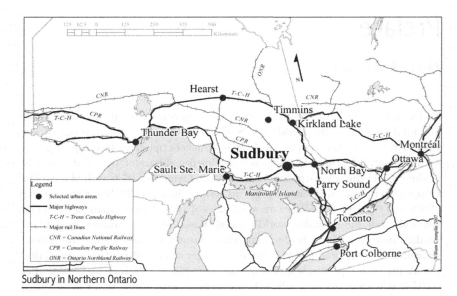

Sudbury in Northern Ontario

ment, poverty, and economic dependency, deteriorating living standards and social programs, and growing social polarization and strife. The current boom in metal prices and production cannot hide the deeper economic and social cleavages forming under the pressures of globalization.

It is not possible to address many important issues and aspects of Sudbury's current life and history within the limits of a single book. The local dimensions of political movements and parties, media concentration, sexual oppression, lesbian-gay-bisexual-trans-gendered rights and family policy, disability history, religious conflict and secularism, immigration and culture, public health, science and arts education, architecture and urban design are some of the many subjects that deserve detailed and critical study. For those who want to explore these and other issues further, several chapters contain references that can be useful points of departure.

Unless otherwise noted, the name "Sudbury" as used in this book refers to the area approximated by the City of Greater Sudbury (formed January 1, 2001) or Statistics Canada's Greater Sudbury Census Metropolitan Area, though boundaries for "the region" have varied over time. This region includes such communities as Azilda, Blezzard Valley, Boninville, Capreol, Chelmford, Coniston, Copper Cliff, Creighton (now demolished), Dowling, Falconbridge, Frood Mines, Garson, Hanmer, Levack, Lively, Onaping, Val Caron, and Val Thérèse, as well as such amalgamations as Valley East, Nickel Centre, Rayside-Balfour, and Walden. The region also includes at least two First Nations that are politically independent of the City. The region arose as a multi-centred area of geographically separated communities, developed around local mine sites, rail and agricultural infrastructure, and with particular cultural histories different from Sudbury proper. The use of the name "Sudbury" is a convenience and is not intended to diminish the concerns of smaller communities about regional inequities, forced amalgamations, or bigger-city chauvinism. Most residents, not known for formalism or pretence, do not refer to themselves as Greater Sudburians, and neither does this book.

Any discussion of the region and its name needs to emphasize that in and around the Sudbury area are several First Nations territories, the nearest two being Whitefish Lake First Nation and Wanapitei First Nation. Of course, the whole area was Aboriginal territory prior to colonization. In classic colonial form, the British-Canadian colonial state removed Aboriginal peoples from their lands and concentrated them into "reserves" to facilitate European resource exploitation, settlement, and expansion, particularly after the signing of the Robinson-Huron Treaty of 1850. Sudbury's name itself reflects that colonial past: it was named in 1883 by a CPR superintendent of construction after his wife's birthplace: Sudbury, England. There is an alternative, indigenous name. The Ojibwe name for Sudbury is N'swakawok (pronounced "swak-a-muk") meaning "where the three roads meet" (Jim Eshkawkogan, personal communication).

This project has benefited from the efforts, support, and knowledge of many individuals active in the Sudbury community, Laurentian University, and the labour movement, especially in the Sudbury and District Labour Council and in Mine Mill Local 598/CAW. Whether for their suggestions, stimulating discussions, manuscript feedback, organizational support, or thoughtful recollections, I would like to acknowledge, in addition to all the chapter contributors, Julian Ammirante, Sandy Bass, Bob Beck, Kaili Beck, Dieter Buse, Carrie Chenier, Pat Chytyk, Stuart Cryer, Charles Daviau, Peter Desilets, Buddy Devito, John Filo, Wayne Fulks, Marie-Luce Garceau, Peter Hudyman, Dan Hutchinson, Narasim Katary, Jennifer Keck (now deceased), Gary Kinsman, Joan Kuyek, John Lindsay, Brennain Lloyd, Brian MacLean, Frank Martins, Barbara Marion, Ralph Marion, Brian McDonald, Joanne Morassutti, Jules Paivio, Michèle Parent, Jane Pitblado, Mary Powell, Geoff Rheaume, Oryst Sawchuk, Laura Schatz, Alan Shandro, Daryl Shandro, Mike Solski (now deceased), Michael Southworth, Dave Starbuck, Mercedes Steedman, Mike Stolte, Peter Suschnigg, Jim Tester (now deceased), Terry Thompson, Sue Vanstone, Anne Watelet, Schuyler Webster, Harvey Wyers, and my Davenport friends. Kathleen Lord offered useful suggestions on my Preface and Introduction. Before he died, Ray Stevenson kindly granted me interviews and let me read a valuable section in manuscript form of his memoirs related to Sudbury, where he was a miner, communist, and elected Mine Mill leader. As is the required caveat, none of the above persons can be held responsible for what is said or not said in the following chapters: that responsibility belongs to the editor and the authors of each chapter.

A word about Laurentian University. Despite problems of corporatization and anti-labour bias common to many universities, it has faculty and staff unions and a significant number of faculty and staff members who work to provide a public space for free discussion, library and archival support, research expertise, and educational programs important to the region, including the Labour Studies program. The Laurentian University Research Fund has helped with funds in support of publication of this book as well as of some of my earlier research on mining communities. In hinterland communities burdened by heavy corporate and media monopoly power and dependency, the social value of such educational and research resources should not be underestimated.

The maps on pages 6, 8, 12, and 180 were produced by William Crumplin, a faculty member in the Department of Geography at Laurentian University. The maps were produced using ESRI ArcGIS 9.2 software and data, under licence, except for the following two sources. In particular, we acknowledge Statistics Canada's permission to use its boundary file for 2006 City of Greater Sudbury (adapted from Statistics Canada Census Metropolitan Areas and Census Agglomerations Cartographic Boundary Files, Catalogue 92F0166X, reference period), though with the standard provision that "the incorporation of data sourced from Statistics Canada within this product shall not be construed as constituting an endorsement by Statistics Canada of such product." As well, we acknowledge the Ontario Ministry of Northern Development and Mines's permission to reproduce MRD 126-Revised: 1:250 000 Scale Bedrock Geology of Ontario (Ontario Geological Survey, October 2006) © Queen's Printer for Ontario 2006.

During the last nearly two decades I have worked with many members in many unions in the Sudbury area, but I would like to mention with special gratitude the cooperation and support this project and other initiatives have received from Mine Mill Local 598/CAW. Like unions, independent publishers are crucial to sustaining democracy and critical thinking, and I would also like to acknowledge with appreciation the excellent work of the people of Fernwood Publishing, including Brenda Conroy, Cynthia Martin, Debbie Mathers, Scott Milsom, Beverley Rach, Errol Sharpe and John van der Woude. Lastly, and assuredly not least, Jane Leadbeater helped with organization, Kate Leadbeater helped with translation and poetry, and both gave their dad deeper reasons to see this book through.

Much of this book is critical of Sudbury's conditions and its corporate *status quo*. Such a critical stance is needed to develop alternatives to globalization and the corporate agenda, which offer working people, the poor, and youth little but economic insecurity and hardship, few prospects, further political disempowerment, and dollar culture. Sudbury is capable of making needed changes. Though screened out by corporate-dominated media, culture, and education, there is a progressive Sudbury, a Sudbury of working-class and socially progressive traditions, engaged workers, strong women, impassioned young people, feisty elders, free thinkers, and advocates against oppression and for democracy and justice. To this progressive Sudbury, I dedicate this book.

Introduction

Sudbury's Crisis of Development and Democracy

David Leadbeater

A crisis of economic development and democracy is confronting Sudbury and many other mining and resource towns in Canada's hinterlands. This is not simply about yet another boom-and-bust crisis, and not even about the next bust to come, though that too is a serious issue. This crisis is deeper and longer-term, and the current minerals boom will not end it. It is a chronic crisis of deteriorating living standards and social polarization. It is expressed in persisting high unemployment and economic dependency, deepening poverty, deteriorating working conditions and job quality, declining opportunity, and the outflow of the younger generation. The crisis is felt mainly by working people and their families, the poor, women, and Aboriginal people. It affects not only work and incomes, but also conditions of life outside the workplace, including health, education, community services, and public space.

Tied to the economic crisis is a crisis of the political system, of political democracy. The structures of government have become even less democratic, the rights of working people — the majority — have been diminished, as has access to a democratic media, culture, and education. The political crisis makes it more difficult to achieve solutions to longstanding problems of Aboriginal rights, French-English relations, and gender inequities. One does not hear about the nature of this crisis from the corporations that dominate Sudbury, their compliant media, or Sudbury's subservient political elite — in large part because of the vulnerable and increasingly limited democracy in which the people of Sudbury and other single-industry towns live.

Globalization is at the centre of the crisis. Emerging since the 1970s, globalization has profoundly and adversely affected the conditions of hinterland economic development and democracy, particularly by increasing the power of transnational corporations such as Inco and Falconbridge relative to labour and communities. While capitalism's inherent anti-labour and impoverishing tendencies existed long before globalization, globalization has accelerated these regressive tendencies and widened their impacts on larger numbers of people. As more people are affected by it, the crisis is becoming not only a crisis of labour, the poor, women, minorities, and youth and students, but also a *community* crisis.

Compared to other mining communities, Sudbury is actually better off in some ways, particularly with its relatively high level of public employment and services. If a "best case" could be made in Canada for external corporate mining-dependent development, then Sudbury would likely be its poster child.

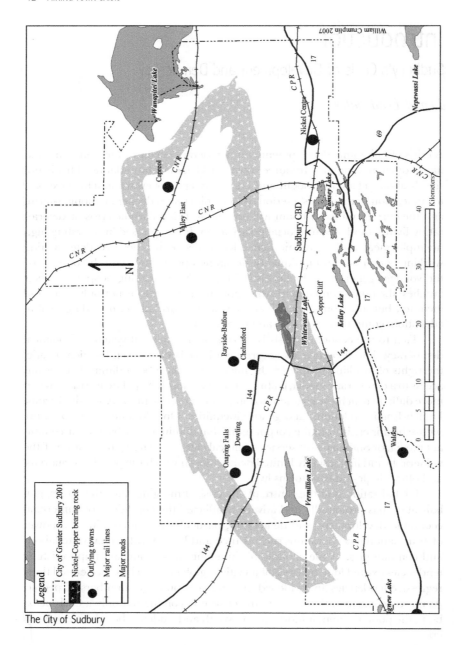

The City of Sudbury

Sudbury has massive reserves, a longer history of mining, larger-scale operations, and a more technologically advanced level of capital accumulation than other mining communities. But Sudbury turns out to also have important and current cautionary lessons about development and democracy in hinterland communities. Sudbury itself, and other communities, might want to ask whether Sudbury expresses a form of future development in kind or scale that other communities truly desire.

At the time of writing, the mining industry is revelling in riches from the current minerals boom. Nickel and other metals prices are at historical highs, demand is generally continuing to grow, and a merger mania has driven up mining share prices. For the moment, Sudbury has had a respite from decline and a small increase in employment and population, but fundamental distributional and social problems remain unresolved. Indeed, the merger mania in which Inco sold out to CVRD and Falconbridge to Xstrata reveals, with excruciating clarity, Sudbury's vulnerability to corporate globalization and to its political sidemen and sidewomen in local, provincial, and federal governments.

Discussing the new crisis helps address a related question resonant in Sudbury: why should a community that has produced so much wealth have so little to show for it? Sudbury is the largest hardrock mining centre in North America, it has one of the world's largest nickel reserves and nickel-copper-platinum group elements mineral deposits (Rousell et al. 2002), it has a large, highly skilled, and productive mine and community workforce, and its heavy lifting has supplied many billions of dollars worth of minerals to Canadian and world markets for well over a hundred years. Yet, as Sudbury enters the new century, it has a long-term pattern of below-average employment rates and employment income, high unemployment and poverty, abject homelessness and hunger, poor job prospects, and a continuing drain of younger citizens. And although much is said, rightly, about Sudbury's highly visible "re-greening," the region is still a major centre of environmental degradation and below-average human health conditions.

In fact, Sudbury fares very poorly on most measures of individual and community well-being. The prominent Sperling and Sander (2007) ranking of best cities to live in in Canada ranks Sudbury among the very lowest (26th) of twenty-seven Census Metropolitan Areas. The *Canadian Family* (2005) rating of the family-friendliness of forty-two Canadian cities has Sudbury in the bottom third, including very low marks for air quality, childcare, diversity, and culture. *Maclean's* 2003 health-care rankings of Canadian regions has Sudbury at fifty-second out of fifty-seven regions (it was sixteenth out of sixteen in 1999). A Statistics Canada study has Sudbury in the bottom 15 percent of Census Metropolitan Areas for the importance of the cultural labour force (Coish 2004: 16). And the list could go on.[1]

A key argument of this Introduction is that, for Sudbury and other hinterland communities, an alternative direction of economic and social development is both needed and possible. Social deterioration and community decline are *not* inevitable. But the necessary changes will not come from mining corporations or the corporate elite as a whole, whose interests since globalization have become even more antagonistic to a majority of the population. Neither is the local business class capable of or interested in leading a fundamental change of direction. The agency for change will have to come from elsewhere, from Sudbury's working people. Why this is and what it means form the main themes that follow.

Mining Towns and the Hinterland

Given the ongoing litany of inadequacy, inferiority, and blame foisted on hinterland communities, it needs to be emphasized at the outset that problems besetting mining communities in Canada and many other areas are not ones of "underdevelopment." Mining is a highly productive and technologically advanced industry: in fact, it is one of the most productive industries by capitalism's normal standards (CLSC 2004; Dungan 1997). A related distortion is that communities with unionized heavy industry are beset with a "sunset" industry or in a "rust belt" or somehow outmoded in a high-tech and "post-industrial" society. All these suggest backwardness and an inevitability of economic and social decline. Compared to many industries, the mining industry does display itself more visibly — in pollution, in decaying structures, in ghost towns, and in ravaged landscapes and bodies. Some images of mining pollution and devastation have become almost iconic, like the Inco "Superstack," or have been raised to the level of high-priced art, as in the photographs of Edward Burtynsky. Such scars, however, are more a testament to the exploitive power of the mining industry and to its considerable political success in shifting — or externalizing — its social costs onto workers and communities. They express little about Inco's or Falconbridge's ongoing high level of productivity, technological capacity, reserves, or profitability. Indeed, what Sudbury reveals is the impact in hinterland conditions of corporate capitalist development at a very high level. It is the opposite of underdevelopment.

Mining and other resource towns like Sudbury are commonly called "single-industry towns." This term reflects the fact that mining is the main or principal industry, as indicated by the fact that mining accounts for a high percentage of total local employment or of total local income. In recent decades, counts of the number of mining communities in Canada have ranged widely, from fifty-four, based on the percentage of local *employment* in mining, to 150 — nearly three times the first figure — based on the percentage of local *income* from mining (Leadbeater 1998: 3–4). Because mining has higher-than-average wages, a definition that uses income rather than employment tends to increase the number of communities identified as mining-dependent, or "reliant," which can boost the perceived importance of the mining industry. In one recent count, for 2001, Natural Resources Canada used an income definition and identified no fewer than 185 "mining-reliant communities" out of a total of 1,997 resource-reliant communities. (The others were 804 communities reliant on agriculture, 207 on fisheries, 652 on forestry, and 142 on energy, with the last including some coal-mining communities [NRC 2006b].) Greater Sudbury is classified as "moderately reliant" (30 to 49 percent of employment income from mining), based on its estimated 44 percent of income from mining: by contrast, direct mining employment has fallen to less than 13 percent of total local employment.[2]

Economically, the single-industry mining town exists as social and physical infrastructure, functioning directly or indirectly to support all or part of the mineral extraction process — the mining, milling, smeltering, refining, and transportation of minerals. Such towns typically have a number of supporting businesses or industries that provide producer goods and services as inputs to the primary industry, as well as consumer goods and services to the local labour force inside and outside the mining industry.[3] In this sense, the costs of such towns are part of the full costs of mining.

Being a single-industry mining town involves much more than simply a particularly high number or percentage of jobs or income from mining. It implies that the town is specialized to the extent that, as a whole, its population and economic well-being — even its very existence — depends on mining and the local export of minerals. If mining declines, other jobs and the local population also decline. In the extreme, without any of the wages, procurement, or profits derived from the mining industry, local demand and employment would decline to the point of disappearing. This has been the fate of the many "ghost towns" dotting hinterland areas, in which the primary industry closed or moved, and the rest — people, housing, and civic organization — disappeared on its own or, at times, by company fiat. Economists have used "economic base" models to help measure and predict the relationship between mining or primary-sector employment and total employment in single-industry towns and regions. The relationship is approximate and changes over time, altering by industry, local conditions, and public-sector presence, but the general pattern is widely known: as mining (or "base") employment declines, so does non-mining (or "non-base") employment, which means the effect on total employment is more than simply the loss of mining jobs, so the effect is "multiplied."[4]

When a town's employment declines so too does its population tend to decline. The effect may be delayed and reduced — for instance, by retirees who stay or by government stabilization policies — but a declining quantity or quality of employment will eventually impact population. Indeed, at times even the announcement or expectation of a future closure or layoff is enough for some people to move elsewhere. However, if unemployment is high across the economy, and particularly if there are not many jobs elsewhere in mining, then out-migration is less, so the community and region becomes a classic "labour reserve," marked by lower employment rates, higher unemployment, lower job turnover, out-migration, higher economic dependency, and poverty. Employment and household conditions have also been sharply marked by the class, gender, and racial hierarchies and segregation of the mining industry.[5]

Single-industry mining towns are also deeply affected by the distribution of "resource rents," which they produce but largely do not receive. Resource rents are that part of corporate profit (or revenue net of production costs) over and above an average rate of profit in the industry. Resource rents can be viewed as above-normal or windfall profits. In 2005, Inco's nickel unit cash cost of sales before by-product credits was US$3.04 per pound.[6] That same year, the average realized price of primary nickel was US$6.73 per pound, leaving a surplus value per pound of well over US$3.50. Nickel production costs in Sudbury at both Inco and Falconbridge have tended to be stable or decreasing, and are lower than the industry average. In 2007, the cash price of nickel reached over US$18 per pound. This big six-fold gap between price and costs — a huge private bonanza from public resources — gives a notion of the magnitude of resource rents that largely flow out of Sudbury and Northern Ontario. Even before the sale to Brazil-based CVRD, over half of Inco's common shareholders were outside Canada. Now, with Inco's shares absorbed and delisted from the Toronto Stock Exchange, the outflow of resource rents will likely be even greater.

The vast majority of these mining and other resource towns have developed and continue to exist as part of a hinterland to a particular metropolitan centre or group of centres. The metropolis-hinterland structure is a relation of both economic exploitation and political power that is fundamental to the pattern of regional inequality in Canada. Metropolitan centres are class centres of corporate power, financial control, and tribute, and a disproportionately large part of the profits and resource rents flow to them. For Sudbury, metropolitan power has been concentrated in Toronto and New York and, to a lesser degree, Montréal. The recent Brazilian and Swiss takeovers of Inco and Falconbridge suggest a shift toward metropolitan centres even farther removed.

Hinterland regions like Northern Ontario have a long history of colonialism (Nelles 1974; Coates and Morrison 1992) driven by resource exploitation. For colonizing or metropolitan capital the hinterland is a frontier for exploitation, for Aboriginal people it is a homeland, and for the permanent settler population it becomes a home region in a larger country. Local interests and external capital inevitably collide over the use, ownership, and control of resource wealth. Yet, in Northern Ontario, with over 80 percent of Ontario's land mass and about 800,000 people (about 8 percent of the provincial population), neither Aboriginal peoples nor the settler population have had any substantial degree of ownership or control over the resource wealth directly through their own democratic or sovereign institutions.

When it comes to evaluating the regional and social outcomes of mining-dependent development, the accumulating evidence is increasingly negative. In the United States, Freudenburg and Wilson (2002) conducted one of the broadest reviews of quantitative studies — amassing 301 findings — of the impact of mining on regional outcomes such as income, unemployment, and poverty. Their review concludes: "Until or unless future studies produce dramatically different findings, there appears to be no scientific basis for accepting the widespread, 'obvious' assumption that mining will lead to economic improvement" (549).[7]

For Canada, Stedman et al. (2004) used cross-sectional 1996 census data on 5,243 census subdivisions (roughly, municipalities), to examine the relation between resource-reliance and community well-being, defined in terms of educational status, five-year migration, family poverty, unemployment, and mean family income. The results were seen to support American research: "Mining places differ very little from rural CSDs [census subdivisions] as a whole: there are no significant differences in education, migration, poverty, and unemployment," except (in 1996) for relatively higher median family income. The point, however, is that such rural areas generally fare worse by such measures than non-rural areas. In an earlier study using community-level census data for 1981 and 1991, Bollman (1999) found that mining areas were associated with relatively lower levels of growth of aggregate community earnings, average earnings per worker, average hourly wage rates, and community employment.[8]

Development, Labour, and the Heavy Burden of Corporate Mining

Community development in mining towns has been shaped not only by resource dependency but also by a history of monopoly power and highly aggressive and exploitive relations with labour and the environment.

By 1900 the rise of the large-scale, highly capitalized, integrated mining and smelting corporation epitomized by Inco and later Falconbridge was requiring a much increased and relatively stable hourly and salaried workforce. This workforce, initially recruited from outside the Sudbury region, was conprised mainly of anglophones from Ontario, francophones from Québec and Eastern Ontario, and European immigrants (Gaudreau 2003). The source countries of these immigrants varied somewhat over the decades, but the immigrant working population was overwhelmingly white and European — mainly British, Finnish, German, Italian, Polish, and Ukrainian. The labour force soon became self-reproducing. By 1941, about half of Sudbury's population growth came from natural increase (Wallace 1993: 139).

Wage and salary earners and their families long constituted the overwhelming majority of the Sudbury labour force and population. The 2001 census found about 91.8 percent of all those engaged in remunerative activities in Greater Sudbury were waged or salaried employees, compared to averages of about 88.2 percent for Ontario and 87.7 percent for Canada. Of those remaining, about 4.3 percent were self-employed, 3.7 percent were employers, and 0.3 percent were unpaid family workers. The once overwhelmingly male working class had also become almost numerically more equal by gender: in 2001, about 49.0 percent of Sudbury wage and salary earners were female, compared to 48.6 percent for Ontario and 48.3 percent for Canada.

As Table 1 indicates, the population of the Sudbury region and city proper increased substantially in every decade from 1891 until it peaked in the 1970s. Through its own population growth and by annexation, the City of Sudbury grew even more rapidly than the region, to just over half the population in the region. In 1973, the region became a new tier of municipal government, the Regional Municipality of Sudbury.

Table 1: Population of Sudbury Areas, 1891–2006

Census Year	Sudbury Census Division (CD) (Territorial District)		Regional Municipality of Sudbury (RMS), 1973–2001	City of Greater Sudbury, 2001-	City of Sudbury (dissolved 2001)	City of Sudbury as % CD	City of Sudbury as % RMS
	pre-1973 Sudbury CD	post-1973 Sudbury District					
1891	4,842				1,000	20.7	
1901	16,103				2,027	12.6	
1911	29,778				4,150	13.9	
1921	43,029				8,621	20.0	
1931	58,251				18,518	31.8	
1941	80,815				32,203	39.8	
1951	109,590				42,410	38.7	
1956	141,975				46,482	32.7	
1961	165,862				80,120	48.3	
1966	174,102				84,888	48.8	
1971	198,079	29,031	169,580		90,535	45.7	53.4
1976	194,983	27,287	167,705		97,604	50.1	58.2
1981	186,847	27,068	159,779		91,829	49.1	57.5
1986	178,241	25,771	152,470		88,715	49.8	58.2
1991	187,388	26,178	161,210		92,884	49.6	57.6
1996	187,880	23,831	164,049	165,336	92,059	49.0	56.1
2001	176,814	22,894	153,920	155,219	85,354	48.3	55.5
2006		21,392		157,219			
2001 land area (km²)		38,350.5	3,365.0	3,354.3	262.7		
density (pop/ km²)		0.6	46.1	46.3	324.9		

Note: Of the three main geographical reference areas for Sudbury, the largest has been the Sudbury Territorial District, which originally comprised the village, town, and then City of Sudbury, as well as communities as far north as Chapleau, as far west as Espanola, Massey, and Webbwood, as far south as Killarney, and as far east as Markstay, St. Charles, and Warren. The next largest was established when the Regional Municipality of Sudbury was carved out of the Sudbury District that surrounded it. The Regional Municipality included the City of Sudbury and the then towns of Capreol, Nickel Centre, Onaping Falls, Rayside-Balfour, Valley East, and Walden. The third is Sudbury proper, which was first settled in 1883, incorporated as a town in 1893, then as a city in 1930. The forced amalgamation effected January 1, 2001, which dissolved the City of Sudbury and other municipalities, made a single-tier municipality covering an area approximating that of the Regional Municipality. Both Statistics Canada's Census Metropolitan Area for Greater Sudbury and its current Sudbury Census Division approximate the

Sudbury's growth came with very high costs. Among the more visible ones were many mine deaths and injuries, degraded environmental conditions, periodic layoffs, and inadequate health, educational, and cultural services. This occurred despite decades of high profits, expansion, and monopoly power — favourable conditions for any industry. One reaction to such criticism of Inco or other mining corporations has been that its behaviour is simply typical of any capitalist mining corporation, and that if Sudbury or any community wants jobs, then this is what one must expect and accept, however reluctantly. This is the classic "TINA" notion — "There Is No Alternative." No doubt there are some strong common tendencies in corporate behaviour — private profit maximization above all — but this does not mean that every existing corporate action is the only or best possible action, nor that the individuals running corporations are absolved of the consequences of their individual or corporate decisions. Comparative analysis across communities and countries shows that — even among mining corporations, as among other capitalist industries — there is a range of possible actions, whether on wages, health and safety, environmental regulation, gender equity, or taxation. Some are better or worse for labour, and some are better or worse for communities. Some actions, such as those with devastating impacts on human health and the environment, are more characteristic of mining or the mining industry, though this too can and has been changed to a significant degree. Some actions are also specific to Inco, which, even by the low social standards of capitalist ethical norms, has become recognized as an extreme case. As Inco's policies were bludgeoning Sudbury in the late 1970s, a leading corporate publication could run a cover story on "The Arrogance of Inco" (Ross, V. 1979). Ironically, the TINA flim-flam not only denies the major social achievements of unions and of environmental and other organizations critical of corporate mining, it also diminishes the efforts of those conscientious managers, geologists, engineers, and other staff who have not followed lockstep behind anti-social corporate policies.

Nonetheless, there are inherent class interests and tendencies in corporate mining that are expressed continually in a range of patterned actions that have debilitating consequences for workers and hinterland communities. Unions, environmental groups, and writers such as John Deverell (1975), Jamie Swift (1977), and Mick Lowe (1998) have documented Inco's and Falconbridge's numerous and continuing legal and contractual violations, destructions, and

---

City of Greater Sudbury. In 2001, the Census Metroploitan Area had a population of 155,601 and land area of 3,536.1 square kilometres, while the Census District had 155, 268 and 3,365.0, respectively. *Sources*: Sudbury CD: 1891–1971, Census 1951 (Vol. X), Census 1971 (92–702). Sudbury District: Census 1976 (92–804); Census 1981 (93–906); Census 1986 (94-111); Census 1991 (93-305). Estimate totals obtained by adding Sudbury District and RMS populations. RMS: City of Greater Sudbury based on Statistics Canada census data, accessed June 2007 at <http://www.greatersudbury.ca/content/keyfacts>. City of Sudbury: 1891, Thomson (1993: 33); 1901–1971, Census 1956 (Bulletin 3-2), Census 1971 (92–702); 1976–2001, City of Greater Sudbury above. Other population, land area, and density data for 1996–2006 from Statistics Canada, Community profiles, accessed June 2007 at <http://www.statcan.ca/>.

anti-social behaviours, in Sudbury and internationally. The pretence trotted out that Inco (or whatever corporate transnational) has a common interest with Sudbury is belied repeatedly by corporate decisions and practices. Here I select four major areas, using the example of Inco, to illustrate that many corporate actions are not merely incidental mistakes or isolated dubious judgements, but are repeated anti-social patterns reflecting the corporate class interest in private profits over workers, community health and the environment, local development, and peace.

First, Inco has shown itself incapable of overcoming its anti-labour interests and roots. From its earliest decades, Inco ran harsh anti-union, anti-democratic, and discriminatory workplaces and company towns. Complaints, union talk, or interest in collective action were met by reprisal and firings.[9] Workers eventually defeated Inco's intimidation, thuggery, and divisiveness and, on February 4, 1944, the International Union of Mine, Mill and Smelter Workers Local 598 achieved certification. But this did not end Inco's anti-labour impulse. In the face of Inco's tenacious opposition, unions won major improvements in wages, benefits, health-and-safety conditions, seniority, rights to grievance, protections against discrimination and harassment, and an important political voice in the community. But it took, and continues to take, innumerable grievances, legal battles, political actions, and strikes. Hans Brasch (1997: 5) estimates that, for Inco and Sudbury alone through 1997, strikes and production shutdowns — in 1958, 1966, 1969, 1975, 1978–79, 1982–83, and 1997 — totalled 847 days, nearly two and a half years.

Perhaps the most telling example of corporate class priorities has been the brutal health-and-safety conditions in Inco's underground and surface operations. Between 1890 and 1997, 674 persons were killed, 144 at the Creighton Mine and its surface operations alone (Brasch 1997: 674). Health-and-safety activists often recall Inco's sintering plant, whose horror of cancer and death Inco doggedly refused to recognize, against evidence and precaution. The 1976 independent Ham Royal Commission showed that Inco's injury rates were much higher even than other mining corporations, and conditons were much more dangerous than they had to be. Though Inco is the focus here, it needs to be said that the human consequences at Falconbridge were no less serious — 84 workers have died on the job at Falconbridge (Brian Macdonald, personal communication).

One must also emphasize the dogged unwillingness of Inco to deal with entrenched male domination in its operations (see Mulroy in this volume; Keck and Powell 2006). It is doubtful one could ever measure all the social subordination, loss of opportunity, harassment, and violence women have suffered as a consequence of this continuing social inequality, which has profited the corporation, and has served as a tool of political division among workers (Steedman 2006). Technological changes long ago eliminated whatever arguments could have been made about the "demanding physical conditions" of mining being a barrier to women entering blue-collar mining jobs, though it is not now and never was primarily a matter of physical conditions. For men too, the macho mentality, maintained in the corporate interest, also does great harm to male bodies (Messing 1995).

Second, Inco's corporate class interest has had a devastating effect on the regional environment and community health. Such environmental questions are not new. In earlier decades, it was evident that Inco's sulphur fumes were destroying local farming. When some farmers sued during the 1910s, Inco relied on establishment courts and on the technique of buying pollution "easements" to continue its destructive practices. This occurred despite the fact that, at the time, less damaging alternatives were not only known but had been implemented elsewhere (Dewees 1992). In later decades, Inco agreed to cover the cost to adjacent residents of repainting their cars corroded by its pollution, but more than a few residents wondered if such pollution could damage auto paint, what might be its damage to human health? After Inco built its Superstack, the tallest free-standing chimney in the world, some claimed it was a sign that the old profits-over-the-environment clash was ending. In fact, the Superstack was built only after major public and governmental pressure, including the passing of Ontario's Clean Air Act in 1967. Although the Superstack helped dissipate Inco's emissions and reduce Sudbury's pollution index, Inco and Falconbridge in 1980 were still releasing over one million tons of emissions annually and were the largest source of acid rain in North America (Buse 1993: 257–58). Even in 2001, Inco was still by far the worst mining polluter in Canada, emitting 704,808 kilograms of poisonous heavy metals, including lead, arsenic, nickel, cadmium, and mercury, and Sudbury was still its major source (EDC 2003).

The full story is still to be told about how successful Inco and corporate mining have been in shifting their costs to the public. In the mid-1970s, a secret federal study estimated the environmental damage done to Sudbury in economic losses, health costs, and reforestation at $465 million annually. When asked who should pay for the clean-up, Inco replied that it should be paid — though it didn't want to say so openly — by the public (Buse 1993: 258). Indeed, these costs were and continue to be largely paid for by the public, both by governments and by individuals through their health care and other costs, some of which are still not fully appreciated. Despite miserable, life-shortening community health indicators (see Nagarajan in this volume), Sudbury still does not have an independent public accounting of the social costs of the mining industry.

Third, Inco and corporate mining priorities have had a stifling effect on Sudbury's, and on Canada's, industrial development and diversification. From the early days of mining in the region, corporate loyalty has been to the flags of profit and empire, and especially the American empire. Inco has resisted efforts to develop refining and value-added activities in both Sudbury and Canada. At first, Inco threatened to close down its Sudbury operations and shift to New Caledonia if it were forced to locate a refinery in Canada (Nelles 1974: 327). It was not until 1918, in the wake of governmental threats and the scandalous wartime export of nickel to Germany, that Inco built a refinery in Canada, at Port Colborne. Inco did not deign to move its headquarters to Canada until 1972,

to Toronto. Inco's major research centre, Sheridan Park, is located in Southern
Ontario, at Mississauga. The centre of its world marketing remains in suburban
New Jersey, though the United States currently has no operating nickel mines.
In 2005, Inco announced the closure of its Sudbury copper refinery, meaning a
loss of 150 well-paid jobs. After many decades, Sudbury still lacks a diversified
industrial base, particularly in value-added industries.

Fourth, corporate mining's interests have repeatedly put it on the side of
profiting from war and empire. Though not all end-use of nickel has been for
military purposes, much has been. In its earliest years, the industry promoted the
use of nickel-steel plate for the American and European navies, and it rapidly
expanded its interest in the armaments race leading to World War I, and in that
war itself. Tanzer (1980: 155–56) observes that in the pre-war armaments race
Inco increased its Sudbury production four-fold and averaged a profit rate of 50
percent, with 40 percent of Inco's production going to the German armament
business prior to the 1914 outbreak of war. The controversy over Inco's involvement in the export of nickel to Germany during World War I is well known
(Bray 1993). Less has been said about its involvement in support of German
remilitarization and fascism, which came out in the Nuremberg war-crimes tri-
als.[10] World War II was another boom for Inco, as were both the Korean War
and the Cold War. During the Cold War, the American government built up
major strategic stockpiles of minerals, including nickel, most of which came from
Sudbury. A royal commission study reported that, as of 1955, about 40 percent
of all new production was for defence and stockpiling purposes (Davis 1957:
75). There is still no public monitoring of military uses of Canadian nickel and
other strategic minerals.

The profit connection to war and empire includes a classic marker of imperi-
alism — securing mineral wealth in foreign countries. There have been numerous
reports of Inco's involvement with brutal dictatorships such as in Guatemala and
Indonesia, neocolonial settings with limited labour and environmental regulations
and enforcement.[11] In 2006, the Sudbury and District Labour Council helped
sponsor a visit and exhibition by Marlon Garcia Arriaga, a Guatemalan artist
and photographer, part of whose work has documented the genocidal actions
of the American-backed Guatemalan governments of the late 1970s and 1980s.
Many indigenous Guatemalans believe Inco was complicit in such atrocities.[12]

These four aspects of corporate mining would be a social indictment of
corporate mining even in conditions of growing employment and community
prosperity. But the new crisis of hinterland development, which offers even fewer
benefits to the community, challenges whatever residue of social legitimacy
remains of corporate mining, and of development based on it.

Globalization and the New Crisis

For the metal mining industry, and for hardrock mining communities like Sudbury,
most decades from the 1940s to the 1970s saw overall growth, despite periodic
booms and busts.[13] Inco's and Falconbridge's monopolistic positions were still

strong. As late as 1961, Canadian sources, which included Inco's Thompson, Manitoba, operations after 1956, still provided about 70 percent of the capitalist world's supply of nickel (Davis 1957: 73). As well, the post-war decades saw a major expansion in government-driven employment and transfer programs, education, health care, social services, transportation, and municipal infrastructure. From a single-industry town, Sudbury — and many other resource towns — became a type of "two-industry" town, maintained by the public sector as well as by mining (Table 2). This two-industry character somewhat reduced, but did not end, dependence on mining employment. It also opened some job opportunities for women, who had been largely excluded from the male-dominated mining industry.

Beginning in the 1970s, however, economic conditions deteriorated sharply. The advanced capitalist countries entered a new phase, one with generally slower growth. Annual GDP growth rates averaging 4.9 percent between 1950 and 1973 fell to 2.6 percent between 1973 and 1989 (Maddison 1991). International competition intensified during this period, and capitalism internationally went through a structural change now commonly called "globalization." Globalization has several features, such as international integration of financial markets, but the one most evident in mining communities and the element on which I focus here is the massive increase in the concentration and centralization of capital, to the point where a relatively small number of transnational corporations have come to dominate production and trade, internationally as well as domestically (Dunning 1997: 16). Transnational corporations still have their ownership bases and control centred in particular countries and metropolitan centres, but a much increased portion of their profits, production, and reserves — for many, a majority, and their largest prospect for expansion — is outside the home country of their ownership base. By 1990, the four largest diversified mining corporations held about 15 percent of capitalization in the mining sector worldwide and, by 2002, about 30 percent (Humphreys 2005). And, the process of concentration and centralization continues. In 2005, before its $19-billion sale, Inco reported assets of US$12 billion and had 11,707 employees, while CVRD had assets of US$22.6 billion and 38,560 employees. In 2006, a matter of months later, CVRD controlled total assets of US$61.0 billion and had 52,646 employees.

It is the class interest of the main owners of these transnational corporations that is the driving force behind globalization and the package of right-wing government policies — called "neo-liberalism" (and "neo-conservatism" by some) — that has extended and reinforced transnational corporate power. Neo-liberal policies include "free trade," deregulation, subcontracting, privatization of public enterprises, weakened regional policy, and reduced social program standards. The economic and political tendencies of globalization have conjoined in Sudbury and other mining communities to create a new crisis in hinterland development. The following are its five key features.

First, there was an increase in mining productivity so massive that it permitted an absolute reduction in employment while production was maintained or even

Table 2: The Sudbury Labour Force by Industry, 1951–2001

	1951	1961	1971	1981	1991	2001
All industries (number of persons)	40,326	38,869	59,215	66,140	81,245	77,640
With industry specified	39,826	37,880	58,365	65,840	80,025	75,945
Mining	11,134	12,450	14,755	10,290	8,725	4,840
Other primary (inc. agriculture, forestry)	3,734	271	255	540		545
Manufacturing	8,146	4,998	8,665	7,920	6,345	4,870
Construction	2,923	2,317	5,940	3,360	5,770	4,415
Transport, communication, utilities	3,867	2,488	3,820	4,370	5,235	5,905
Trade (wholesale and retail)	3,851	5,576	8,115	12,040	14,470	12,595
Finance, insurance, real estate	537	994	1,695	2,810	3,585	3,115
Services	5,634	7,129	12,585	19,940	27,805	33,445
Public administration		1,657	2,535	4,570	8,090	6,215
All industries (percent of specified)	100	100	100	100	100	100
Mining	28.0	32.9	25.3	15.6	10.9	6.4
Other primary (inc. agriculture, forestry)	9.4	0.7	0.4	0.8		0.7
Manufacturing	20.5	13.2	14.8	12.0	7.9	6.4
Construction	7.3	6.1	10.2	5.1	7.2	5.8
Transport, communication, utilities	9.7	6.6	6.5	6.6	6.5	7.8
Trade (wholesale and retail)	9.7	14.7	13.9	18.3	18.1	16.6
Finance, insurance, real estate	1.3	2.6	2.9	4.3	4.5	4.1
Services	14.1	18.8	21.6	30.3	34.7	44.0
Public administration		4.4	4.3	6.9	10.1	8.2

Note: Smelting and refining is considered primary manufacturing and throughout has been by far the largest component of manufacturing in Sudbury. The "services" category includes public-sector funded health, education and social services as well as private-sector business and personal services. In 1951, public administration is included in services. In 1991, other primary is included in mining. During the period, industry classification has had several small changes, especially for services, so intercensal comparisons must be treated as approximate. Statistics Canada uses the experienced labour force concept. This takes in employee and self-employed persons, including some who are unemployed at the census date but who were recently employed in the industry. For 1961 on, the data are for persons 15 years of age and over; for 1941 and 1951 they are for 14 and over; for 1931 they are for 10 and over. Totals may not appear to add due to rounding. Data for 1961 on are for the Sudbury CMA and, for 1951, are for the Sudbury Census Division. *Source*: Statistics Canada, Census of Canada, 1951 (Vol 4, Table 18), 1961 (94-519), 1971(94-757), 1981(93-966), 1991 (95-349), 2001 (95-239).

increased. Total employment in mining fell absolutely from the 1970s through most of the following decades. Sudbury, at peak in the 1970s, had around 25,000 jobs in mining, but by 1991 it had under 10,000, and it currently has below 6,000. Mining towns were confronted, not only with periodic booms and busts, but with a long-term downward employment trend or, at best, stagnation.

Significant increases in productivity were in process before the decisive shift to globalization in the 1970s (Clement 1981: 112), but the growth of nickel production outside Canada, and outside Inco, increased competitive pressures. Inco and Sudbury's near monopoly (outside the Soviet Union) dropped to a world market share under 20 percent by 2005. Increases in productivity would likely have occurred even under conditions of exclusively national or public rather than international corporate ownership. But the pressures of globalization speeded up technological changes such as dieselization, and managerial pressures reduced staffing and intensified work through such programs as "lean production," "team," and "Six Sigma."

Second, there has been a massive increase in the concentration of capital and monopoly power, both domestically and internationally, which has caused a shift in the balance of power toward the transnational corporations, like Inco and Falconbridge in Sudbury, at the expense of labour and local communities. On one hand, workers and communities face poorer employment conditions, while on the other, capital has, for example, more alternative mines, sources of supply, and additional access to finances. When challenged, capital can more easily threaten to go elsewhere, which further strengthens its already substantial power against even relatively strong unions.

An example of this shift was Falconbridge's 2000–01 strike against Mine Mill/CAW. This marked the first time since unionization where one of the Sudbury mining corporations dared to maintain production using scab labour. The smaller size of the Mine Mill bargaining unit and the new availability of feed from Falconbridge's Raglan mine had weakened the union position even before Falconbridge made use of Conservative pro-scab labour legislation and abusive police power.[14] The Mine Mill/CAW union was able to overcome this hostile situation, but it took a bitter seven-month strike, and for a while the union's existence as an effective force hung in the balance. Falconbridge claimed the strike cost it $30 million. For the workers and the community, it was much greater. The CAW alone spent nearly $10 million on strike pay. Despite Falconbridge's anti-social conduct and mismanagement, the corporation's overall reported profits were double those of 1999. This experience also illustrates how the scale of "diversification of risk" by transnational corporations increases costs and reduces accountability to local groups of workers and communities.

Increased corporate concentration and monopoly have gone beyond mining to dominate most parts of the local private sector — from box stores to supermarkets to financial services to hotels and restaurants to fast food to "convenience" stores — whether through directly managed operations, or distributor or franchise arrangements. Though these corporate operations are generally larger than local businesses, workers have so far been able to unionize only a small number. Weakened bargaining power for workers, whatever the sector, has negative distributional effects, such as lower local wages, poorer working conditions and benefits, decreased employment security, and increasing subcontracting. For the resource sector, it further disadvantaged labour and communities in the distribution of the benefits of productivity gains and also on who shouldered the huge community costs of mining industry "downsizing."

Third, there has been as a major shift in government policy toward cutbacks in social programs and public employment. Even as economic conditions in hinterland areas have deteriorated, federal and provincial governments have reduced standards in a variety of social programs (particularly social assistance and unemployment insurance), weakened labour and collective bargaining standards, eliminated or diminished support for social housing and regional development, privatized a range of public enterprises such as Air Canada, CN, and PetroCanada that are of importance to hinterland areas, reduced funding to education and healthcare, and cut or subcontracted jobs in public administration. The initial sharp edges of cuts were most visible federally under the Mulroney Conservatives (1984–93), the Chrétien Liberals (1993–2003), and also provincially under the Harris Tories (1995–2002). But even the provincial NDP government of Bob Rae (1990–95) shifted toward neo-liberal policies, though less rapidly (Walkom 1994), or saw centre-left policies later reversed (Haddow and Klassen 2006). What has been crucial, however, has been not so much the pace of change as its direction, which has been in a systemically anti-labour and anti-community distributional direction in terms of social program standards, taxation policy, worker rights, and social ownership.

The efforts of neo-liberal governments to reduce access to social programs and to further stigmatize welfare and the poor has hit hard in the high-unemployment hinterland areas. These changes have come as no surprise. With the Liberal federal government's cutbacks to unemployment insurance effected July 1, 1996, it was actually known in advance in Parliament that forestry and mining would be the industries with the two largest cuts to benefits. By 1997, only 33 percent of unemployed workers in Sudbury were receiving benefits (CLC 2005). Sudbury has a large number of injured workers, so the provincial Harris Conservatives' attacks on workers' compensation had major significance. As compensation activist Peter Hudyman recounts, the Conservatives "gutted benefits, reduced retraining, reduced the pensions, contracted out services, the tone changed with the Board, and they eliminated labour representation, made it more difficult to appeal, and got rid of the Occupational Disease Panel" (Hudyman, personal communication July 2007).

Fourth, the growth of resource extraction and consumption has faced more environmental limits, both at the local and national levels. Not only has the number of large, easily accessible mineral deposits diminished, but environmental legal restrictions, health concerns, and conflicts with other industries, such as tourism, have also increased. Further, there has been rising social concern, not only about local or regional issues such as acid rain, but also about global impacts, most notably climate change. The shift has been reflected in environmentalists' challenges to resource industries such as those brought by organizations like Northwatch and MiningWatch Canada, in stronger environmental policies in the labour movement, and in widening public support for "sustainability." Such resource and societal limits continue to emerge in contradiction to and despite the still-dominant neo-liberal trend.

Fifthly, extensive resource development has faced increased political and legal resistance from Aboriginal peoples over fundamental questions of sovereignty and land claims. The fact that the ownership and governance of resource lands are contested by actual or potential sovereign peoples is not necessarily, in itself, an absolute limit to the expansion of corporate resource exploitation: capitalist mining corporations have long conducted production and export across sovereign frontiers. However, within Canada, as limited as this emerging sovereign power may currently be, it has altered the reach of corporate power and forced a degree of redivision of the profits and economic benefits from resource exploitation. An example of the change since the 1990s is the emergence of so-called "Impacts and Benefits Agreements" negotiated by Aboriginal peoples with mining corporations. The terms of such agreements and the strategy behind them are the subject of some debate, including among Aboriginal peoples themselves, but the existence of such a negotiated process puts Aboriginal peoples ahead of most non-Aboriginals and local and regional governments in challenging the power of mining corporations.

Overall, the new conditions of globalization since the 1970s have fundamentally transformed development prospects for hinterland communities and labour. Not only has the balance of power shifted further away from labour and communities, but simplistic growth policies based on expanded resource extraction have also lost credibility. Resource extraction has either been increasingly constrained by availability or access or, when permitted, has been much more limited in its local employment and income benefits.

Consequences

The crisis of hinterland development has had adverse long-term consequences for most of Sudbury's people, and it has done so by intensifying the impoverishing tendencies of capitalism. The effects have been numerous, though here I can summarize only some major consequences: employment, unemployment, bankruptcy, economic dependency, relative and absolute poverty, incomes, earnings, and distribution.

There has been a long-term decline in employment rates, in both the quantity as well as the quality of jobs. There have been major losses of higher-paid and unionized jobs, as employment has become more insecure and local prospects have diminished. This has occurred mainly through massive job cuts in the mining industry, but it also occurred in the 1990s with job cuts in the public sector. As can be seen in Table 3, male employment rates shifted sharply downward,

Table 3: Employment and Unemployment Rates for Sudbury, Ontario, and Canada, 1951–2001

	1951	1961	1971	1981	1991	2001
Employment rates (%)						
Both sexes						
Sudbury	54.3	54.7	57.2	56.6	59.9	56.3
Ontario	54.1	55.0	57.8	63.4	63.6	63.2
Canada	51.8	52.0	53.4	60.0	61.0	61.5
Males						
Sudbury	84.1	81.1	78.7	70.9	67.0	59.9
Ontario	82.6	78.2	75.4	76.0	70.7	69.1
Canada	80.0	74.9	70.8	73.1	68.6	67.2
Females						
Sudbury	16.7	26.0	33.5	42.7	53.1	52.9
Ontario	25.6	39.1	40.6	51.3	56.9	57.6
Canada	23.1	28.8	36.4	47.3	53.8	56.1
Unemployment rates (%)						
Both sexes						
Sudbury	1.2	3.3	6.2	8.2	8.6	9.2
Ontario	1.0	3.3	6.9	5.6	8.5	6.1
Canada	1.7	3.9	7.9	7.4	10.2	7.4
Males						
Sudbury	1.1	3.1	4.6	6.4	8.2	9.9
Ontario	1.0	3.5	6.0	4.6	8.6	5.8
Canada	1.8	4.2	7.3	6.5	10.1	7.6
Females						
Sudbury	1.7	4.1	10.0	10.8	9.1	8.4
Ontario	1.1	2.8	8.2	6.9	8.4	6.5
Canada	1.6	2.9	8.8	8.7	10.2	7.2

Note: The table uses Ontario for comparison, not only because Sudbury is in this jurisdiction, but also because until recently Ontario has been considered one of Canada's two most wealthy, or "have," provinces.. *Source:* Census of Canada 1951 (Vol. 5, Table 2), 1961 (94–533), 1971(95–749, 94–772), 1981(93–966), 1991 (93–338), 2001 (95–220).

from being above or at the average for Ontario and Canada from 1951–71 to below it in 1991 and much below it in 2001. Female employment rates tended to rise over the period until hit with public-sector and service-sector job cuts: however, female employment rates, reflecting the segregating effects of the mining industry, tended to be below the rates for Ontario. Overall, Sudbury went from having a higher employment rate than the average for Canada and one similar to Ontario in 1971, to a situation, in 2001, of more than 5 percentage points below the average for Canada, and even further below the average for Ontario. Though the gap has since narrowed in light of the current mineral boom, the Sudbury employment rate is still below the Ontario and Canadian averages. The Northern Ontario and Northwestern Ontario employment rates are even further behind.

There has been an upward shift in rates of unemployment, for both men and women, but experiences by gender have been different (see Table 3). For men, unemployment rates in the earlier decades were below the averages for Ontario and Canada, but by 1981 rose rapidly above both those averages. For women, the segregating effects of the mining industry led to unemployment rates that were higher than average for Ontario and Canada in all census years, except for 1991 for Ontario, likely due to then increasing public-sector employment. Overall, mining areas like Sudbury became more like other low-employment-high-unemployment hinterland areas.

Bankruptcy rates were also much higher than average. In 2001, Sudbury had about 645 consumer bankruptcies or 4.2 per thousand of population, nearly double the average for Ontario (2.2 per thousand, while Canada was 2.6 per thousand). Business bankruptcies were also significantly higher: 64 or 0.41 per thousand of population compared to 0.27 for Ontario and 0.33 for Canada. Such high levels of bankruptcy have high household and community costs. They are also a salutary warning to those who simplistically promote small business start-ups as the key solution to Sudbury's economic development.

Economic dependency on social programs has increased from below to well above federal and provincial averages. In 2004, the economic dependency rate on government transfers for men for Greater Sudbury was 14.5, compared to 9.3 for Ontario and 10.8 for Canada. For women, the rate was 29.3, compared to 21.2 for Ontario and 24.1 for Canada. These factors help account for the higher rate: lower average labour earnings, more people needing social programs such as unemployment insurance, and, for those using social programs, more benefits were needed, due, for instance, to longer durations of unemployment.

Poverty rates, as indicated by Statistics Canada's Low Income Cut-Off, suggest that Sudbury's overall poverty rates are near average for Ontario and somewhat below the average for Canada (Lee 2000). However, much depends on Sudbury's relatively low rate for older age groups, which is bolstered by Sudbury's large number of retirees living on employer and union-negotiated pension plans. Poverty rates for younger persons (below 35) tend to be higher than average for Ontario and similar to those for Canada. Unattached younger persons, especially women, have higher rates than both Ontario and Canada. Further, Kauppi (1999) has shown that child poverty rates were higher in Sudbury than both Canada and Ontario (30.2 percent for the City of Sudbury and 22.4 percent for the Sudbury Region in 1996).

Absolute destitution is also substantially present in the midst of Sudbury's enormous mining wealth. Several surveys of homelessness in the early 2000s found that, even using a conservative service-use-based measure, there were nearly 500 homeless persons, and the situation was persisting if not increasing (Kauppi 2002). Hunger and food insecurity is also much greater than is generally appreciated (see Suschnigg in this volume).

As might be expected, higher unemployment, poverty, reduced job quality, and cuts to social program standards have led to both relative and absolute declines in incomes and earnings. In earlier decades, Sudbury and other mining communities tended to have much higher than average wages and incomes. But in 2001, the census estimated average earnings from full- and part-time employment in Sudbury to be $31,063, about 12 percent lower than Ontario's average and 3 percent lower than Canada's. Women in Sudbury earned about 62 percent of men. Even those who worked full-time and year-round were below the Ontario average and only slightly above the Canadian average. My analysis of income tax return data shows that average real income in Sudbury has either stagnated or declined over most years of the1990s and into the 2000s. In 1993, real average wage and salary income was $28,800, higher than the averages for Ontario and Canada, while in 2003, adjusted for inflation, it had dropped to $24,150, or about 20 percent, to below both the Ontario and Canadian averages. Even in the mining sector, where in the past unions had more bargaining power, analysis of collective agreements shows there was a stagnation of base rates, and even some years of real decline, from the late 1980s to the early 2000s.[15] These earning patterns occurred despite increasing productivity. If one goes beyond market income to include pensions and social-program income, the picture is somewhat better, though only for families: for single parents it is sharply lower. However, market income is generally a clearer long-term indicator of tendencies in the labour market.

Social disparity within Sudbury has also grown. Looking at earned wage and salary income, the disparities are major. In 1993, the lowest 60 percent of earners made 25.9 percent of all earnings, while the highest 20 percent made 47.8 percent. In 2003, the share of the lowest 60 percent had fallen to 21.7 percent, while the highest 20 percent had increased to 51.7 percent — over half of all wage and salary earnings in the community. Even the average of this highest-paid 20 percent declined in real terms and relative to the high-earner average for Ontario and Canada. This reinforces how poorly the majority of Sudbury's wage and salary earners fared. Without social programs, there would have been mass and rapid impoverishment of a kind not seen since the Great Depression. The current boom in mining earnings and bonuses as well as the new medical school and some hospital expansion may alter this pattern for upper incomes, at least in the short-run, but the disparity will remain large and could increase further.

The above patterns have their human side in many individual and family stories of hardship, loss, and broken hopes of those who have been subjected to the capitalist "adjustment" process in hinterland areas. Neo-liberal cuts to social program are making the consequences worse, even deadly, such as in the tragic case of Kimberly Rogers (see Kuyek in this volume).

Democracy and Merger Mania

Globalization is having a destructive effect on democracy, including local democracy, which is especially important in mining communities, where corporate power is more concentrated and where the local business class has tended to collaborate with the transnational corporate agenda.

Sudbury is a class-divided community with a deep experience of struggle between labour and capital. To paraphrase Marx's well-known observation, the history of Sudbury has been a history of class struggle. The complex and clashing forces of the mining corporations, the local business class, and labour are central to understanding community power in Sudbury as well as the direction of local development and well-being. On the face of it, mining communities have an interest in strong unions: union bargaining power redistributes a portion of the benefits of mining productivity increases and resource rents not only to union members but to the larger community. More money in pockets and purses increases local demand for the goods and services of local businesses and, through increased tax revenues, improves public services. Union gains also exercise an upward pressure on the wages, benefits, and workplace rights of other workers, which some local employers actively resist. Sudbury unions have seen numerous examples of material and moral support from some individual local business owners, but they have also seen examples of local businesses fighting union recognition, harassing union supporters, using scabs to break strikes, and other typical and often illegal measures to deny workers' rights.

In municipal politics, the community interest of labour and local business sometimes converges against transnational corporate interests. In 2005, under pressure from the labour movement, City Council felt compelled to assert a community interest and declared its opposition, by resolution, to Inco's closure of the Copper Refinery and the loss of 150 jobs. However, more often the corporate class interest reasserts itself against local labour and the community interest. A majority of Council a year earlier supported a strike against its own workers at Greater Sudbury Utilities, which aimed to take away retiree benefits. The same Council, responding to a corporate request, also weakened the municipal retail closing by-law against the clear opposition of the RWDSU, the main retail union, and the Sudbury and District Labour Council. Overall, the corporatized view of municipal government as a service-delivery organization to local "customers" has been replacing the concept of municipal government as a centre of democratic political expression and action.

While local labour has resisted numerous elements of globalization, the local business class has accepted and even openly supported the expansion of transnational control from outside the community. In one form or another, its dominant outlook has been "What's good for Inco (or corporate mining) is good for Sudbury." This outlook reflects the trend of growing corporate monopoly together with local business dependency. In earlier decades, the local business class, usually organized through the Board of Trade or Chamber of Commerce or the Conservative or Liberal parties, was relatively larger and included more independent elements. Today the local business class has been so displaced and tied in dependency to transnational corporations through franchising, licencing, and supplier relationships that it is incapable of concerted, independent action in the community interest to curb or reverse transnational domination.

Take a 2006 survey by the City of Greater Sudbury of major employers with 200 or more employees. Of the total 24,370 jobs in twenty-nine operations, 56 percent (in fourteen operations) were in the public sector, such as the Sudbury Regional Hospital, municipal government, and school boards, and this count did not include about 1,500 provincial government employees. Of the rest, 32 percent worked for non-Canadian transnationals (about three-quarters of all private-sector employment, including Inco and Falconbridge), 9 percent worked for non-local Canadian corporations, and only 2 percent worked in locally controlled corporations.[16] Among the twenty-nine operations is a call centre, the new industry most promoted locally as an alternative to mining employment. Tele Tech, the largest private-sector employer outside the mining industry, with about 800 employees, is incorporated in Delaware, headquartered in Colorado, has about 47,000 employees worldwide, and is highly mobile. However, the survey did not include foreign transnationals such as Wal-Mart, the virulently anti-labour American company with assets of over $40 billion, which already has nearly 200 stores in Canada and 1.4 million employees worldwide. Nor did it include Costco, which, like Wal-Mart, drains retail activity from smaller businesses, with its 374 stores and about 92,000 employees internationally.

The orientation of Sudbury's dependent business class is evident in its economic analyses and policies, particularly in its uncritical acceptance of globalization, with its intensified corporate concentration and resource exploitation. While promoters of globalization and models of intensified competitiveness such as Michael Porter (GSDC 2003) are viewed approvingly, those critical of globalization or who take seriously the international struggles of unions and indigenous peoples for greater local control and public ownership of mining are ignored. Above all, there is a subservient support of corporate mining: "There is no other significant mining region outside of Australia, as welcoming to the mining sector as the City of Greater Sudbury" (CSTF 2006: 7). Issues of Canadian sovereignty and community democracy are secondary to supporting Canadian corporate expansion in Latin America and elsewhere. This is what a 2006 Community Stakeholders' Task Force on the Future of the Local Mining Industry had to say:

> It would be preferable to see both companies [Inco and Falconbridge] stay under Canadian ownership; however, Canadian mining, exploration and mining supply and service companies have a major international presence, operating in more than 100 countries around the world.... It is not feasible in the interconnected, global economy not to allow foreign ownership of Canadian assets. (CSTF 2006: 13)

These self-serving claims conveniently ignore the reality that some industries in Canada have foreign-ownership and other restrictions, that the ownership of assets and interconnectedness across countries is highly unequal, and that several countries elsewhere are moving toward greater, not less, control of their natural resource industries. Of course, mining is important to Sudbury, but so is a balanced discussion of the mining corporations' real harm to workers and the community, as well as the need for much tougher limits on corporate mining's power and exploitation.

On the crucial question of the distribution of resource profits, or rents, the local elite mentions the need for "resource revenue sharing" (NOLUM 2007; APMMR 2008) and that "[p]eople want a more equitable sharing of the benefits of resource extraction" (CSTF 2006). But the focus is not on greater local or provincial control over industry rents from public resources, or even on compensation for the industry's enormous social or environmental costs. Rather, it is on pleading with provincial and federal governments for a greater share of existing government revenues. However, Ontario provincial mining revenues are low relative to the needs of mining communities, low relative to the social and environmental costs of mining, and low relative to the revenues of the industry.[17] Neo-liberal provincial and federal governments have been lowering the general rates of corporate taxation, including for resource extraction corporations, and this means increased tax pressures at the provincial and federal levels are likely to fall more on personal (worker) income taxes than on corporate ones. Nor is there any questioning of federal or provincial subsidies to the mining industry, estimated at over $67 million for Ontario in 2000 (Winfield et al. 2002: Ch. 4). In some years, such subsidies exceed royalty revenue.

Recently, Sudbury's municipal property tax collected from Inco and Falconbridge totalled only about $11 million, or 7 percent of total municipal taxes, which is down from 25 percent a decade ago. Yet Sudbury's new mayor, as reported by Denis St. Pierre, says that he:

> does not believe the solution should include taxing underground assets or increasing the overall level of taxation of mining companies, even in boom times such as the current nickel industry supercycle. "I think they do pay healthy taxes.... The issue is getting the other levels of government to share it. (*The Sudbury Star,* Sept. 8, 2007)

The apparent reversal of policy on taxing underground assets of mining corporations, something advocated by Northern mining municipalities for decades, is a notable step backward, as is the concept that mining is taxed sufficiently. Policy statements don't question their own logic, such as when the City's main strategy document proclaims "Nickel has become the metallic version of oil" (CSTF 2006: 4). When it comes to oil, about 77 percent of the world's hydrocarbon supplies are controlled by national petroleum companies (Séréni 2007), and this will likely increase. Even in Alberta, one of Canada's most right-wing provincial governments saw fit to review its royalties policy. For oil, too, there is debate about "peak oil," yet we hear no concerns that only 100 years of mineral reserves exist in Sudbury. Without a transparent review and increased public capture of resource rents and profits from mining corporations, and without some recognition of the full social costs of mining, communities like Sudbury are unlikely to see the major increases in revenues that are needed.

The current fashion in regional development policy in Sudbury is to create a local mining "cluster" to make Sudbury the "Silicon Valley of the Mining Industry" and Laurentian University a "Harvard" of the mining sector (CSTF 2006). This re-treaded concept aims to concentrate a larger share of mining activities and research in Sudbury to make the region an international pole of attraction for mining. Once again, the role of government is to provide policy and funding support, such as for "centres of excellence," in what is effectively a more aggressive model of state support for corporate mining expansion and globalization. One hears no questioning of how the touted cornucopia of benefits would be shared, how the approach might negatively affect smaller mining communities, or how corporatization damages independent university research and teaching. The analogy to Silicon Valley is not comparable in terms of industrial and technological significance, capital ownership, and the local level of scientific and cultural resources: even leading proponents of clusters warn against overselling their benefits (Wolfe and Gertler 2003).

Such class attitudes and values permeate many areas of local development. For example, municipal planning has been aggressively oriented toward a retrograde corporate developer-driven commercial and residential expansion that encourages wasteful sprawl, suburban malls at the expense of vibrant downtowns, drive-throughs galore, and other practices increasingly discredited for their costly, health-debilitating car dependence. In the case of the Millennium Centre, a major suburban big-box development, the local elite carried out the corporate vision at the expense of small local businesses. As one city official commented:

> We aggressively went after big box stores, for example. There were opponents to that. There were people that — downtown merchants, for example — that were opposed to it, people that just didn't want to see us become a big box city, who wanted the mom and pop stores, the small businesses, that kind of thing.[18]

One could go on to other such issues, from transportation to housing to culture. There is hardly a sphere where the anti-working class, anti-female, and anti-environmental bias of the ruling corporate power and policy outlook does not have an impact. However, two events in recent history are especially telling — Sudbury's twin merger manias.

The first was the 2001 forced amalgamation of the five municipalities surrounding the City of Sudbury into the City of Greater Sudbury (see Table 1 note). Following their 1995 election in Ontario, the Harris Conservatives pursued a stridently pro-corporate platform that featured municipal and school board amalgamation. Taking this opportunity of a rightward lurch in the provincial government, a local group of "concerned citizens" agitated for an amalgamated, single-tier municipality for the Sudbury region. The demand was backed in lemming-like fashion by leading municipal political figures claiming it would bring more efficient and less costly municipal services. The largely foreordained process was conducted under legislation arrogantly named The Fewer Politicians Act, 1999 (Sancton 2000: 101–11).

Forced amalgamation was about restricting democracy and centralizing power to cut services. The new municipality of "Greater Sudbury" savagely cut democratically elected representation from sixty-eight to thirteen councillors. The new structure had no authentic democratic basis, whether in a referendum or in a broadly based regional movement. Apart from annihilating meaningful representation for smaller outlying communities, it made election more difficult for candidates with less money or those not favoured by the local corporate media. Forced amalgamation was also a major anti-democratic insult to francophone communities in the region. Unfortunately, francophone corporate-oriented leadership (see Dennie in this volume) largely capitulated. Once the amalgamation was imposed, the promised large savings did not materialize, but centralizing service cuts did occur and the corporate talk of the "customer" started replacing that of the "citizen." As well, the door was opened to "area rating" (differential taxes by neighbourhood) and further inequality within the region. After the provincial Conservatives were driven from office in 2003, the McGinty Liberals added insult to injury by moving to extend municipal councillors' terms from three to four years, thus making municipal political change even more difficult.

The second merger mania featured municipal leaders as passive spectators to a costly global-level corporate struggle for control over the world's nickel mining industry. The main act began in 2005 with Inco proposing to take over Falconbridge (McNish 2006). This massive consolidation would mean more job losses and even greater monopoly power in Sudbury. Yet the municipal council was supine. As Inco's bid proceeded, I personally contacted the two regulatory bodies most involved in reviewing the proposed merger — one relating to competition issues, the other to foreign ownership — both under the federal Minister of Industry. In keeping with how both Conservative and Liberal federal governments have gutted and redefined corporate regulation to favour globalization, monopoly power today is defined so narrowly as to effectively ignore local monopoly effects on the labour market, the media, and some suppliers. Further, I was told there would be no public hearings, even in Sudbury. As for foreign ownership, it turns out that approval details are secret and whatever limited conditions might be required of the merger are not disclosed publicly by Canadian government officials. I was told explicitly that "we don't do transparency," and so, in order to get information on the government's decision, I had to rely on an Inco press release. I was informed that the Ontario government, now under the McGinty Liberals, had been contacted and voiced no objection to the takeover.[19]

In the end, the sales of Inco to CVRD and of Falconbridge to Xstrata not only ended whatever Canadian ownership and control of the nickel industry remained, it also blew away any pretence of corporate loyalty to the community. The enormous wealth built up for Inco and Falconbridge at great cost to Sudbury was flipped to Brazilian and European capitalists even farther removed from the consequences of their actions. One of the few local business leaders who dared to raise public doubts about the whole process, Michael Aitkins, opined in his *Northern Life* paper on September 6, 2006, that "The sell-out of Sudbury is all over but the whimpering." As for the municipal government of Greater Sudbury, it utterly failed to act independently and decisively to assert a community interest. By the time some critical voices had started to penetrate the corporate fog, it was too late, and politics were reverting to "collaborating with the new owners" and yet another futile "multi-stakeholder" process.

The Labour Movement

Sudbury is often seen as a "labour town."[20] There is truth to this in terms of Sudbury's class character and rooted union presence, but less so in terms of effective political power, which globalization is making increasingly clear. Still, in what could otherwise be bleak, fatalistic times, the working-class character of Sudbury comes through in the sparks of collective resistance in strikes, demonstrations, popular art, and petitions, as well as in thousands of individual acts of solidarity and protest. This resistance has occurred *despite* the many ways in which the labour movement has been, at times, divided, deflected, and co-opted. The question why, even in such a labour town, power has shifted against workers and how it could change is controversial and requires discussion.

First, the deterioration of labour market conditions since the 1970s, as described earlier, has increased insecurity and disparities among workers. Although this was a major change from the preceding post-war decades with their overall increases in employment, real wages, social programs, and in-migration, the roots of the weakness were present earlier. While the post-war decades in Canada were generally ones of expansion, unemployment was still climbing, as was the disparity between higher paid union jobs and the growing number of lower-paid and minimum-wage jobs (Leadbeater 1992). Since the 1970s, even the stronger unions, such as those in mining, have found it more difficult to bargain a share of their increasing productivity. Wage growth slowed and at times stagnated or fell. The conditions of unorganized and marginalized workers deteriorated even further. So, while workers as a whole were doing worse relative to corporations, disparities among workers also increased. The current nickel boom has not altered that fundamental pattern, especially as the current higher bonuses and settlements are going to an ever smaller fraction of workers. Pro-corporate and conservative forces used the growing disparities to sow falsehood and division, to blame public-sector workers for conditions of private-sector workers, welfare recipients for causing high taxes, women for taking the jobs of men, francophones for taking the jobs of anglophones, Aboriginal peoples for not paying taxes, immigrants for taking jobs from the Canadian-born, and so on.

Further, social and workplace changes have negatively affected social engagement. While women made progress in job opportunities and greater economic and personal independence, there was no comparable progress in reducing the working week or increasing child-care benefits. Workers today face a much-increased burden of work hours, less free time, and increased stress. Indeed, on-the-job work hours and shift lengths actually increased for some workers. For instance, in 1984, after many decades, Falconbridge was able to increase the eight-hour maximum working day in its surface operations. As well, in many workplaces the pace of work was intensifying under new technology and lean production management strategies, while commuting and shift-work spread in communities. Among the effects of these developments was to make personal and group participation in union and community activities more difficult. Further, there was increased monopolization of mass media, which was already most serious in hinterland communities, restricting parameters of debate, weakening independent working-class culture and education, and encouraging a growing consumerism that dulled class awareness of these changes and of any alternatives to them.

While unions and workers tried to resist several of these negative trends, pro-corporate governments have deployed their power in an increasingly anti-democratic way. Unions face growing government restrictions on organizing, and the right to strike, as well as increased use of state coercion, police power, and violence, which has aided and abetted intensified corporate opposition to worker power and rights (Panitch and Schwartz 2003). This has contributed to a precipitous decline in the percent of workers in unions ("union density"), especially in the private sector. In mining, a traditional bastion of union strength, union density in Ontario in 2003 was only 45.5 percent (personal inquiry to Statistics Canada).

As if weakened labour conditions coupled with increased state and corporate coercion were not enough, Sudbury also has had a political and social history that has weighed heavily on its labour movement. Sudbury was later in achieving successful labour organization than many other mining communities in Canada, and later than Inco's American refining operations in Bayard, New Jersey. Prior to the 1940s, Inco's firings, ethnic prejudice, company informers, and the social controls of company towns defeated several union efforts to organize Inco. It also gave Sudbury a reputation of being a "scab town." Once legally recognized, Mine Mill Local 598 made enormous progress, not only at the bargaining table, but also in solidarity actions with other unions and in community cultural and recreational programs. However, Mine Mill Local 598 was also the largest union local in Canada in an industry that was strategic for the American military-industrial complex and, for the establishment, it was disturbingly progressive.

The Pittsburgh-headquartered United Steelworkers of America (USWA) came to Sudbury in the 1950s as part of American-based, continent-wide Cold War union raids to halt Mine Mill's successes and destroy the left-wing union. With the backing of Sudbury's business elite, the francophone elite, the Catholic Church, and Laurentian University, in 1962 the USWA raid succeeded narrowly in taking over Mine Mill at Inco, while the latter retained bargaining rights for hourly rated workers at Falconbridge. The USWA raids were the single most divisive action in the history of the working class in Sudbury, with an impact far beyond the city and those years.[21] The division has since narrowed, and the two unions have often supported each other in strikes and negotiations. In 1993, Mine Mill/CAW Local 598 at Falconbridge, after affiliating with the Canadian Autoworkers Union, joined the Sudbury and District Labour Council and was again in the same labour central as the USWA and Inco workers.

But the raids (or "the split" as it is also called) did not end the division between the Steelworker and Mine Mill unions, nor did it end left-right struggles within each union. Within the USWA, the progressive tradition reasserted itself in Sudbury when Dave Patterson, a young and radical activist, was elected President of Local 6500. Patterson led the local in its longest and most difficult strike against Inco, in 1978–79. With or without the raids, the strike and Inco's job cuts put in focus the exploitative nature of corporate mining and raised again the question of nationalization of nickel (Tester 1994: 100–102). The struggle between capital and labour was fundamental and incessant. As Patterson himself noted "the struggle continued after the split for both locals" (Swift 1977: 11).

Within both unions there existed two opposed approaches to unionism and corporate capitalism, often called "social unionism" and "business unionism." Social unionism emphasizes unions as a movement of the entire working class for social change, a high level of rank-and-file participation, union democracy, external organizing, and actions not only for its own members but for all workers wherever solidarity is needed. It also is more critical of corporate collaboration and capitalism. The Western Federation of Miners, who created the labour slogan, "An Injury to One is an Injury to All," embodied a strong anti-capitalist social unionism, which was carried into the Mine Mill union. By contrast, business unionism has more limited social goals (a "pure and simple" unionism), a narrower focus on the interests of its own members alone, a lesser role for rank-and-file participation, and an acceptance of collaboration with employers and of capitalism. During the Cold War, with its anti-communist expulsions and witch hunts and growing economic prosperity, business unionism achieved dominance in most unions in Canada, and even more so in the United States and in American-based unions: "Business values predominated, and unions were seen as institutions (businesses) providing special services to members (a contract, contract enforcement) for a fee (dues)" (Nissen 2003: 138). The rank-and-file and "movement" character of unions declined and was replaced primarily by a "servicing model." The self-concept of the leaders of the Steelworkers union is a type of social unionism, though the union's actual practices have tended to be more conservative and business-unionist than Mine Mill. This is reinforced by the more conservative pattern of unionism in its American base over the last half century.

The Patterson period reflected a major upsurge in militancy and offered the possibility of a change in direction for the labour movement in Sudbury and beyond. However, the shift in union leadership was short-lived, as the right-wing union staff led by Leo Gerard isolated and defeated Patterson. The return to business unionism at USWA Local 6500 was followed by a long-term decline in union activity, further corporate collaboration, and increased local division (see McKiegan and Mulroy in this volume). One serious consequence was that the labour movement was unable to unify around a strong common policy and program of action to confront the massive job cuts at Inco and Falconbridge during the 1980s and 1990s. Downsizing became acceptable if corporations did it by "attrition" (not replacing those retiring or leaving their position). While better than outright layoffs, this situation did not help younger workers or the community, and it gave legitimacy to Inco's and Falconbridge's dumping of their social costs onto the community.

During this period, the general character of Sudbury's labour movement was changing, particularly with the growth of public-sector union membership, such as in the Ontario Public Service Employees Union (OPSEU), the Canadian Union of Public Employees (CUPE), and the Public Service Alliance of Canada (PSAC), and with a much larger number of unionized women workers (see Closs in this volume). In 2003, about 36 percent, or 27,000, Sudbury workers were unionized within 224 bargaining units (Whynott 2003). The sectors with the highest unionization rates still included mining, but now also health, social services, education, and public administration. Among unions, the largest was still the USWA (including its non-mining locals), but they were now both absolutely and relatively smaller, at 22.5 percent of union members, while CUPE was the second-largest at 18.1 percent. Union members are about evenly split between the private and public sectors, with the latter including many blue-collar as well as white- and pink-collar workers. Since the 1990s, the main labour central in Sudbury, the Sudbury and District Labour Council, was joined, not only by Mine Mill, but also by two teachers' unions, the Laurentian University faculty union, and the nurses' union. Positively, no single union or sector had the numbers or authority to dictate its views and the internecine tumult of the period of the raids was fading. However, some of the old left-right divisions still erupt in new forms.

One of the most visible clashes developed in 1993 over the provincial NDP's Social Contract legislation, which was fiercely resisted by public-sector unions and Mine Mill/CAW, but supported by the more conservative Steelworkers and other so-called "pink paper" unions (Reshef and Rastin 2003). Then came the "Days of Action" in 1996. The public-sector unions and Mine Mill, making up a majority of the Labour Council, backed the Days of Action, but the Steelworkers pulled out and did not support it. Then came the corporate merger mania of 2005–06. When Inco proposed its takeover of Falconbridge, the Steelworker leadership lined up to support Inco and was clearly enthused by the prospect of taking over Mine Mill members at Falconbridge. Not only did the top Steelworker leaders start commenting aggressively about how the USW (the United Steelworkers of America in Canada dropped the "America" from its name in 2005) would be a better union for Mine Mill workers, but they also claimed to establish "a Steelworker Inco/Falconbridge Council to advance our building power program."[22] The Mine Mill/CAW union urged caution and questioned whether community benefits were being protected in the proposed Inco merger, and it also began to hoist its flag as a Canadian union (in contrast to the American-based Steelworkers). For a period, the possibility of a destructive replay of the raids hung over the Sudbury labour movement. More loyal to profits, Inco soon jilted the Steelworkers, first in a plan to merge with Phelps-Dodge, a company infamous among American mine workers (Rosenblum 1998), and then in folding for even more money from Brazil-based CVRD.

Such divisions in the labour movement are likely to continue, even though they have little member support, until another progressive upsurge like the one represented by Patterson can compel steps forward. The current mindset and organization of much union leadership were largely formed in a period of capitalist expansion and prosperity. Economic and environmental conditions have changed dramatically, though the thinking at the top of the labour movement has not, and not only in the USW. As working people see the need for stronger policies to confront corporate power and globalization, one might expect to see new debates and changes in power unseen before in Sudbury. As part of developing a new labour strategy, some policy and organizational divisions of the past need to be addressed. Labour policy directions could include:

- a progressive economic and regional policy for hinterland areas to protect, improve, and expand jobs, social programs, environmental conditions, and community participation, all anchored around greater public ownership and community control of natural resources;
- support for the multinational character of Canada, particularly the collective rights of Aboriginal and francophone minorities, as well as the rights and contributions of immigrants. Dealing with language and cultural issues within unions is part of the question, but so is local solidarity against the forced amalgamation of francophone communities into Sudbury or the City Council's insulting flag debates;
- completing the desegregation of male-dominated workplaces and unions, as well as strengthening protections against discrimination and harassment of all kinds, including those based on disability, age, sexual orientation, or race. Sexism, homophobia, racism, and ableism are part of the package of

right-wing ideology and power used to provoke deflecting issues and divide collective action;

- democratization of the mass media and greater access to non-commercial culture, education, and training, which is crucial for a sustained development of critical awareness, solidarity, and alternative directions in community development;
- a policy for peaceful uses of metals and against the support of militarism. Metals are as basic to war as water is to agriculture. No labour movement with any international perspective can avoid issues now generated by the increased destructiveness of war and the role of mining transnationals in support of brutal militarist regimes internationally.

The organizational direction of a new labour strategy must also address the need for a single industrial union in mining that adopts the perspective of social unionism and is headquartered in a hinterland city. The new union could be independent of both the USW and Mine Mill/CAW, centred on mining workers but also including groups of workers related industrially or geographically to hinterland areas. Local and international solidarity and affiliations would be basic, but not the concept that sees ever-larger unions and international bargaining as its main strategy to deal with transnational corporations. Within Canada, organizing the unorganized and winning company-wide and industry-wide bargaining would be major goals. The possibility of these and other policy and organizational goals are a key part of the need for discussions and actions to build greater unity in mining communities and hinterland regions against corporate globalization. Each mining and resource community and hinterland region has its particulars, but the anti-labour and anti-community consequences of globalization are a shared experience.

Which Future?

Two seemingly opposed views now dominate thinking about the future prospects of Sudbury and other mining communities. The first view foresees continual growth in population and employment, at least following a period of restructuring or temporary decline. The second view foresees inevitable decline, perhaps to a more stable, lower level. However, both views accept corporate globalization, and neither treats seriously its impoverishing effects on community conditions, democracy, or the environment. For working people, this is another Hobson's choice.

The continual growth view is typical of the local business class and commercial media. Often larded with boosterism, the central belief is that growth will happen through more pro-corporate policies, incentives, and values, particularly focussed on even more aggressive corporate and community competitiveness (such as through a mining cluster policy). Community-building and the role of local government is reduced to or rationalized as competitiveness-building, whether in social and labour policy, education, sports, or culture. Advocates of this view often preach about working in "partnership" with transnationals to revitalize community prospects without questioning whether corporate domination is itself a major part of the problem.

In a more thoughtful expression of the growth view, Saarinen (1992) has argued that by the middle and late 1980s Sudbury had overcome the mining staple trap and shifted toward self-sustainability through diversification in health, education, tourism, and administrative sectors: "Once known only as a resource community, it has since developed as a major regional service centre for northeastern Ontario" (Saarinen 1992: 182). True, increases in public-sector and services employment have been significant, though there were also cuts (Table 2 and Closs in this volume). However, this has not meant a shift beyond mining dependency nor to self-sustained growth, let alone to more social equality. Sudbury has a higher, not lower, level of social-program dependency and the overall employment rate has fallen. And, Natural Resources Canada's estimate of mining employment income at 44 percent of total income illustrates that mining is still by far the most important sector apart from the public sector.

The second view of Sudbury's future foresees population and employment decline. Arguably, this is the dominant view, though it is not publicized in senior levels of the Canadian state, whose policies encourage metropolitanization and that for decades have been content to manage decline, largely ignoring numerous reports on conditions of mining towns (Leadbeater 1998). In one of the clearest decline positions, Polèse and Shearmur (2006) argue that decline is inevitable in regions outside major metropolitan areas.[23] Given that total population growth in Canada is close to zero, they argue that achieving population growth in particular regions (like Sudbury) is a zero-sum game that depends on attracting migrants and immigrants from other areas. This in turn depends mainly on the distribution of employment opportunities across regions of Canada. Because of the structural trend of increasing employment in major metropolitan areas, the situation of hinterland areas cannot be "easily altered by public policy" and "it is unreasonable to expect local economic development strategies to halt decline" (Polèse and Shearmur 2006: 24). Polèse and Shearmur see Northern Ontario (including Sudbury) as limited by distance from major markets and by resource conditions. They reject the idea that new information technologies (IT) will overcome the costs of distance, because IT has not been shown in practice to reduce the need for face-to-face contacts, nor to have much effect on transportation costs. Contrary to much local economic development practice, they refuse to blame the lack of local growth on a lack of social capital or local entrepreneurship: this idea is "not only misleading, but may be counterproductive" (Polèse and Shearmur 2006: 43). The key policy problem becomes "devising positive decline strategies" to a new, lower equilibrium size (Polèse and Shearmur 2006: 44).

Neither the decline nor growth views capture the depth of the developmental crisis confronting hinterland areas. On the one hand, the growth view emphasizes a type of corporate competition that reverts inevitably to reducing labour costs (whether reducing jobs, job quality, pay, or benefits) or to increasing government subsidization of capital's costs (such as deregulation, free-trade zones, tax concessions, or higher tuition costs). In other words, it proposes even greater redistribution to capital and more social disparity. On the other hand, the notion that there might exist some lower and socially positive equilibrium in population or employment is delusional about the capitalist adjustment process. Decline in mining communities is strongly associated with lower incomes, more unemployment and poverty, and further polarization of income and wealth. The decline view is disempowering in that it offers little more than lower incomes, more poverty, fewer local opportunities, and reduced expectations. While growth hardly trickles down to the majority, decline usually makes conditions even worse.

Both the growth and decline views avoid other major issues, such as sustainability in resource extraction and use. Increased investment in mining and more rapid rates of resource exhaustion and use are not sustainable in the long term, especially given the tendency for shorter durations of mine life, the reduced likelihood of finding new large-scale ore bodies, and growing global environmental concerns. Unaddressed too is continued metropolitanization. A complex range of federal and provincial policies, dominated by a metro-centric outlook, have reinforced this trend, despite its enormous social and environmental costs.

As for the issue of growth or decline, there can be no resolution unless a far greater emphasis is placed on living standards and the distributional consequences and fairness of particular forms of community development. In the short term, efforts need to focus on protecting existing jobs, living standards, social programs, and community rights in the face of the impoverishing pressures of globalization. A labour-oriented perspective tends to measure developmental success by higher rates of employment, reduced poverty, stronger social protections, and a broader sharing of productivity gains and resource rents, through governmental as well as union action. If communities could achieve much higher rates of employment and job quality, stronger social protections, and more equitable sharing of the costs of adjustment, some shrinking — or increases — in population, or even employment, would not be so critical.

The central economic issue for the future of mining-dependent communities like Sudbury still remains: how and by whom are resources to be owned, controlled, and developed? The combined economic, environmental, and political crises require a break with the policies of corporate globalization. Corporate mining has demonstrated vividly that corporate ownership does not assure social responsibility or stewardship of the resource. As Blackmar (2005: 98) comments: "Absentee ownership gives lie to property rights advocates' invocation of stewardship of the land as a feature of proprietorship." With globalization removing power even further from the people of hinterland communities — those most directly affected — the time has come for a renewed demand for greater public ownership and community control of mining and mineral resources, for a major portion of resource rents for hinterland regions, and for a planned use of resources that protects future as well as present generations. Such a demand needs to go further than the pattern with earlier state mining companies — such as in coal or asbestos — that too often were formed to remediate and rationalize corporate failure and that often aped the environmental and social practices of private corporations.

Stronger elements of democratization and accountability are crucial for the future, including a legislated role for mining communities in the long-term planning of resource development and the monitoring of environmental and health impacts. Other related measures would include full public disclosure and independent verification of reserves; public setting of rates of exhaustion and protections against high-grading; inventory planning to modulate boom and bust cycles; prioritizing of recycling, waste reduction, and sustainable uses to minimize use of remaining resources; gradual incorporation of the full costing of environmental and social costs of mining; and regulatory support for the higher metals prices that full costing would entail.

A shift toward the economic and social rights of hinterland regions would also be an important step toward more peaceful and equitable relations among countries. Mining has long had, and continues to have, an association with empire, oppression, and war, from gold and silver in the conquest, to colonization and enslavement of the "New World" and Africa, to oil and diamonds in the current bloodshed in the Middle East and Africa. There is a need to work toward an international treaty prohibiting extraterritorial ownership of resource lands and mineral rights, including leases and joint-production sharing arrangements, together with a greater emphasis on regional self-sufficiency in resource use. The positive contributions of mining experience in engineering, geology, production, and remediation could continue to develop and be used through fair exchange and mutually beneficial cooperation in consulting, technology transfer, and international training and research projects and institutions. Ultimately, mining does *not* need to continue under the control and in the form of transnational corporations: resources *can* be used more rationally for present and future generations in ways that help to overcome international inequalities, rather than to exploit and aggravate them.

For Sudbury and other hinterland communities, there will have to be much stronger requirements set on mining operations, as well as ongoing regulation to retain and develop refining, secondary industrial linkages, and research. Provincial action is needed for an independent public investigation, free of corporate interest or pressures, of community health issues. As well, more open and rigorous monitoring of soil, water, air, and other environmental conditions are called for. Equally, the social character of mining must change, especially with decisive steps in hiring and promotion of women and other equity groups, because corporate mining has shown itself, over many decades, to be unwilling to desegregate its workplaces. There must be government-enforced measures — in cooperation with the unions — in areas ranging from equity quotas to reductions in the working week to family- and community-friendly shifts and workplace policies.

Many aspects of mining communities need changing, from town planning to food systems to democratizing mass media to cultural policy to the national question. But the key to achieving such changes lies in transforming the mining industry itself. Much of what needs to be done is already known. A raft of progressive policies is available from mining and other hinterland unions, as well as from numerous studies.[24] Many other policies and initiatives will evolve through the skills and enormous creativity of working people that a progressive reorientation of the industry would create. Mining communities *do* have real choices available, at least once it has been decided they have had enough of corporate globalization.

Notes

1. Of course, these indicators can and have been criticized as rough and biased, which they are. But the bias usually understates the problems, especially by their general exclusion of distributional measures, including disparities relating to class, gender, age, disability, race, and language. For some local views, in a framework of community competitiveness, see GSDC 2003 and Robinson 2003.

2. The definition for 2001 is based on 30 percent or more of employment income from mining or other resource industry relative to total income, including transfer income. The 44 percent figure is from a personal communication with Natural Resources Canada. The employment figure for the mining industry here is defined to include mining (6.4 percent) plus, generously, all manufacturing (6.4 percent) (see Table 2 for 2001). The latter includes smelting and refining. Most mining communities are characterized by Stage I (Primary) or Stage 2 (Smelting and Refining), or both, in Natural Resources Canada's four-stage classification of the mining production process: the other two stages are of semi-fabricated and fabricated products.

3. Using data from the 1980s, one study for Northern Ontario has estimated that for every $100 of output in mining, about $24.16 went to wages and salaries and $24.19 went to purchases of inputs in other industries (or "backward linkages") in Ontario (Jankowski and Moazzami 1993: 42–45). The other industries include travel and advertising ($0.94), maintenance and support ($3.50), services ($3.18), electric power ($3.16), transportation and storage ($1.42), repair and construction ($1.73), chemicals ($2.65), gasoline and fuel ($1.57), machinery ($2.66), iron and steel ($0.73), mining services ($1.71), non-metallic minerals ($0.50), and natural gas ($.045).

4. Assuming the above Natural Resources Canada estimate of 44 percent resource-export dependence, Sudbury's base multiplier would be about 2.3 or lower, given leakages.

5. The growing body of research on the relation of women and men in mining, and in mining communities, includes Forestell (1999), Kechnie and Reitsma-Street (1996), Klubock (1996), Peck (1993), Seager and Perry (1997), Tallichet (1995), and Yount (2005).

6. From Inco's 2005 SEC report (accessed May 2007 at <http://www.inco.com/investorinfo>). This is a report required by the American government, which has stronger corporate reporting requirements than Canada. Estimates of economic rents and their flows are made difficult in part because much corporate cost, revenue, and ownership information remains proprietary. This is yet another reflection of the fact that pro-corporate federal and provincial governments have been unwilling to

take action to protect public rights in natural resources, particularly in the interests of mining communities.

7. The review, which included oil-extraction, compared strictly non-metropolitan mining regions to other non-metropolitan regions. About half of all published findings showed negative economic outcomes, with those remaining divided between favourable and neutral/indeterminate outcomes. The limited positive outcomes were more associated with incomes than with unemployment rates or poverty, with the western United States (relatively large new coal strip mines), and with years prior to 1982. The observation of higher average or median income, together with higher unemployment or poverty, is consistent with a point I will make later — that among the impacts of resource-export development is that it typically increases socioeconomic inequality.

8. Methodologically, longer-term patterns can be obscured in narrowly cross-sectional studies, which are usually based on data for a single year of the evolution of an industry, region, or community. Cross-sectional studies have also tended to favour the use of mean (average) and median values in variables, rather than distributional impacts or structural trends, and they have avoided measures of what is sometimes called the economic "adjustment process." Longer-term historical and longitudinal studies can give a clearer picture of the consequences of the resource-extraction cycle and development arc of resource-dependent local development.

9. "Bosses roamed the working places with 'blue slips,' termination notices, and issued them as they wished. The whip of speed-up cracked all around harried workers, accidents and fatalities were plentiful, while 'stool pigeons' and informers kept the Company informed in the fight to keep unionism off the mines and plants" (Brasch 1997: 18). Among other actions against growing union support, Inco funded a divisive company union, dubbed the "Nickel Rash." Inco was widely believed to be behind the February 1942 attack by a dozen goons who destroyed the Mine Mill office and seriously assaulted two union officers (Solski and Smaller 1985: 103–105). On ethnic and occupational segregation and corporate control through housing in the Inco company town of Copper Cliff, see Goltz 1992.

10. According to Norden (1970, accessed May 2007 at <http://shunpiking.com>): "At the Nuremberg trial against the IG Farben directors, the court confirmed that the International Nickel Company of Canada (Inco), which controls 85 percent of the nickel production in the capitalist world, delivered nickel to the Hitlerite state for political-military reasons. On 29 September 1947, in the course of the trial, a declaration of the accused director, Paul Hafliger, was read out which stated that in 1934, that is to say, one year after Hitler's rise to power, a treaty was signed between IG Farben and the nickel trust which permitted IG Farben to cover a good half of the German needs with only 50 per cent of the costs paid in foreign currency. In addition IG Farben AG was able to have the nickel trust stockpile a substantial supply of nickel in Germany at its expense."

11. For example, Swift 1977. Blocked by the corporate-controlled mass media, expressions of international solidarity have been most visible on the Internet, for example, on the Mines and Communities Website or, for Canada, the webpages of Mining Watch Canada or the international pages and links of several unions including the CLC/CTC, CAW, and Steelworkers.

12. Challenges are also coming from Canadian and American activists: "We asked questions about well documented abuses related to Inco's operations in the 1970s and early 1980s: community social disruption; lack of consultation with local com-

munities; forced relocation of communities; Inco's infamous relationship with the military; repression in Guatemala City against activists and academics criticizing the country's fire sale of mining concessions; repression against local activists in the El Estor region; low profile remittances to the local government; etc." Accessed February 2007 at <http://web.unbc.ca/geography/whatsnew/guatemala2004/photoessay.html>. See also Gedicks 2001.

13. In terms of mining in Canada, the total employment in mineral industries rose from its 1941 wartime peak of nearly 56,000 to over 86,000 in the early 1970s, while coal mining employment declined almost continuously from its peak levels in the 1920s of over 30,000 to less than 9,000 by the early 1970s (Leacy 1983: P15, Q13). In terms of employment in metal mining alone, and excluding smelting and refining, employment reached a peak about 1974 at around 70,000. By 2000 it had plummeted by more than a half to under 28,000 (NRC 2006a: Table 23).

14. On the strike, see Grylls and Kuyek in this volume. See also Macdonald and Chammus (2001), Lowe (2001), and Beck et al. (2005). At the time, Falconbridge was owned 55 percent by Noranda, which was in turn owned 40 percent by Brascan. CBC News, Feb. 21, 2001, reported Falconbridge's $30 million claim. The actual figure is likely higher.

15. The unadjusted average for Sudbury in 2003 was $29,000, indicating stagnant money earnings. A similar pattern occurred with Sudbury's median wage and salary income, which in 1993 was $23,300, above the medians for Ontario and Canada. But in 2003 the Sudbury median, even unadjusted for inflation, had dropped to $20,000, well below the median for Ontario and Canada. The inflation adjustment uses the annual Consumer Price Index (2002=100) of Statistics Canada. The wage and salary data used here, as well as on distributive measures and for the economic dependency data above, was retrieved through special orders with Statistics Canada's Small Area and Administrative Data Division. The analysis of mine wages is based here on Mine Mill contracts, which is complicated by strike and lockout time lost, COLA adjustments, productivity and nickel bonuses, and overtime earnings. The last of these probably declined over much of the period, but has increased in the recent nickel boom, bringing some catch-up for unionized mine workers, though less than would previously have been shared of productivity gains.

16. The last were two contracting or construction companies heavily dependent on mining and the public sector. Survey accessed July 2007 at <www.city.greatersudbury.on.ca/keyfacts>.

17. Ontario's taxes on mining lands (leases, licences of occupation, and patents) are minimal, only about $1.7 million on 675,395 hectares in Ontario in 2007, of which the Territorial District of Sudbury returned about $713,000 (personal communication with the provincial Department of Northern Development and Mines). Ontario's Mining Profits Tax on profits in excess of $500,000 returned only about $52 million in 2006 for the entire province, which has the most mining in Canada, and Ontario's entire revenue from the mining industry was said by the industry itself to be around $180 million in 2005 (NOLUM 2007). For Inco alone in 2005, for example, reported net sales were US$4,518 million and net earnings US$836 million, for a return on equity of 17 percent. In 2005, Sudbury accounted for 52.7 percent of Inco's world annual mine production. Some infrastructural costs of mining are noted in APMMR 2008.

18. Personal communication with Laura Schatz, from interview as part of research for Schatz and Johnson (2007).

19. By contrast, the Mine Mill/CAW union published a booklet calling for a review and particular conditions for any merger plan, including local government approval, to ensure benefits for workers, communities, and Canada. It noted some of the self-serving corporate greed in the process, for example, the 2004 corporate pay of Inco Chief Executive, Scott Hand, at $5.36 million, and of Falconbridge Chief Executive Derek Pannell at $4.98 million. This included stock options that would give them an interest in engineering financial deals that would bring higher share prices even if gains are short-lived (CAW 2006).

20. In this chapter, the term "labour" has two main meanings, at times overlapping, distinguished by the context. The first, which is my preferred use, refers broadly to workers (employees) or the working class, or in an economic context to labour as opposed to capital. In the second, labour refers more narrowly to unions or union-ized workers. The active movement for worker rights and union organization is often referred to as the "labour movement," which can include workers whether in unions or outside them.

21. Labour activists and historians continue to study "the raids" in Sudbury as among the most momentous events in labour history. On the history of Mine Mill and the raids, from persons with local Mine Mill experience, see Lang (1970), Solski and Smaller (1985), Tester (1980), and Stevenson (1993). A pro-Steelworker view is found in Southern (1982) and Gilchrist (1999). See also Arnopoulos (1982: Chapter 7), Laite (1985), and Steedman et al. (1995). Among others, the work of Mercier (1999) on the Steelworker raids in Montana provides useful parallels.

22. USW Canada press release, Dec. 7, 2005. The USW was likely assuming that, in a combined vote of the two locals, the much larger USW Local 6500 would outvote Mine Mill even if, as most observers believe, a large majority of Mine Mill mem-bers would prefer Mine Mill over the USW. Either the USW leadership understood this situation and disregarded the views of Mine Mill members or it overestimated USW support, including in its own union. Whatever, this was not a democratic or progressive way to heal wounds or to turn what was potentially a brutally divisive struggle into something constructive.

23. For Polèse and Shearmur, who use a centre-periphery concept, central urban re-gions have a minimum threshold of 500,000 people. Saarinen (1992: 175) considers 250,000 "the population size often considered necessary for self-sustainability." In both analyses, the Sudbury area, even at roughly 160,000 people, is well below these somewhat arbitrary thresholds.

24. In Canada, union policies on mining and mining communities have not been cen-trally collected but are available over the decades in resolutions, convention minutes, press releases, policy brochures, and, now, union websites. For studies, see also, for example, Tanzer (1980: Chapter 19), Leadbeater (1998), Winfield et al. (2002), Kuyek and Coumans (2003), and Sampat (2003).

Chapter 1

Mine Mill Local 598/CAW Reaches a Turning Point

Rick Grylls

Jim Tester, our Past President and a labour activist in Sudbury, used to make the point that we as workers are not afraid to work, to produce the wealth, and make the company successful — the difference with the company comes in how we share the wealth. I think that's what we are seeing with globalization and the wealth of the world. Globalization is bringing the struggle over the sharing of wealth right down to us here in Sudbury. It's a struggle over power and control. Globalization has pushed the corporate agenda of more for less — they want more, and they want to give workers less.

The 2000–2001 Strike

The 2000–2001 strike was the longest and hardest our local ever had at Falconbridge. The company was out to break our union, to weaken it with ineffective workplace language in the collective agreement. They put an agenda on the table that was unacceptable after almost sixty years of collective agreements. They were out to take a *lot* more and give a *lot* less. The bean counters, as we call them, the financiers in Toronto, were out to maximize, to take control, to take our collective agreement far away from what the union had established over many years.

Falconbridge started by demanding all sorts of concessions: downsizing union health-and-safety representation, denying union time off the job, increasing contracting out, and diminishing job security, seniority, and the ability for members to move from site to site.

We weren't on strike for money. The company had come to take control. In early 2000 they built a fence around the smelter, changed the road entrance, and built a new entrance building, which we found out later featured near bullet-proof glass. At the time, Falconbridge told us it was just for upgrading the security perimeter of the property.

Once they got us out on strike, they brought in a private security company called Accu-Fax. The change to the picket line was stunning. It was a paramilitary effort, with jackboots and uniforms. In previous strikes we used to play horseshoes and interact with company security and supervision personnel. I lived just one house away from the gate at Falconbridge, so I got to see the strike first-hand. Before I went to bed, I'd look out my window and see the Accu-Fax patrol. I saw it when I got up in the morning, and a lot of times when I got up in the middle of the night, when as strike coordinator I went down to see the guys. This was the result of the corporate agenda. It took us by surprise. Its message: workers would have to pay for globalization.

Several things happened that led to this strike. The question has been raised, "Why was there a strike with scabbed production?" Up to 1999, Mine Mill members were the basis of Falconbridge's Sudbury operation because our members mined 100 percent of the ore used in the smelter. In 1999, Falconbridge's Raglan Mine went on stream in Northern Québec. By 2000, Raglan was producing about 45 percent of the feed (the ore) that went through the Sudbury smelter. This feed was transported down from Raglan to Québec City by boat and then by rail cars to Sudbury.

Falconbridge said they could run the smelter without the unionized workers. In the first week of the strike, they told us, "If you don't settle the strike soon we are going to continue operating." What they needed was a little Sudbury ore, which contained sulfur that Raglan slurry lacked, to make the smelter process work. To get the ore, the company used shifters and scabs in the mines. They blasted long-hole stopes that had been pre-drilled before the strike, then mucked and milled the ore and sent the slurry to the smelter. With the mixture of Sudbury and Raglan feed, the company was able to run the smelter. They claimed 65 percent of normal production with scabs, but stats later showed production was a lot less.

That was one of the reasons Falconbridge put us on strike and scabbed it up. Of course, they also had the help of the Harris Conservative government, which wanted to break labour rights and had taken away anti-scab legislation to allow Falconbridge the opportunity to do it. Right now, Inco doesn't have the same opportunity, but if it gets Voisey's Bay on line, if it gets that rail supply coming in, the Inco workers in Sudbury will be in the same situation we were.

We didn't really see this long strike coming. We didn't think the company would do what they did — scab and run the smelter. Looking back, we can see that the company's first volley was the little strike of about three weeks that began in August 1997. The main issues then were pensions and job evaluation. Falconbridge had spent hundreds of millions of dollars rebuilding the smelter in the 1990s. The smelter was very efficient, with fewer workers. The company was very angry that workers withdrew their labour for short periods. They lost more money after the costly rebuilding.

Soon after the 1997 strike, the company carried out a workplace audit that included asking the workers about their union. They interviewed everybody, and found there was some dissatisfaction with the union. In 2000, they used this survey, thinking that the workers would abandon the union during a big strike. While workers did feel some dissatisfaction with the union, they weren't ready to give up union values or principles.

Then Falconbridge hit hard in 2000. Noranda had bought control of Falconbridge in 1989 but was just establishing full management change. Noranda was known historically as a company with a poor employee relationship. Their management style was confrontational and dictatorial by design, their stock ratings were just above junk bonds, and their environmental trail of disasters is well documented. Falconbridge historically had better relations with employees and the community. But particularly after the death of Falconbridge CEO Frank Pickard in 1996, the management style at Falconbridge became overrun with the Noranda management style.

Noranda, which itself was controlled by Brascan, engineered the strike of 2000–2001 as an outright attack on employees and their collective agreement. The main structural change they wanted was to separate the company in Sudbury into seven individual business units. The four mine sites, the mill, the smelter, and central services (mostly surface maintenance) would all be separate businesses. The new language the company proposed would have allowed them to lay off workers in any of the proposed seven units without allowing workers to use their seniority to move into other work sites.

The company attacked health and safety. They really hated one of our health-and-safety reps, Ernie Taylor, and they literally took away his full-time union position of Health-and-Safety Coordinator. They actually said, "We don't want to see that man on the job." This is because he had stood in their faces for so long and made them live up to the Health and Safety Act. There used to be four health-and-safety reps, now there are three.

The company openly attacked the union. They cut the number of stewards' meetings. They cut union-leave time: "We're not paying you any more company-paid union leave, because you guys went up and organized Timmins." They were upset because our Sudbury union had gone up to Timmins and organized 600 Falconbridge workers at their smelter into CAW Local 599. So now it was a real grudge match. They were going to teach us a lesson. After six and a half months on strike, the union forced changes in the company's language of attack. While not the same as before the strike, the final offer was safe enough to preserve the rights of workers. We broke their all-out death hold on the union.

Globalization versus Community and Solidarity

One of the things that has happened at Falconbridge through globalization is the parachuting in of a lot of non-local and foreign management. The home-grown element of our society is slowly being taken over by globalization. We consider Frank Pickard the last home-grown CEO of Falconbridge. He raised his kids here in Sudbury, in the town of Falconbridge. He worked in the mill. He was a guy you could interact with. He worked his way up the line, and that was good. As you see, the new CEO was less than forty, and a money manager extraordinaire who already had massive mergers and acquisitions in his portfolio.

The out-of-towners who sat at the bargaining table had no association with Sudbury. They didn't raise their children here, they didn't know the neighbours, and they didn't live in a small town like Falconbridge or Onaping or Copper Cliff. I think the loss of hometown strength is really going to hurt the North. There are second-, third-, and fourth-generation workers working at Falconbridge. This is our community, this is our home. We want to make it strong and viable for ourselves, our children, and our pensioners. I think that's a source of strength for a socially active union.

The company didn't care whether you lived here or not: they had their own agenda. I remember them saying they have to make cold, hard decisions — so don't get personal. These guys were all taking orders from the top to maximize their profit. Labour is about 50 percent of their costs. The other 50 percent, like hydro and steel, is pretty stable or rising and out of their control. So the main way they feel they can cut costs is cutting back on the amount and price of our labour, by denying raises, by contracting out, and by cutting back on the amount of maintenance work. But they also know they're short of skilled labour, so there's a whole conflict caused by trying to keep control of the workers and the union. They want to control every last ounce of our labour. They said, "We're tired of the union running the place." The truth is the workers are far from controlling the workplace — though that would be a good idea!

The same things were happening with other corporations. We heard from the Steelworkers during bargaining in 2003 that Inco asked for something and the union said "no": the union considered it a concession. The Inco guy, who had just come from Ford, said, "You know the raise you want — we consider that a concession from our profits." The corporations are representing the wealth of the industry, and they're getting very tight. They want to maximize their wealth. So I think that's what we've seen come down the line from the corporate globalization agenda: more control of workers and profits.

Media coverage was a big factor in the strike, and we learned lots of lessons. The media is on the side of the capitalists who own the news media. The company lied and misled in order to control public opinion. They had a public relations guy named Craig Crosby. People here asked, "Who is Craig Crosby — who is that guy?" Actually, he was one of our best allies in the whole event, because the public saw right through him. He was a Toronto jock, one of the guys parachuted in. He didn't know what he was talking about. He came off as an arrogant SOB. We just said, don't attack Craig, he's one of the better assets for us. If he opened his mouth, we looked better and better.

The company lied often, so getting the facts strengthened our position — we used facts to challenge them. We quickly learned some inside stuff about what the company was doing. One of the things Falconbridge didn't do was take us off the fax machine. (The union has interaction with their offices during regular operations.) We received all the first-aid reports during the beginning of the strike. Rolly Gauthier, our union President during the strike, was getting faxes that "contractors" — scabs — had been hurt in the smelter, so we were challenging them on contractors. Their Human Resources spokesperson, Carol Casselman, who was one of the parachuted managers, said there were no contractors, only company personnel. Rolly was challenging them on injuries. Carol said, "I don't know of any injuries or any contractors on site." But they had forgotten to take us off the fax. Some scabs in the smelter did get hurt. So Rolly jammed the fax into her face. That was early on in the game.

We learned how to influence the public in the media coverage. There were a lot of things in our strike the media controlled big time. Another little incident: I got a call from MCTV and the reporter said, "Falconbridge is on the horn here and they're saying you're causing all kinds of trouble, you're causing all kinds of problems at the Onaping gate. They're really having lots of problems there, and they're holding back trucks." So I learned those guys' game. I said, "I don't know of any problems at the smelter. Why don't you go check?" I knew there were no problems at the smelter. Instead of going to the West End where the only trouble really was, the media went to the smelter. When they got to the smelter they found a truck sitting peacefully at the picket line. The news reporter went over and talked to the picket captain, Roy Gideon.

So the six-o'clock news said, "The company has said the union is causing lots of problems…. And here we are at the picket line." It's very quiet, sunny. There's a truck sitting there all by itself, nobody blocking its path. The picket captain comes over and says, "What do you mean, the company's saying there is trouble?" Roy walks back to the truck and waves at the driver to proceed, then walks back to the camera. The truck just sits there. Roy says "That's the third time I've told that truck to go in (to the plant) and he won't go in — see, I don't know what the company's talking about." That was one of the bright moments in the strike. We watched the news and had a good laugh. The company was mad as hell.

That's the importance of people getting the *whole* picture, of not getting only the corporate stuff. We have to learn to make sure that the workers' message gets out there. One of the real problems labour has to look at is a communications system to get our message out.

We also learned lessons out of the strike about the importance of open channels and communications *within* labour and the community. We had tremendous community support. People donated tons of food. There was so much food brought to the picket line it seemed like during the first couple of weeks we all gained weight. We had a number of rallies and received moral support from many unions. Community support has a long history here. The last big strike in mining in Sudbury was in 1978–79 at Inco. My brother worked at Inco then. I have a son-in-law who works at Inco now. So there is that relationship in the community. You wouldn't have believed how many people came to the picket line just to bring food and money, whatever they had. That really opened my eyes.

The new employees learned a lot of lessons. About seventy-five employees had never been on strike and 190 had only experienced the three-week strike in 1997. They really got an education about what the company was. As a result, we have a much stronger union today.

Other workers supported the strikers. Interaction grew among the labour groups that came to support us. Our biggest supporter was the CAW Local 599 in Timmins, which sent $40,000, mostly for our 2000 Christmas party. These were workers we had helped organize, and they stood with us throughout the strike.

The biggest rally was on January 28–29, 2001. A video was made, called "One Day Longer." CAW President Buzz Hargrove, Rolly Gauthier, and community activists spoke. The workers were convinced they would stand until hell froze over. The company saw that the workers would not back down — that we weren't coming back.

We had international support, too. In November 2000, the 350 brothers and sisters at Falconbridge's Nikkelverk refinery in Kristiansand, Norway, of the Allied Chemical Workers Union Local NKIF 40, had gone on strike for five days, a symbolic strike of solidarity. They had the right to do it, to withdraw their labour — and they did it. They didn't know us personally, but they knew we were fellow Falconbridge workers. They have a real social conscience in Norway, and they knew the company was wrong. They didn't like the idea of scabs in our workplace. They didn't like the idea that the nickel coming from Sudbury, the matte they were working on, was produced with scab labour. Their national union in Norway paid them 60 percent of wages for strike pay for the week. So those guys took a pay cut of two days each, because they withdrew their labour in solidarity with us. I sometimes ask how many of us would you take a pay cut of two days to support someone as an act of solidarity, someone you didn't know?

In 2002, we brought two key members of the Norwegian union, Lief Gusland and Terje Naesse, to our Mine Mill solidarity conference. From that conference, we created a strike solidarity fund. The workers put in one cent per hour worked. Today we have about 1,000 workers at Falconbridge, or 1,700 including all of our ten affiliated units, so we put in about $30,000 a year for direct support to people on strike. I think that's one of the ways of building a defence — we have to have a war chest. With the CAW, we have our strike fund and we have our international funds. (The Falconbridge unit workers also have been giving twelve cents an hour to our local strike fund, which has over a million dollars in it.) But the workers at Mine Mill are willing to put in more, and at about 2,000 hours a worker, everybody puts in $20 a year.

Lief died in 2004. The fund is now called the Lief Gusland Solidarity and Social-Justice Fund. It's become one of our things. When we get a call that there's a union on strike, we can send them $500. We can also take a busload of workers and go down and visit them — it's the moral support as much as the cash. In fact, I think the moral support is a lot stronger than the cash support. So that's one of the lessons that came out of our union. We're trying to push it with the CAW. We've mentioned it a number of times, because we have to give our support to the people, our brothers and sisters, who are on the picket line, who are standing against this corporate control of the people. I think Sudbury is one of the last bastions of union strength in North America.

Aftermath of the Strike

In its 2001 *Annual Report*, Falconbridge said that the strike cost them $94 million, plus there was the lost production. So they lost a tremendous amount of money. But as a global whole, the corporation still had a record year for profits. And that's what they said, "Oh, it's a year of record profits." That's the image they want to control. For Sudbury, it was not only that the workers lost six and a half months' wages, it was also that the community lost business from our members and the city even had to pay additional costs of policing. Falconbridge had nothing to say about what its unnecessary behaviour did to the community. Record profits didn't mean that things would get better.

Management directives were completely taken over by Noranda in 2001, after the discovery of the Nickel Rim South ore body. The discovery of Nickel Rim South shifted the attitude of the company and set new investments into high gear. They used a stage-gate program to construct new projects like Nickel Rim and a Six Sigma program to redesign workplace policies, practices, and employee relationships. In 2005, Noranda completed the takeover of Falconbridge and joined the two companies into one. The new company was called Falconbridge because of its historically good name, but under that name live Noranda's corporate practices and attitudes.

Beginning in 2001 and 2002, management started attacking work hours by rearranging shift lengths and schedule rotations. Then they stopped summer maintenance shutdowns after 2003 and wanted to do repairs on the run. We believe they have been using a run-out theory for the ore bodies. This maximizes the company's profits but jeopardizes the integrity of the mines. It has caused the biggest problem with the mines. This is evident in the Fraser Mine shafts, where we have many maintenance issues. The number of maintenance workers was cut from four to two. According to reports, the manways need maintenance and repair. There are cases where the dividers in the shaft have shaken loose and fallen down. Now, workers don't have the summer vacation time that the shutdowns used to allow. We recommended they should keep the summer maintenance shutdowns.

Grievances have increased. In the five years since the 2000–2001 strike, Mine Mill/CAW has filed over 780 grievances. Currently there are over 150 grievances dating back to 2001. As Richard Paquin, Falconbridge Unit Chair, points out, CAW members in the "big three" automakers have over ten times the Mine Mill/CAW membership at Falconbridge, but their outstanding grievances and/or arbitration cases are less than 5 percent of ours.

Another Strike: 2004

Two years later we came to Round Two. In December 2003, we went back into negotiations and in eight weeks had twenty-seven hours of face-to-face talks. Another strike began on February 1, 2004, and lasted twenty-one days. The 2004 strike was about two main issues. The first was to get the company to back off on contractors doing production and maintenance work within the collective

My Apologies to the Members of
Mine Mill and Smelter Workers Union 598/CAW

Sunday February 1, 2004, 7:40 a.m.
4 Lindsley St.
Falconbridge, Ontario

While I sit here writing, I can look out my window though the leafless trees and see my fellow Sisters and Brothers on our smelter picket line. It is an inspiring picture, the temperature is around twenty-five below Celsius, the dawn starting to chase away the darkness. The first sunlight casts long shadows of the two smokestacks across the fences into the town site. The eastern hills are frost-laden and a misty fog arises from the valley, reflecting the face of the sun.

It seems like yesterday that we settled the bitter seven-month strike of 2000/2001 and returned to *our* workplace. This morning my view is that I must apologize for some of the positions that I have taken over the last three years. In February 2001 I became the President of this proud and historical local, and I took on the task of building an on-the-job, working relationship with management.

The early months were difficult, as they attacked the injured and accommodated workers, refused to follow the collective agreement in the worksites, and abused the workers with an irrational discipline policy. Their front-line supervision policies have resulted in hundreds of grievances, and an increase in the workers' distrust of this company. The stewards have, and continue, to do a good job protecting the *rights* of the workers.

In time, management appeared to begin working with us through the Health and Safety programs. Today, because of the dedication of the Union safety reps we have some of the best programs and accident statistics ever.

On the communications of the business strategies and policies, I promoted with management the fact we had to work together on the issues that would lead us to a better relationship and a secure future for us all. I stood with them at employee meetings, at city council, at business... meetings promoting a working relationship for all stakeholders.

The company's mission statement is, "for all the stakeholders, the employees, the community, and the shareholder."

The last nine weeks of sitting at the hotel waiting to bargain with these people, who in the end forced us onto the picket line once again, brings me to my apology.

I apologize for thinking that these people would live up to their mission statement, would think of all three parts of this company in their dealings and work with us to secure our future together. Somewhere deep in the heart of this management group there are people who will not deliver, in practice, what they preach.

Rick Grylls

(*This was written by Rick Grylls to members of the Mine Mill/CAW Local 598 during the 2004 strike at Falconbridge.*)

agreement and instead to hire new employees, including apprentices, on site. The second was to secure union work in future mines like Nickel Rim South.

The company agenda was again on contracting out, as much as possible, all future work, including the work under our Mine Mill collective agreement. While this may sound like a good business strategy to increase profitability for the company and its financial investors, we must not forget that Sudbury, the province, Canada, and their citizens are the second half of the equation. The rich natural resources that lie below our feet belong to all the people of Canada, and they should be developed in the interest of everyone, including the people of Sudbury.

We asked the company to hire the contractors doing Mine Mill work so they would become employees and benefit from the standard of living our union members have achieved, which allows the community to prosper. We made a commitment to work with the company at increasing production and maintenance efficiencies to allow more profitability, but we refused to increase their share of the wealth by taking wages, benefits, and pensions away from the people doing the work.

Again, the company hired a strikebreaking security company — LPI, the most notorious strike-breaking private police force. The company was again prepared to run operations with scab labour if need be. But this time, they decided to settle, because the price of nickel was rising and the company's fortunes were turning, and they knew the union was resolved and united.

Aftermath of the 2004 Strike

Soon after the 2004 strike, we had to put in a grievance against the company. They were not following the contracting-out language in the collective agreement they had agreed to. In February 2005, when we had our first day of arbitration hearings, the arbitrator told the company they were in violation of the contracting-out language. The arbitrator told the company they would have to hire between 30 and 130 employees. He asked: why not talk to the union and come up with the number of people to hire?

The company then said to us, "Let the arbitrator tell us how many." We have had a number of hearing dates in 2005 and 2006. More dates will be needed. It takes time to arrange open dates where all parties are available and some arbitrations, like this one, take several years. Again, this shows the company does what it wants, even when third parties indicate how to settle issues.

Our union has put up a tough defence against all the company's workplace changes and attacks. The number of arbitration wins — 18 of 19 in two years by the chief stewards and Unit Chair — prove that company actions are wrong, but they continually do as they please.

The company has a "tough love" approach and disciplines every little thing in order to force workers into believing that if you speak up you will be disciplined. Middle-line supervisors continually tell the workers the union agreed to the changes — though we did not — and this causes a great deal of workplace confusion. There are a few really bad supervisors who continually blame the workers for their mismanagement, but the Human Relations department believes that workers are liars and that management always tells the truth.

There has been a steady decline in the flow of information from management to the union since the 2004 strike ended in February of that year. The Mine Manager refused to talk to me until May 2004 and prevented the union from attending the Manager's meetings at which the union was able to follow company dealings at a closer level. Company communications are at a historical low for the five years I have been President, while the grievance wins are at a high point. We interact on the basis of: they act and we grieve. For the meetings we have, they hear our concerns and then turn around and ignore them. Then we grieve.

Merger Mania

In this last year the workers and community have been thrown into the midst of huge takeover struggles that could have a major effect on our union and on Sudbury for decades.

The first takeover talk came in 2004 from Min Metals, a Chinese state-owned company that wanted to buy Falconbridge. This really exposed us to Canada's hollow foreign investment regulations. For unknown reasons, however, Min Metals withdrew their proposal.

Then, in October 2005, Inco proposed a "friendly" takeover of Falconbridge. In November, Mine Mill/CAW said publicly it would support the proposed $13 billion merger only if the two companies negotiated a mutually acceptable merger plan with affected unions, communities, and other stakeholders. This position was outlined in a detailed joint statement on the proposed merger released in February 2006 by Buzz Hargrove, CAW President, by myself as President of the Sudbury Mine Mill Local 598, and by Jeff Martin, President of CAW Local 599 in Timmins.[1] According to the statement:

> The Inco-Falconbridge merger presents Canadians with both opportunities and threats. Whether the net benefits, on balance, are positive or negative for the broader industry and the communities which rely on it, depends on whether the merged company is held accountable to the longer-run economic interests of Canada — as opposed to being guided solely by profits.

The statement outlined an eight-point process that the unions proposed should guide the merger of the two companies. This plan included a moratorium on facility closures or layoffs until a merger plan is mutually negotiated between the two companies, their unions, and other affected stakeholders; clear targets for Canadian re-investments and supply purchases by the merged company; downsizing through attrition only; and the full recognition of existing pension and post-retirement benefit commitments by the merged company.

Buzz spoke on behalf of the unions:

> This is no knee-jerk rejection of change by the union. We clearly recognize
> there is a potential upside to this merger, as well as a downside…What is
> crucial, however, is that Inco and Falconbridge be required to negotiate
> with stakeholders to ensure that both the costs and the benefits of the
> merger are fairly shared. The federal and provincial governments could
> enforce this process through their existing regulatory powers, including the
> federal competition and investment review divisions, and the provincial
> development permit process.

Despite the efforts of our union, not one level of government — federal,
provincial, or municipal — took any action. In the meantime, Swiss-based Xstrata
had an opportunity to submit a competing offer for Falconbridge. Bids also came
from other suitors, including Teck Cominco for Inco and Phelps Dodge for the
combination of Inco and Falconbridge. This pushed up the price of Falconbridge
shares as investors speculated on further bids.

Sky-high metal prices have generated super-profits for the mining companies and spurred the drive to further acquisitions. In many cases, executives
and shareholders face a "no-lose" proposition in the current takeover battle.[2]
Xstrata has already enjoyed a 100-percent return on its $2 billion investment
in Falconbridge last summer — even before its takeover offer succeeded. And,
Inco could receive $450 million in break-up fees, even if its takeover bid is ulti-
mately defeated. It's outrageous that Falconbridge would pay Inco more money
in a "divorce" settlement than it spent last year in capital investments in all its
Canadian operations. It's proof that the real interests of our industry and our
community are being ignored in all this speculative fever.

With the entry of Xstrata, Teck Cominco, and Phelps Dodge into the fray,
the stock market shenanigans have become more complicated, but the basic
principles at stake are the same. Our union can't trust the investors or executives
of any of these companies to do what's right for Sudbury or our industry. These
corporations are all trying to fatten their pockets through paper transactions,
and it's up to other stakeholders — including government — to hold them accountable to the public interest. The eventual winner of the battle may be so
laden down with takeover-related debt and other obligations, that it will suffer
major damage from an inevitable future decline in mineral prices.

Every one of these takeover offers must be subject to full public scrutiny of
their costs and benefits. We need to attain binding commitments that Canadian
mines, Canadian smelters, and Canadian jobs won't be lost — whichever company ends up on top. We need our governments to take action.

Sudbury has seen what leaving things to corporate power has meant. In the
late 1980s, I stood before City Council and wrote local politicians to urge them to
use their power to force Inco and Falconbridge to make a deal that would allow
an ore body beside East Mine to switch hands — from Inco to Falconbridge —
to save 250 mining jobs here in Sudbury. Our argument was that the ore body

of the Sudbury Basin is non-renewable, and that nothing of value should be left in the ground. The government could pass laws to make sure we maximize our natural resources for the long-term development of our communities and Canada. But the politicians — except one NDP member — basically shrugged their shoulders. No government took action. East Mine closed, 250 jobs were lost, and that ore body remains wasted in terms of potential Canadian betterment.

We have also faced some speculation about the impact of an Inco-Falconbridge merger on labour relations, in the form of extensive published comments by leaders of the United Steelworkers — who endorsed Inco's proposed takeover — which indicate that union's desire to represent all workers at a merged company. Instead of jumping on the bandwagon of any particular takeover bid, we should all be working together to win as much protection for jobs and investments in Sudbury as we possibly can. Any union official who starts to dream about capturing new members is missing the more important question: how can we hold all of these investors accountable to the Canadian public interest? In the event a merger results in representation elections for workers at Inco and/or Falconbridge, I believe workers would choose a Canadian union to represent them.

Our Future

The corporate agenda, I think, is starting to be viewed differently by a lot of people. In the last few years, many people, including in our union, have been awakening. The attacks on our medicare, energy resources, fish harvests, water, lumber, and minerals have to be stopped, and development has to be controlled. As a social group and as a country, we own the natural resources — they're ours and we need better laws. They are supposed to be developed in a shared way for the company, for the employees, for the community, and for the country. But that is not what is happening. The corporate agenda is to take as much as possible for its own class. We have to force the agenda to be restructured, to make the viability of our communities and our country the central purpose and principle.

The unions believe the merger proposals going forward could have major costs for Sudbury — such as job losses — and there is nothing in place to guarantee Sudbury benefits from its resources. We simply can't trust any of these huge companies to do the right thing for Sudbury, or for Canada. We have to hold them accountable. Our unions have called on Canadian regulatory authorities to play a more active role in reviewing the impact of any proposed merger. For instance, the Investment Review branch of Industry Canada should question the implications of the mergers on foreign ownership levels. So far, the federal and provincial governments have rubber-stamped everything the companies want. It is embarrassing that these mega-mergers have received a more thorough review from foreign regulators than from our own Canadian ones.

What is in the interest of the company is not necessarily in the interest of the community. Falconbridge and other mining corporations are willing to push the system. We, the men and women who produce the wealth through our labour,

Taking a Stand Does Make a Difference

Our Union, through the Bargaining Committee, has brought us a tentative agreement that not only serves to reinforce our sixty-year-old collective agreement, but also provides language that carries us well into the next decade, to the mining of Nickel Rim South. In addition, this language deals with any new ore bodies in existing mines such as at Fraser-Morgan.

We have language that deals with contractors and the hiring of new employees. We have held our ground against the company's attempts to reduce the effectiveness of our contract language and to achieve concessions from our benefits and pensions packages. Our Negotiating Team was able to achieve these goals through the strong support of the rank-and-file membership and the active support of the retirees of this local.

This generation of Mine Mill/CAW Local 598 workers has fought the corporate agenda, and we have held our ground. Looking back to the three-month strike which created our defined pension plan, our six-and-a-half month strike of 2000–2001, and now this three-week struggle, we can truly see that, "Taking a stand makes a difference in the shaping of our futures."

Our collective agreement is the basis of our rights on the job.

It is the responsibility of each and every one of us to learn the context of our Collective Agreement.

It is the responsibility of each and every one of us to live our Collective Agreement on the job. If there is a violation — grieve. Support your stewards and health-and-safety reps when they ask.

It is the responsibility of each and every one of us to protect our Collective Agreement, even if it means that we must go on strike every three years.

Taking a Stand Makes a Difference.

It is the rank and file of our Union, standing side-by-side in solidarity, that gives us our strength.

Rick Grylls, President,
February 2004
(*Written by Rick Grylls to Members of Mine Mill/CAW Local 598 at the End of the 2004 Strike.*)

who have built this community, and who pay the price of dying before our time, will not allow the corporate globalization agenda to erode our community. It's our community and our resources — we really have to take control.

Notes

1. This statement, "Two Sides of the Coin: The Opportunities, and Risks, of Creating the World's Largest Nickel Producer," is available at <http://www.caw.ca/whatwedo/bargaining/bycompany/falconbridge/CAWJointStatementIncoFalconbridge.pdf>.

2. Rick Grylls completed this chapter in 2006 shortly before Xstrata defeated Inco and took over Falconbridge.

Chapter 2

Strikebreaking and the Corporate Agenda at *The Sudbury Star*

Denis St. Pierre

In a "union town" branded by the historical struggles of workers in its mining industry, it might come as a surprise that the employer with the worst record for labour disputes in Sudbury history is the city's daily newspaper. In the last three decades, workers at *The Sudbury Star* have been relegated to the picket lines on six separate occasions.

After surviving the likes of newspaper barons Lord Thomson of Fleet and Lord Black of Crossharbour, *Sudbury Star* employees might have been forgiven for entertaining fanciful notions of a more benevolent master in mid-2001, when the daily newspaper's sale was announced.[1] Regrettably, if not predictably, it wasn't long before *The Star's* new ownership demonstrated it would be every bit as ruthless and reactionary as its predecessors. So it was in the fall of 2002, barely one year into its stewardship of the newspaper, that the fledgling Osprey Media Group added a new chapter to *The Sudbury Star's* notorious history.

In fact, Osprey Media took *The Star's* dreadful labour relations record one step further, engineering a premeditated lockout, calling in strikebreakers, and hiring a private security force to publish the community's first-ever scab newspaper. To the seventy employees victimized by the four-month lockout, it soon became clear that their predicament coincided with the fact they were the first group of unionized workers to face Osprey Media at the collective bargaining table. It appeared this new corporate master was intent on sending a message to all of its unionized outposts, and if it took a misguided, costly, and damaging labour dispute in Sudbury to do so, so be it.

Nor did it take long for the employees beset by the lockout and Sudburians in general to realize the behaviour of *The Star's* new owner appeared rather incongruous with its corporate motto — "Building Better Communities." Just as Thomson and Black had done for decades before, Osprey served notice that it planned to continue *The Star's* tradition of sucking as much money out of the community as possible, and damn the consequences. Improving the collective lot of employees and their families, fostering genuine community-building — even advocating for a better-quality newspaper — would, as always, be left to the unions, their members, and supporters. To place the lockout of 2002–03 in its proper context, a brief examination of *The Star's* labour relations history is in order.

For decades, the city's only daily newspaper belonged to the Thomson chain, whose small-town monopoly newspapers were once characterized by a Royal Commission as "a lacklustre aggregation of cashboxes" (Royal Commission on Newspapers 1981: 177; also Siegel 1883: 122–23 and Burris and Puhala 1987). During the Thomson reign, *Sudbury Star* employees were embroiled in five strikes or lockouts over a seventeen-year period, from the early 1970s to 1990. In one case, workers endured an eight-and-a-half month strike before Thomson decided it would make the extraordinary concession of giving its employees a disability insurance plan.

In 1995, yet another labour dispute with Thomson was averted when *The Star's* unions accepted a less-than-generous, four-year collective agreement. The deal was forged on the premise — actually a pledge (not committed to writing, of course) — that the company needed long-term labour peace in order to proceed with a multi-million-dollar expansion and upgrading of its Sudbury operations. The ambitious plan included construction of the most advanced printing plant in Northern Ontario, a facility that would vastly improve *The Star*, attract new business, and enrich the company and even its employees. So convinced were some union leaders at the time that they engaged in the unseemly spectacle of a champagne toast with management, in anticipation of their pending mutual prosperity. However, as the months passed and signs of the promised investment failed to appear, *Star* employees began to realize there would be no reciprocation for the concessions and good faith they had offered at the bargaining table. The other shoe finally dropped in 1996, with the announcement that *The Star* and most other Thomson newspapers had been sold to Conrad Black's Hollinger empire.

Given Black's well-documented record with respect to community dailies, it probably goes without saying that the huge investment promised for *The Sudbury Star* never materialized. To the contrary, more money than ever was squeezed from the newspaper and spirited out of the community to Black and cronies such as David Radler. Black never darkened *The Star's* hallways during his brief reign over the newspaper. But soon after the 1996 takeover, Radler was dispatched to inspect the operation and presumably reassure anxious employees who were well-acquainted with Black's job-slashing tendencies.

While it would be another eight years before Black and Radler would be taken to court and accused of running their newspaper empire as a "corporate kleptocracy," their arrogance and profligate ways were apparent even to menial *Sudbury Star* employees in 1996. As part of a whirlwind tour of his and Black's most-recent acquisitions, Radler flew into Sudbury one day on a corporate jet, met briefly with *The Star's* publisher and granted an even-shorter audience to employees. Holding court in *The Star's* cheerless, 1950s-era newsroom, Radler regaled employees with his version of nirvana — the tax-free haven of the Cayman Islands. He also amused the group with quips about the inability to find a decent meal in Sudbury and how dearly he was looking forward to jetting back to New York that evening for a dinner that suited his refined tastes.

Before Radler made his getaway, a precocious employee asked the question on everyone's minds: what were the new owners' plans for the newspaper and its workforce? *Star* employees were well-acquainted with tales of the Black-Radler regime's *modus operandi* when it came to sizing up new acquisitions — walk around the building, count desks, then slash a pre-determined percentage (often one-third) of those desks — that is, jobs. However, Radler assured his Sudbury employees there were no plans to alter the *status quo* at *The Star*. In fact, his assessment was that the operation was already on the lean side — even by his and Black's standards — and there would be no need for job cuts.

No sooner had Radler left and the hot air dissipated than *The Star's* publisher announced the newspaper's profit margins had been deemed too low for the new ownership's liking. Not to worry, however. The management brain-trust had — without consulting employees or unions, of course — devised an innovative solution to the problem: the largest layoff in the newspaper's history, roughly 20 percent of the unionized workforce. Such draconian measures allowed Black to squeeze tens of millions of dollars of additional profits from *The Star* and other Canadian newspapers, not only to pad his personal coffers, but also to finance his mega-ego-sustaining pet project, the *National Post*. Before the *Post's* first edition was printed in late 1998, Black already had spent $10 million on advertising alone. Following its launch, the *Post* proceeded to incur huge losses under Black's leadership — reportedly as much as $50 million a year. All the while, newspapers such as *The Sudbury Star* and their employees bore the burden of the financial disaster by subsidizing the *Post* at the expense of the quality of their own publications.

The bright side of the Hollinger era for *Sudbury Star* employees (or so they thought at the time) was it was short enough that they had occasion to negotiate only one collective agreement with the Black regime — a 1999–2002 deal that somehow was struck without a labour dispute. *Star* employees were therefore understandably relieved when Black's reign ended in 2001. Black sold his Canadian assets after realizing he was unlikely to secure the Order of Canada he so dearly deserved. He turned his back on this colonial backwater and headed to Great Britain to solicit entry into the House of Lords.

The majority of Black's large Canadian newspapers were purchased by Izzy Asper of the CanWest Global conglomerate, which was not interested in smaller holdings such as *The Sudbury Star*. As a result, in mid-2001 Black sold twenty-eight provincial newspapers to Osprey Media Group, headed by an aspiring publishing mogul named Michael G. Sifton. The arrival of Osprey and Sifton came with promises of bigger and better things for the new chain's employees. Sifton, a young man born with the proverbial silver spoon in his mouth, came from a wealthy family that had amassed its fortune through newspaper, television, radio, magazine, and airport holdings. The family's media empire was founded in the late nineteenth century by Sir Clifford Sifton, who began with two newspapers, including the *Manitoba Free Press* (precursor to the *Winnipeg Free Press*). Other major assets included Saskatchewan's two largest newspapers, Regina's *Leader Post* and

Saskatoon-based *The Star Phoenix*, which were added in the 1920s.

For decades, the Sifton family was known as a benevolent employer and a good corporate citizen. The family maintained a no-layoff policy at their newspapers, even amid the rampant unemployment of the Great Depression. Sir Clifford Sifton, Michael's great grandfather, eventually passed along the business to two of his sons, including Clifford Jr. In the mid-1950s, the family business was split in two, with Clifford Sifton Jr. taking the *Leader Post* and *The Star Phoenix* as well as several radio and television stations and other interests. Maintaining the family tradition, Clifford Jr. eventually brought his son, Michael C. Sifton, into the business. After working various industry jobs such as small-town newspaper reporter and advertising salesman, Michael C.'s thirty-two-year-old son, Michael Jr., received the well-deserved appointment as publisher of the *Leader Post* and *The Star Phoenix* in the early 1990s.

It wasn't long before the new publisher either forgot or rejected his ancestors' values of commitment and loyalty to employees. In early 1996, Michael Sifton Jr. sold the Saskatchewan newspapers to Conrad Black. The deal not only put lots of cash in Michael Sifton's pocket, it also gave the ambitious young man a job as one of Black's top executives — Chairman of the Sterling group of newspapers. Sifton wasted no time demonstrating his mettle as a Black lieutenant. Within days of assuming his new post, he announced a massive firing at the Saskatchewan newspapers. About 170 workers, who had long enjoyed a shared sense of loyalty with their employer and had eschewed the thought of unionization, were called into hotel ballrooms and unceremoniously informed they no longer had jobs. Union organizing drives were subsequently launched at the newspapers, but with limited success.

The newspapers' sale to Conrad Black and the subsequent job cuts created a firestorm of controversy in Saskatchewan, where many citizens still bear a grudge against Sifton. But young Michael, who flies his own airplane and cites the bourgeois pastime of polo as a favourite hobby, seemed unfazed. He was charting his own course to newspaper barondom. The opportunity presented itself in 2001 after Conrad Black, engaging in more of his infamous financial shenanigans, began divesting himself of his Canadian newspapers. Sifton seized the opportunity, parlaying his ambition as well as his inherited wealth and influence to secure a financing partnership to buy twenty-nine of Black's Ontario papers — including *The Sudbury Star* — for a reported $220 million. Funding partners included the Bank of Nova Scotia and the Ontario Teachers' Pension Fund. Following the initial purchase, more than thirty other newspapers were gobbled up by Sifton's chain, including a $194-million purchase of four dailies and twenty-one weeklies in southern Ontario in early 2003.

When Osprey Media announced its purchase of *The Sudbury Star* in 2001, it billed itself as a progressive newspaper company, proud of its corporate motto: "Building Better Communities." It later gave *The Star* an equally promising, if not self-serving, slogan to advertise daily on its pages: "A Proud Community Partner." But signs of community building and partnerships were scarce as far as Osprey employees in Sudbury and other towns were concerned. After making his various acquisitions, Sifton visited each newspaper in his chain. In the process, he positively shunned the unions in these workplaces. In a number of visits to *The Star*, for example, he never once acknowledged the presence, let alone the roles, of the unions representing the newspaper's employees. He never attempted to engage the unions in any kind of dialogue, let alone partnership. He did not seek the unions' views, concerns, or suggestions regarding labour relations or the newspaper's operations in general. In fact, he never bothered to introduce himself to union leaders.

Sifton's father was known for visiting each of his newspapers several times per year and knowing every employee by name. Michael Jr. has attempted to portray himself in the same light. In a number of self-serving interviews, Sifton has characterized his leadership style as a "folksy" CEO who, like his dad, greets employees on a first-name basis. In reality, however, he has not even attempted to introduce himself to employees at many of his newspapers. Years after taking over these newspapers, he still would not recognize many long-term employees' faces, let alone their names. Like Thomson and Black before him, Sifton has left no doubt that he has little use for unions and their frivolous demands for job security, cost-of-living protection, pensions, and benefits. In a feature article in the *Ryerson Review of Journalism,* Sifton acknowledged his "deep distaste for unions." He said he "prefers dispensing gifts to loyal employees rather than negotiating with union bosses" (Clarke 2003).

Sick-leave benefits don't appear to be among the gifts Sifton likes to dispense to his employees, however. He has unabashedly justified his demands for clawbacks to such benefits, even at his smallest newspapers, where employees are entitled to as little as nine days of paid sick leave per year. "Sick days are 'x' number of days that an employee gets to claim that they're sick," he said in the *Ryerson Review.* "So they're really additional holidays." Not surprisingly, when the time came for the first round of contract negotiations with Osprey Media, union members at the affected newspapers were skeptical about this allegedly enlightened corporation. Their skepticism was well-founded, as Osprey provoked labour disputes at the first three newspapers where it was required to negotiate new collective agreements.

A Premeditated Lockout

The first such dispute was orchestrated at *The Sudbury Star*, in the early-morning hours of October 5, 2002, when Osprey Media decided to lock out seventy unionized employees. Following several rounds of negotiations, bargaining committees for The Newspaper Guild of Canada and the Graphic Communications International Union agreed to Osprey's request to submit the company's "final" contract offer to a vote by union members. The vote would be scheduled for the following day.

However, unbeknownst to union negotiators and rank-and-file members alike, the company was not particularly interested in waiting for the results.

Before it even tabled its final offer, Osprey had hired strikebreakers and private security officers who were already in *The Star's* downtown building, preparing for publication of a scab newspaper. No sooner had the unions agreed to Osprey's request for a contract vote by rank-and-file members than the employees were locked out of their jobs and forced onto the picket line. The company justified its actions by claiming it had to protect the safety of its "assets and staff" from potential job action by the unions. Osprey's real motives were clear, however. It was sending a message throughout the chain that it could — and would — be as lean and mean as Thomson and Black ever were. Within days of engineering *The Star* lockout, Osprey's hard-line tactics would produce strikes at the *Cobourg Daily Star* and the *Port Hope Evening Guide*, where employees were seeking meagre workplace improvements that even their colleagues in Sudbury took for granted. While another labour dispute at *The Sudbury Star* may not have been earth-shattering news, the nature of the 2002 lockout shocked and angered many city residents.

Sudburians were genuinely offended that a new corporate citizen would swoop into town and at the first opportunity lock out local employees and publish the community's first-ever scab newspaper. Never before in *The Star's* sordid history, not with Thomsom nor Black, had a company attempted to publish a scab newspaper. But Osprey Media was intent on breaking new ground, regardless of the consequences for the newspaper, let alone the employees or the community. Osprey hired scabs locally — at one point advertising such jobs on a Human Resources Development Canada website — and recruited others from management and non-union ranks at its newspapers in Timmins, North Bay, Sault Ste. Marie, and a number of southern Ontario cities. The recruits included perennial scabs who a few years earlier had participated in Black's notorious union-busting campaign at the *Calgary Herald*. Over the next four months, Osprey would spend at least $800,000 on lockout-related expenses over and above regular operating costs at *The Star*, according to information obtained by the union. Settling the outstanding issues at the bargaining table would have cost a small fraction of that amount.

The dispute revolved around monetary issues and demands for improvements to working conditions, although the unions did have to contend with demands for concessions from the company in areas such as paid sick leave. Given that they had fought an eight-and-a-half month strike to win a sick-leave plan almost twenty years earlier, the unions steadfastly rejected demands for such concessions.

With regard to monetary issues, union members had seen their standard of living decline over more than a decade and they were intent on ending that trend, if not reversing it. The plight of a newly organized group of part-time workers was particularly appalling. The mailroom workers had only recently joined the union, after years of toiling in what amounted to a minimum-wage job ghetto, with no annual pay hikes, no benefits, and no job security. Another pressing monetary concern for employees was their chronic subsidization of the company's operations as a result of an outdated reimbursement system to pay expenses such as mileage costs for the use of personal vehicles.

Aside from the meat-and-potato issues, the unions, incredibly, had to negotiate for such mundane items as standard health-and-safety language and the provision of adequate numbers of telephones, desks, and computers for journalists to do their jobs. The absence of basic equipment and furniture was symptomatic of *The Star's* decline over a period of many years. Unions had long expressed concern over the lack of attention to the problems and challenges facing the newspaper. But such concerns were routinely dismissed and belittled by management, even as the newspaper's circulation dropped from year to year. Employee concerns culminated in the fall of 2002 when frustrated rank-and-file union members demanded that their union executive committees send a letter to the corporation's CEO outlining the chronic problem of management bungling and its impact on the newspaper's operation. The letter was sent, but Sifton never replied nor acknowledged the employees' concerns in any way. The letter illustrated in painful detail *The Star's* decline over the years, as more and more community citizens turned their backs on the newspaper. It noted how *The Star's* circulation decline had exceeded by far the industry-wide trend of lower readership. For example, on a per-capita basis, *The Star's* circulation was allowed to drop more than 50 per cent lower than its sister dailies in Sault Ste. Marie and North Bay. In other businesses, such glaring underperformance would be seen as a crisis worthy of dramatic action. Why was that not the case at *The Star*, employees wondered?

"Why has our newspaper been allowed to flounder and stagnate?" the workers asked Sifton in their letter, which continued:

> Sudbury is the business, education, and health-care centre of northeastern Ontario. We have the largest economy in the North. We also should have the largest and best newspaper in the region, but we don't. That is a shame, but it is understandable, considering what has happened to this newspaper over the last several years. The circulation numbers unequivocally demonstrate that *The Sudbury Star* has alienated and failed our community.

The letter called for a significant investment in the newspaper and its employees from the (self-proclaimed) progressive Osprey corporation. While Sifton opted not to respond to the employees' concerns, there was nevertheless a clear, if not demoralizing, explanation for the corporate disinterest in *The Star's* day-by-day troubles.

The fact was that management was able to consistently deliver considerable profit margins over the years, and so keep head office happy. This was accomplished by the ingenious means of continually cutting costs — particularly staff — while increasing advertising and subscription rates. "We have to do more with less" became *The Star* management's unofficial slogan. So, while circulation, staff morale, and *The Star's* place in the community sagged year-by-year, the revolving door CEOs were kept placated by healthy profit margins, reported to be in the 20 to 30 percent range. As the employees told Sifton in their letter:

> it appears to us that the margins delivered by *The Star* have not been realized through an aggressive, long-term plan for growth, but through a self-defeating, short-term strategy of cutting expenses to keep pace with the continual decline in our circulation.

The newspaper's profitability didn't prevent the company from crying poor at the bargaining table in 2002. That tactic was short-lived, however, after the unions cited internal information suggesting *The Star* was the second most-profitable newspaper in the Osprey chain. The claim was neither refuted nor denied. But as negotiations came to a head, the company held fast in rejecting union demands that would have amounted to an estimated $25,000 in additional costs annually. It was prepared to spend $800,000 over the next four months to prosecute a lockout that served its corporate agenda. For the early part of the labour dispute, as they did throughout the bargaining process, union members often made the observation that they appeared far more worried than manage-ment about the newspaper's direction and fate. "Never before have there been such widespread feelings of concern, frustration, disillusionment, and outright despair at the state of our newspaper," the employees wrote in their letter to Sifton. The employees' concern was such that in the early stages of the lockout, the unions opted not to attack the scab newspaper's circulation and advertising revenues, in the hope of negotiating a quick settlement. But as the dispute wore on and that hope grew faint, and as they were confronted daily by the scabs and security guards, it became clear to the locked-out workers that the company's agenda did not include an imminent resolution. With no prospect for a negoti-ated settlement, the unions became resigned to launching a public campaign to bring down the city's first-ever scab newspaper.

Almost immediately, the campaign drew widespread community support. In addition to the local labour movement, support came from small business people, professionals, and ordinary citizens. City councillors agreed unanimously, as did the local members of provincial and federal parliaments, not to grant interviews to what soon became known throughout the community as *The Scab Star*. Most advertisers, whether they overtly supported the locked-out workers or not, pulled their business from *The Star*, recognizing the community's poor appetite for a scab newspaper. Many retailers also refused to carry the newspaper in their stores. More than 3,000 readers signed subscription cancellation forms.

The Star responded to its plummeting readership with a coldly calculated, cynical ploy that eventually would add to the company's tainted reputation in the community. It launched a promotion in which it pledged to donate a portion of the price of every newspaper sold in stores to a local food bank. The publisher of the day insisted this newfound corporate benevolence would continue well after the lockout was over. It did not. Following the dispute's resolution, the company decided it no longer needed the food bank to help sell newspapers,

and the donations ceased. But *The Star* had never been big on corporate donations to worthy causes anyway. Indeed, over the years, virtually all requests for
charitable assistance were rejected. The company's typical response was to offer
"free publicity" — publication of a brief item in the newspaper to promote the
community group or project in question. In contrast, *The Star's* unions and employees had long epitomized the concept of "Proud Community Partners." In
simple terms, *The Star's* ownership was intent on squeezing as much money out
of the community as possible. But the unions and their members have always
had the opposite goal, to contribute as much as they could to the community's
economy and social fabric.

Informal research conducted by the unions has shown that their collective
bargaining struggles and victories over the decades have translated into millions
of dollars of additional economic activity in the community, compared to the
wages and benefits earned by their peers at non-union newspapers elsewhere.
The Star's unions and their members have also been among the community's
largest per-capita supporters of local charities, donating hundreds of thousands
of dollars over the years to numerous causes, including a children's telethon, the
United Way, and cancer research programs.

Furthermore, whereas *The Star's* management has consisted largely of out-
of-towners who forge few community ties before leaving for their next corporate
assignment, union members are homegrown folk who have long taken active
volunteer roles in charities, non-profit agencies, community and church groups,
minor sports organizations, and the like. In short, despite *The Star's* cynical
attempts to gain support for their scab newspaper in late 2002, it was already
clear to most Sudburians who in this labour dispute was the "Proud Community
Partner."

As readers cancelled their subscriptions and stopped buying *The Star* at retail
outlets, the unions turned their attention to the few advertisers who continued to
support the scab newspaper. Secondary picketing began outside the premises of
advertisers and had an almost-immediate impact. The first few businesses targeted
quickly pulled their advertising from *The Star* after being publicly condemned
for supporting a scab employer in its lockout of local workers.

As the lockout entered its fourth month and the company continued to lose
advertising and circulation revenue and its public image became increasingly
tarnished, the unions began planning for a major event in support of their
cause. Officials with the Mine Mill and Smelter Workers Union Local 598/CAW
proposed a demonstration of solidarity for the locked-out newspaper employees
by staging a rally outside *The Sudbury Star* offices. The rally would be part of the
CAW's province-wide campaign to pressure the provincial government to reinstate
labour laws — which had been scrapped by the former Conservative government
of Mike Harris — to outlaw the use of strike-breaking scab labour.

Indeed, *The Sudbury Star* picket line would provide a compelling backdrop
for a public rally demanding progressive legislation to outlaw scab labour. The
scene created by Osprey Media featured scabs, hidden from view in vans with

dark-tinted windows, being ferried to and from *The Star* every day, escorted by crews of black-uniformed, private security guards who patrolled inside and outside the building, video-taping any and all activity in sight, round the clock, seven days a week.

(Whether the company received any value from the prohibitive price tag for its private security force would appear highly questionable. One of the few, tangible uses the company made of the thousands of hours of surveillance tapes provided one of the more ludicrous anecdotes from the lockout. *The Star's* publisher ordered a review of the tapes after he noticed a sign on the door of the portable outhouse used by picketers that read "This is where [the publisher's] career is heading." The publisher was intent on learning who put up the sign, although it was never clear if the crack security team was able to resolve the caper.)

In any event, planning progressed for a huge rally outside *The Star* building that would attract CAW leaders and members from across the province, as well as local union members, community activists, and the general public. With the proposed rally approaching and the lockout nearing four months in length, Osprey Media decided it was time to resume bargaining. Whether it was the implications of the rally or the lockout's effect on the company's business or image — or a combination of those factors — the company wasn't saying. But it was more anxious than ever to settle the dispute. Long gone were any demands for concessions and any hope of breaking the unions. The company tabled a new offer for settlement, containing modest improvements to previous proposals.

Union negotiators decided to bring the new offer of settlement to the membership for a vote, with no recommendation from the bargaining team. The locked-out employees, who had rejected two previous contract proposals, clearly were unimpressed with Osprey's latest offering. At the same time, employees were feeling the effects of a sixteen-week dispute, most of which they had endured during bitter winter conditions on the picket line. When the contract offer was put to a vote, it was rejected by a slim majority of the overall union membership. However, legally, the vote had to be broken down to reflect the positions of the three different bargaining units in the Joint Council of Newspaper Unions. Two of the bargaining units voted to accept the contract offer by the slimmest of margins — a single vote in one case. The third unit — representing mailroom employees — soundly rejected the proposal.

Historically, the bargaining units in the Joint Council at *The Star* always supported the position of any unit that could not accept a proposed contract. To maintain their solidarity and bargaining power, no unit would ratify a contract unless all other units were prepared to do the same. But in January 2003, to their considerable credit, the mailroom workers did not ask their sisters and brothers in the other bargaining units to prolong the labour dispute on their behalf. Instead, the mailroom workers reconsidered their vote and accepted the contract offer, allowing the lockout to end on January 27.

Within days of *The Star* employees return to work, cash-strapped, penny-pinching Osprey Media announced it was spending $194 million to purchase more than thirty newspapers in southern Ontario from CanWest Global.

The new, four-year agreement at *The Star* was considered one of the best in the newspaper industry in recent years. It fended off demands for concessions while providing wage increases ranging from 9.2 to 15 percent, and brought improvements in areas such as pension contributions, mileage rates, and vacations. In a telling and embarrassing footnote for Osprey, the union also won contract language stipulating that each reporter would be provided with his/her own desk, telephone, and computer — something the company had previously been unable or unwilling to do.

The lockout's conclusion also represented a victory for employees who stood up to the unprecedented strike-breaking tactics used by Osprey, and who beat back any notion the company entertained about breaking the unions at *The Star*.

At the same time, any hope employees harboured that *The Star* might commit to better labour relations and improve its standing in the community was soon dismissed after the lockout. On their first day back at work, several employees were targeted for retribution for their activist roles during the lockout. The union President and Vice President, as well as two employees who were among the most active and vocal picketers during the dispute, were immediately informed that their duties and work schedules were being drastically and arbitrarily changed. A fifth union activist was also informed he was being laid off, even though such a layoff clearly violated the collective agreement. The union filed grievances on all these matters that culminated in an indisputable victory for the affected employees. The disputed layoff was categorically rescinded, while the other employees were granted the right to resume their former duties and schedules.

Next on the company's post-lockout agenda was the cancellation of *The Star's* Sunday edition, in April 2003. For years *The Star* took pride in the fact it was the only daily newspaper in Northern Ontario to publish seven days a week. But for more than a decade the company invested little, if anything, in its Sunday edition, seemingly being content for it to stagnate rather than become a centrepiece publication. In announcing the Sunday cancellation, *The Star's* publisher pledged to employees and the community that the quantity and quality of news content would not suffer. Lost content from the Sunday edition, in terms of sports and news coverage and various features, would be added to *The Star's* new, six-day publication schedule. That undertaking was short-lived, as news coverage soon tailed off and promised targets were abandoned.

Still, *The Star* insisted it was committed not only to improving its in-house labour relations, but to building a bigger and better community newspaper. The veracity of that commitment was soon belied, not only by a lack of investment in the newspaper but by a series of devastating job cuts. Through attrition, firings, and layoffs, job losses occurred in most areas of the newspaper's operation, including the editorial department — contradicting the company's claim of increasing its focus on local news coverage.

As the job cuts continued, the company at least had the courtesy of eliminating the corporate motto that featured so prominently in the newspaper: "A Proud Community Partner." The most shocking attack on *The Star's* workforce came in the spring of 2005. As *The Star's* press staff were preparing to head to work on the evening of May 24, they were contacted at home and ordered to assemble at a local hotel for a special staff meeting. Inside a small hotel meeting room, they were informed they no longer had jobs. *The Sudbury Star* would henceforth be printed in North Bay, beginning that evening, company officials said. The eight press staff, whose service to *The Star* ranged from a few years to more than four decades, were advised against visiting their workplace. Private security guards were on the premises to dissuade them from entering the building, they were told. When asked to justify the decision, company officials refused to answer questions from the shaken press workers that night, as well as those of other employees in subsequent days.

To employees and much of the community, this company decision was a shock that made little sense unless it was viewed through Osprey's anti-union prism. At the time, *The Star* was equipped with a modern, high-speed, high-capacity, full-colour press capable of printing multiple newspapers daily, if required. In contrast, the printing press at the Osprey-owned *North Bay Nugget* was small, outdated, and incapable of printing multiple daily newspapers. To be able to print more newspapers in North Bay, Osprey would have to make a sizeable investment to upgrade the *Nugget's* press facilities and to hire several more press operators.

The apparent deficit of logic behind this decision led many in Sudbury — including community leaders — to conclude that Osprey had based the move on unspoken factors other than press capabilities and technology. The fact was that in Sudbury, Osprey had to contend with unionized employees who had proven time and again they would respond militantly to protect their interests and working conditions. Such militancy was not as great a problem in North Bay, where the company enjoyed greater freedom in terms of imposing various demands on press operators.

"We all know that Sudbury is a labour town: North Bay isn't," Greater Sudbury City Councillor Ron Dupuis said at a Council meeting in June 2005. *The Sudbury Star's* press operators, Dupuis said, "are victims of somebody who is not happy with how healthy the union is at *The Sudbury Star*. That's the bottom line."

Like much of the community, Sudbury city councillors took offence with Osprey's decision and its underlying motivation. Council requested that *The Star's* publisher or another Osprey representative appear publicly before Council to explain the decision and the company's plans for its local operations. On June 29, 2005, Council unanimously passed a resolution calling on Osprey to account for its actions. Council urged Osprey to resume its press operations in Sudbury and to reverse its trend of taking jobs out of the community. Osprey, councillors said, should be committed to creating "a better, more successful, committed local newspaper." Osprey management declined requests to appear before Council to justify its persistent job-cutting in Sudbury. They may not have been too keen to let on that greater slashing and burning were on the horizon.

By late 2005, with Michael Sifton citing a need for "greater efficiencies" within his would-be empire, Osprey launched a campaign of outsourcing jobs from many of its provincial newspapers. This time, in addition to Sudbury, numerous communities would be affected, including Sault Ste. Marie, Timmins, North Bay, St. Catharines, Barrie, Belleville, Orillia, Chatham, Cobourg, Cornwall, Kingston, Port Hope, Owen Sound, Pembroke, Brantford, and Lindsay.

Sifton set up call centres in Niagara Falls and Sarnia to handle customer service calls for circulation and classified ad business. Osprey began axing long-term, well-paid employees at several newspapers, including *The Sudbury Star*. The work — but not a single one of the displaced employees — was transferred to the southern Ontario call centres, which Osprey staffed with part-time workers receiving low pay and no benefits. The latest round of layoffs at *The Sudbury Star* saw three customer-service clerks lose their jobs in April 2006. As of that date, more than thirty jobs had disappeared at *The Star* since Osprey Media took over the newspaper.

Osprey's outsourcing of local jobs to low-wage call centres prompted Newspaper Guild locals in Sudbury and several other cities, supported by their national body, TNG Canada, to launch community-based protest campaigns. The outsourcing was condemned by politicians, as well as by labour and community leaders. Osprey employees and their supporters picketed outside affected newspapers in several cities. The campaigns won broad public support and infuriated Osprey management. But Sifton was adamant about staying the course, for he was in a self-made bind, resulting from a decision in 2004 to convert Osprey to an income trust.

The Osprey Media Income Fund was launched amid much fanfare, with promises of generous returns and monthly cash payments to investors, or "unit holders." But, in short order, the Osprey fund ran into serious difficulty. Although the company was profitable — with double-digit profit margins — its net income was still not high enough to meet the payments it was promising investors. Analysts predicted Osprey would have to reduce its payouts to unit holders. Unit prices fell. The Osprey fund's value dropped well below its initial public offering price. But Sifton insisted Osprey would meet its distribution obligations. Any shortfalls would be covered by more cost-cutting at already profitable newspapers.

For employees at Sifton's newspapers, it wasn't difficult to conclude that Osprey's income-trust experiment was a disaster. Many industry analysts appeared to agree with that assessment. "Michael Sifton wanted to become a newspaper mogul," the *Globe and Mail's Report on Business* stated in February 2006. "Instead, he became a warning to investors who thought a security containing the cheery words 'income' and 'trust' could do no wrong" (Reguly 2006). Bay Street forensic accountant Al Rosen listed Osprey Media among his top five income trusts that investors should be wary of.

McLean & Partners Wealth Management of Calgary released a "red flag" list warning investors of income trusts at risk of suspending cash distributions. The analysts used three key criteria, or red flags, to evaluate 200 income trusts. A total of eighty-three trusts raised at least one flag: Osprey Media set off all three.

For virtually all of 2006, Osprey's income-trust woes provided fodder for analysts and the business press. Speculation was rife that Sifton was trying to sell the newspaper trust but was having difficulty finding buyers.

Employees at *The Sudbury Star* likely won't be shocked if — or when — their newspaper, having been suitably milked, is again "flipped" from one corporate master to another. But they certainly would be pleasantly surprised to someday be correct in the time-honoured lament, "this one just can't be as bad as the last one."

Note

1.   In 2007, shortly after the author completed this chapter, *The Sudbury Star*, then owned by Osprey Media Income Fund (2004), was the subject of another corporate takeover, this time by Québec Media Inc. of Montréal.

Chapter 3

Public-Sector Unions in Sudbury

John Closs

For decades, the mining industry was the driving force behind Sudbury's economy. For Sudbury residents, the plumes of toxic smoke that poured from chimneys at Inco's nickel smelter signaled jobs and prosperity. By 1975, the well-paying unionized jobs in the nickel mines and mills had made Sudbury one of the wealthiest cities in Canada on a per capita basis, and, at the time, the community enjoyed almost full employment. When Walter Stewart (1975), writing in "Canada's national newsmagazine," described Sudbury as "squatting in its glum background like a whore in a hovel," the observation outraged some Sudburians, but there was little real concern that the condescending description would have any effect on Sudbury's booming economy (Sudol 2004).

At the time, there was no apparent apprehension in Sudbury about the future prospects of the mining industry. In 1975 an economic study commissioned by the Planning and Development Department of the Regional Municipality of Sudbury reassuringly predicted the possibility of only slight declines in mining employment over the next twenty years (Peat, Marwick, and Partners 1975: III–17). It was not until after major layoffs by Inco and Falconbridge, the two major employers in Sudbury's mining industry, in 1977 — as it became apparent that employment in the mining industry was declining precipitously and permanently — that the development of a diverse economy became a priority for the community (Project Group on Urban Economic Development 1985: 14).

Sudbury's mines and mills had experienced temporary workforce reductions before, but increasing mechanization and automation meant that the mining companies could maintain and even increase nickel production with a much smaller workforce than had been required in the past (Clement 1981: 83). The effect on employment in the industry, which was the core of Sudbury's economy, was devastating. In 1972, Local 6500 of the United Steelworkers of America represented 14,500 hourly rated workers at Inco's Sudbury operations, but by 1982 Local 6500's membership in Sudbury had dropped to 10,000 (Brasch 1997: 81, 94).

In response to this crisis, some politicians called for nationalization of mining operations in Sudbury. At a packed meeting in the Steelworkers Hall, Stephen Lewis, Leader of the Ontario New Democratic Party, accused Inco of firing an arrow into the heart of the community and called on government to take away Inco's corporate bow. In the provincial Legislature, Floyd Laughren, the member for the Nickel Belt riding, which includes much of the region of Sudbury, called for an immediate public takeover of Ontario's nickel resources (Swift 1991). However, the demand for public control of the mineral wealth that Sudbury was built on was not broadly accepted outside the labour movement, and most local politicians decided to adopt a more accommodating strategy. In the short term, they would depend on government benevolence to replace the jobs that were being lost and, at the same time, they would attempt to diversify Sudbury's economy to ensure the long-term survival of the community (Tester 1994: 101).

Local government decided to concentrate its economic development efforts in five areas: mining-related technology, health services, tourism, government services, and higher education and training. Local political leadership also sought and was able to secure the commitment of every sector of the community — business, labour, and the media — to work together to respond to the crisis (Project Group on Urban Economic Development 1985: 23, 30). This remark-able coalition of groups reflected the depth of the crisis the community faced. Attempts to attract private industry to Sudbury were generally unsuccessful, but, through a determined campaign of lobbying, local leaders were able to increase public-sector employment in the region, and the public sector became the one bright spot in the regional economy during the 1980s.

Public-Sector Expansion and Contraction

During the 1980s, the growth of the public sector in Sudbury was dramatic. Between 1981 and 1991, over 3,500 jobs were added to the government service sector of Sudbury's labour force. Those jobs represented a 76.8 percent increase in employment in the public sector, which contributed to the 18.4 percent increase in Sudbury's total labour force. In contrast, during the same period, employment in the mining sector fell by 29.0 percent (Statistics Canada 1983, 1994).

The growth in public-sector employment was the result of new public services being located in Sudbury and the expansion of established ones. The most sig-nificant addition was the federal Taxation Data Centre. Opened in 1981, it is still one of the major employers in the area, with 1,500 full-time workers, along with another 1,300 part-time workers hired during the three- to four-month period when the bulk of the income tax returns are processed (Gilbert 2004). During those months, the entrance to the Taxation Data Centre is a very busy place. The day shift starts at 7:00 a.m., but even that early in the morning workers have to park blocks away from the Centre because the large parking lots surrounding it are already full.

Local politicians were also able to convince the provincial government to move major portions of some provincial ministries to Sudbury. The province constructed a new building to house the Ministry of Northern Development and Mines in downtown Sudbury and, in 1990, most of the Ministry's head-office employees were moved to Sudbury. The same Ministry also built the Willet Green Centre near Laurentian University to house testing and research facilities for the Ministry's mining branch and the Ontario Geological Survey, which moved into the new facility in 1992 (Smith 1992: 15).

Sudbury was also able to get funding for economic development projects such as Science North, a science centre and family tourist attraction that opened in 1984. Science North would not have been built without the combined efforts of the federal, provincial, and municipal governments, and government funding is still essential for its survival. In the post-secondary education sector, both Laurentian University, established in 1957, and Cambrian College, established in 1966, expanded during the 1980s and took on greater economic importance. As a result, Sudbury was the natural location for the main campus of a new French post-secondary institution, Collège Boréal, established in 1995.

In the health sector, Laurentian Hospital was opened in 1975 to serve the districts of Sudbury and Manitoulin, securing Sudbury's position as a regional health centre. As a result, the Northeastern Ontario Regional Cancer Centre was built in Sudbury to provide cancer treatment for the residents of northeastern Ontario. It opened in November 1990.

One notable effect of the increase in public-sector employment in Sudbury was the increase in women's employment. The increased importance of the public sector has had a profound effect on the gender composition of the labour force in Sudbury. Women's participation in the labour force has increased to the point that almost half the workers employed in Sudbury are now women (Statistics Canada 2004). What success local leadership achieved in diversifying Sudbury's economy was dependent on the federal and provincial governments' interest in and support of economic development in the region, but even before the end of the 1980s it became apparent to local leaders that government support for community economic development was drying up (Davies 1988: 6).

In the late 1980s, the federal government began to adopt neo-liberal policies designed to reduce the size of government and its influence in the economy. In 1988, for example, the newly elected Conservative federal government backed out of a commitment to build a new federal building in downtown Sudbury. In Ontario, these policies were adopted by a Conservative government led by Mike Harris, which was first elected in June 1995, and they have continued under the Liberal government of Dalton McGuinty, elected in October 2003.

Government intervention in the economy was seen as counter to the natural efficiency of the market. Labour market, regional development, and welfare programs that attempted to alleviate the worst inequities of the market were seen as creating disincentives to work (Bradford 2000: 68). The federal government cut many of the programs designed to support the peoples of disadvantaged areas like Sudbury, as the government sought to dismantle the welfare state (Russell 2000: 41).

In the late 1980s, the federal government also started pulling money out of the public sector through reduction in transfers to the provinces. Despite the reductions, the NDP provincial government, elected in September 1990, continued to intervene in the market by supporting regional development in the face of the economic recession and pressure from the business community (Rae 1997: 225). However, the NDP also chose to abandon its position that jobs in the public sector have the same value as those in the private sector. Instead, the NDP began to adopt the right-wing rhetoric that bestowed greater value on the private sector. In the face of the recession, NDP Premier Bob Rae said it was necessary to cut back on the public sector in order to allow the private sector to lead the economic recovery (Walkom 1993).

When the Mike Harris Tories replaced the provincial NDP government, the attack on the public sector increased in intensity. One of the new government's first acts was to cut welfare payments by 22 percent. The Tories also started a systematic reduction in the size of the public sector. Sudbury was particularly vulnerable to reductions in government spending because so much of its economy was dependent on government funding. From 1991 to 2001, Sudbury lost 1,920 public-sector jobs (Statistics Canada 1994, 2004).

In education, government cutbacks meant that Cambrian College, which had employed over 300 full-time professors, counsellors, and librarians in 1989, retained fewer than 200 full-time academic staff by the end of the nineties, despite the fact that the College had the same number of full-time students enrolled. The reduction in full-time staff was mainly accomplished by increasing class sizes and decreasing students' contact time with their professors. Overall, since 1989, in the college sector in Sudbury, despite the addition of Collège Boréal, the number of academic employees has decreased even as student numbers have risen.

During the 1990s, the combined effect of cutbacks in the public sector and continued decline in employment in the mining industry resulted in an overall decline in the Sudbury labour force. However, Table 3.1 shows that, despite the cutbacks, the public sector continued to be an important part of Sudbury's economy, while employment in the mining sector continued to fall dramatically.

During the 1980s, Sudbury had come to rely on expansion of public-sector employment as a way to maintain its economic growth. With the cutbacks by both the federal and the provincial governments, expansion of the public sector was no longer a viable means of replacing the jobs that were draining out of the mining sector. But public-sector workers had become and would continue to be a large and vital portion of Sudbury's workforce.

Sudbury's Public-Sector Unions

The public sector now plays a much larger role in the Sudbury economy than it did in 1975 and, as it has grown in importance, public-sector unions have become more significant in the local labour movement. In 1972, the United Steelworkers of America Local 6500, which represents the hourly paid workers at Inco, and the Canadian Union of Mine Mill and Smelter Workers Local 598, now part of the Canadian Auto Workers, which represents the hourly paid workers at Falconbridge, were the dominant labour organizations in Sudbury. Now, while

Table 3.1: Comparison of Sudbury's Labour Force, by Selected Industry and Gender, 1991 and 2001

	1991		2001	
	Number of persons	Percent of total labour force	Number of persons	Percent of total labour force
Total labour force	81,245	100	77,475	100
Primary industries (includes mining, forestry, agriculture, and fishing)	8,725	10.7	5,370	6.9
Government service industries	8,095	10.0	6,175	8.0
Educational service industries	7,280	9.0	5,905	7.6
Health and social-service industries	7,610	9.4	8,680	11.2
Subtotal for education, health, and government	22,985	28.3	20,760	26.8
Males	43,710	53.8	40,090	51.7
Females	36,315	44.7	37,390	48.3

Source: Statistics Canada 1994 and 2004

they remain important parts of the labour movement, they no longer hold a pre-eminent position. In 2002, while there were 4,654 employees in the two main bargaining units at Falconbridge and Inco, there were 7,141 employees in bargaining units in the health-care sector and 4,690 employees in bargaining units in the education sector in the Sudbury area (Whynott 2003: Table 1).

Several unions represent public-sector workers. The largest public-sector union in Sudbury is the Canadian Union of Public Employees (CUPE), which represents employees in health care and municipal services. Other public-sector unions with significant memberships are the Ontario Public Service Employees Union (OPSEU), which represents workers in provincial government ministries, jails, social-service agencies, health care, and colleges; the Ontario Nurses' Association; the Public Service Alliance of Canada, with its component the Union of Taxation Employees, which represents the workers at the Taxation Centre; the Laurentian University Faculty Association, which represents academic employees at the university; and the Laurentian University Staff Association, which represents non-academic staff there. There are also a number of unions that represent workers in elementary and secondary education: the Association des Enseignantes et des Enseignants Franco-Ontariens, the Elementary Teachers' Federation of Ontario, the Ontario Secondary School Teachers' Federation, and the Ontario English Catholic Teachers' Association.

Members of public-sector unions have borne the brunt of the attacks on the public sector by neo-liberal governments. Cutbacks in the public sector have led to layoffs, deteriorating working conditions, and alienation, as the value of public services and public-service workers are denigrated by the champions of private enterprise. In response to the constant attacks on public services, public-sector unions have begun to develop more militant resistance to the corporate agenda of privatization, contracting out, and downsizing of public services.

OPSEU has been one of the leading unions in the fight to preserve public services. The OPSEU symbol is a stylized trillium representing Ontario, surrounded by three lines representing the members of the three components of OPSEU, the Ontario public service, the broader public sector, and the colleges of applied arts. For years, the border had a broken line at the bottom indicating that the members of OPSEU employed in the Ontario public service did not have the right to strike. That line was joined in 1993 when those OPSEU members won that right. Since then, OPSEU members in the Ontario public service have been forced to go out on strike twice as the Harris Tories attacked public services and the workers who deliver them. The number of workers involved in the two strikes bear witness to the devastating effects of the cutbacks on the public service. The first strike in 1996 involved over 65,000 members (Rapaport 1999: Table 2). Six years later, in 2002, cutbacks in the public sector meant that only 45,000 members were involved in a strike that year.

Other public-sector unions have also felt the effects of government cutbacks. CUPE represents workers in the municipal sector and health care in Sudbury. The forced amalgamation of the smaller municipalities that made up the Region of Sudbury into the City of Greater Sudbury has affected the jobs of many CUPE members. The amalgamation of the three local hospitals — St. Joseph's, Memorial, and Laurentian — into the Sudbury Regional Hospital forced CUPE to compete with OPSEU, which represented the clerical workers at Memorial, for the right to represent clerical workers at the new hospital. CUPE had the majority of the clerical workers and eventually won a representation vote, but the campaign was costly and divisive.

In the education sector, the teachers' unions were among the leaders of the resistance to the Harris Conservative agenda between 1995 and 1999. They led the fight for public education and took on the Harris government in an illegal strike in the fall of 1997 (Camfield 2000: 309–10). Teachers' unions have also seen the value of aligning themselves with the broader labour movement and have affiliated with the Canadian Labour Congress and the Ontario Federation of Labour. In Sudbury, the Ontario Secondary School Teachers' Federation and the Ontario English Catholic Teachers' Association are now active members of the Sudbury and District Labour Council.

During the 1990s, public-sector unions also had to adjust to the privatization and downloading of the costs of government services. While the number of employees directly employed by government fell steadily, the broader public sector grew rapidly. This forced public-sector unions to become more involved in organizing. After shrinking a bit, OPSEU's membership actually grew under the Harris government because OPSEU organized almost everybody who went from direct government employment to the broader public service. In the past, public-sector unions had been able to rely on the growth of the public service to increase their membership. OPSEU in particular had been able to rely on the fact that almost everyone hired as a full-time employee of the public service was going to become a member of the bargaining unit and a source of dues revenue. As a result, OPSEU had little reason to get involved in the expensive and often unrewarding task of organizing workers.

Now, if OPSEU wants to keep growing as a union, it has to keep organizing. One of the main forms organizing has taken is campaigns to ensure that workers affected by the divestment of public services will maintain their union rights and benefits and will not lose the protection of the union. These campaigns often combine opposition to the privatization of the public service with a drive to ensure that if the services are privatized OPSEU will retain the employees as members. One example of this is the OPSEU campaign against the downloading of ambulance services to the municipalities by the provincial government, announced in 1997. Despite OPSEU's opposition, the downloading went ahead, and OPSEU had to fight to retain representation rights for ambulance paramedics who had formerly been part of the Ontario public service (OPSEU 2001).

The need to organize also means that OPSEU and other public-sector unions are going to be more active in meeting the needs of people in the community. For example, OPSEU led a campaign in support of community mental-health services in Sudbury, organizing public forums to highlight the cutbacks that reduced the region's seventy-two beds for acute care mental-health service to thirty-nine (OPSEU 2002). OPSEU also campaigned against the privatization of jails, holding a rally in Sudbury in January 2000 to educate the community about the hazards of for-profit corrections services (OPSEU 2000). But when the provincial government determined to go ahead with private prisons, OPSEU organized the workers in the first private prison.

The Harris years made public-sector unions aware of how difficult it is to make gains when the government abandons any pretence of building consensus and working with the unions. During the first years of resistance to the Harris Tories, public-sector unions, along with the Canadian Autoworkers, called for extra-parliamentary resistance to the government and sought to build support through "Days of Action" in individual cities. Most private-sector unions were more comfortable with re-establishing strong links to the New Democratic Party that had been severed over the Rae government's "Social Contract" legislation, and with building electoral support for the NDP (Rapaport 1999: 58). Sudbury was one of the main arenas for this debate.

In October 1996, a huge turnout for the Toronto Day of Action appeared to lay the groundwork for a province-wide general strike. However, some of the more conservative private-sector unions — dubbed the "pink paper unions" and including the United Steelworkers — announced that they would not support future Days of Action. The next Day of Action was scheduled for February 28, 1997, in Sudbury. and the pink paper unions, led by the United Steelworkers, were able to ensure that the local Labour Council did not support the event. Despite this, public-sector unions, social activists, and sympathetic private-sector unions such as the Canadian Autoworkers organized a major march and rally in Sudbury, but resistance to the Harris Tories never regained the vigour it had shown in Toronto (Camfield 2000: 309).

During the 1990s, public-sector unions also became more active in electoral politics. This has been the subject of considerable contention within and among unions. Some members are uncomfortable with any union involvement in electoral politics. Once those objections have been overcome there has been much debate over how unions can be most effective in influencing the political process, because public-sector unions' attempts at engaging in politics have not always been successful. One commentator pointed out the flaws in a strategy that was adopted by the teachers' unions during the 1999 provincial election campaign in an attempt to defeat the Conservative Party led by Mike Harris:

> Toward that end, they followed a vengeful and ill-advised strategy of pouring enormous resources (specifically volunteers) into a campaign to defeat then-Education Minister Dave Johnson.
>
> The problem was that Johnson was not only a relative moderate around the Cabinet table, but also a talented minister who was highly popular amongst his colleagues. So when the Tories won another majority government, even as Johnson went down to defeat, the teachers had clearly won the battle while losing the war. (Holcroft 2001)

While the first campaign to defeat the Harris Tories was unsuccessful, public-sector workers and their unions realized that they needed to continue to defend public services in the face of the advocates of deregulation, privatization, and downsizing. As they gain more experience in politics, public-sector unions are exploring different strategies. For example, in April 2006 OPSEU's Central Political Action Committee (CPAC) presented a resolution to the OPSEU Convention that OPSEU should formally affiliate with the NDP. In preparation for the convention, CPAC had consulted extensively with union members and their leadership, and at the convention each CPAC member spoke in support of the resolution and pointed to the benefits of affiliation. The resolution was fiercely debated, and there were long lines of speakers still standing when debate was closed. The vote on the resolution was so close that a standing count was ordered. In the end, there were 349 votes in favour of affiliation and 378 against. The resolution was defeated by only twenty-nine votes. While the delegates rejected the resolution, the debate demonstrated a mature attitude toward political involvement. The delegates who opposed the resolution were not arguing that OPSEU should disengage from politics: rather they were debating the merits of party affiliation as a tactic in furthering the union's agenda politically.

In whatever way they choose to engage in politics, public-sector unions understand that they can no longer stand aside from the political process and hope that the government will work in their favour. Public-sector unions will have to engage in the political process, and, as the debate on how to do so continues, so too will the debate about what policies need to be promoted. This policy debate will encourage members of public-sector unions to think about how they and their unions can create alternatives to the dominant neo-liberal ideology.

Public-Sector Unions and the Labour Movement in the Community

As has been seen, events far removed from the community and the influence of local intervention can have significant local effects. For Sudbury, decisions made in Queen's Park and Ottawa have been, and will continue to be, critical to the future direction of the community. When the provincial government decided to move a substantial number of government jobs to Sudbury, it had a positive effect on the community. But, when federal and provincial governments began to dismantle the welfare state by reducing welfare rates and dismantling regional development programs, the community suffered. The importance of government funding can lead communities to support only those political parties likely to form the government. The economic situation of Sudbury makes it difficult for voters to support alternative candidates or parties because of the fear that the governing party will not favour opposition ridings and might withhold public-sector jobs and investment from the community.

Another challenge is that most union leaders and members are mainly interested in supporting their union when it is attempting to make gains in the workplace. Unions are able to mobilize members around collective bargaining, but are less successful in engaging their members with community issues. Union members are most supportive of their union when it fights for better wages, benefits, and working conditions. They are willing to get involved in issues in the workplace or that directly affect the workplace, but once the issues go beyond the imperatives of the workplace members are less willing to participate. For example, OPSEU represents many of the professional paramedical staff at the Sudbury Regional Hospital. In 2003, hospital professionals across the province were so upset with the government that they went on an illegal strike. To protest staff shortages that put hospital health care at risk, they risked lost pay and even jail. But, later that year OPSEU could not mobilize those same workers to attend a one-hour rally to support the recommendations in the Romanow Report on the future of health care in Canada, which stoutly defended medicare.

Public-sector workers who engage in strikes quickly realize that, to be successful, they must involve the community's, the province's, or the country's political leadership, and labour disputes in the public sector quickly become politically significant. In the spring of 2004, the local electrical utility, Greater Sudbury Utilities (GSU), which is governed by a board appointed by the municipal council, demanded that the members of CUPE Local 4705 accept a contract that included the concession that new employees would not be eligible for the same retirement benefits as current employees. The local went on strike to ensure that future employees would enjoy the same benefits current employees are entitled to when they retire. The strikers were strongly supported by the local and the provincial labour movement because their fight was emblematic of the challenges the whole labour movement faced as the health-care and retirement benefits that unions fought for over decades were being whittled away through the various cost-saving and profit-making measures of contemporary corporations (O'Flanagan 2004).

After a summer on the picket line, the striking workers and their supporters realized that they needed to step into the political arena to motivate the GSU board to settle the dispute. A number of city councillors, including the Mayor, sat on the GSU board and, despite the municipal council's supposed neutrality, it was clear that the strikers needed to mobilize political pressure to settle the dispute. The local Labour Council had been actively involved in recent municipal election campaigns and during the previous municipal campaign it had publicly endorsed a number of successful candidates who had agreed to a platform that included a commitment to honour workers' rights and oppose concessionary bargaining. Disappointingly, only one of those councillors honoured their commitment and stood firmly with the strikers. However, local labour leaders worked together to put pressure on the municipal council to resolve the dispute, and the Ontario Federation of Labour threatened a boycott of the city (Carmichael 2004). Within a month, the GSU removed the demand for concessions on retiree benefits from the bargaining table and the strike was settled.

That strike demonstrated that when the labour movement works together it can exert substantial pressure on the local political leadership regarding particular issues. Motivating workers and their unions to support positive changes will be key to developing a more progressive Sudbury, and public-sector workers are going to be particularly important because of their numbers, their organization, and their interest in the political process. The confluence of the workers' interests and the broader political agenda shows how important the public sector can be in promoting political engagement that is key to building a more democratic community.

Public-Sector Unions and the Public Interest

One issue that has resonance for members of public-sector unions is the defence of a strong public-sector presence in our community. If you visit the offices of any public-sector union, you will see information promoting well-funded public services. One such publication from the National Union of Provincial Government Employees describes the value of public services in our society as follows:

> public services have a value that is both undeniable and perhaps even beyond estimate — not only to us as individuals eager to get on with our own private, day-to-day lives in safety and comfort; but also as a society, as a people, as a community of friends and neighbours with a distinct and

definite collective vision of who we are, who we want to be, and how we want the rest of the world to know us. (NUPGE 1998: 5)

Public-sector unions and their allies in the labour movement will fight to maintain public services in our community, and, for Sudbury to continue to prosper, a strong public sector is essential.

One way that public-sector unions and the labour movement can enhance the value and legitimacy of public services in the community is by advocating a role for labour in the governance of all public services. Currently, boards appointed by the provincial government usually control organizations active in the public sector. If these boards have any recognized labour representatives, the local Labour Council has rarely selected them, and they often have little or no connection to the labour movement. Also, few of these boards include representatives of their organization's employee groups. The organizations' managers usually dominate these boards because board members predominantly come from management backgrounds and are sympathetic to management's goals. As a result, these boards focus on fiscal responsibility rather than on public service and community benefit.

For example, in 2003, the provincially appointed board of the Manitoulin-Sudbury Community Care Access Centre, which had been set up by the Harris Tories to manage the delivery of home and school health care in the region, awarded a contract to provide home nursing care in Sudbury to a profit-making, non-union nursing company because its bid was lower than the bid of the not-for-profit Victorian Order of Nurses (VON), a unionized employer that had provided quality home nursing care in the community for decades. The Chair of the Centre's board, a former Conservative Party candidate, stated that services would not be affected by the change, but the new service provider paid its nurses by the visit rather than by the hour, which discouraged the nurses from spending time with their patients and was ill-suited to such a widely spread-out community. Services to those in need of home nursing care quickly deteriorated and patients in outlying areas were forced to pay for private nursing care. In addition, the VON's other services to the community — a nurse practitioner clinic, an adult day centre, and offices in Espanola and Manitoulin Island that offered services like Meals On Wheels, transportation, and home support programs — were affected, because the loss of the contract threatened the continued existence of the Sudbury branch after eighty-two years of service to the community (VON 2004).

The effective involvement of the labour movement in the governance of organizations such as the Manitoulin-Sudbury Community Care Access Centre, which are entrusted with the provision of public services in the community, would ensure that the community's interest would not be subsumed by narrow fiscal considerations. The participation of the labour movement would increase local control of public services, enhance local participation in decisions about the future of public services, and strengthen the link between public services and the community's interests.

While the dominant neo-liberal ideology worships the market and denigrates the role of public services, the latter are a key component in the growth and development of a community (Hall 2003: 12). Public services reflect commitment to community. The people of the community own the public services and we can take pride in the quality and breadth of public services available in our community. Private enterprise will quickly abandon a community if it cannot make a profit, and multinational corporations certainly owe no allegiance to a municipality.

In Sudbury, public-sector workers are employed in the health-care, social-service, education, and government service sectors. These services are essential to our community and these jobs provide good wages and benefits that in turn benefit our local economy. Despite the obvious importance of the public sector in the Sudbury economy, local leaders have adopted the same neo-liberal disdain for the public sector that is evident in the federal and provincial governments. When Sudbury was first faced with the decline in mining employment, local leaders were not afraid to call for government help to relieve the crisis. Now, despite the importance of the public sector in Sudbury's economy, the city's establishment is unwilling to acknowledge that governments can create economic growth in the region. The "New Way," a recent initiative focussed on wealth creation and economic growth in the region, was intended to mobilize the community to create a shared vision of the future, but after the requisite community forum to develop the shared vision it was clear that it would not include more government-led growth. Instead, the community was told that government should not lead the way, and that the community needed to invest in itself (Carmichael 2000).

Public services do represent the community investing in itself, and they are one of the best ways for the community to reflect its belief in its future. Instead of slavishly following the trend of corporate adoration, Sudbury should look to its early efforts at economic diversification, when the community worked together to create economic growth in both the public and private sectors. The best way for the community to invest in its future is through its local public services. The labour movement must be present to ensure that that investment is to the benefit of all of the people of Sudbury.

Chapter 4

The State and Civility in Sudbury

Don Kuyek

On May 3, 1994, the Ontario Progressive Conservative Party under the leadership of Mike Harris issued a Party platform called *The Common Sense Revolution.*
It encapsulated both an election strategy and a statement of neo-conservative
political philosophy and policy. It promised fundamental change. No tinkering,
incremental change, or short-term solutions. The political system was considered
"captive to big special interests... full of people who are afraid to face the difficult
issues, or even talk about them... full of people doing all too well as a result of
the *status quo*" (Ontario Progressive Conservative Party 1994).

An extensive portion of the platform emphasized "welfare reform," and
included promises of a substantial reduction in assistance levels and the implementation of workfare, and identified welfare fraud as a serious problem. It
unabashedly invoked the stereotypical image of the overindulged, lazy, and
cheating welfare recipient.

Harris also promised to repeal labour-law reform introduced by the previous labour-friendly NDP government, including repeal of provisions prohibiting replacement workers, commonly referred to as "scabs," during strikes.
According to the platform, it was time to "restore the balance between labour
and management, to shift power from labour bosses to union members." The
anti-union animus was palpable and real. In Mike Harris's world, there were
no union leaders, only "union bosses." The platform made many promises, but
this chapter will focus on the impact of certain aspects of the promised welfare
and labour-law reforms.

The Common Sense Revolution document was prepared in the early months
of 1994 by the Bradgate Group, a collection of about ten, mostly young, neo-
conservative (often also referred to as "neo-liberal") ideologues close to Mike
Harris. It was the product of brainstorming ideologues and certainly not, as it
stated, "a solid plan based on four years of study, analysis, and consultation with
workers, employees, Party members, and ordinary Ontarians."

In his book *Promised Land: Inside the Mike Harris Revolution,* John Ibbitson (1997:
73–74) described the challenge of the document as follows:

> With *The Common Sense Revolution* [CSR], Harris nailed a thesis to the door
> of Ontario's sacred political edifice. It was now for the other two par-
> ties to challenge it. At a fundamental level, however, the contest would
> be not between the Tories and the other parties, but between the Tories

and the electors themselves. The CSR challenged Ontario voters to decide whether they truly had the courage to embrace a political program most of them claimed they wanted. The program itself was a relatively complex articulation of water-cooler wisdom, of locker-room punditry, of dinner-table debate. It was what the broad middle class of society had always said they desired but were afraid to demand. The CSR massaged their resentments, comforted their fears, and stoked their longings. But it was an ideology that heretofore in Ontario had dared not speak its name, that the mainstream media, the academic, social, and political elites, even much of the business community, had dismissed as unjustified, petty, divisive, mean-spirited, and cruel — something to be ashamed of, something not even to be said out loud. Now it had been said. And there was an election coming up.

The *Oxford English Dictionary* defines "revolution" as "an instant of great change or alteration in affairs or in some particular thing." "Common sense" is defined as "the general sense, feeling or judgment of mankind, or a community."

The document promised "revolution," but was it a revolution based on the general experience and/or judgment of the community? Was the promised revolution in accordance with the public's sense of civility, civic obligation, and social justice?

On June 8, 1995, Mike Harris was elected Premier, winning 82 of 130 seats. The new government immediately demonstrated a commitment to quick implementation of *The Common Sense Revolution* manifesto, typical of the neo-conservative "cold shower" strategy. Move quickly. Damn the consequences. Trust in your ideology. The ends justify the means.

Political scientists David Cameron and Graham White, who studied the 1995 transition, observed the following about the Harris government's approach, as quoted by Ibbitson (1997: 115):

> We were struck on several occasions to find both political and bureaucratic interviewees voicing what to our minds was a naive distinction between policy and implementation.... Policy was what was in the CSR. It had been constructed and "road-tested" by the Party before and during the election campaign. Implementation was what came after the election, once the Tories had formed the government. The election meant that the policies of the Conservatives had been approved by the electorate and now implementation could begin. There was no need for policy committees of Cabinet, no need for papers presenting options or exploring the costs and benefits of alternative courses of action, apparently no significant issue for decision which had not been prefigured and pre-determined by the CSR policy framework. Action was what was required; public servants were simply to get on with the job, and politicians were there to see the job was done. It is not difficult to see how this conception of the distinc-

tion between policy and public administration could lead a government to serious errors in judgment and vexing political problems.

The public challenge to the implementation of the CSR manifesto was immediate. Queen's Park was closed for security reasons when the government was sworn in on June 26, 1995. There was widespread outrage and demonstrations when, on July 21, 1995, the government reduced social assistance by an unprecedented and startling 21.6 percent. There was a pitched battle at Queen's Park between demonstrators and police on September 27, on the occasion of Harris's first throne speech.

The challenge to Harris's CSR was not limited to broad policy issues and general mobilized action. Occasionally, communities were uniquely touched by policies that challenged their sense of civility, civic obligation, and social justice. Sudbury did not escape this unique challenge.

Attacking the Poor: The Kimberly Rogers Case

The Harris government quickly and aggressively dismantled fifty years of social assistance (welfare) policy. Its "reforms" were miserly, punitive, and demeaning. In addition to the reduction of assistance levels by 21.6 percent; the "man in the house" rule was restored; workfare was imposed; recipients who attended school were disentitled to social assistance; loans and gifts were now treated as income; "zero tolerance" of welfare fraud was imposed, with three months disentitlement — later amended to a lifetime ban — for those convicted, whatever their personal circumstances; and administration of welfare assistance was downloaded to municipalities, though the province maintained control over statutory and regulatory frameworks.

These reforms were oppressive to those living under already trying circumstances and were a real challenge to community values. The citizens of Sudbury were directly and uniquely confronted with this challenge.

Kimberly Rogers, born on July 20, 1961, was raised in the Sudbury area. She had a troubled youth, did not complete high school, spent a number of years in a youth facility as a result of non-criminal behaviour, and, at age eighteen, gave birth to a child who was raised and adopted by her parents. She left Sudbury to live in Toronto, where she primarily lived until returning to Sudbury in 1996. She suffered from a number of medical problems, including chronic insomnia, panic disorder, chronic anxiety, migraine headaches, and a significant knee injury involving chronic pain.

Kimberly enrolled in a social-work program at Cambrian College, a local community college, and graduated in May 2000. While attending college, she received what was known as "Ontario Works," Harris's version of social assistance. Attending school while in receipt of social assistance was prohibited, and she failed to disclose the fact to welfare authorities. Her social assistance was terminated on October 31, 1999, and she was charged with fraud in September 2000 for attending school while in receipt of social assistance. She supported herself by a combination of student loans and work until January 2001, when she quit her job for health reasons. She was unable to support herself, and again applied for and was granted social assistance in January 2001 of $520 per month.

On March 5, 2001, her family doctor confirmed that Ms Rogers was two months pregnant. She was living alone, unemployed, on social assistance, pregnant, and facing the still pending welfare fraud criminal charge.

On April 25, 2001, she pleaded guilty to the fraud charge and received a six-month conditional sentence, sometimes known as "house arrest," and eighteen months probation. The house-arrest conditions restricted her to her residence at all times except for medical and religious purposes, to shop for necessities of life between the hours of 9 a.m. and noon on Wednesdays, or for any other purposes permitted by her sentence supervisor. As a result of her conviction, her social assistance, including the drug plan, was cut off for three months under the zero-tolerance rule.

She was now three months pregnant, without income, without medication that she regularly required, largely restricted to her residence, over $30,000 in debt for student loans, and ordered to reimburse Ontario Works $13,372.67 for the overpayment of benefits received while disentitled.

A group of citizens quickly rallied around her and the case became a searing example of the consequences of the anti-poor welfare reforms. Sudbury welfare administrators were obviously embarrassed by the application of the zero-tolerance rule but had no choice under provincial government regulations. An application for judicial review of the decision to terminate benefits was filed, and an interim order restoring benefits was granted on May 25, 2001. In her judgment, Judge Epstein (2001) stated:

> In my view, this is one of the "clear cases" where the applicant has demonstrated that the balance of inconvenience favours the granting of an order exempting the applicant from the operation of the Regulations pending the final determination of the application.
>
> In the unique circumstances of this case, if the applicant is exposed to the full three-month suspension of her benefits, a member of our community carrying an unborn child may well be homeless and deprived of basic sustenance. Such a situation would jeopardize the health of Ms Rogers and the fetus, thereby adversely affecting not only mother and child but also the public — its dignity, its human rights commitment, and its health-care resources. For many reasons, there is overwhelming public interest in protecting a pregnant woman in our community from being destitute.
>
> While the integrity of our social-assistance programs must be respected and maintained, it simply has to be that the "inconvenience" of a pregnant woman living on the streets is far greater than is the "inconvenience" of any threat, perceived or real, that the order exempting Ms Rogers from the operation of the Regulations may seriously jeopardize

that integrity. I have considered the argument that an exemption may be a "slippery slope" leading to a suspension of the operation of the Regulations but there is no convincing evidence in the record before me of the real likelihood of such a consequence. More importantly, the order is being granted in light of the particular facts in this case that centre on Ms Rogers's medical condition.

Ms Rogers was now in receipt of social assistance and medication but faced a bleak and desperate future. On August 9, 2001, amid a sweltering heat wave, Ms Rogers committed suicide. The cause of death was unknown at that time, but a coroner's jury eventually determined she died by suicide.

Her death occasioned public outrage locally, provincially, and nationally. The circumstances of her death were closely reported and discussed in the media. On March 25, 2002, the Ontario Coroner's Office announced an inquest into her death to commence in October of that year.

Under the leadership of the Sudbury Committee to Remember Kimberly Rogers, a "Justice with Dignity Campaign" was launched on May 14, 2002, the anniversary of her court challenge, to advocate for social-assistance reform. White roses were planted in her memory in Thunder Bay, Sault Ste. Marie, Sudbury, Toronto, Ottawa, and London.

The government was not without its supporters. The flavour of the public debate is caught in the exchange of the following letters to the editor published in the local daily, *The Sudbury Star*:

Kim Rogers was Unfairly Punished
On March 2, the Laurentian University Faculty Association/L'Association des professeurs de l'Universite Laurentienne (LUFA-APUL) voted unanimously to endorse the recommendations of the Committee to Remember Kimberly Rogers. In contrast to the tone of the editorial, "Crime Cannot Go Unpunished" — February 27, this association considers these recommendations to be reasonable advice for city council in the period leading up to the inquest. Sudburians were outraged last summer's tragedy could take place in our city, in our province, in our Canada. But many do not realize the conditions are still in place for similar tragedies to occur again. Rogers's circumstances help to illustrate the dire straights that post-secondary education students are facing with rising tuition costs and increasing debt loads; situations confirmed at the LUFA-APUL hearings held in Sudbury only last week. She collected social assistance and student loans and for this she was given a conditional sentence of house arrest with absolutely no means to support herself and her unborn child. An appallingly punitive penalty, smacking of draconian, Dickensian work-house era laws and justice. It reflects the Progressive Conservative government's efforts to criminalize the poor and needy, apparently a policy direction supported by *The Sudbury Star*? We salute and support the work of the Committee

to Remember Kimberly Rogers and thank them for reminding our community leaders, and the community-at-large, of our social responsibilities. (Letter to the editor, *The Sudbury Star*, March 14, 2002)

Rogers Created Her Own Predicament
Re: The letter... regarding Kim Rogers ("Kim Rogers Was Unfairly Punished" — March 14). The issue that seems to have been forgotten is Rogers was under house arrest being punished for a crime she had committed. Being needy and poor does not put one above the law. If one breaks the law, punishment is the consequence that has to be faced. Rogers was an educated person who had to have known she was committing fraud. I don't feel she was a victim of the system, she created the situation herself. Yes, she did die and that is tragic, however, I don't feel the government should be held responsible. Perhaps she could have served a jail sentence, but I'm sure the public outcry would have been loud and clear as well. House arrest was probably considered a "kinder" incarceration. Beating the system is a way of life for some people; they become masters of the game. But, what I don't understand is, when one is experiencing difficulty in one form or another, the government is often blamed and is then expected to bail you out even if you are the one who made the bad decisions. We have lost sight of responsibility and accountability for our own lives. Perhaps this is why we are so over-legislated — we have to be protected from ourselves. (Letter to the editor, *The Sudbury Star*, April, 2002)

The Coroner's inquest commenced October 15, 2002, and wrapped up on December 19, 2002. Detailed evidence of Ms Rogers's background was presented challenging the pervasive stereotypes of social-assistance recipients. There was nothing socially perverse or unforgivably irresponsible about her. Stereotypes of the poor and welfare recipients rarely survive a detailed examination of the realities of their lives. The inquest provided a unique opportunity for such examination.

The jury heard evidence of her personal background, the setbacks that led to her being on social assistance, the harsh realities of living on assistance, the difficulties in getting off welfare, welfare cheating as a survival technique, the low incidence of welfare fraud, and the overwhelming harshness of the zero-tolerance policy.

Despite the evidence criticizing the government's welfare policies, the Ministry responsible for social assistance presented no evidence to justify its policies. It participated in the inquiry only indirectly through counsel for the Ministry of Correctional Services, which was mainly concerned about the administration of the house-arrest sentence. It is widely acknowledged that the Harris welfare reform was not based on careful research and balancing of interests, but on neo-conservative ideology. Any attempt to participate meaningfully in the hearing would have quickly disclosed the meanness and shallowness of their policies.

The Harris Conservative government literally had nothing to say.

In their verdict, the five jurors flatly rejected the neo-con welfare agenda and, among other things, recommended the following:

- the zero-tolerance lifetime ineligibility for social assistance as a result of the commission of welfare fraud, pursuant to Ontario Works Act, 1997, O. Reg.134/98 Section 36, should be eliminated. The temporary ineligibility in the instance of offences that have occurred prior to April 1, 2000, should also be eliminated;
  Rationale: evidence indicates that this would have a devastating and detrimental effect on our society. To prevent anyone from having to go without food and/or shelter, to be deemed homeless and therefore and most importantly, to prevent the death of impoverished individuals;
- a provision should be added to the Ontario Works Act permitting the local Ontario Works Administrator to exercise discretion in the use of any suspension of Ontario Works benefits, in instances that could be life threatening to the client and/or dependants;
  Rationale: evidence indicates that suspension of benefits is detrimental to the client and the community;
- the Ministry of Community, Family and Children Services and the Ontario Works Program should assess the adequacy of all social assistance rates. Allowances for housing and basic needs should be based on actual costs within a particular community or region. In developing the allowance, data about the nutritional food basket prepared annually by local health units, and the average rent data prepared by the Canada Mortgage and Housing Corporation, should be considered;
  Rationale: to ensure that social assistance rates are adequate and adjusted annually if necessary. (Ontario Ministry of Public Safety and Security 2002)

In their submissions to the Coroner, both the City of Sudbury and the Sudbury Police Services Commission recommended that the zero-tolerance policy be eliminated.

The overwhelming response to Ms Rogers's criminal prosecution and death was to condemn the Harris welfare reforms, not only because of their impact on individuals, but also, as noted by the jury, that they "would have a devastating and detrimental effect on our society" and were "detrimental to... the community."

But the neo-con agenda is deeply entrenched, and the successor Liberal government elected in October 2003, although it eliminated the zero-tolerance policy in December 2003, has only slowly and incrementally set aside some of the Harris amendments. Workfare remains intact, and only some of the rough edges of the "man in the house" rule have been changed. Assistance levels remain low and fail to keep up with inflation. Other than those in receipt of disability benefits, recipients are unable to attend school. Only nominal loans and gifts are not regarded as income. However unpalatable they may be to the general public, the Harris Conservative welfare reforms remain largely intact, even though they were conceived and fashioned out of a mean and ill-informed prejudice against the poor.

The stubborn survival of the Harris welfare reforms cannot be explained simply as catering to pervasive ill-informed prejudice. The citizens of Sudbury had an opportunity to widely debate and study the underlying issues, and they concluded they could not stomach the impact of the reforms. They were contrary to their community values and common sense, that is, "the general sense, feeling of judgment of mankind, or a community."

Neo-conservative welfare reforms help establish the two cornerstones of the free-market global economy — lower taxes and a flexible, compliant workforce. A stingy, harsh social-assistance program forces people to work for lower wages and under harsher work conditions, which produces what is euphemistically called a "more flexible" workforce. Less money for the poor finances lower taxes. Welfare and other social-program cuts were followed by significant tax reductions, especially for those in upper-income brackets, as promised by the Harris government. These tax cuts came at a cost that Sudbury found unpalatable.

Strike-Breakers and the 2001–2002 Falconbridge Strike

On August 1, 2000, 1,250 members of the Sudbury Mine Mill and Smelter Workers Union Local 598/CAW, the certified collective bargaining agent for the production and maintenance employees of Falconbridge at its mining and smeltering operations in Sudbury, went on strike.

Falconbridge had been mining and smelting nickel and copper in Sudbury since 1928 and was regarded as one of Canada's premier mining companies. In 1988 Noranda, another prominent Canadian mining company, effectively took control of Falconbridge by purchasing 19.9 percent of Falconbridge. Noranda had been controlled since 1981 by Brascan, which morphed into Brookfield Asset Management after purchasing 58.4 percent of Falconbridge in 2002. In 2005, Brookfield merged Noranda and Falconbridge under one operation called Falconbridge Limited. On November 2, 2006, Falconbridge Limited was purchased by Xstrata, a major global diversified mining group headquartered in Zug, Switzerland.

Brascan was not a mining company but a holding company, buying and selling other companies like commodities. It had no long-term commitment to Falconbridge. Xstrata has promised to treat Falconbridge differently.

Typically, the controlling corporation imposes objectives and strategies and closely supervises the controlled company. Union officials claim that Noranda and Brascan brought an anti-union attitude to Falconbridge and that the union-company relationship deteriorated under Noranda's influence.

Mine Mill had previously struck Falconbridge in 1969 (for three months), 1975 (three months), 1985 (three days), 1988 (ten days) and 1997 (three weeks). The Sudbury community was no stranger to strikes at both Falconbridge and

Inco, including a nine-month strike at Inco in 1978–79. Falconbridge and Inco strikes were dreaded, because of the numbers on strike and the resulting economic impact. Inco and Falconbridge are major local employers and Sudburians generally understand the importance of maintaining good wages, benefit plans, pensions, and working conditions for the economic and social health of the community. Inco and Falconbridge strikers ordinarily enjoy widespread community support.

Strikes are usually orderly — even the tough, long strikes. Incidents are rare and seldom go beyond minor vandalism and unruliness. Facilities and picket lines would be installed on company property. Management access to company facilities and maintenance of mines and smelter facilities would be assured. Mines must be constantly maintained or they become flooded and badly damaged. Smelter furnaces must be protected and maintained if they are to be available at the end of the strike. Mine rescue crews need to be maintained in case of accidents. Normal operations and production would cease.

The 2000 strike was to be like no other strike at Inco or Falconbridge, at least in recent history. Falconbridge decided to maintain operations at its smelter. Ore from its open-pit mine in Raglan, Québec, was smeltered in Sudbury, but it required a mixture of about 20 percent local Sudbury ore for its added sulphur content. Raglan ore was transported by ship to Québec City and from there by train to Sudbury.

Prior to the strike, the company had prepared extensive "bulk mining areas" that only required blasting, scooping, and transport of the ore to the mills for preparation of "slurry." This could be done by non-striking employees and management, occasionally supplemented by a small number of scab labourers. The slurry from the mills was trucked to the smelter by independent contractors, as was the case before the strike. So long as bulk-mining areas were available and drilling wasn't required, these operations could continue. Maintaining full mining and milling operations would be costly and difficult, and would be fiercely resisted by the union.

Smelter operations could not continue without a significant number of scab labourers, who were transported to the smelter primarily by helicopter. Specifically licenced personnel, such as crane operators and electricians, were needed, as well as general labourers. They lived on-site for extensive periods, with relief workers coming in periodically. The union was not intimidated by the ongoing smelter operations, believing that, at worst, profits would be marginal and eventually serious production problems would develop. Their views turned out to be correct. Why then would the company decide to continue production?

One should not assume that corporate strategy is always the product of intelligence and measured judgement moulded by broad experience. The boys at Brascan enjoyed only a mixed reputation on Bay Street. Given the labour climate perpetuated by the Harris Conservative government and its repeal of anti-scab legislation, the company probably thought this was a strategic opportunity to challenge the power of the union and enhance Falconbridge's value and marketability by producing a more compliant workforce. The corporate strategists were not about to respect Sudbury's history of union resistance and community support of striking miners. Their strategy failed, but at the cost of a seven-month strike, which severely damaged both Falconbridge's corporate reputation and its relationship with its employees.

The Sudbury community quickly understood the implications of Falconbridge's strike strategy. The Sudbury Regional Municipal Council passed the following resolution on September 27, 2000:

> Whereas the citizens of the Regional Municipality of Sudbury have grave concerns respecting the ongoing strike at Falconbridge and the hardships that the strike is causing for workers, their families, and the community at large;
>
> And whereas Falconbridge has retained *scab* labour for the first time since Mine Mill became certified in 1944;
>
> And whereas the employment of *scab* labour only escalated the dispute, causing the parties to become more and more entrenched in their respective positions, thereby minimizing the opportunity for a negotiated settlement;
>
> And whereas Falconbridge has a responsibility to both its own workforce and the community at large to minimize the potential for conflict and to show leadership and good faith to make every reasonable effort to end this strike;
>
> And whereas the employment of *scab* labour by Falconbridge creates a climate of conflict, mistrust, and uncertainty, which is counterproductive to the negotiating process;
>
> And whereas, with the existence of *scabs*, there is the imminent possibility of violence and conflict on the picket lines, which will involve the *police*;
>
> And whereas the *police* have more important tasks to perform, such as resolving the unsolved murders of several citizens of this community;
>
> Therefore be it resolved that the Regional Municipality of Sudbury demand that Falconbridge reverse its decision to employ *scab* labour during this dispute;
>
> And be it further resolved that the Regional Municipality of Sudbury encourages Falconbridge to show good faith and leadership by terminating its usage of *scab* labour;
>
> And be it further resolved that the Regional Municipality of Sudbury encourages Falconbridge to return to the bargaining table and, in good faith, resolve their differences with Mine Mill, putting an end to this unnecessary strike that has and will continue to damage the economy of our community.

As in any other community, municipal council members represent a variety of political views, and in Sudbury they had a reputation for being pro-labour. But they had a clear sense of the potential impact of strike-breaking and scab labour on the city and its citizens. The economic hardships of a long strike could be stoically tolerated and resisted, as in 1978–79, but strike-breaking and scab labour introduced a new dimension.

The use of scab labour and the decision to maintain operations contrary to long-established tradition was uniquely offensive and challenging to the striking workers and other Sudburians, and it offended their sense of civic propriety and responsibility. Here, we examine two aspects of this challenge and experience: the role of private armies and the role of injunctions, police, and the courts.

Private Armies

If Falconbridge planned to continue production, security services beyond its own regular personnel would be needed. The company retained Accufax Investigation Inc., a company whose website self-describes its core business as "focussed exclusively on services that enable employers to manage work stoppage due to strikes, lockouts, or plant closures safely and securely." Accufax advertises that it provides a full panoply of strike-breaking services, including advance planning, security, workplace access, product diversion, and replacement workers. They offer performance monitoring and the administration of payroll and benefits, removing clients from all direct responsibility for the temporary workforce.

It was known from a copy of a cheque given to the union that Falconbridge paid at least $400,000 to Accufax in early July, well before the start of the strike and the breakdown of negotiations. Obviously, the company had planned and committed to its strike-breaking strategy long before the summer of 2000. Falconbridge was now in bed with a notorious strike-breaking corporation.

Accufax personnel arrived in Sudbury in their black uniforms and black SUVs, and probably numbered no less than eighty to hundred at any given time, compared to about 220 officers in the Sudbury police force. Most were recently recruited specifically for the Falconbridge strike and they came from throughout Ontario. Tellingly, no Sudburians were identified among their ranks. They occupied various motels and hotels, circulating to avoid notice. They escorted the slurry trucks delivering the Sudbury ore to the smelter. Accufax personnel drove the buses delivering non-striking workers, contractors, and scabs to the Falconbridge sites. They provided security at all picket-line sites and at the airport for company helicopters used to transport scabs, provisions, and equipment. They patrolled company property and closely watched scab labour at the smelter. They were not shy about insulting and taunting picketers and were also known to follow union members away from the picket lines. Strikers were under constant video surveillance at the picket sites and from Accufax vehicles. Accufax had a communications and command centre, and it carefully maintained and catalogued its video records. Its presence was highly visible and controversial.

The strike lasted from August 1, 2000, to February 20, 2001. Union officials report that, generally, striking workers were more unsettled and disturbed by the company's use of Accufax than by the economic deprivation of a long strike. They were insulted their employer had introduced Accufax into the employer-employee relationship. Many Sudburians were offended by its presence and considered Accufax as Falconbridge's private army. The enduring visual image of the strike for Sudburians was a video recording of an Accufax employee in uniform and black vest with a full balaclava pulled down over his face escorting a journalist off company property. This was Falconbridge's new corporate image.

The Accufax website, now under the name AFI International Group Inc., quotes from the 2006 Canada Conference Board report on Industrial Relations, which suggests that as globalization increases there will be more union-management strife as unions struggle to maintain working conditions. AFI's analysis of the Conference Board report progresses to an advertisement for its strike-breaking, anti-union services and a statement from its President that "this year will be an ideal time for employers to obtain consultation to be prepared for a labour dispute." This is an implicit promise that communities facing these struggles can also expect to be invaded by private corporate armies, as Sudbury was in 2000–2001.

Injunctions, Police, and the Courts

Picket lines during strikes are mostly symbolic, though they are important tools in maintaining union morale and commitment. During long strikes, unions will arrange the occasional show of force by increasing the number of picketers and perhaps by denying or delaying access to management and engaging in a bit of measured unruliness. Although not legal, such activity is, in the general course of events, socially and civilly accepted, and it is considered necessary to protect and improve working conditions.

That protocol changes when management decides to maintain production with scab labour. The picket line becomes a more important union tool to limit or stop production. Resistance is more forceful and, if resistance is effective, employers resort to the courts to obtain injunctions to restrict the effectiveness of the picket line.

Prior to the strike, the union and Falconbridge entered into an agreement or protocol for the conduct of picket-line activities, including the temporary stopping of entering vehicles in order to obtain access to the occupants for the ostensible purpose of conveying information about the strike and obtaining their support.

Shortly after the strike began, the union and Falconbridge disagreed about the meaning of some of the terms of the protocol, and the company alleged that vehicles transporting non-striking employees and replacement workers were unduly delayed. Although the strike had only begun on August 1, the company was already applying for an injunction on September 7, alleging that transportation delays were causing production difficulties and irreparable damages.

Historically, Canadian courts, mirroring English courts, have considered unions unlawful conspiracies. Early labour legislation focussed on legalizing unions and union activity, and protecting unions and union activity, including picketing, by minimizing or even denying the courts' jurisdiction in industrial disputes.

In 1970, Ontario passed legislation limiting the court's jurisdiction to grant interim injunctions to circumstances where the police, after making reasonable efforts, failed to protect persons or property, or failed to prevent obstruction of, or interference with, lawful entry or exit. The message here was that the courts are to issue injunctions in industrial disputes only if there are serious and continuous breaches of the peace beyond the police's ability to control. At first, the courts respected this caution, but, certainly since the 1980s, the limitations have been almost universally disregarded and interim injunctions have been routinely granted.

In their first application for an injunction, Falconbridge made a number of strategic errors. Because the strike was barely one month old and picket-line incidents were not serious enough to alarm even the most prissy judge, the application was based on disruptions to production caused by delays in crossing the picket line. Companies almost never base an injunction application on disruption of production, because it opens their records to examination.

Also, because of the short notice of the application given to the union, company officials were forced to testify in open court and were subjected to cross-examination. Their evidence of disruption to production and irreparable damages was seriously undermined when they were confronted with contradictory company-generated evidence that came into the hands of the union. The application was denied, a rare event.

In this first injunction application, the presiding justice summarized the test for an interim injunction as follows:

> the applicant must show that the claim is not frivolous but reflects serious issues to be tried; that if the injunction is not granted, it will suffer irreparable harm which cannot be adequately compensated by damages; that the balance of convenience favours the granting of the injunction. (*Falconbridge Limited v. Sudbury Mine Mill* et. al. 2000)

In this context, the term "irreparable" has a specific, more qualitative meaning that "refers to the nature of the harm suffered rather than its magnitude. It is harm which either cannot be quantified in monetary terms or which cannot be cured, usually because one party cannot collect damages from the other" (Dukelow 2004).

Further applications were heard and granted on October 20, 2000, and February 16, 2001. They were based not on disruption to production but on alleged strikers' illegal and violent behaviour. Accufax was instrumental in these two applications.

Under "Crowd Control Services," the current Accufax website states:

Your local Police Services will not open picket lines. Should pickets block entrances, it may be necessary to seek relief through the court. A court injunction serves this purpose.

An injunction investigator will gather evidence and deliver detailed documentation of picket activities to support your request for an injunction. The evidence will be presented in an organized, categorized, court-ready format that will save your legal counsel valuable time and help expedite your injunction application.

This division is completely equipped with portable communication centres, surveillance vehicles, video cameras, tape-to-tape copiers, video still printers, escort vehicles, and long-range digitally encrypted radio communications.

The Accufax strategy is to overwhelm the local police force with complaints in order to obtain an admission from the local police before the courts. In Sudbury, Accufax was successful in this, as Sudbury police testified in court:

Due to overwhelming volume of reports and complaints that have been received and are continuing to be received by the Sudbury Police Service, police officers with the service are no longer able to attend on calls concerning complaints of delay in entering or exiting Falconbridge business premises due to picket-line activities.

This direct quote is from the affidavit of the labour liaison officer assigned to the strike by the Sudbury Regional Police Service, filed by the company in support of their injunction application.

All three injunction applications were heard by the same judge, who before her appointment was a well known local lawyer. Typically, such hearings are attended by a small group of union and company officials and their lawyers. In Sudbury, the hearings were well attended, especially the second one, when strikers, their spouses and children, company officials, strike supporters, and other local citizens jammed the courtroom to capacity.

It was more than idle curiosity or commitment to one side or the other that brought people to the hearings. It was an opportunity to observe how their institutions protected or advanced their interests. Would their struggle be seen, not as one of narrow self-interest, but as a struggle for social justice that should take priority over control of unruliness or breach of the peace that may have caused offence, but little physical harm? Would unruly picket-line activity be characterized as "mob rule" and an invitation to anarchy? Would the use of scab labour be legally sanctioned? If "irreparable harm" *must* be found before granting an injunction, how can an applicant whose sole purpose is *profit* and who cannot be assaulted or physically harmed suffer irreparable harm from unruly and/or "criminal" picket-line behaviour? Will the corporate applicant be allowed to plead on behalf of persons directly affected by picket-line conduct even though they may not be named as parties to the proceeding? Would the courts stress the need to "preserve law and order" over the realities of the strike and the community's interest in the outcome? Sudburians had a first-hand opportunity to observe how the judiciary and police would balance the various interests, administer the law, and dispense justice.

The injunction proceedings received a lot of attention, but apart from the first injunction application that was denied, the injunctions probably had very little impact on the strike. If the first application had been granted it would have caused morale problems and forced the union to quickly reorganize its strike actions. At the time, picket lines were the focus of the strike. By the time of the second application, the union strategy was already switching to other actions, such as secondary picketing.

By the time of the third application, picketing was a minor strategic factor and the union had developed widespread local, provincial, national, and international support, especially from a sister union in Norway at a Falconbridge-owned refinery.

The injunction proceedings, although they had only a marginal impact on the strike, did have a more subtle and unexpected impact on Sudburians. Instinctively, unionists know that the law and policing are stacked against them when it comes to strike activity, an instinct corroborated by history and experience. Perhaps buoyed by the unexpected results of the first application, the strikers and the community at large closely followed the injunction proceedings, seeking and receiving a lesson in civics and accounting of the behaviour of their police and judiciary. This was a lesson, and an accounting, they would rather have avoided, but nonetheless it was an important lesson to experience first-hand.

Conclusion

The impact of the Harris Conservative government's welfare and labour "reforms" on the Sudbury community was the logical outcome of the neo-conservative agenda. The tentacles of this agenda spread, and take hold deeply in a community, threatening not only its economic well-being but its sense of community and civility. The unique nature and scope of the threat, as Sudbury experienced, must be understood if it is to be successfully resisted.

Chapter 5

Environmental Impacts of Nickel Mining

Four Case Studies, Three Continents, and Two Centuries

Evan Edinger

Nickel mining has been the basis of regional development in a number of areas around the world, bringing with it considerable environmental damage and sometimes social disruption. This chapter considers four cases: two massive sulphide deposits in boreal to sub-arctic Canada — Sudbury, Ontario, and Voisey's Bay, Labrador — and two laterite deposits in the tropics — Soroako, Indonesia, and Goro, New Caledonia.[1] This review of environmental impacts is aimed at a general audience. Readers wishing further technical depth can explore the references.

The four case studies are chosen on the basis of my experience. They are not necessarily the most egregious examples of the environmental impacts of nickel mining. Many other regions could be studied, especially Norilsk in Russia, which has great climatic and geologic similarities to Sudbury (Vilchek et al. 1996). Similarly, experiences in Guatemala, Cuba, and the Dominican Republic could be compared with Indonesia and New Caledonia. Although all four examples involve Inco, this chapter is not intended as "Inco-bashing." The disastrous environmental record in Norilsk demonstrates that the environmental legacy of nickel mining and smelting is a product of three factors: the mining and metallurgical process, the geographical and geological setting, and government policy, regardless of the particular company involved (Blais et al. 1999).

Environmental Problems Associated with Sulphide Ore Mining and Processing

Well-known environmental problems associated with sulphide ore mining and processing include tailings dust, acid mine drainage, smelter fallout, and acid rain.

Tailings Dust

Although most of the metals in the mined ore are sent to the smelter, significant amounts of metallic sulphide minerals remain in the waste rock and tailings, which have been finely crushed and usually floated to the tailings dam as a watery slurry. As the tailings are exposed to air, two environmental hazards emerge. First, fine dust blows off the tailings. This dust is an irritant and can create a health hazard in the form of particulates, which contribute to silicosis or "brown lung." Most long-time residents of Sudbury are familiar with this problem in the form of the tailings dust that frequently accumulated on their gardens, laundry, and houses before the tailings were revegetated. Second, the tailings contain metals, which can react when the dust falls into lakes, streams, or soils.

Acid Mine Drainage

Acid mine drainage is the result of the weathering of sulphide minerals that remain in mine tailings, mine runoff, slag, or some abandoned mines. As the tailings are exposed to oxygen in the air, the remaining sulphide minerals are oxidized to form free metal cations and sulfuric acid in a process catalyzed by bacteria (Gould and Kapoor in Jambor et al. 2003). The sulfuric acid then further accelerates the oxidation of sulphide minerals, freeing more and more toxic metals into tailings runoff. If left unchecked, acid drainage from tailings, mine runoff, and slag can become a runaway train of toxic metals release in local watersheds (Belzile et al. 1997). In Canada, Northern Ontario and British Columbia are the regions with the greatest acid mine drainage problems, although there have been local concerns at active and abandoned mines in every province except Prince Edward Island. Although low pH levels can kill many fish and aquatic invertebrates, the long-term environmental and health impact of acid mine drainage comes from the metals release, which poisons waterways, destroys habitat for fish and other aquatic organisms, and can pose significant human health threats. For example, arsenic and lead concentrations can be highly elevated in groundwater affected by acid mine drainage.

Smelter Gas Emissions and Fallout

Sulphur dioxide gas is released from the smelter as a by-product of sulphide ore smelting. It is a highly toxic gas, and with acute or chronic exposure can cause health problems. Smelter fallout consists of the particulate matter released to the air from the smelter, and includes rock dust, metal spherules (solidified droplets of molten metal), and sulphur dioxide adhered to rock dust. This dry deposition of sulphur dioxide is a major contributor to localized soil acidification around smelters, leading to soil pH and metals concentrations poisonous to many plants (Maxwell in Gunn 1995). Smelter fallout creates an environmental and human health hazard through both particulate dust and toxicity, due to the heavy metals in the fallout.

Acid Rain

Acid rain is the most widely known environmental hazard from sulphide ore smelting. Sulphur dioxide gas released from the smelter is further oxidized to sulphur trioxide in the atmosphere, then hydrated to produce sulfuric acid. This acid returns to ground as rain or snow. The original description of acid rain as an environmental problem comes from the Sudbury region (Beamish and Harvey 1972), and the Sudbury nickel smelters still account for a large portion of Canada's total sulphur dioxide emissions, despite the cleaner production technologies introduced since the 1970s. The health implications of acid rain are usually less severe than its environmental effects, such as the dead lakes in Killarney Provincial Park. Nonetheless, acid rain with attendant metals deposition can increase the metals concentrations in surface waters beyond safe levels for human consumption. Furthermore, metals contamination and mobilization in soils affected by acid rain can poison food crops grown in that soil.

Environmental Problems Associated with Laterite Ore Mining and Processing

Environmental problems associated with laterite mining and ore processing are somewhat similar, and at the same time somewhat different, than those associated with sulphide ores. They are similar in that both sulphide and laterite ore mining and processing can cause extensive soil erosion and heavy metal contamination of watersheds. They differ in several important ways.

First, laterite deposits are soil-borne, so mining them is more akin to an earth-moving operation than to the infrastructure-intensive hardrock mining for sulphide ores. The "earth-moving" approach to laterite mining means that the safety and environmental issues associated with mining laterites are quite different from those involving sulphides, and that the overhead costs of laterite mining are usually much lower than those of hardrock mining of sulphides. Most laterite mines do not produce large volumes of tailings, because it is not necessary to crush host rock to separate the ore from host ultramafic rocks. The unweathered host rock is less reactive than tailings from sulphide ores, because the metals are not bound, as sulphide minerals are (hence avoiding the dangers of acid mine drainage), and also because the rock has not been crushed. (Crushing creates a larger surface area, therefore increasing the speed of reactions.)

Second, because most laterite mining is effectively strip mining, large areas of vegetation are removed, causing extensive soil erosion and high siltation in surrounding watersheds. Pits are usually relatively shallow and are operated for short periods of time, after which revegetation is necessary but not always successful. Because large amounts of tailings are not generated, and because the ore itself is not sulphide-rich, tailings dust and acid mine drainage are not usually concerns, except possibly from slag piles (Dagenais and Poling in Goldsack et al. 1999).

Third, laterite ore processing by pyrometallurgy (from the Greek, meaning "making metals by fire") still produces smelter fallout, with the attendant particulate hazards, metals deposition, and potential local acid precipitation. Hydrometallurgical processing of ore can consume vast amounts of water, which can cause conflicts over water use in arid regions, such as Western Australia, where a pressure acid leach (PAL) process is used for some laterite nickel ores (Storey 2001). In some cases, acid aerosols are released from the hydromet facilities.

The following four case studies examine how differences in geology, climate, mining history, and regulatory regime have influenced the pattern of environmental degradation in four nickel-mining districts.

Map of Northeastern Ontario, showing area of terrestrial and aquatic ecosystem damage caused by Sudbury mining and smelting. Ecosystem damage areas after Keller et al. (1999).

Sudbury, Ontario

Sudbury is a textbook case in industrial degradation of the environment, one of the most studied cases of environmental degradation and recovery. The Sudbury basin remains one of the world's largest nickel deposits, second to Norilsk. There is an extensive technical and popular literature on the environmental impacts and history of mining in Sudbury. The story of acid rain, deforestation, soil erosion, and the Sudbury "moonscape" of the 1940s to 1970s has become part of Canadian legend, and it is frequently cited in environmental science or resource management textbooks (Dearden and Mitchell 2002). More recently, the much-publicized re-greening programs around Sudbury have also attracted international attention, and are again a textbook case (Lautenbach 1987; Ross et al. 2001).[2]

Environmental damage from mining and smelting in the Sudbury basin began shortly after copper ore was rediscovered during the construction of the CPR railroad in the 1880s, having first been encountered during geological exploration in the 1850s. The environmental impacts in the Sudbury area came first through deforestation for timber production, and then through deforestation to fuel the ground-level roasting beds (Winterhalder in Hynes and Blanchette 1995). Roasting beds caused three forms of damage: cutting trees to fuel the roasting process; ground-level release of sulphur dioxide clouds, which killed most vegetation and animals; and heavy metals release into the soil beneath and adjacent to the roasting beds. The last roasting beds ceased operation in the late

1920s. Vegetation surrounding them began to recover shortly thereafter, where not affected by smelter fallout from the Copper Cliff, Coniston, and Falconbridge smelters. Levels of nickel, copper, and other heavy metals in soils below and immediately adjacent to roasting bed sites still remain at toxic levels, and vegetation recovery of the roasting beds themselves has been slow to non-existent.

With construction of smelters in Copper Cliff, Coniston, and Falconbridge, sulphur dioxide emissions and particulate-metal fallout were concentrated in those three areas, but with some longer-distance transport of all three forms of pollution. It was in this period of expansion and smelting in low-stack smelters that large areas of the Sudbury landscape were made barren or semi-barren (see Photo 1). Sulphur dioxide clouds killed vegetation, and smelter fallout containing both acids and metals poisoned soils, preventing re-establishment of any plant life. As long as soils remained acidified, heavy metals deposited to them remained mobile and biologically available — that is, in forms readily absorbed by plants and animals (Negusanti in Hynes and Blanchette 1995). Intensive liming of soils beginning in the 1970s brought soils to neutral or basic pHs, which immobilized most metals, such that biologically available nickel and copper are now reduced to acceptable levels in most soils, and vegetation recovery has proceeded well in many areas. Liming soils was key to the much celebrated "re-greening of Sudbury" (Lautenbach 1987; Beckett et al. in Hynes and Blanchette 1995).

Sulphur dioxide from the Sudbury smelters acidified more than 7,000 lakes over an area of 17,000 square kilometres (Keller et al. 1999b). In the Killarney case, as in many others, the nature of the bedrock below each lake determined its "buffering capacity" — its ability to absorb acid rain without acidification and biological effects. The lakes occurring on the bedrock types most resistant to weathering, like the 99.9-percent-pure quartz Lorraine Quartzite of the LaCloche Mountains, had the least buffering capacity, were acidified fastest and most intensely, and remain dead lakes to this day (Snucins et al. 2001). Diatom (micro-algae) skeletons in sediments of these lakes show that lake acidification may have begun as early as the 1920s (Dixit et al. 1992; Smol 2002). Many other lakes throughout the Sudbury region felt the effects of acid rain, and have yet to return to their normal pH level of less than six (Keller et al. 2001). Other lakes were subject to very high sulphate and metal loadings, yet did not acidify. For example, Ramsey Lake, near the centre of Sudbury, was protected from acidification by diabase (volcanic rock with feldspar and amphibole minerals) dykes underlying the lake, which neutralize acidity as they weather.

Some lakes in Killarney and the Sudbury region will probably never recover. Today approximately 18 percent of the sulphur deposition to Sudbury area lakes comes from the nickel smelters, with the balance from long-distance transport of atmospheric sulphate from other sources, mainly coal-fired power plants in the United States. The Sudbury area smelters supply approximately 70 percent of the airborne nickel and copper deposition to the region, particularly within a forty-kilometre radius of the smelter (Chan et al. 1984). Removing long-distance sources of acidification from multiple sources will be very difficult, both techni-

Photo 1: The Inco Superstack on the author's first visit to Sudbury, May 1989. Although this photo was taken nearly fifteen years after the beginnings of the re-greening effort in Sudbury, extensive barren areas still surrounded the smelter. The revegetation has made great progress, but most of the area immediately surrounding the smelter and subject to the most intensive acidification and soil metals pollution, remained barren as late as 2001.

Photo 2: The Soroako smelter and its plume settling over the town of Soroako, June 2002. Foreground shows houses built over the water.

cally and politically (Schindler 1999). Furthermore, many lakes that have been limed to achieve chemical restoration, or that have naturally returned to normal pH levels following emission reductions, remain biologically impoverished, and may never return to their original condition (Keller et al. 1999a).

The closure of the Consiton smelters, redesign of the Falconbridge smelter, and construction of the Superstack in 1972 reduced local emissions, but also sent the pollutant effects farther afield. Installation of pollution reduction technologies at the Superstack ultimately reduced total emissions by about 90 percent. This reduction in total emissions has been crucial for the dramatic success of the re-greening programs, and for the beginnings of lake recovery in the regions surrounding Sudbury (Keller et al. 1999b). Despite the 90-percent reduction in emissions levels, sulphur dioxide emissions still fluctuate above provincial air-quality guidelines, and Sudbury residents complain that, when downdrafts occur, the sulphur smell in downtown Sudbury is intolerable. In 2003, Inco was fined $375,000 for large-scale sulphur dioxide gas releases in the late 1990s, one of which was severe enough to cause hospitalizations and even the evacuation of a hospital. Both Inco and Falconbridge continue to be convicted of a wide range of environmental violations, on various scales, for which they pay fines. These violations underscore the importance of government intervention: the mining industry needs to be monitored closely. This point is particularly important given the current mining industry pressure for deregulation or self-regulation, which is discussed later in this chapter.

The health implications of sulphur dioxide gas releases and other environmental violations require more study. The fact that Inco compensates employees and residents of Copper Cliff and the West End of Sudbury for damage to the paint on their cars caused by smelter fallout, but not for damage to their lungs, illustrates the low attention given to health impacts of smelter operations.

The Inco tailings area northwest of Sudbury covers nearly twenty square kilometres of land, large areas of which remain unvegetated, and hence unstabilized (Puro et al. in Hynes and Blanchette 1995). Unstabilized tailings present the problem of wind-blown tailings dust that includes heavy metals in or adhered to dust particles. Efforts at stabilizing the tailings area through revegetation have focussed on liming soil to reduce acidity, thus immobilizing metals and enabling plant growth, followed by seeding with grass and planting trees (Peters in Gunn 1995). These efforts are hindered when plants develop thick taproots that draw metal-rich water from below the zone to which lime has penetrated. Other more recent efforts at neutralizing tailings to enable plant growth have used compost, pulp mill waste, and other organic materials to increase soil pH enough to enable plant growth.

Successful revegetation can address the dust problem, but not the acid mine drainage problems associated with mine tailings. Most responses to acid mine drainage, including Sudbury area tailings, focus on keeping tailings piles water-saturated to ensure that metal sulphides have minimal contact with oxygen, thereby preventing oxidation of sulphide minerals. Acid mine drainage from

Sudbury tailings remains a serious environmental concern that has not been adequately addressed (Blowes et al. in Jambor et al. 2003).

The Regulatory Environment

Public pressure, increasingly strict government regulations, and cleaner production technologies have largely driven reductions in sulphur, metals, and particulate emissions in Sudbury (Keller et al. 1999b). Shockingly, the mining companies argued against emission reductions on the basis that the lands and lakes were irreparably damaged, and that therefore the cost of implementing emissions reductions would not yield any benefit in terms of landscape recovery (Keller et al. 1999a).

As emissions have been reduced, lakes have begun to recover, particularly those more distant from the smelters that received lower amounts of acid deposition. In the cases of both the vegetation and the lakes, further interventions were necessary, in the form of liming soils and lakes to increase soil and water pH levels, in addition to seeding and planting vegetation. The speed of lake recovery was controlled both by proximity to the source of — now reduced — contamination and by the nature of the bedrock underlying, and in the watershed draining into, each lake (Keller et al. 1999a; Snucins et al. 2001).

Recovery also has several dimensions. Chemical recovery of a lake refers to its return to its normal, pre-industrial pH levels and concentrations of dissolved sulphate. Biological recovery applies to the restoration of lakes to their pre-industrial levels of biological diversity, and of ecosystem function. Biological recovery is more complex than chemical recovery, usually takes longer, and is more difficult to achieve by human intervention. In many cases, lakes around Sudbury that were acidified and subsequently limed have achieved chemical recovery but incomplete biological recovery, as aquatic invertebrate, amphibian, and fish species have not yet re-colonized these lakes (Keller et al. 1999a).

The importance of the terrestrial and aquatic recovery patterns is that environmental restoration depends first and foremost on reducing contamination at source. Neither the re-greening nor the lake recovery efforts would have succeeded without reduced levels of acid deposition from the Sudbury smelters, which were mandated by government. As long as the Sudbury smelter operations continue, there will continue to be a finite level of soil and water contamination, which will require abatement in one form or another. Ongoing Sudbury pollution, combined with general patterns of acid deposition from industrial sources in Canada and the United States, will probably prevent some of the most sensitive lakes from ever recovering to their pre-industrial chemical condition, let alone allow them to achieve biological recovery (Snucins et al. 2001).

Employment and production in Sudbury are covered in other chapters of this volume. Both Inco and Falconbridge resisted environmental controls for many years, and finally implemented them because they were required to do so. When the companies implemented cleaner production and reduced emissions from the Sudbury smelters, they independently increased mechanization of the mines and reduced the size of the workforce. Inco mine and smelter operations today, with a workforce of less than 5,000 (not including contractor employees), produce more ore than was produced in the 1960s with a workforce of nearly 30,000.

Soroako, South Sulawesi, Indonesia

In striking contrast to Sudbury, virtually no research has been published on the environmental impacts of nickel mining and smelting in Soroako (Robinson 1986; Edinger and Best 2001; Haffner et al. 2001; Glynn 2006). The following review is based largely on interviews with Soroako residents and Inco environmental staff, on field observations in 2000, 2002, and 2004, and on the research of Tracy Glynn toward her Masters of Science degree, conducted in Soroako under my supervision.[3]

Nickel deposits in the Soroako region were known to the Dutch before Indonesia gained independence, but large-scale mine development took place only after the Suharto government seized power in the bloody *coup d'état* of 1965–66. The laterite nickel mines in Soroako, South Sulawesi, Indonesia, were established in the late 1960s, with construction proceeding through the early and mid-1970s, and opening in 1977. The Soroako mine and smelter currently produces approximately 70,000 tonnes of nickel matte per year.

Inco's contract with the Indonesian government was the second mining agreement negotiated in the country under the Suharto regime, which was desperate to attract foreign investment. The royalties and taxes Inco paid were extremely low, environmental regulations were lax — with virtually no enforcement — and the government dictated the compensation package offered to local landowners, which was so low that many refused to accept the compensa-

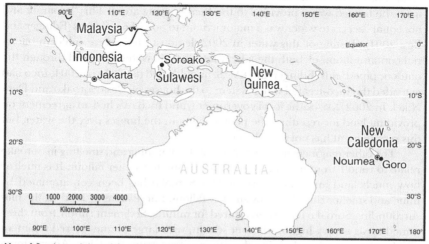

Map of Southeast Asia and Oceania, showing location of Soroako, Indonesia, and Goro, New Caledonia.

tion (Robinson 1986). Land tenure in the Soroako region was further confused during that time by the conflict during the late 1950s and early 1960s between government troops and local militias fighting for an Islamic state in Sulawesi. This fighting forced many people to flee Soroako, particularly the majority Christian Karonsi'e Dongi ethnic group. Although this fighting had largely ended before the 1965–66 *coup*, people displaced by the fighting mostly remained displaced until the late 1960s and 1970s. When the Karonsi'e Dongi began to return to the Soroako region in the late 1960s and early 1970s, the land that had been theirs was controlled by Inco, and no land compensation was offered to them.

Control of land lies at the centre of one of the most critical environmental and health hazards associated with mine development in Soroako: fecal contamination of lake water, and subsequent contamination of drinking water. When Inco negotiated its contract with the Indonesian government, most of the land surrounding the old village ("kampung lama") of Soroako and Desa Nikel was ceded to Inco (Robinson 1986). During the construction phase of mine development, thousands of people migrated to Soroako from other parts of Sulawesi and other Indonesian islands seeking work in the mines. Many of those employed received housing from Inco, but many others crowded into the kampung lama. Eventually, migrants to the region who did not have access to Inco housing began building houses over the water on the lakefront, because there was no available land in the region, since virtually all the land was controlled by Inco. Approximately 1,000 people live in houses over the water. Human waste from these houses is dumped directly into the lake.

Lake Matano is the source of drinking water for both the Inco housing areas and for the communities of Desa Soroako and Desa Nikel. Until the late 1970s, residents of Desa Nikel took their water directly from the lake. In the late 1970s, Inco put pipestands into Desa Nikel to provide outdoor water to the village, but sourced this water directly from the lake through a separate system from the treated water provided to the Inco housing areas. This "separate and not equal" access to water was a major irritant to Soroako residents (Edinger and Best 2001). Testing of this water in 2002 demonstrated severe coliform bacterial contamination of both the lake water and the water delivered through the outdoor pipestands (Edinger and KWAS, unpublished data). As of 2004, Inco had extended the Inco-treated water system to the houses of Desa Soroako and Desa Nikel. In 2002, KWAS, the local government, and Inco reached an agreement on providing land for resettling the people living in the houses over the water, but this resettlement has not yet taken place.

The other major environmental threats from mining and smelting in Soroako relate to runoff from the mines and smelter, and to smelter fallout. It is unclear how much land and water surrounding Soroako has been contaminated by mine and smelter runoff and by smelter fallout. Large areas of land on the hills surrounding Soroako have been cleared for mining. Sediment runoff from these mined areas is very high in the wet season, with large plumes of red sediment visible where streams draining the mining areas enter the lakes. After mining

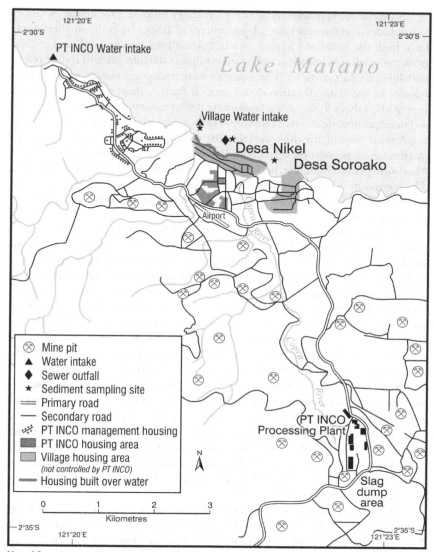

Map of Soroako area, showing mines and smelter, areas of water polluted by bacteria and heavy metals, and residential areas referred to in text. Base map from the Indonesian mapping agency, BAKOSURTANAL.

areas are closed, they are revegetated with grass to allow eventual recolonization by trees. Nonetheless, torrential rains bring large amounts of topsoil down into streams during the rainy season. In 2004, Inco built small check-dams along the major streams draining the smelter and active mines to catch some of the sediment. These check-dams appeared to dramatically reduce sedimentation following major rain events.

Soroako ore is processed by pyrometallurgy following reduction of oxides to sulphides in reduction kilns. Major sources of fallout from the smelters come from both the reduction kilns — which release large amounts of soot — and from the smelter furnaces, which release sulphur dioxide gas and red or yellow metalliferous dust particles. These particles are transported as far as twenty-two kilometres away, the direction depending on shifts in local winds (Edinger and Best 2001; Glynn 2006). Inco environmental monitoring reports indicate that airborne particulate levels in most areas of Soroako town are within Indonesian regulations most of the time, and that the composition of smelter fallout is approximately 2 percent nickel (P. Sampetoding, personal communication 2002). Monitoring efforts continue, both by Inco staff and the local village organization. The composition of dust accumulated on tree leaves is consistent with the composition of smelter fallout as reported by Inco (Edinger and Best, unpublished data; Glynn 2006).

Smelter fallout levels reaching the town of Soroako, lying six and a half kilometres northwest of the smelter site, vary depending on the direction of local winds. Daytime winds usually blow from the northwest or northeast, but nighttime winds often blow from the south, bringing smelter fallout directly to Soroako. Smelter fallout — or dust — has been one of the principal environmental complaints of Soroako villagers, much as in Sudbury. Although airborne particulate levels in the communities surrounding Soroako are usually below the Indonesian standard, airborne nickel concentrations are as high or higher than concentrations immediately surrounding the Sudbury smelter in the mid-1980s, and are high enough to constitute a potential health concern (Glynn 2006).

Smelter fallout has certainly contributed to the high concentrations of nickel, manganese, cobalt, and chromium reported in Lake Matano sediments, but the extent of this contribution is not known. On calm mornings, an oily film with red particles of smelter fallout can be seen on top of Lake Matano waters (Edinger and Best 2001). Lake Matano bottom sediments have nickel, manganese, and chromium concentrations over 1,000 parts per million, and iron concentrations over 10 percent (Haffner et al. 2001). These levels all far exceed Ontario Ministry of Environment lowest effect levels.[4]

In a small pilot project, we collected paired water and sediment samples in October-November 2000, June 2002, and August 2004. Sediments in Lake Matano in the area of lakebed nearest Soroako come from two rivers that drain mine and smelter areas. These sediments contain much higher concentrations of nickel, cobalt, zinc, and other elements than lake sediments far from the town. The highest concentrations were found close to the mouth of the Capra River, which drains the smelter effluent. Neither Canadian nor Indonesian regulations cover nickel or cobalt concentrations in freshwater sediments, but Ontario's sediment quality guidelines for nickel are exceeded by approximately 150 times, and copper and zinc concentrations in sediments immediately off the Capra River exceed Canadian sediment quality guidelines. Dry-season water samples from Lake Matano indicate that concentrations of nickel, copper, and cobalt in lake waters collected near Soroako are all below the Environment Canada recommended guidelines for freshwater, but dissolved zinc concentrations are high (Glynn, Edinger, and KWAS, unpublished data). Water samples show much more temporal variability than sediment samples, and it is not possible to draw conclusions on metals contamination of lake water based on the few samples collected to date.

The Malili Lakes are not dead, despite the high levels of metals in them. Bedrock geology has protected them from the devastation inflicted on many Sudbury area lakes, in a manner similar to Ramsey Lake's resistance to acidification. The western half of Lake Matano is underlain by limestone, giving the lake a pH of 7.4 and infinite buffering capacity. The slightly basic pH of Lake Matano ensures that most metals entering the lake, either as dissolved metals or particulates, do not remain in solution, but precipitate and settle to the bottom, so dissolved concentrations of metals remain low, and the transmission of metals into plankton and surface-dwelling fish is limited (Haffner et al. 2001). Bottom-dwelling invertebrates and near-bottom-dwelling fish still face high concentrations of metals in lake sediments, in addition to the dangers posed by bottom-dwelling prey. Analysis of nickel levels in fish tissue collected from Lake Matano did not find abnormally high levels. Nickel concentrations were not correlated with fish length or weight, indicating that the fish were able to eliminate some of the nickel from their bodies (Glynn, Edinger, and KWAS, unpublished data).

Smelter effluent drains into Lake Matano via the Capra River and into Lake Mahalona via the artificial catchment in Lake Lamuloi (Fiona Dam). Villagers reported fish kills in Lake Mahalona during the dry season, with the last fish kill in 1997 or 1998. These fish kills may result from oxygen consumption by reduced metals (iron or other metals) in smelter runoff, rather than from direct metal toxicity. Deformed fish with abnormal tooth development, or lacking teeth altogether, have been observed in Lake Mahalona and Lake Towuti farther downstream (Edinger and Best 2001; Glynn 2006). Nickel concentrations in Lake Towuti sediments are higher than in Lake Matano, but most other metals are lower in Lake Towuti than in Lake Matano (Haffner et al. 2001). This pattern may reflect the dominant airborne transport of smelter fallout toward Lake Towuti rather than Lake Matano, but other processes could also account for the differences observed.

Employment and Labour Rights

Employment and labour conditions in Soroako have been one of the major points of contention between Inco and Soroako villagers. Inco proudly notes that 99 percent of its staff in Soroako are Indonesians. Nonetheless, most of these people are not derived from local populations. The bulk of employees involved in building the mine and processing plant in the 1970s, and the bulk of current Inco employees, migrated into the Soroako region from other parts of Sulawesi, or even from other Indonesian islands (Robinson 1986). Currently, about 3,000 people are employed at Inco, of whom about 150 are native to Soroako (KWAS, personal communication 2002). Most of the rest of the industrial workforce migrated into Soroako from other parts of Sulawesi. Most of the professional and managerial positions not staffed by expatriates are held by Javanese and other Indonesian migrants.

Because the Soroako mine is essentially a strip mine, it has a much better safety record than underground mines in Canada. Injury rates are relatively low, and mostly involve heavy equipment accidents (Edinger and Best 2001). Both Inco and contractor employees are covered by safety statistics. By contrast, Inco health records cover only Inco employees, and include examinations by company doctors only. Some people interviewed complained that Inco doctors gave employees a clean bill of health while independent doctors identified illnesses in the same patients, some of which could have been work-related (Glynn 2006). Although there is a trade union for Inco employees in Soroako, it is regarded as a "company union."

The ability of village organizations such as KWAS to protest against Inco or government decisions has improved dramatically since the demise of the Suharto regime in 1998. Shortly after their first visit to Canada, which included meetings with the Innu Nation in Labrador (see below), KWAS blockaded the access road to Inco's Soroako offices, successfully demanding access to Inco's hospital, school, and recreational facilities in Inco housing areas. KWAS and the Karonsi'e Dongi participated in a community mapping exercise that documented the locations and extent of traditional Soroako and Karonsi'e Dongi lands now occupied by Inco. Following community-based water testing in 2002, Inco extended its water service to the Soroako kampung lama, ending "water apartheid" that had prevailed for more than two decades. As many of the most egregious water rights and access issues were resolved, the leadership of KWAS has, in the period after 2003, become steadily more closely aligned with Inco. Soroako's business class and traditional nobility, which constitute the leadership of KWAS, enjoy Inco connections, positions for family members in various capacities, and other company perks. KWAS has continued to lobby for more positions at Inco for native Soroakans, including promotion of some Soroakans to management positions.

Since 2003, cooperation between KWAS and the Karonsi'e Dongi has largely broken down. Starting in 2004, some of the latter's members occupied land close to Inco's golf course and the site of their pre-1955 village, an abandoned mining area known as Kurate Lawa. The Karonsi'e Dongi have been offered land elsewhere in the region, and the community is split between those who have accepted the alternative land offer and those who continue to occupy the land in Kurate Lawa. KWAS has not publicly sided with either Inco or the Karonsi'e Dongi in this dispute and has not come to the aid of the Karonsi'e Dongi. The apparent co-optation of the KWAS leadership, and Inco's successful divide-and-conquer strategy regarding the KWAS and the Karonsi'e Dongi, both work to its benefit, and are consistent with mining companies' approaches to community relations elsewhere.

Regulatory Environment

Environmental regulations in Indonesia look good on paper, but are less demanding than those in Canada. A crucial problem is that enforcement tends to be lax. In relatively remote locations such as Soroako, neither regional nor national governments have the infrastructure, training, or personnel to monitor pollution, so *all* monitoring is conducted by Inco alone. Inco makes quarterly reports to the regional government's department of planning summarizing the environmental data it has collected, but these reports are difficult for the public to access. Inco monitors airborne particulates, chemistry in streams draining the smelter complex and the principal mines, and near-shore lake sedimentation rates where those streams enter Lake Matano. However, Inco's monitoring is concentrated almost entirely on its worksites, with relatively little monitoring in the residential areas surrounding the mine and smelter. Only recently, with financial support from the Steelworkers Humanity Fund (Canada) and technical support from Memorial University of Newfoundland, has the village organization, KWAS, begun independent environmental monitoring. This community-based monitoring collected the basic data on air pollution and water pollution, and included a health questionnaire survey (Glynn 2006).

Goro, New Caledonia

New Caledonia has the longest history of nickel mining among the four regions under consideration, with the initial discovery of nickel ore there in the 1870s (EPS 1982). Strip mining for laterite and garnierite nickel ore throughout New Caledonia caused extensive soil erosion and deforestation from the 1910s onward (Bird et al. 1984). Most ore concentrate from mines was shipped to the capital, Noumea, for smelting by pyrometallurgy. There are health concerns for Noumea residents who live in the areas of highest smelter fallout (Rick Anex, personal communication 2002).

The proposed Inco mine at Goro would be the first of a new generation of very large mines in New Caledonia, and the third largest of the mines discussed in this chapter. Inco estimates the size of the deposit at 54 million tonnes, and it forecasts annual nickel matte production at 55,000 tonnes. Inco plans to use hydrometallurgy to extract nickel from laterite ore, and is constructing a production-scale PAL processing plant.

One major environmental concern is the amount of dissolved metals that would be released to the ocean from the hydromet effluent pipe. The effluent would be released about five kilometres from the Yves Merlet marine reserve, the largest and oldest Marine Protected Area in New Caledonia. Although Inco claims that its environmental models predict reduction of metals levels to background levels within twenty metres of the pipe diffuser, this model has not passed any independent peer review. Another concern is acid aerosol release from the PAL plant. The Goro region hosts seven botanical reserves for rare endemic plants, mainly serpentine or nickel-rich soil endemics. These botanical reserves could potentially be endangered by soil acidification caused by acid aerosol deposition from the PAL plant (R. Anex, personal communication, 2002). Native Kanak residents already complain about the acid smell from the PAL pilot plant, which would be increased in scale by a hundred times or more for the actual production plant.

There has been relatively little study of the impact of nickel mining on the marine environment in New Caledonia (Labrosse et al. 2000). Many rivers and coastal lagoons have been contaminated by metals from nickel mines throughout the island. One study of reef fish in New Caledonia showed that they were less diverse, but more abundant and larger, on reefs subject to high soil erosion from strip mining. This pattern is explained by higher nutrient flux with terrestrial runoff, and by lower fishing pressure in turbid waters (Letourneur et al. 1999).

Regulatory Environment

New Caledonia remains a semi-autonomous French possession. The Kanak people participate in New Caledonian governance through the Kanak Customary Senate, which has advisory power only. For environmental purposes, French law is meant to apply to mines such as Goro, but enforcement is often lax.

Inco prepared a limited environmental impact assessment for the Goro project, referred to as an *installation classée*. Local environmentalists, the Kanak Customary Senate, and international environmental non-governmental organizations have questioned various aspects of the *installation classée*. Inco then commissioned a review of the *installation classée* by the Institut National de l'Environnement et des Risques (National Institute of Environment and Risks). This review found a number of errors or inadequacies, mostly in aspects of the review that had insufficient detail to assess the risks and impacts of the project. Areas of particular concern were key component studies that were not made public; insufficient data on the physical and chemical stability of dams and other waste storage structures, under predicted and catastrophic conditions; insufficient data to adequately assess possible chemical impacts on groundwater; insufficient information on dry covers over tailings impoundments; insufficient background information on ocean currents near the effluent pipe outfall and inappropriate modeling of the effluent plume from this pipe; insufficient range of factors considered in the risk assessment; and insufficient baseline data on terrestrial flora in the vicinity of the mine and processing plant (Halifax Initiative 2003).

The *installation classée* was also reviewed by the Parks and Territorial Reserves Service of the Southern Province of New Caledonia. Its review was severely critical, particularly with respect to impacts on rare and endangered plants in the vicinity of the Goro development (Halifax Initiative 2003). New Caledonia is well known for its diverse endemic flora (Myers et al. 2000), including seven botanical reserves for endemic plants in the vicinity of the Goro mine and processing plant.

The Goro project has been held up for three reasons. First, Inco has had some trouble securing financing for the project. Second, the local Kanak leadership wants to negotiate more secure benefit arrangements with Inco, analogous to the Impacts and Benefits Agreements (IBAs) Inco has had to negotiate with Innu and Inuit groups in Labrador (see below). Finally, environmental concerns not adequately addressed in the *installation classée* have come back to haunt Inco. Starting in 2001, a coalition of local Kanak leaders known as Rheebu Nuu has intermittently blockaded the road going to the construction site, seeking a greater share of the benefits to local Kanak landowners and a more rigorous environmental review. These protests included some acts of theft and vandalism in which heavy equipment was either removed from the site or destroyed. The French military was called in to quell the protests, but the situation remains tense. In November 2006, the Tribunal de Grande Instance de Paris (a French court) ruled that European environmental laws apply to New Caledonia, therefore setting dramatically lower limits to manganese concentrations in effluent than outlined in Inco's *installation classée*. Although one French court ordered a halt to construction of the processing facility at Goro pending more appropriate environmental assessment, this decision was overturned on appeal, and mine construction continued.

Voisey's Bay, Labrador

Voisey's Bay is Inco's latest large purchase in North America. The massive sulphide deposit in Northern Labrador is accessible only by air or sea, with land-fast ice and pack ice in coastal waters for much of the year. Construction of the open-pit mine, mill, and associated infrastructure has begun, and ore production began in late 2005. Ore is milled to concentrate on site, and the concentrate is shipped out by barge. Inco forecasts an annual production rate of 50,000 tonnes of nickel matte.

Tailings are deposited into a local lake (Nicholson et al. in Goldsack et al. 1999). Fish from this lake were transplanted to a nearby lake of similar species composition. One of the major environmental concerns raised by the Innu Nation is acid mine drainage, more from the mine itself than from the tailings, which will be underwater. Subaqueous tailings dumping is a controversial mining practice: the mining industry likes it for its low cost, for not having to build and maintain tailings dams, and because "out of sight is out of mind."

Like the Goro mine, Voisey's Bay has been the subject of an extensive environmental impact assessment (EIA), and Voisey's Bay is the only site of the four considered in this review for which accurate data on pre-industrial environmental conditions were collected (Veinott et al. 2001). The EIA included both scientific and socioeconomic impacts and a mine closure plan, and was reviewed and severely criticized. The Innu Nation retained biologists from Memorial University to review portions of it, and they found several areas of concern. A review of the avifaunal (birds) portions of the EIA done for the Innu Nation identified many deficiencies (Goudie 1998). Because this review of the EIA was commissioned by the Innu Nation, it had no legal standing and did not necessitate a reassessment of the project's environmental impacts or a more complete assessment of avifaunal information.

The Voisey's Bay development sits near the boundary between land claimed by the Innu Nation and the Labrador Inuit Association (now Nunatsiavut). Inco has negotiated IBAs with both the Innu and the Inuit, though the details of these agreements are not public. The Innu Nation IBA includes provisions on Innu employment levels, Innu involvement in environmental monitoring, and a number of other provisions. About 40 percent of the mine and concentrator construction workforce is Aboriginal, and approximately 1,350 people are currently employed on the project. These workers are represented by the United Steelworkers, and they went on strike for several months in 2006. Inco receives a federal wage subsidy for Aboriginal workers, part of a federal program to encourage hiring of newly trained Aboriginal workers. Nonetheless, the Innu Nation remains concerned that relatively few Innu have been employed at the mine.

One of the major issues surrounding the Voisey's Bay development has been the location and type of ore processing. From the beginning, there were suggestions that ore concentrate from Voisey's Bay would help feed the Sudbury smelter, but the Newfoundland and Labrador government has insisted that ore mined from Voisey's Bay should be processed in the province as a condition for allowing the mine development to proceed. Inco plans to use PAL hydrometallurgy to process the ore. The adaptation of the PAL process to Voisey's Bay ore remains in the experimental stage, but it appears to be operationally feasible. The province resisted the PAL approach due to uncertainties about its feasibility for large volumes of sulphide ore, and it argued for construction of a traditional pyrometallurgy smelter. Despite the province's insistence on ore processing in Newfoundland, Voisey's Bay ore is currently shipped to Sudbury for smelting.

Inco is now in the process of building a pilot hydrometallurgy facility in Long Harbour, Newfoundland, having given up on the planned site in Argentia, the site of a former American naval base. Long Harbour and Argentia are both situated on Placentia Bay, the richest and most diverse large bay in Newfoundland. It hosts the only remaining commercially viable cod stock in eastern Newfoundland, but more than 350 oil tankers ply its waters each year, the highest concentration of tanker traffic anywhere in Canadian waters.

The provincial government waived the requirement for a separate EIA for the Placentia Bay ore-processing facility. Instead, Inco prepared a much less detailed environmental protection plan for the site. Inco has agreed to construct a traditional smelter if the hydromet process cannot be adequately modified to treat Voisey's Bay ore. Approximately half the province's remaining 500,000 people now live on the Avalon Peninsula, within a hundred kilometres downwind, and so they would potentially be affected by the PAL facility or smelter. There is some local opposition to a smelter or PAL plant in the region on environmental grounds, but for the most part there is public support for *any* development that might bring more jobs to the province. In order to gain provincial approval for Voisey's Bay, Inco has donated large sums of money to various parts of the provincial economy, including $13.2 million to Memorial University. An existing building on the Memorial campus has been renovated and re-named the Inco Innovation Centre.

Considerable progress has been made toward making nickel mining and processing less environmentally damaging, largely as a result of government regulation, which in turn largely resulted from observations of disastrous past effects of mining and smelting. The regulatory process around the Voisey's Bay development, for example, is quite rigorous, and has included extensive negotiations toward IBAs with both local groups of indigenous peoples as well as environmental assessments of various phases of the project. This does not mean that there will be no adverse environmental consequences of the Voisey's Bay mine and concentrator, or of the Long Harbour PAL plant, if it is ever built. Rather, it means that many of the environmental consequences can be predicted, and governments have deemed those consequences to be acceptable.

Summary

There are six major lessons that can be gleaned from all this. First, the legal requirement for mine-closure plans, and the requirement that mining companies post mine-closure bonds, is very important. Having predicted the consequences of a mine, the mining company assumes legal and financial responsibility for restoring the landscape to an agreed-upon level after the mine has closed. Mine-closure plans may not be sufficient, however. How will a mining company ensure that mine tailings left at a closed mine will remain free of oxygen in perpetuity, and so prevent acid mine drainage? Mine-closure plans are required in Canada, the United States, and many European countries, but they are not required in Indonesia, New Caledonia, or many other developing world sites of base metal mining.

Second, standardizing environmental legislation by raising standards worldwide will help ensure that mining companies do not flee to the developing world as a refuge from environmental legislation and labour unions. Many local mining communities in developing countries are demanding just this: they want environmental protection at standards of the developed world, along with employment and investment. Although the EIA requirements have improved our understanding of the impacts of mining and regulations have lessened the impacts, there are still tangible and long-term consequences of mining operations.

Third, there are flaws in the EIA process. The client-vendor relationship between the mining company and the consulting company sets up an inherent conflict of interest. Mining companies pay environmental consultants to write EIAs with a tacit understanding that the consultant's role is to acquire the necessary permits so the mining company can do what it wants. True alternatives to a mining company's proposal are rarely considered, even though EIA regulations require consultants to do so. This tunnel-vision approach to assessment is not surprising: the assessment process is usually initiated after the project has been fully designed and engineered, so the proponents are loath to return to the drawing board. It is uncommon for a consulting company to return with an alternative suggestion on how to solve a problem, and virtually unheard-of for a consulting company to recommend that a project not proceed on environmental grounds.

The EIA is reviewed by a government-appointed review panel, and proponents are sometimes required to produce addenda to certain sections of the EIA, but review panels rarely require a proponent to actually change its development plans. Review panels are often under intense political pressure to approve the EIA because of the economic incentives to governments in allowing mining to proceed (royalties, taxes, etc.). As seen in the case of Voisey's Bay, the final decisions on whether a mine will be permitted to proceed are often political, and not based on scientific or environmental factors.

In Canada, EIAs have a thirty-to-forty-five-day public comment period. Though this is a legal requirement, it is rarely implemented in an effective manner. It is very difficult for citizens' groups to accurately review a document hundreds or thousands of pages long in thirty to forty-five days. Local citizens' groups can hire consultants to review or critique an EIA, and they can sometimes even receive government funding to prepare such reviews, but their reviews have no legal standing. Usually, these citizens' reviews are completely ignored by the proponent, as happened with the review of the Voisey's Bay EIA presented by the Innu Nation.

To resolve the conflict of interest and other systemic problems in the EIA process, a mandatory arms-length peer review process with legal power to require revisions or reassessments, or to block the project altogether, could be applied to EIA documents. Such an arm's-length review system could be similar to those used in publishing scientific research. This could ensure the validity of pollutant dispersion models, population and habitat assessments, and other aspects of the EIA, and could require proponents to pursue alternative designs when impacts are too severe. Alternatively, mining companies and other project proponents could pay a tax to a special government department whose role would be to conduct environmental assessments. Although a government department might be less prone to corporate pressure, it might be more prone to political pressure, as observed with the political influence on Department of Fisheries and Oceans catch limits during the years leading up to the cod moratorium in 1992.

Fourth, the mining and smelting of base metal ores bring *inherent* environmental threats. Mining companies, being for-profit enterprises, seek to extract the most ore and metal for the least cost. Mining companies invest in environmental protection or in clean-production technologies primarily because they have been required to do so. The government-controlled mining industry in the former Soviet Union, although not strictly for-profit, left an environmental legacy as bad or worse as that in Sudbury. Government regulation and pressure from trade unions, environmental non-governmental organizations, and local residents are crucial in protecting the environment from the potential damage from base metal mining and smelting.

Fifth, there is too much mining of raw minerals. Nickel is extracted from the ground, refined, used in many forms of steel, in electronics, and other products that are eventually discarded in landfills. This one-way conveyor belt of metals from ore deposits to industrial uses to landfills needs to be closed into a circle. Rather than developing new ore deposits, mining companies should focus on developing clean technologies for recovering metals from garbage. Such efforts will reduce the toxicity of landfills by removing heavy metals and will reduce the environmental impacts of mining by having fewer mines in operation. This sort of metal recycling is already happening, but not to the extent necessary. While recycling could diminish the amount of raw ore required, informal estimates from within the mining industry suggest that it could probably supply much less than half of the metals required at current consumption rates. On a cautionary note, however, it is important to separate metallic from non-metallic components of waste in order to ensure that other toxins are not generated through plastics combustion. The recent attention to electronic waste illustrates the hazards of poorly regulated metals recycling from computer components.

Sixth, in all four case studies considered in this chapter, the wealth generated by mining has largely left the region where the mines are, and are concentrated in financial centres where mining companies have their corporate headquarters. Sudburians complain that the their mines made Toronto rich, but that Northern Ontario is still poor. Soroako natives complain that they have largely been shut out from the economic benefits of jobs, yet they have lost their land and previous livelihoods as farmers and fishermen. The profits of the Soroako mines flow to PT Inco in Jakarta, and to their majority shareholder, Inco in Toronto. In New Caledonia, Kanak leaders oppose the Goro project on environmental grounds, and on the grounds that not enough economic benefits will be returned to their people, who will lose some of their agricultural land. Within New Caledonia, the wealth that stays in New Caledonia stays in the capital, Noumea, rather than in the mining region itself. In Voisey's Bay, a major part of the IBAs with the Labrador Inuit Association and Innu Nation focus around jobs and compensation for loss or degradation of other natural resources in the area of the mine and smelter. The Newfoundland and Labrador government insisted on ore processing in the province to ensure value-added production in that province, with attendant jobs and infrastructure development.

Ensuring that the majority of the wealth created by mining remains in the region of the mine, and with the people on whose land the mine stands, and with the people who have done the mining, is a difficult challenge within the context of capitalist mining development. A strong labour movement is essential. Trade unions must make the environment a priority, along with the health and safety of workers, and they must forge alliances with indigenous peoples in areas where mineral deposits occur.

Notes

Friends in Sudbury, Soroako, New Caledonia, and Newfoundland and Labrador generously shared their experiences and clarified many of the environmental issues surrounding their regions. In particular, I thank Andi Baso Am, Naomi Mananta, Umar Ranggo, and Yusri Yusuf for their patient answers to my many questions in Soroako, and for their commitment to the community-based environmental monitoring program there. Tracy Glynn contributed to this research in many ways, including allowing me to cite some of her thesis data. Rick Anex explained some of the complexity of the politics surrounding the Goro mine in New Caledonia. Larry Innes provided insights into the Innu Nation's environmental concerns about the Voisey's Bay mine, and about the impacts and benefits agreement between the Innu Nation and Inco. This chapter benefited from discussions with R. Anex, N. Catto, T. Donaghy, I. Goudie, L. Innes, M. Lowe, A. Peach, J. Rendell, and R. Sproule. Soroako research was supported by the Steelworker Humanity Fund (Canada) and the Environmental Defense Fund.

1. Massive "sulphide" deposits, such as the Sudbury, Thompson (Manitoba), Norilsk, and Voisey's Bay deposits, contain nickel, copper, and iron as metal sulphides hosted in igneous rock, usually ultramafic igneous rocks. "Laterites" are soil-borne deposits of iron oxides containing small amounts of nickel, and smaller amounts of cobalt, zinc, and other metals, typically found in the top three to ten metres of soil, and formed by intense weathering of ultramafic igneous rocks. "Igneous" rocks are those that form from molten rock, while "ultramafic" rocks have low silica content and high content of iron and magnesium-rich minerals such as olivine, pyroxene, and metalliferous ore minerals.

2. For reviews of impacts and recovery in Sudbury, readers are referred to the *Proceedings of the Mining and the Environment* conferences (Sudbury '95, Sudbury '99, and Sudbury '03), Jambor et al. 2003, and Gunn 1995. Only journal articles are cited individually.

3. Environmental research in Soroako is a cooperative effort with the Native Soroako Association, Kerukinan Wawoinia Asli Soroako, known by its acronym, KWAS.

4. Although these data were collected using a gravity corer, enabling retroactive analysis of pre-mining metals levels in the lake, temporal variation in metals levels have not yet been published (Haffner et al. 2001). These cores are currently under study as part of a doctoral project through the Great Lakes Environmental Research Institute at the University of Windsor.

Chapter 6

Some Aspects of Health and Health Care in the Sudbury Area

K. V. Nagarajan

Introduction

The health status of the people of Sudbury and Northern Ontario is relatively poor. Most health indicators generally lie below provincial levels. Standardized mortality ratios in Northern Ontario are "20 percent greater than expected all-cause premature mortality relative to the province" (Altmayer et al. 2003). The Ontario Ministry of Health and Long-Term Care has observed that "[P]eople living in the northern District Health Council regions have a lower life expectancy than the provincial average" (OMHLTC 2002: 12, 14). Sudbury residents, like other Northern Ontario residents, are also at a distinct disadvantage in terms of access to physicians, nurses, and health-care facilities.

This chapter brings together selected, publicly available data bearing on the health and health care of people in the Sudbury area. My objective is to find answers, however tentative, to a number of basic questions. First, how does the Sudbury area compare with the province as a whole in terms of important indicators of health? Second, how does the Sudbury area compare with the province as a whole in terms of availability and access to health-care resources? Based on this comparative data, we can point to important challenges confronting our community and suggest why these challenges arise and how to face them.[1]

The "Sudbury area" has been defined differently for different data-gathering purposes. Most of the data I use are for the Sudbury and District Health Unit (SDHU) area so, in this chapter, the Sudbury area means the SDHU area, unless otherwise noted. This SDHU area covers 46,121 square kilometres, or 5.1 percent of Ontario's landmass, and is made up of the City of Greater Sudbury, the District of Sudbury, and the District of Manitoulin. Within this area, the City of Greater Sudbury has the largest population (81 percent of the SDHU's 190,840 population by the 2001 census) and an area of 3,354 squire kilometres.[2] The health status of the Aboriginal population is of particular concern. According to the 2001 census, the City of Greater Sudbury has 7,020 self-identified Aboriginal persons, or nearly half of the 14,210 Aboriginal population of the SDHU area.

A Changing Demographic Picture

Between 1996 and 2001, the Sudbury area's population declined by 5 percent. By contrast, the province of Ontario as a whole registered a gain of 6.1 percent over this same period, reaching over 11.4 million. Along with the size of the population, its age and sex distribution also have important implications for understanding health-care needs.

As shown in Table 6.1, the Sudbury area has a bulge in the twenty-five-to-forty-four age group, though this group is slightly smaller as a percentage of the total population than for the province as whole. In this age group, the Sudbury area had a 13 percent decline between 1996 and 2001. There was also a significant decline in the number of young people aged twenty to twenty-four, particularly males, whose numbers fell from 7,487 to 5,720. This was a major decline, amounting to a loss of 24 percent of males in this age group. The exodus of young people has serious implications for the health, both physical and economic, of Sudbury area communities. Not surprisingly, the Sudbury population is becoming slightly older compared to the province as a whole. The median age for males is thirty-nine (while it is thirty-six years for Ontario), and for females it is forty (compared to thirty-eight for the province). Overall, it is thirty-nine, compared to thirty-seven for the province.

Table 6.1: Population Distribution for the Sudbury Area, 2001

Age Groups	Male	Female	Total
0–4	5,150	4,855	10,005
5–9	6,290	6,045	12,335
10–14	6,500	6,405	12,905
15–19	6,810	6,585	13,395
20–24	5,720	5,800	11,520
25–29	5,110	5,265	10,375
30–34	5,750	6,130	11,880
25–39	7,550	8,065	15,615
40–44	7,815	8,345	16,160
45–49	7,200	7,740	14,940
50–54	7,320	7,020	14,340
55–59	5,675	5,665	11,340
60–64	4,615	4,770	9,385
65–69	4,060	4,360	8,420
70–74	3,460	3,825	7,285
75–79	2,345	3,210	5,555
80–84	1,180	2,015	3,195
85+	6,95	1,510	2,205
TOTAL	93,240	97,600	190,840
Median Age	39	40	39
% population 15+	80.8	82.3	81.5

Health Indicators of the Sudbury Area

There are a vast array of generally accepted health indicators that are very useful to measure the health status of a community. In this section, I have selected thirteen categories of health indicators to understand the health profile of Sudbury area residents.[3]

Child Health Indicators

Childhood health indicators for Sudbury show a situation worse than for the province as a whole (Table 6.2). Especially worrisome are infant mortality rates (the death of a child under one year of age) and peri-natal infant mortality rates (the total number of stillbirths and deaths in the first week of life). Also of concern are gaps between male and female rates, including for low birth weights. The numbers in parentheses are 5 percent confidence intervals. Statistically, the higher the number of observations, the smaller the confidence interval, so it is not surprising that the Sudbury area figures show a larger range than the Ontario figures. When the range is large, the data are to be interpreted and compared with greater caution.

Table 6.2: Childhood Health Indicators, Sudbury Area and Ontario, 1997

Ontario	Sudbury area	Indicator
5.9 (5.8–6.0)	6.1 (5.6–6.8)	Total: Low birth weight rate
5.5 (5.4–5.6)	5.8 (5.0–6.60)	Male: Low birth weight rate
6.3 (6.1–6.4)	6.5 (5.7–7.5)	Female: Low birth weight rate
4.3 (2.7–6.5)	6.5 (4.7–8.7)	Total: Infant mortality rate per 1,000 live births
4.8 (2.5–8.2)	6.3 (3.9–9.4)	Male: Infant mortality rate per 1,000 live births
3.9 (1.9–7.1)	6.8 (4.3–10.2)	Female: Infant mortality rate per 1,000 live births
6.2 (4.3–8.8)	8.2 (6.2–10.7)	Total: Peri-natal mortality rate per 1,000 total births
4.0 (3.0–5.2)	8.1 (5.4–11.6)	Male: Peri-natal infant mortality rate per 1,000 total births
6.2 (5.1–7.5)	8.4 (5.6–12.1)	Female: Peri-natal infant mortality rate per 1000 total births

Notes: Low birth weights refer to babies born at less than 2,500 grams (5.5 pounds). Infant mortality refers to the death of a child less than one year of age. Peri-natal mortality is the total number of stillbirths and deaths in the first week of life. The numbers in parentheses are 5 percent confidence intervals.

Table 6.3: Life Expectancy Indicators, Sudbury Area and Ontario, 1997

Ontario	Sudbury area	Indicator
78.8 (78.8–78.9)	76.8 (76.4–77.2)	Total: Life expectancy at birth
76.2 (76.2–76.3	74.0 (73.5–74.5)	Male: Life expectancy at birth
81.4 (81.4–81.5)	79.6 (79.1–80.1)	Female: Life expectancy at birth
18.2 (18.1–18.2)	17.1 (16.9–17.4)	Total: Life expectancy at age 65
16.3 (16.2–16.3)	15.2 (14.9–15.6)	Male: Life expectancy at age 65
19.9 (19.9–20.0)	18.9 (18.5–19.2)	Female: Life expectancy at age 65

Table 6.4: Aggregate Mortality Rates, Sudbury Area and Ontario, 1997

Ontario	Sudbury area	Indicator
649.0 (646.5–651.5)	762.4 (741.5–783.3)	Total: Total mortality, age-standardized rate per 100,000 population
825.3 (820.8–829.6)	968.4 (931.3–1,005.4)	Male: Total Mortality, age-standardized rate per 100,000 population
520.5 (517.5–523.5)	602.7 (578.2–627.2)	Female: Total mortality, age-standardized rate per 100,000 population

Life Expectancy

Life expectancy is defined as the number of years a person would be expected to live, starting from birth, on the basis of mortality statistics for a given period. Similarly, life expectancy at age sixty-five refers to the number of years a person of that age is expected to live on the basis of mortality statistics for a given period. Life expectancy figures for the Sudbury area are worse than the provincial figures — there is almost a two-year gap in total life expectancy (Table 6.3). A recent study of the health of Canadians living in Census Metropolitan Areas put Greater Sudbury in last place in terms of life expectancy (Gilmore 2004). Between Vancouver, the first-place holder (81.1 years) and Greater Sudbury (76.7) there is a 4.4-year difference in life expectancy. This finding provides further evidence of the lower life expectancy in the Sudbury area. Life expectancy at age sixty-five is also lower than the provincial figures for the total population, for both men and women.

Aggregate Mortality Rates

Total mortality figures for the Sudbury area are much higher than the provincial figures (Table 6.4). The total mortality rate is 17.5 percent higher. The male rate

Table 6.5: Cardiovascular and Cerebrovascular Mortality Rates, Sudbury Area and Ontario, 1997

Ontario	Sudbury area	Indicator
255.4 (247.0–269.8)	292.7 (279.5–305.9)	Total: All circulatory disease deaths, age-standardized rate per 100,000 population
319.8 (299.9–339.8)	366.4 (342.5–390.2)	Male: All circulatory disease deaths, age-standardized rate per 100,000 population
206.4 (193.2–219.6)	231.2 (216.0–246.4)	Female: All circulatory disease deaths, age-standardized rate per 100,000 population
160.1 (151.0–169.2)	167.3 (157.3–177.4)	Total: Ischemic heart disease deaths, age-standardized rate per 100,000 population
207.3 (191.2–223.5)	221.1 (202.7–239.4)	Male: Ischemic heart disease deaths, age-standardized rate per 100,000 population
119.7 (109.6–129.9)	121.4 (110.3–132.5)	Female: Ischemic heart disease deaths, age-standardized rate per 100,000 population
48.0 (43.0–53.0)	51.8 (46.1–57.5)	Total: Cerebrovascular disease deaths, age-standardized rate per 100,000 population
53.9 (45.5–62.4)	61.0 (50.8–71.1)	Male: Cerebrovascular disease deaths, age-standardized rate per 100,000 population
42.7 (36.6–48.7)	44.8 (37.9–51.6)	Female: Cerebrovascular disease deaths, age-standardized rate per 100,000 population

is 17.3 percent higher. The female mortality rate is 15.8 percent higher. As we will see, disease-specific mortality rates are also higher for the Sudbury area for most illnesses.

The aggregate figures in Table 6.4 are age-standardized. This means we can directly compare two areas with different age structures.[4]

Cardiovascular and Cerebrovascular Deaths

These cover deaths from circulatory disease, ischemic heart disease, and cerebrovascular accidents, which are mostly strokes. The total death rate from circulatory disease for the Sudbury area population is 15 percent above the provincial rate, 16 percent higher for males and 12 percent higher for females. Circulatory disease includes, among other conditions, rheumatic fever, hypertension, atherosclerosis, angina, and heart attacks. For this category of disease-specific deaths, as for several others that follow, it is important to note that the rate of death for males is significantly higher than for females, even before considering the adverse regional differential for the Sudbury area.

The total death rate from ischemic heart disease (clogged arteries) for the Sudbury area is about 5 percent higher than the provincial figure. For males, it is about 7 percent higher, for females about 1 percent higher.

The total death rate from cerebrovascular disease for the Sudbury area is 8

Table 6.6: Cancer Deaths, Sudbury Area and Ontario, 1997

Ontario	Sudbury area	Indicator
187.3 (177.1–197.4)	196.0 (185.3–206.6)	Total: All cancer deaths, age-standardized rate per 100,000 population
221.6 (205.0–238.1)	240.8 (222.2–259.5)	Male: All cancer deaths, age-standardized rate per 100,000 population
162.0 (149.1–175.0)	165.7 (152.4–179.0)	Female: All cancer deaths, age-standardized per 100,000 population
46.2 (41.2–51.2)	52.7 (47.02–58.2)	Total: Lung cancer deaths, age-standardized rate per 100,000 population
56.8 (48.6–65.0)	72.5 (62.7–82.4)	Male: Lung cancer deaths, age-standardized rate per 100,000 population
37.8 (31.5–44.1)	37.1 (30.8–43.4)	Female: Lung cancer deaths, age-standardized rate per 100,000 population
19.3 (16.0–22.5)	21.0 (17.5–24.60)	Total: Colorectal cancer deaths, age-standardized rate per 100,000 population
22.4 (17.2–27.6)	25.1 (19.2–31.0)	Male: Colorectal cancer deaths, age-standardized rate per 100,000 population
16.1 (12.1–20.1)	17.6 (13.3–22.0)	Female: Colorectal cancer deaths, age-standardized rate per 100,000 population
27.3 (26.6–28.1)	26.9 (21.5–32.3)	Female: Breast cancer deaths, age-standardized rate per 100,000 population
28.2 (27.3–29.1)	29.4 (22.1–36.8)	Male: Prostate cancer deaths, age-standardized rate per 100,000 population

percent higher than the provincial figure. For males, 13 percent higher and for females 5 percent higher (Table 6.5).

Cancer Deaths

Death rates from all cancers in the Sudbury area exceed the provincial average by 5 percent (Table 6.6). For males the rate exceeds the provincial average by 9 percent and for females it exceeds it by 2 percent. The total lung cancer death rate in the Sudbury area is 14 percent above the provincial figure. Male lung cancer death rates are substantially higher than the provincial figure — about 28 percent higher. For females, death rates are about 2 percent below the provincial average. The total colorectal cancer death rate for the Sudbury area is 9 percent above the provincial rate, with the male rate exceeding the provincial figure by 12 percent and the female rate by 9 percent. The female breast cancer death rate is actually a little below the provincial figure, by about 2 percent. The male prostate cancer death rate, on the other hand, exceeds the provincial figure by 4 percent.

Table 6.7: Respiratory Disease Deaths, Sudbury Area and Ontario, 1997

Ontario	Sudbury area	Indicators
76.6 (70.0–83.3)	67.2 (60.7–73.7)	Total: All respiratory disease deaths, age-standardized rate per 100,000 population
113.8 (100.4–127.2)	96.6 (83.2–110.0)	Male: All respiratory disease deaths, age-standardized rate per 100,000 population
55.4 (48.1–62.6)	50.1 (43.0–57.3)	Female: All respiratory disease deaths, age-standardized rate per 100,000 population
31.3 (27.1–35.5)	27.7 (23.5–32.0)	Total: Pneumonia and influenza deaths, age-standardized rate per 100,000 population
35.5 (28.2–42.8)	36.7 (27.9–45.5)	Male: Pneumonia and influenza deaths, age-standardized rate per 100,000 population
28.0 (23.0–33.0)	23.2 (18.3–28.0)	Female: Pneumonia and influenza deaths, age-standardized rate per 100,000 population
4.9 (4.7–5.1)	5.6 (3.8–7.4)	Total: Bronchitis, emphysema and asthma deaths age-standardized per 100,000 population
6.5 (6.1–6.9)	7.6 (4.4–10.8)	Male: Bronchitis, emphysema and asthma deaths, age-standardized per 100,000 population
4.0 (3.7–4.2)	4.1 (2.0–6.2)	Female: Bronchitis, emphysema and asthma deaths, age-standardized per 100,000 population

Table 6.8: Suicide Death Rates, Sudbury Area and Ontario, 1997

Ontario	Sudbury area	Indicators
8.6 (8.3–8.9)	15.3 (12.2–18.3)	Total: suicide deaths, age-standardized rate per 100,000 population
13.8 (13.2–14.4)	26.2 (20.5–31.8)	Male: Suicide deaths, age-standardized rate per 100,000 population
3.8 (3.5–4.1)	4.6 (2.2–7.0)	Female: Suicide deaths, age-standardized rate per 100,000 population

Respiratory Disease Deaths

More positively, total death rates, as well as both male and female rates, for all respiratory diseases for the Sudbury area are well below provincial rates, by 12 percent, 15 percent and 5 percent respectively (Table 6.7). As well, the total death rate from pneumonia and influenza is below the provincial figure, by 12 percent. For females, the rate is 17 percent below the provincial figure, though for males the rate is 3 percent higher. Due to the unpredictability of these diseases, these figures can fluctuate from year to year. While the figures for pneumonia and influenza are encouraging, the total death rate due to bronchitis, emphysema, and asthma are 14 percent higher in the Sudbury area than the provincial figure.

Table 6.9: Unintended Injury Death Rates, Sudbury Area and Ontario, 1997

Ontario	Sudbury area	Indicators
23.2 (22.7–23.7)	35.1 (30.4–39.8)	Total: Unintended injury deaths, age-standardized rate per 100,000 population
31.3 (30.4–32.2)	50.3 (41.4–59.1)	Male: Unintended injury deaths, age-standardized rate per 100,000 population
16.0 (15.5–16.5)	22.6 (17.6–27.7)	Female: Unintended injury deaths, age-standardized rate per 100,000 population

Table 6.10: Chronic Conditions, Household Population 12 Years and Over, Sudbury Area and Ontario, 2000/2001

Condition	Ontario (percent)	Sudbury area (percent)	Condition	Ontario (percent)	Sudbury Area (percent)
With arthritis/ rheumatism: Total	16.6	21.8	Without arthritis/ rheumatism: Total	83.3	78.5
Males	12.6	18.2	Males	87.3	81.7
Females	20.5	23.6	Females	79.4	76.1
With Diabetes: Total	4.2	5.9	Without Diabetes: Total	95.7	94.1
Males	4.6	6.7^E	Males	95.3	93.3
Females	3.8	5.1^E	Females	96.2	94.9
With asthma: Total	8.5	9.7	Without asthma: Total	91.5	90.3
Males	6.8	9.0^E	Males	93.1	91.0
Females	10.1	10.4	Females	89.9	89.6
With high blood pressure: Total	13.0	16.9	Without high blood pressure: Total	86.8	83.0
Males	12.1	14.5	Males	87.6	85.4
Females	13.9	19.3	Females	86.0	80.6

Note: E signifies that the coefficient of variation (CV) was from 16.6 to 33.3 percent. These figures must be interpreted with caution.

For males, the rate is 17 percent higher, while for females the figure is only 3 percent higher.

Suicides

The suicide rate for the Sudbury area is alarming — almost double the provincial rate. The total rate exceeds the provincial figure by 78 percent (Table 6.8). For males, it is 90 percent above the provincial figure, for females 21 percent higher.

Table 6.11: Injuries Causing Limitation of Normal Activities, Household Population 12 Years and Over, Sudbury Area and Ontario, 2000/2001

Condition	Ontario total (percent)	Sudbury area total (percent)	Ontario males (percent)	Sudbury area males (percent)	Ontario females (percent)	Sudbury area females (percent)
Injuries in past 12 months, sought medical treatment	8.3	7.7	9.5	9.9E	7.1	5.6E
Injuries in past 12 months, did not seek medical treatment	4.9	5.0E	5.6	6.2E	4.1	3.8E
No injuries in past 12 months	86.8	87.3	84.8	83.9	88.7	90.7

Note: E signifies that the coefficient of variation (CV) was from 16.6 to 33.3 percent. These figures must be interpreted with caution.

Unintended Injury Death Rates

Also alarming is the fact that unintended injury death rate for the Sudbury area is 52 percent above the provincial figure (Table 6.9). For males, it is 61 percent above the provincial figure, for females, 41 percent higher.

Short of death, people also suffer from chronic conditions. Next, I present data on a number of selected clinically diagnosed chronic conditions.

Chronic Conditions

The percentage of cases for both males and females of arthritis/rheumatism is above the provincial average (Table 6.10). The total figure exceeds the provincial figure by 31 percent, being 44 percent higher for males and 15 percent higher for females.

The occurrence of diabetes, another chronic condition with complex outcomes, is much higher in the Sudbury area than in the province as a whole. The total figure for the Sudbury area is 40 percent above the provincial figure. For males, it is 46 percent higher, for females, 34 percent higher. As in the cases of arthritis/rheumatism and diabetes, the figures for asthma are higher in the Sudbury area than the provincial figure. Overall, asthma cases are 14 percent higher than the province rate, being 32 percent higher for males and 3 percent higher for females. While the male population living with asthma in Sudbury exceeds the provincial average, the percent of females with asthma in Sudbury is higher than the percent of Sudbury males with that condition.

Figures for high blood pressure, which is one of the risk factors for both cardiovascular and cerebrovascular diseases, are higher in the Sudbury area than in the province as a whole. The Sudbury area incidence for the total population

Table 6.12: Severity of Pain or Discomfort, Household Population 12 Years and Over, Sudbury Area and Ontario, 2000/2001

Condition	Ontario Total (percent)	Sudbury area Total (percent)	Ontario Males (percent)	Sudbury area Males (percent)	Ontario Females (percent)	Sudbury area Females (percent)
No pain or discomfort	83.6	78.3	85.6	77.5	81.7	79.2
Mild pain or discomfort	5.2	4.4ᴱ	5.0	4.5 ᴱ	5.4	4.3 ᴱ
Moderate pain or discomfort	8.3	13.3	7.1	12.7	9.8	13.2
Severe pain or discomfort	2.6	4.3	2.1	5.2 ᴱ	3.0	3.4 ᴱ

Note: E signifies that the coefficient of variation (CV) was from 16.6 to 33.3 percent. These figures must be interpreted with caution.

Table 6.13: Functional Health Status by Sex, Household Population 12 and over, Sudbury Area and Ontario, 2000/2001

Sex	Moderate or severe functional health problems (percent)		Very good or perfect functional health (percent)		Functional health not stated (percent)	
	Ontario	Sudbury	Ontario	Sudbury	Ontario	Sudbury
Both	20.1	23.3	79.1	76.1	0.8	F
Male	18.5	23.0	80.7	76.1	0.9	F
Female	21.7	23.6	77.7	76.1	0.6	F

Note: F signifies that the CV exceeds 33.3 percent and hence the percent is not reported due to extreme sampling variability.

is 30 percent higher than the provincial figure. For males it is 20 percent higher, for females 39 percent higher.

Injuries Causing Limitation of Normal Activities
In terms of injuries causing limitation of normal activities, the Sudbury area figures do not differ much from the provincial figures (Table 6.11).

Severity of Pain and Discomfort
As we go up on the scale of pain or discomfort, Sudbury area residents fare worse than their provincial counterparts (Table 6.12). It is noteworthy that both males and females in the Sudbury area suffer higher levels of pain or discomfort than residents of Ontario as a whole. Nearly 13 percent of males in the Sudbury area reported suffering from moderate to severe pain or discomfort, a level almost double that for the province.

Table 6.14: Self-Rated Health Status by Sex, Household Population 12 and Over, Sudbury Area and Ontario, 2000/2001

Sex	Excellent self-rated health (percent)		Very good self-rated health (percent)		Good self-rated health (percent)		Fair-to-poor self-rated health (percent)	
	Ontario	Sudbury area	Ontario	Sudbury area	Ontario	Sudbury area	Ontario	Sudbury area
Both	26.5	25.2	36.6	35.0	24.7	22.9	12.2	16.8
Men	27.7	24.3	37.0	34.1	23.7	23.4	11.6	18.1
Women	25.3	26.1	36.3	3 6.0	25.6	22.4	12.7	15.5

Functional Status

As a result of the fact that Sudbury area residents suffer chronic conditions at higher levels than those in the province as a whole, the functional status — a person's ability to perform daily activities, cognition, mobility, psychosocial state, and so on — of Sudbury area residents is below the provincial average (Table 6.13). There is a formal review process to measure functional status.

Self-Rated Health

Finally, the Canadian Community Health Survey regularly asks people for their own rating of their health. The percentage of Sudbury area residents rating their health status as "excellent" is slightly lower than the provincial figure, much lower for males and a little higher for females (Table 6.14). For the "very good" and "good" categories, Sudbury area men and women both have lower ratings, while the percentage rating themselves as "fair to poor" is in excess of the provincial figures. These figures indicate that Sudbury residents are lower in self-rated health status compared to the provincial figures. This difference is sharper in the "fair to poor" category.

Determinants of Health

To explain the health status of a population such as Sudbury's, a "determinants of health" approach (also called a "population health" approach) holds that we must look beyond medical services and consider also the socioeconomic and environmental characteristics of regions.[5] The key factors this approach uses to explain differences in health status are lifestyle, environment, socioeconomic conditions, human biology, and health services. Researchers look at income and social status, social-support networks, levels of education and employment, working conditions, the social and physical environment, personal health practices, early childhood development, biological and genetic endowments, health services, and gender and cultural practices, and the relationship of all of these factors to health status. Unfortunately, data at the local level are not available for all the key factors. However, I have brought together a select set of local-level data that are available from the Ontario Health Survey and the Canadian

Table 6.15: Body Mass Index (BMI) by Sex, Household Population Aged 20 to 64, Excluding Pregnant Women, Sudbury Area and Ontario, 2000/2001

Sex	Underweight: BMI under 20 (percent)		Acceptable weight: BMI 20–24.9 (percent)		Some excess weight: BMI 25–27 (percent)		Overweight: BMI 27 or higher (percent)	
	Ontario	Sudbury area	Ontario	Sudbury area	Ontario	Sudbury area	Ontario	Sudbury area
Both	8.2	7.2ᴱ						
Male	4.3	6.7ᴱ	38.6	25.6	19.4	19.9ᴱ	36.9	47.5
Female	12.1	7.6ᴱ	45.4	41.2	11.7	15.4	28.2	29.8

Note: E signifies that the coefficient of variation (CV) was from 16.6 to 33.3 percent. These figures must be interpreted with caution.

Table 6.16: Smoking Status by Sex, Household Population 12 and Over, Sudbury Area and Ontario, 2000/2001

Sex	Daily smokers (percent)		Occasional smokers (percent)		Former smokers (percent)		Never smoked (percent)	
	Ontario	Sudbury area	Ontario	Sudbury area	Ontario	Sudbury area	Ontario	Sudbury area
Both	20.1	28.1	4.4	4.0ᴱ	35.1	37.4	40.2	30.1
Male	22.7	29.1	4.6	F	38.2	41.5	34.2	24.5
Female	17.6	27.1	4.2	3.5ᴱ	32.1	33.5	46.0	35.6

Note: E signifies that the coefficient of variation (CV) was from 16.6 to 33.3 percent. These figures must be interpreted with caution. F signifies that the CV exceeds 33.3 percent and hence the percent is not reported due to extreme sampling variability.

Community Health Survey to look at how the Sudbury area is doing in terms of non-medical determinants of health. Biological and genetic endowments are complex issues and beyond the scope of this study. Health care is treated in a separate section below.

Lifestyle Factors
The set of lifestyle factors commonly associated with poor health status includes excess body weight, heavy smoking, high alcohol consumption, poor nutrition, and lack of exercise. Let us consider these factors from the Canadian Community Health Survey.

Table 6.15 shows that the proportion of people in the Sudbury area at "acceptable weight" is below the provincial average and that the proportion of people in the "excess weight" and "overweight" categories are above the provincial average. The "overweight" figures for males are especially noteworthy. Body weight is usually measured with the Body Mass Index, which is calculated by

Table 6.17: Frequency of Heavy Drinking by Sex, Household Population 12 and Over Who are Current Drinkers, Sudbury Area and Ontario, 2000/2001

Sex	5 or more drinks on one occasion, never (percent)		5 or more drinks on one occasion, less than 12 times a year (percent)		5 or more drinks on one occasion, 12 or more times a year (percent)		Drinking frequency not stated (percent)	
	Ontario	Sudbury Area	Ontario	Sudbury Area	Ontario	Sudbury Area	Ontario	Sudbury Area
Both	57.9	48.0	22.1	23.8	19.3	27.6	0.8	F
Male	47.5	36.2	24.1	22.6	27.6	40.2	0.9[E]	F
Female	69.0	60.9	19.9	25.1	10.4	13.9	0.7[E]	F

Note: E signifies that the coefficient of variation (CV) was from 16.6 to 33.3 percent. These figures must be interpreted with caution. F signifies that the CV exceeds 33.3 percent and hence the percent is not reported due to extreme sampling variability.

dividing an individual's weight in kilograms by the individual's height in metres squared. These data do not address the even more widely acknowledged increase of obesity among children.

As well, the proportion of people who smoke every day in the Sudbury area is higher than the provincial average, while the proportion of people who never smoked is lower (Table 6.16). One positive feature is that the proportion of ex-smokers is higher than the provincial average, indicating that there has been an effort on the part of Sudbury area residents to quit smoking. Of course, this trend has to continue in order to substantially cut the proportion of daily smokers, which is almost 10 percent higher than for the province. Public health officials hope that a recently enacted local by-law that restricts smoking in public places will make a dent in these figures.

Another problematic area is excess alcohol consumption or binge drinking, defined as drinking five or more drinks per occasion. Frequent binge drinking is an issue for both men and women, but especially for men, in the Sudbury area (Table 6.17)

Most nutritionists advise people to eat more fruits and vegetables. In Sudbury, the consumption of fruits and vegetables is below the provincial figure (Table 6.18). In particular, the proportion of people eating fruits and vegetables fewer than five times per day exceeds the provincial average, while the proportion of people who consume fruits and vegetables more than ten times per day is less than the provincial average.

Regular exercise has been shown to reduce the occurrence of many chronic conditions. Residents of the Sudbury area are comparable, if not more active, in their physical activity levels, to the provincial average (Table 6.19). However, this is no reason to celebrate, since almost half of the provincial population is physically inactive.

Table 6.18: Dietary Practices by Sex, Household Population 12 and over, Sudbury Area and Ontario, 2000/0001

Sex	Consume fruits and vegetables less than 5 times per day (percent)		Consume fruits and vegetables 5 to 10 times per day (percent)		Consume fruits and vegetables more than 10 times per day (percent)		Fruits and vegetable consumption not stated (percent)	
	Ontario	Sudbury area	Ontario	Sudbury area	Ontario	Sudbury area	Ontario	Sudbury area
Both	61.5	69.6	33.4	27.8	4.1	2.3^E	1.0	F
Male	66.5	75.2	.28.5	22.8	3.7	F	1.2	F
Female	56.6	64.1	38.1	32.6	4.4	F	0.8^E	F

Note: E signifies that the coefficient of variation (CV) was from 16.6 to 33.3 percent. These figures must be interpreted with caution. F signifies that the CV exceeds 33.3 percent and hence the percent is not reported due to extreme sampling variability.

Table 6.19: Leisure-Time Physical Activity by Sex, Household Population 12 and Over, Sudbury Area and Ontario, 2000/2001

Sex	Physically active (percent)		Moderately active (percent)		Physically inactive (percent)		Physical activity not stated (percent)	
	Ontario	Sudbury area	Ontario	Sudbury area	Ontario	Sudbury area	Ontario	Sudbury area
Both	21.3	24.5	21.3	23.0	49.8	48.6	7.6	F
Male	24.0	30.2	21.0	19.7	44.8	44.0	10.1	F
Female	18.6	18.9	21.6	26.2	54.6	53.1	5.2	F

Note: F signifies that the CV exceeds 33.3 percent and hence the percent is not reported due to extreme sampling variability.

Overall, in terms of lifestyle factors, Sudbury area residents tend to be heavier, smoke more, drink more, and eat less nutritious food than other Ontarians. These lifestyle factors have to be considered for both their short-term and long-term health effects. One encouraging factor is that in terms of recreational physical activity, Sudbury area residents are at par with the province, if not more active, although Ontarians as a whole need to increase their level of physical activity.

Environmental Factors
It is well-known that our physical environment is an important determinant of health. Still, there have been few publicly available studies of the health impact of Sudbury's environment. The Ontario Ministry of the Environment has been sampling soil and vegetation in Sudbury and surrounding regions since 1971. In a 2001 report (Ontario Ministry of the Environment 2001), the Ministry found

that, in "soil in Sudbury and surrounding areas, metals are present in concentrations exceeding the Ministry's 'Guidelines for Use at Contaminated Sites.'" The report notes that elevated levels of heavy metals, such as nickel, copper, cobalt, selenium, and arsenic are commonly found in Sudbury and surrounding regions. The levels are especially high in the communities of Falconbridge, Copper Cliff, and Coniston, as well as at the roasting yards.

In response, "The Sudbury Soil Study" was launched with corporate, community, and other partners. A Sudbury Area Risk Assessment Group (SARA Group) was formed in 2003. In the spring of 2008, the SARA Group released the results of the soil study (SARA Group 2008). Its main conclusions were:

- based on current conditions in the Sudbury area, there is little risk of health effects from metals in the environment;
- there were no unacceptable health risks predicted from exposure to arsenic, copper, cobalt, and selenium;
- exposure to lead within the Greater Sudbury area was within acceptable benchmarks for the protection of human health. However, there were some soil samples from Copper Cliff, Coniston, Falconbridge, and Sudbury Centre that may pose a potential risk of health effects for young children;
- there was minimal risk of respiratory inflammation from lifetime exposure (seventy years) to airborne nickel in Copper Cliff and the western part of Sudbury Centre;
- First Nations people who may consume more local fish and wild game are at no greater risk of health effects due to metals in the environment than is the general population.

These conclusions appear to give positive, reassuring news to the community. Mayor John Roderiguez and Chief Medical Officer of Health Dr. Penny Sutcliffe accepted and applauded the results (Bradley 2008a). The community at large, however, remains skeptical. A local newspaper, *The Northern Life*, conducted an informal Internet poll and found that 68 percent of the respondents were not reassured by the results (Bradley 2008b). Homer Seguin, a retired union expert on occupational health and safety, questioned the neglect of the risk in past years of the accumulation of metals in the environment in the region, because the Sudbury Soil Study considered risk only as of 2005, when the SARA Group set up monitoring devices (Bradley 2008c). Mine Mill Union Local 598/CAW President Rick Grylls expressed the view that the terms of reference were narrow and, as a result, important questions were not considered, such as the synergistic effects of the metals on human health (Grylls 2008).

Furthermore, the study did not look into the health of workers involved in mining and smelting operations. The SARA Group, of course, did not have a mandate to study occupational health-and-safety issues, because those concerns come under the Ministry of Labour. This study was not a health study, but a risk-assessment study. National Coordinator of MiningWatch Canada and former Sudbury resident Joan Kuyek raised the issue of the choice of cut-off point for deciding the acceptable risk level for lead presence in soil. The study chose 400 parts per million (ppm) for the Sudbury region, whereas the provincial guideline calls for 100 ppm. She urged the formation of an independent panel to take a look at the presence of contaminants in area residents' bodies. "Unless blood and hair testing are undertaken," she wrote, "we should not trust the risk assessment model that has been used" (Kuyek 2008).

In sum, despite publication of the results of the Sudbury Soil Study, no definitive statement can be made about the Sudbury environment's impact on the health of area residents. I have not found any other recent studies of the health effects of the Sudbury environment, particularly for air and water pollution. However, there likely are problems, as is suggested by another chapter in this volume (see Edinger), and by the health indicators noted above, especially in the case of respiratory illnesses.

Socioeconomic Factors

Socioeconomic factors such as educational attainment, income levels, and unemployment rates are also determinants of health. Educational attainment indicates income-earning potential, while income level and its adequacy determine whether individuals and families can afford a nutritious diet, adequate housing, education, and other necessities of life. As for the link between unemployment and health status, studies have shown that unemployed persons face many physical, social, and mental health issues (Catalano 1991; Dooley et al. 1996; Mathers and Schofield 1998).

The Sudbury area has generally below average socioeconomic levels. In terms of educational attainment, the Sudbury area has a higher percentage of people with less than a high-school graduation certificate, according to the 2001 census, about 24.4 percent, compared to 19.9 percent for the province as a whole. Average earnings for males in the Sudbury area are 13 percent below the provincial average, while females earn 15 percent less than the provincial average (see Leadbeater in this volume). A substantial proportion of families and unattached people live below the low-income cut-off level: in 2001 it was about 15 percent in the Greater Sudbury area, slightly higher than the provincial rate. Unemployment rates are higher in the Sudbury area than provincially. These indicators show that the socioeconomic environment in the Sudbury area is generally harsher than in the province as a whole.

The State of Aboriginal Health

The task of studying the health status of Aboriginal people, including Métis people, is made difficult due to the lack of systematic and detailed local-level data. Also, responsibility for health care of Aboriginal people is splintered among various levels of government, starting at the federal level and going all the way down to band councils. Further, in the Sudbury area (as elsewhere in Canada)

Aboriginal residents are differentiated by whether or not they have Treaty status, by where they live, and by whether they live on reserves or not. Because of this, data specific to all the Aboriginal people living in the Sudbury area are not available. That said, it is well known that the overall health status of Aboriginal people is far below the Canadian norm (Health Canada 2003; CIHI 2004).

There are some data available for one of the local areas within the Sudbury region — the Wikwemikong Reserve — that illustrate the poorer health status of local Aboriginal people, a condition they share with Aboriginal people across Canada (Health Canada 2003; Statistics Canada 2003). The Aboriginal Peoples Survey reported that 55 percent of the Wikwemikong population suffered from one or more long-term health conditions. For example, 14 percent of Wikwemikong residents were reported to have diabetes, compared to 4 percent for Ontario and 6 percent for the Sudbury area. Among Wikwemikong residents, 22 percent were diagnosed with high blood pressure, compared to the Ontario rate of 13 percent and the Sudbury area rate of 17 percent. The proportion of adults who rated their health as "excellent" or "very good" was 51 percent, while 28 percent rated their health as "good" and 21 percent rated their health as "fair to poor." Comparing these numbers to the data presented in Table 6.19 (which covers persons twelve and over), those reporting "fair to poor" health in Wikwemikong are more numerous than both the Ontario (12.2 percent) and the Sudbury area (16.8 percent) rates.

Health Care in the Sudbury Area

Although the health of individuals does not depend entirely upon the health-care system, we need an adequate health-care system to take care of those who fall ill and to maintain a healthy population. When we talk about the health-care system, the most important factors are the availability of adequate health-care human resources and health-care facilities. I will take a brief look at these two factors.

Health-Care Human Resources

The main focus here is usually on the availability of physicians, with a secondary focus on the availability of nurses. But the availability of other health-care professionals, such as pharmacists, physiotherapists, occupational therapists, and so on is also important.[6]

For the Regional Municipality of Sudbury, the number of physicians per 100,000 population showed a modest increase between 1995 and 2000 (Table 6.20). By contrast, there has been a province-wide decline in the number of physicians per 100,000 people, even though the absolute number of physicians has risen slightly in most years. This shows that, while the province has not kept up with the supply of physicians in relation to population growth, the Regional Municipality of Sudbury has made a small relative improvement. Although the city's all-physician ratio may have actually risen above the provincial average in 2000, non-specialist physicians (family doctors) are still below the provincial average.

Table 6.20: Physicians per 100,000 Population, Specialists and Non-Specialists, Sudbury Regional Municipality (SRM) and Ontario, 1995–2000

Year	Non-Specialists				Specialists				All Physicians			
	Number		Number per 100,000		Number		Number per 100,000		Number		Number per 100,000	
	SRM	Ont.	SRM	Ont.	SRM	Ont.	SRM	Ont.	SRM	Ont.	SRM	Ont.
1995	130	9,695	77.0	88.4	161	10,115	95.4	92.2	191	19,810	172.4	180.7
1996	131	9,870	77.7	88.9	162	10,183	96.0	91.7	293	20,053	173.7	180.6
1997	130	9,843	77.6	87.5	157	10,290	93.8	91.5	287	20,133	171.4	179.0
1998	130	9,841	78.6	86.4	153	10,424	92.5	91.5	283	20,265	171.0	178.0
1999	132	9,807	81.1	85.2	152	10,673	93.4	92.7	284	20,480	174.4	177.8
2000	132	9,828	82.1	84.2	160	10,524	99.5	90.3	292	20,370	181.7	174.6

Health-care services available to Sudbury residents are partly distorted by the fact that the city is a regional centre for health-care services. Physicians, especially specialists, in Sudbury treat many patients from outside the Sudbury area. In fact, all these physician numbers must be interpreted with caution. They do not show the number of hours physicians work, nor do they show whether the physicians work full-time or part-time. It is, therefore, difficult to determine the adequacy of physician resources. In some areas, the situation may be much worse than these numbers indicate.

Health-Care Facilities

Health-care facilities represent a vital part of a community's infrastructure. Hospitals and long-term care facilities are needed to provide acute and chronic care. Table 6.21 immediately brings to attention the fact that outlying areas have serious gaps in available beds and services, other than acute care (ACMS 2002). Other services are all concentrated in Sudbury.

In view of the fact that the hospital system is caught in the throes of transition, even in Sudbury the adequacy of the number of beds available to serve its referral area is in question. The Sudbury Regional Hospital went through substantial changes following recommendations made by the Health Services Restructuring Commission in 1996. One of its key recommendations was to move hospital services to the site of the former Laurentian Hospital. A major capital building project was launched to house the single-site facility. The project ran into severe cost over-runs, construction was suspended, and is still incomplete. As of October 2005 the province gave the green light to continue with construction. However, the number of beds is set to drop to 429 from the current 500-bed capacity.

The availability of long-term care facilities in the Manitoulin and Sudbury Districts in 2001 is shown in Table 6.22. Another 256 beds were added in 2004, for a total of 1,500 beds. This amounts to 117.2 beds per 1,000 senior citizens over seventy-five years of age. The Health Services Restructuring Commission

Table 6.21: Beds in Operation, Manitoulin and Sudbury Districts, 2001

Hospital institution and location		Acute care	Psychi-atric	Rehabil-itation	Chronic care	Eldcap	Total
Service de Santé Chapleau Health Services	Chapleau	14			6	19	39
Manitoulin Health Centre	Little Current, Mindemoya	20 12					32
Espanola General Hospital	Espanola	14			6	30	50
Sudbury Regional Hospital	Sudbury RM	412	24	20	52		508
Sudbury Algoma Hospital	Sudbury RM		44				44
Total		472	68	20	64	49	673

Table 6.22: Long-Term Care Institutions, Manitoulin and Sudbury Districts, 2001

Facility	Community	Short-stay beds	Total operating beds
Extendicare Falconbridge	Region of Sudbury	3	234
Extendicare York	Region of Sudbury		288
Finlandia Hoivakoti Nursing Home	Region of Sudbury	2	108
Pioneer Manor	Region of Sudbury		340
Espanola Nursing Home	Espanola		30
Manitoulin Centennial Manor	Little Current	1	59
Manitoulin Lodge	Gore Bay	2	59
Wikwemikong Nursing Home	Wikwemikong	1	60
Bignucolo Residence	Chapleau	2	18
Sudbury Regional Hospital	Sudbury		40
Total		11	1,236

benchmark guideline calls for 99.1 beds per 1,000, so, by this yardstick, the Manitoulin and Sudbury Districts are considered "over-bedded." Yet, there are many complex continuing-care and alternative-level-of-care patients still occupying beds in the Sudbury Regional Hospital (Bostrom 2004), referred to as "bed blockers." There are also waiting lists. The situation remains unresolved.

Health Policy Actions

This survey of health and health care in the Sudbury area has demonstrated that the health status of Sudbury area residents is below the provincial average in most ways and that the state of Aboriginal health is cause for special concern. In the short run, the immediate problem that has to be addressed by the provincial government is the shortcomings of our health-care facilities as well as the coordination of their functioning. This study did not discuss home care. As pointed out by the Romanow Commission (2002), home care will become an important issue, especially given the high average age and the incidence of chronic disease and disability in the Sudbury area.

In the long run, the lower health status of Sudbury area residents must be addressed. The determinants-of-health approach underlines the need for taking preventive action through improvements in socioeconomic and environmental conditions. These fall into the category of preventive care, so that health problems can be avoided before they manifest themselves in individuals (Barlow 2002). The figures on the health status of the Sudbury area population argue for the need to expand preventive programs. The fee-for-service payment system for physicians does not encourage them to undertake such preventive care. When it is provided, preventive care comes from the Sudbury and District Health Unit, which, among many other activities, undertakes a variety of preventive educational programs.

Another important measure is primary care reform. The Sudbury area population, as is the case for most of the rest of the provincial population, does not have twenty-four-hour, seven-day access to primary care. The current model of practice by physicians under the fee-for-service system encourages limited office practice and the proliferation of walk-in clinics. These walk-in clinics also operate during limited hours, forcing many patients to seek care at other times in expensive emergency rooms. The health status of the population is likely to improve if a multi-disciplinary team of health-care professionals provides round-the-clock care. The Romanow Commission (2002) recommended such a reform.

In terms of health-care facilities, it is imperative that the one-site model be implemented as soon as possible if Sudbury area communities are to realize its benefits. And, with the establishment of the new Northern Ontario School of Medicine, the one-site model becomes even more in important in attracting and retaining faculty. Completion of the super-hospital as soon as possible is crucial.

Another area of concern is the coordination of acute, long-term, and home care activities. If our health-care system is to function in an integrated fashion, there must be sufficient attention paid to continuity of care. Currently, the province of Ontario has set up Local Integrated Health Networks and Family Health Teams. It remains to be seen whether these initiatives will deliver better care.

Toward an Explanation of Health Disparities

Along with these suggestions, some examination is called for of the reasons for the Sudbury area being left behind in terms of health and health care. One avenue of inquiry is to use a "core versus periphery" framework (Wallerstein 1979). According to this approach, in the modern capitalist system systematic inequalities emerge, with benefits flowing in the direction of the core, with the periphery kept in a disadvantaged state. In the case of Ontario, for example, much of the population and wealth can be found in Toronto and surrounding areas, so southern Ontario can be considered the core. The vast, but sparsely populated, northern part of the province is home to extractive industries as well as to the majority of First Nations people. With a less diversified economy and fewer employment opportunities, Northern Ontario can be considered the periphery. Political power is also limited, due to the smaller number of voters in Northern Ontario. The conditions of First Nations people in an advanced nation such as Canada can be viewed as a result of neo-colonialism.

Another approach is to view the health of residents of the Northern regions as part of the inherent inequalities generated by the capitalist system. This argument is advanced by Vincente Navarro (2002). Despite the fact that Canada has a universal, publicly funded system of health care, several studies have documented that inequalities persist. For example, a strong correlation has been found between the income level of a community and the health status of its residents (McLeod et al. 2003; Gilmore 2004: 29). Given the adverse economic conditions, the Sudbury area population is bound to have poorer health outcomes. Some studies have suggested that inequalities in income distribution can also be correlated with health status (Wilkinson 1992: 165–68), although the Canadian evidence is not very strong as far as mortality is concerned (Wolfson 1999; Ross and Wolfson 1999; Ross et al. 2000).

Recently, in a series of studies, Coburn (1999, 2000, 2004) argued for the relevance of the neo-liberal economic policies of recent years in contributing to health inequalities. He points out that with the rise of neo-liberalism, the power of the business class has strengthened while the power of the working class has weakened. This trend, he contends, has led to increasing income inequalities, poverty, and unequal access to health-care resources. The Sudbury area is known to have more unequal income distribution than the province as a whole. The Gini Coefficient of income disparity in the Sudbury area has been calculated to be 0.4123, compared to the provincial figure of 0.3882, based on 2001 census data (Wong 2003).

These approaches suggest new avenues for further research. Politico-economic studies on the distribution of power in society and its impact on health outcomes are needed. We also need to study the performance of the health-care system under the neo-liberal and budget-cutting policy environment. Further detailed studies of the links between income inequalities and health outcomes are also worth pursuing. Such studies may point to ways public policies need to be changed to improve the health status of Sudbury area residents and other Canadians.

Conclusion

The overall picture that emerges about the health of Sudbury area residents is one of relatively poor health. They face a higher mortality rate across almost all major illnesses. They also suffer a disproportionate occurrence of chronic diseases. The determinants-of-health approach can provide some explanation. Lifestyle choices in terms of eating, drinking, and smoking are far from optimal. There have been serious concerns raised about the area's physical environment, and the socioeconomic environment is also rather harsh, with higher unemployment, lower education, and lower income levels than provincial averages.

Both in terms of health and health care, there is a lot of work to be done in the Sudbury area. Morbidity and mortality levels have to be brought down. Given the limited availability of some health-care resources, one of the principles of the Canada Health Act of 1984 — accessibility — still remains a dream for many residents in the Sudbury area. It is high time that the provincial government act to improve the health status of Sudbury area residents and make the dream of accessibility to high quality health care a reality.

Notes

I wish to thank Elaine G. Porter and Raymond W. Pong for their comments on the initial draft. Isabelle Michel and Lianne Valiquette helped with data collection. None are responsible for any interpretations and views expressed here.

1.   The data for this paper come from a variety of reports produced by the Sudbury and District Health Unit and the Algoma, Cochrane, Manitoulin, and Sudbury (ACMS) District Health Council. The reports draw from the census, the Ontario Health Survey, the Canadian Community Health Survey, and other sources. Given the nature of the data-gathering cycle, most of the data pertain to the years 1996 or 1997. These are the latest available data for certain variables reported here. More recent data are used wherever available. This study uses aggregate level data.

2.   The District of Sudbury (2001 Census Division) has a population of 22,894 and an area of 38,351 square kilometres. It covers the largest area, extending all the way to Chapleau in the north, Cosby, Mason, and Maitland and some unorganized area in the south, Casimir, Jennings, and Appleby in the east, and Baldwin in the west. The District of Manitoulin has a population of 12,679 and a land area of 4,760 square kilometres. It covers Manitoulin and surrounding islands.

3.   The original sources for these data are Statistics Canada and the Canadian Institute for Health Information. The latest data are compiled at the Statistics Canada website at <http://www.statcan.ca/english/freepub/82-221-XIE/01002/about.htm> (accessed July 24, 2006).

4.   To calculate age-standardized figures, the 1991 census population structure is used.

5.   The original impetus for this approach in Canada came from the famous Lalonde Report (1974). Then came the World Health Organization document, *The Ottawa Charter for Health Promotion* (1986). The approach was further elaborated in the Epp Report (1986). In 1994, official endorsement of this approach came in the form of a document prepared by the Federal/Provincial/Territorial Ministers of Health titled, "Strategies for Population Health: Investing in the Health of Canadians." The National Forum on Health (1997) brought together much of the evidence underlining the importance of non-medical determinants of health. There is now a growing literature studying the determinants of health (Evans et al. 1994; Hayes and Dunn 1998; Health Canada 1999).

6.   The data for this section are drawn from ACMS District Health Council (2002) based on data from the Canadian Institute for Health Information (CIHI).

Sudbury Sleep

Kate Leadbeater

The daycares spoke two languages
in the place that I left. The streets echoed
strange with the lonely noises of pocket change
and pick-up trucks. Winter was unforgiving as hell.

Santa Claus men with calloused hands
and union bellies cradled Bell Canada
telephones between their stocky shoulders
and thawing ears, trying humanly hard not
to hear the credit card sounds of Christmas.

They were deaf, I thought.

In the place that I left, wildcat words danced
often on the radio, the thumping fists of collective
agreements shook snow from trees' branches
and promised new teeshirts dressed in bright block-letter
acronyms. Letters that would've crushed my soaring
pre-teen heart, had I known the weight of them.

I was eighteen when I left.

I left in favour of taller things, brighter
People with properly thought out plans
Of attack. Libraries like neighbourhoods.

I had more to say, I thought. More to say
for myself and my cervix than cancer. More
to know than a hard luck, hardrock town.

And as I scrubbed myself clean of my history,
gathered my most urban parts and boarded the Greyhound
bus, I secretly wished they had screamed:

we know

the sky is black here, like a Milne watercolour in a gallery
too small for its city but it is well-intentioned like the rest of us,
tired and trying like the rest of us, in the stormy epilogues
of sunlight our queens and our men (jokers all of them) seek to

invade some warmer place decked in brightly coloured lights
but those city signs will not trick us, friend,

will not have us

believe

that we've arrived. We know better, the rest of us, having been
deprived, having tried the honest costume and having been
discovered in the most painful circumstance (bare) and so we plead

stay, friend

together we will afford the rest of them no grace and no advance
we will orchestrate this war from beneath our birth-town black skies
and we will be victorious, friend, together we will swell and fade
victorious, the guilty blood of our slashed and borrowed futures
testifying to our glory, testifying to a breed of success

so long-since lived as to be foreign,

together

we, the trampled spirits of our generation will know
an honest celebration, will know the caves we have built
in these afterthought years, bound and blistered by this Progress
(and what should follow) only we will know the brick to lay,
the pride and secret, the dry slag-filled breath

and at last

they

will see that we've kept at bay the demons of our black skies
for one day, more, fighting with the cruel vigour of orphaned warriors
the sparkle of our unborn babes sharpening our dirty blades

o friend, hear our cry

But instead, they told me it was best. Ushered me to the city limits,
where evergreens screeched — in a single lonely language — that I
would never wake rested from Sudbury sleep.

I was eighteen when I left.

(2007)

Chapter 7

The Failing Health of Children and Youth in Northern Ontario

Kate C. Tilleczek

This chapter addresses my concerns about the failing health of children and youth in Sudbury and Northern Ontario. These concerns are founded both on research and on my personal observations as a sociologist of childhood, a parent, and a former teacher. I argue that child and youth health is failing in a number of ways. It is failing relative to other areas of the province (regionally), failing by social class and socioeconomic gradient effects (class polarization), failing absolutely (declining over time), and failing in relation to the needs and rights of children (by ethnicity, gender, and age).

The Meanings of Child and Youth Health

The World Health Organization (WHO) defines "health" as "a state of complete physical, mental and social well-being and not merely the absence of disease or infirmity" (WHO 1946). This definition identifies health as a positive entity, which suggests that the absence of disease by itself does not necessarily mean that a child is healthy. While this classic definition has not been amended since 1946, a 2003 WHO document, *Strategic Directions for Improving the Health of Children and Adolescents*, identified several indicators of child health: maternal and newborn health, nutrition, communicable diseases, injuries and violence, physical environment, adolescent health, and psycho-social health and development. Consistent with the WHO, *The Northern Ontario Child and Youth Health Report* (NHIP 2003), whose data I use here, chose a broad definition of child and youth health that includes psycho-social, physical, political, economic, historical, health behaviour, and environmental factors (Bronfenbrenner 1979; Tilleczek 2006).[1]

Despite the desire to measure child health in this comprehensive fashion, the provincial and federal governments most often keep social statistics only on mortality (death) and morbidity (illness). Data that allows for the differentiation of outcomes by social class or ethnicity is often not kept, and when it is kept may not be easily analyzed. The dearth of child data suggests that children are a "muted group" (Hardman 1973) and subject to numerical marginalization (Qvortrup 1997).

Like "health," the meanings of the terms "child" and "youth" also vary culturally and historically. "Children and youth" are often defined for statistical purposes as people between the ages of seven and nineteen. This period is commonly referred to as the "between years," falling between early childhood (up to and including age six) and emerging adulthood.[2] However, this statistical definition is only a shell. The terms "youth" and "child" are societal labels or representations with roots in history (Hendrick 1997; Riegel 1972). How we have defined childhood has been prone to cultural fluctuation and interpretation.

During World Wars I and II, adolescence was seen as adult-like in manner, a stage that developed quickly, and that should be accelerated (Enright et al. 1987: 541). It would be much more troubling to be publicly seen sending children to the front lines of war than to send the same individuals seen as adults. During the depressions of the 1890s and 1930s, adolescence emerged as a phase both stressful and childlike. Since work was scarce for adult males, youth were protracted in a back-to-school sweep, safely away from the labour market. These images reversed under changed economic conditions.

Currently, societal representations of children and youth are understood to be about setting them apart from adults, the inevitability of trouble, and the need for surveillance and protection (Boyden 1997; Kelly 2000). Popular images about youth are rife with dichotomies of active-passive, good-bad, innocent-evil, and capable-incapable. These binary images should be challenged. They have been shown to arise mainly from psychological and pathological models of children (Jenks 1996). Childhoods are complicated ensembles and assumptions about "childhood" therefore require careful study, especially as they relate to child health.

Threats to the Developmental Health of Young Persons

Social scientists have amassed a good deal of data about the optimal conditions within which children and youth flourish. For children and youth, becoming competent adults is a long-term process that is most often gradual but is also marked by periods of rapid development and reorganization (Case 1991). Optimal environments are those that foster critical developmental transitions (Keating 1996) and have in them secure and loving attachments with nurturing adults (Suomi 1999). Social connections and the perception of control over one's life are also protective factors against later health problems (Kiecolt-Glaser et al. 1995). Child health is important not only for children but for adults, because good child health is a powerful determinant of good adult health (Hertzman 1999).

In this pathways model, understanding and fostering children through critical periods are necessary. The factors most able to protect vulnerable children are considerable individual attention and a society able to support families and schools (Keating 1996). With this support, young people can gain the power, belonging, and identity crucial to their well-being while actively negotiating their various transitions into adulthood (Tilleczek 2003).

We know, however, that many children and youth have considerable trouble negotiating these transitions. For children with chronic health conditions, daily life can be a struggle. For all children, erosion of social connectedness, alienation, disempowerment, and separation from supportive individuals create risks

(Keating 1996). An emerging and powerful body of evidence links both poverty and the growing unequal distribution of income to a host of child and youth health outcomes. For example, long-term negative outcomes have been documented from such factors as low standard of living, low maternal education, and family instability in the first two years of life (Werner and Smith 1992). Children living in poverty face poor prospects as basic food security is compromised, the possibility of exposure to community violence rises, and the development of aggressive behaviour rises in response to difficult daily concerns (Offord et al. 1992). Research from the Canadian Institute of Child Health (Kidder et al. 2000) demonstrates, for example, that:

- the poorest 20 percent of children are at greater risk of dying in a fire or a homicide than other children;
- the higher rate of death from injury among male children in low-income families may be attributable to unsafe housing, a lack of safe play spaces, and limited access to supervised recreation and sports; and
- children living in households with incomes less than $20,000 per year are at a considerably elevated risk of being labelled with "hyperactivity" and "delinquent behaviours."

The pervasive finding of the relation between poverty and ill health in children has now been termed the "socioeconomic gradient" in health status, and has been shown to exist for behavioural problems (Trembley 1999), achievement in mathematics (Case et al. 1999) and literacy, including receptive vocabulary and reading (Willms 1999). In each case, children from families with the lowest incomes have the highest rates of failure and chronic health conditions, an effect that accumulates over life (Case et al. 1999). Moreover, societies in which the gap between rich and poor is greatest demonstrate a more pervasive social class gradient in each of these outcome measures (Keating and Hertzman 1999). Relative income equality in a society predicts improved population health status for its members such that "equality is good, not only for the vulnerable but for the privileged too" (Hertzman 1999: 25).

There is also evidence of absolute deterioration in children's health. At the global level, WHO data on infant mortality shows some gains have been made, but there have also been losses: "While major gains were made in reducing childhood mortality during the previous decades, stagnation or even reversal of trends has been observed in many countries since the 1990s. In 2001, almost 11 million children died before reaching the age of five" (WHO 2003: 5).

However, infant mortality should not be the whole picture. Just "being born" is not enough when speaking about child health in the way it is defined here. We are moving to a defined quality of daily life encompassing physical, social, and psychological health for our young. In this case, as Keating and Hertzman (1999: 1) attest, there is "troubling scientific evidence that points to a societal breakdown in the process of making human beings human. The signs of this breakdown are seen in growing rates of alienation, apathy... and violence we have observed in youth... in recent decades." In their work with the Canadian Institute for Advanced Research, a group of researchers from diverse scientific disciplines have begun to cite the evidence of decline, especially for the most vulnerable children: "In particular, labour market policies that do not recognize the extensive demands of families with young children, combined with the dearth of good affordable child care, create a situation in which adequate nurturing of the next generation cannot be assured" (Keating and Mustard 1993: 88).

These child health outcomes exist within "modernity's paradox," in which massive expansion in global wealth generation exists alongside growing incidences of health deterioration, especially for those already marginalized by social class, gender, and age (Keating and Hertzman 1999). This marginalization takes place at precisely the same time that developmental needs for inclusion and empowerment become present for children (Tilleczek 2003). Like wealth and access to care, health threats are unevenly distributed along lines of social class, with the least advantaged being further marginalized.

One major threat to child and youth health is the presence of the "risk society" (Beck 1992), characterized by an eradication of social networks and a set of risks and uncertainties such as high unemployment and an increasingly burdened public school system. These trends place increasing pressures on families with young children and reduce the possibility of secure income and of providing optimal care such as high quality child care, especially for those living in poverty (Ross and Wu 1995). Further, this unsettled cultural context, including parental unemployment, results in youth transitions through secondary schools that are becoming increasingly difficult to negotiate (Tilleczek and Lewko 2001), especially for young people marginalized by social class, ethnicity, and region (Tilleczek et al. 2006). Keating and Mustard (1993: 88) conclude that: "Although economically poor families are at the highest risk of this form of family insecurity, the changes we are currently experiencing are so widespread that negative consequences are occurring even for the families of children that are moderately secure economically."

For example, in public schools in Ontario during the Conservative government reforms in the 1990s, the burden of added standardized testing, larger class sizes, and fewer years to complete a secondary school diploma led to higher drop-out rates for vulnerable students (King 2004). This conservative direction in day-care and schooling saw needs for care being replaced by a production mentality. New data from Ontario youth who have left secondary school before graduating indicates that the majority are struggling with poverty, the need to assume adult roles while in school, and school-related issues such as inflexible structures and negative school cultures, including violence and bullying (Tilleczek et al. 2006). Aboriginal, rural, visible minority, and immigrant youth face further burdens having to do with isolation, racism, and classism in their schools and communities (Ferguson et al. 2005).

A second major and related threat to child and youth health is that the expansion of capital takes primacy over the needs and rights of the environment, land, and children (McNally 2002). This has led to the pervasive culture of commodification and consumption. Especially for youth who have access to media technology and disposable income, lives are gated into low-paid "McJobs" and mass consumption of the latest American invention. Youth culture has become synonymous with purchasing ever-changing fashion, music, and technologies (Latham 2002). Television advertisements no longer attempt to hide the agenda, as an ad for a new Barbie Doll who "loves to go shopping" suggests, "You can never have too much stuff!" Yet evidence suggests that the more children engage in consumer culture, the greater their depression, anxiety, and feeling of helplessness (Schor 2004).

Outcomes for Child and Youth Health in Northern Ontario and Sudbury

There has been a scarcity of data on Northern or rural children in Ontario, though such data are crucial for sound planning, discussion, and action. Those data that do exist provide only a fragmented signpost to social and regional issues that deserve further study. Given the limitations of existing data, it is a concern that they can at worst suggest a static representation of childhood as necessarily bad, incomplete, and unhealthy. With this caution in place, we now examine a selection of statistical data on Northern Ontario's child and youth health. (See NHIP 2003 for the complete report.[3]) As Aboriginal children are not specifically included in the data in the above named sections, NHIP gathered a separate section on Aboriginal children, and selected data are reported here in a final section.

Regional Population Characteristics and Rural Realities

There are approximately 220,000 children and youth under twenty years of age living in Northern Ontario (NHIP 2003). Geographically, this is a highly dispersed population, making service delivery problematic. The proportion of male children aged nineteen years and less comprises 28 percent of the Ontario population and 27 percent of the Northern population. The proportion of female children aged nineteen years and less is 25 percent for both the province and the Northern region. The children of baby boomers (the "echo") are now in the ten-to-nineteen age group.

Northern Ontario has a greater proportion of its population living in rural and small-town areas relative to the entire province, approximately 40 and 15 percent respectively. Rural and small-town areas are defined here as those communities that have fewer than 10,000 people and are at least 80 kilometres from an urban centre with a population of more than 50,000 (Pitblado and Pong 1999). Although an idyllic image exists of the countryside, many rural communities and smaller Northern cities such as Sudbury are facing demographic, ecological, economic, and social challenges due to geographic and social isolation, the depletion of natural resources, boom-and-bust cycles in primary industries, chronic high unemployment, out-migration of the young, population aging, environmental destruction, and inadequate municipal infrastructure.

These problems have profound implications for the health and well-being of rural Ontario (Pong 2001; Pong et al. 1999), such as poorer health status, lower life expectancy, higher accident and injury rates, and higher levels of disability (NHISSC 2003). There are major problems in rural health-care delivery. The lack of ready access to health services is a common complaint of rural and small-town residents, with smaller and more remote communities having greater problems of access (Pitblado et al. 1999; DesMeules et al. 2003).

Mortality and Morbidity

Infant mortality rates are often used as an indicator of the state of maternal and child health. Canada's infant mortality rate has declined dramatically over the past years (Government of Canada 1998). International comparisons of infant mortality rates prepared by the March of Dimes (2002) using WHO data suggest that Canada is ranked fifteenth among selected countries, with a rate of 5.3 per 1,000 live births. But the infant mortality rate is higher in Northern Ontario, at 6.6 per 1,000 live births, compared to the provincial rate of 5.8 per 1,000.

Unintentional injury remains the leading cause of death for children aged seven to nineteen, accounting for 70 percent of all deaths within this age group in the North and 58 percent provincially between 1987 and 1999. Injuries accounted for as much as 85 percent of deaths in the seven-to-nineteen age group within the Northwestern Health Unit Area during the same period. After motor vehicle accidents, suicide is the second-ranked cause of death due to injury.

For morbidity — sickness and injury — one can look at hospitalization data. During the period 1997–2001, there were 73,361 hospitalizations in Northern Ontario for children less than seven years old. This represents a rate of 1,995 per 10,000, higher than the equivalent rate for Ontario of 1,876 per 10,000. The overall hospitalization rate for the seven-to-thirteen-year-olds is significantly lower than for those under the age of seven. However, the Northern rate of 251.7 per 10,000 remains significantly higher than the provincial rate of 178.7 per 10,000. Injury and poisoning were the leading causes of hospitalization for both the province and the North, responsible for 19 and 22 percent respectively of all hospitalizations. Diseases of the respiratory system were the second-leading cause of hospitalization in this age group in both Ontario and Northern Ontario. Mental disorders were the fourth-leading cause, accounting for 5 percent both in the North and the province within the seven-to-thirteen age group. (The third-leading cause was "symptoms, signs, and ill-defined" disorders.)

For the fourteen-to-nineteen age group, injury and poisoning were the second-leading cause of hospitalizations for both Ontario and the North, accounting for 15 percent of hospitalizations in the province and 17 percent in the North. Pregnancy and childbirth, the leading cause of hospitalization in this age group, accounted for 25 percent and 27 percent of hospitalizations for Ontario and the North respectively. In the North, mental disorders accounted for 17 percent of all hospitalization in this age group and 15 percent for the province. While teen pregnancy is usually represented as a moral issue, sex education clearly deserves more attention for young women. The long-term implications of teen pregnancy and childbirth are obvious, as they impinge upon educational and life pathways. For example, Tilleczek et al. (2006) report that for young Ontario women who left school early the main risk factor cited was teen pregnancy and the inability to complete school while caring for a child. The young women cited bullying during pregnancy and the inability to take on adult roles of motherhood and schooling simultaneously as the sources of their daily struggles.

Child and Youth Mental Health

A recent study of the pathways and barriers to mental-health care for rural Ontario children and youth suggests that the system lacks both funding and integration of services, making access difficult and services inadequate (Boydell et al. 2004). Health Canada's (2002) *Report on Mental Illness in Canada* and a recently released report by the Canadian Senate (Kirby and Keon 2006) offer further insights into this issue:

- children and youth are among the most vulnerable groups for mental-health challenges;
- the onset of most mental illnesses occurs during adolescence and young adulthood;
- the school is the most undeveloped site for child mental-health care;
- there are severe shortages of child and youth mental-health human resources, especially in rural and Northern areas;
- approximately 20 percent of Canadians will experience mental illness during their lives, and only 20 percent of these persons will ever receive the care they need; and
- social factors related to mental health for children and youth are those that negate their ability to belong, and to form an independent identity.

It is difficult to determine the exact prevalence of mental illness in Ontario. We know that approximately 61,200 Ontario youth aged twelve to nineteen reported having spoken to a health-care professional regarding their mental or emotional health in the past year. This amounts to 5.2 percent of the youth population. In Northern Ontario, it is estimated that only some 2,000 youth — approximately 1.7 percent — have done so (Barnett and Fearn 2003). However, given that access to service providers is limited in rural Northern Ontario (Boydell et al. 2004), this figure is likely an underestimate of those wanting to speak to such a professional. Ferguson (2006a) estimates that close to 300,000 Ontario children and youth appear in school each day with a mental-health challenge that has not yet been treated.

As youth approach secondary school, self-esteem and access to a confidant declines markedly. Approximately 9 percent of Ontario youth in grades seven to twelve report low self-esteem, with a significant plunge occurring among first-year high-school students. Moreover, approximately 4 percent of Ontario youth report not having a single person they could speak to about their problems, with a peak in grade nine, the first year of high school. This suggests the importance of further understanding of school culture as it relates to mental health. About 11 percent of Ontario youth in grades seven through thirteen seriously contemplated taking their own lives. Young women were more likely than young men to contemplate this act.

In Northern Ontario, only 82.2 percent of women aged fifteen to nineteen reported "never" having experienced suicidal ideation, while 91.7 percent of young men surveyed claimed to have never considered taking their own lives. This discrepancy in rates is understandable, given the higher attempted suicide rate of females (NHIP 2003). However, it points to the need for more study of gender issues in mental health. For example, suicide attempts, hospitalization for self-inflicted injury, and suicide contemplation are all different measures used in the literature. In each case, there are variations in rates by gender. This needs to be explored and understood in order to gain an understanding of, for example, whether young women attempt suicide for different reasons and to different effect than young men.

We do know that, overall, 15 percent of Ontario youth enter hospital with a mental disorder as the main diagnosis. This figure increases to approximately 21 percent if we include all noted patient diagnoses and developmental/emotional issues, as defined by the American Psychiatric Association's DSM-IV-TR (APA 2000). Hospitalizations for children and youth with mental-health issues in Northern Ontario occur at approximately 60 percent higher than the provincial rate. This age group is also the most at risk for hospitalization due to intentional self-injury. However, suicide mortality alone does not accurately represent the prevalence of suicidal ideation or suicide attempts in the population. Further, research suggests that Canadian hospitalizations for suicide attempts are under-reported by a full 63 percent, suggesting that even the above-noted hospitalization numbers are undercounts (Rhodes et al. 2002). Both hospitalization and death due to intentional self-injury are approximately three times more frequent in Northern Ontario youth than in the rest of Ontario. Further, while both provincial hospitalization and death rates due to suicide attempts have been decreasing over the past decade, in Northern Ontario they have been increasing (Table 7.1).

Chronic Disease

While the above data point to the main causes of mortality and morbidity for children and youth in the Sudbury area, perhaps the most shocking situation is the chronic conditions of twelve-to-nineteen-year-olds. Table 7.2 suggests that nearly 60 percent of children and youth in the Sudbury area are living their daily lives with a chronic illness such as allergy, asthma, high blood pressure, migraine headaches, cancer, or epilepsy, and that the rates are higher than in other areas of Northern Ontario. Chronic conditions impact significantly on the quality of a child's life, and they represent a significant burden on families and the health-

Table 7.1: Hospitalization Due to Intentional Self-Inflicted Injury in 10–19 Year Olds, by Gender, Comparing Ontario and Northern Ontario, 1987–1999 (rate per 100,000)

	1987	1989	1991	1993	1995	1997	1999
Ontario							
Males	5.8	6.9	4.7	4.5	5.5	4.8	4.5
Females	1.6	1	1.1	2.2	1.7	1.2	0.8
Both	3.8	4	3	3.4	3.7	3	2.7
Northern Ontario							
Males	12	23.1	12.3	12.4	23	17.5	14.2
Both	7.8	13	8.6	12.8	14.7	11.3	8.5

Note: the rate is the number of deaths in 10-to-19 year olds due to suicide from 1986 to 1999 divided by the age-specific population for each year. *Source*: NHIP (2003) from Vital Statistics, 1987 to 1999.

Table 7.2: Self-Reported Chronic Conditions in 12–19 Year Olds by Public Health Unit, Percent, 2001

Ontario	45.9
Northern Ontario	51.4
Algoma	46.9
Muskoka-Parry Sound	42.2
North Bay	51.2
Porcupine	53.1
Sudbury	58.5
Thunder Bay	52.5
Timiskaming	48.1

Note: Proportion of 12-to-19 year olds who report having (or are reported by proxy as having) a health condition that has lasted over six months that has been diagnosed by a health-care professional, including allergies, asthma, fibromyalgia, arthritis or rheumatism, back problems, high blood pressure, migraine headaches, diabetes, chronic bronchitis, chronic obstructive pulmonary disease, epilepsy, heart disease, cancer, ulcers, incontinence, bowel disorders, thyroid conditions, chronic fatigue syndrome, and multiple chemical sensitivities. For Muskoka-Parry Sound, the coefficient of variation is large and the estimate must be used with caution. *Source*: NHIP (2003) from Canadian Community Health Survey, Cycle 1.1, 2000/01.

care system. As Hertzman (1999) suggests, this is itself a testament to the failing health of young people, and we must work backwards in time to find the origins of these maladies. As yet, the data are not available to allow such analysis, but environmental conditions, poverty, and access to health care are obvious avenues for further exploration. It will also be important to monitor these chronic conditions in both quantitative and qualitative ways to understand their origin and impact on the everyday lives of young people. For example, how are these chronic conditions treated? How is access to such treatment distributed locally? How do communities, schools, health systems, families, and children respond to and cope with these chronic conditions?

Food Security, Poverty, and Northern Families

Food is a necessity of life usually provided in a family environment, so family structure and income are important to child health. Single-parent families accounted for 15 percent of all family units in both Ontario and the North. In 1997, the rate of poverty for Canadian children in single-mother families was 60 percent, compared to 13 percent for children in two-parent families.[4] Thus, living in a single-parent family represents a 4.6-fold increase of risk of poverty (Kidder et al. 2000).

According to the Canadian Community Health Survey, 19 percent of the low-income group and 2 percent of the upper-income group in Ontario stated that they sometimes worried about not having enough to eat (Statistics Canada 2000/01). Nearly 9 percent of households with children in Northern Ontario have reported not having enough money to buy food. There are also a significant number (26,673) of Northern Ontario children under the age of seventeen who are living in families dependent on social assistance benefits as family income. This number includes nearly 6,000 children in Greater Sudbury.

A related but understudied issue is the kinds of food young people eat. The Ontario Ministry of Health and Long-Term Care (2001), in its Mandatory Health Programs and Services Guidelines, aims to have "increased the proportion of the population age four and older who consume five or more servings of fruit and vegetables daily to 75 percent by the year 2010." Currently, 37 percent of Ontarians aged twelve to nineteen eat five or more servings of fruits and vegetables daily. The equivalent figure in the North is 38 percent. None of the areas in the North come near to the provincial target: close to 62 percent of youth are not receiving proper nutrition, even though nutritious food is available.

Health and School Systems

Children from advantaged homes, who first present themselves at schools with hours of reading, nurturing, and stimulation behind them, tend to do better at school than less advantaged children (McCain and Mustard 1999). Research has shown that nurturing is a key component in creating the foundation for brain development. A key activity related to nurturing is parental reading: a child's progress in school is related to his or her parent's literacy and encouragement in learning.

Success in school is also related to parental social class and socioeconomic status. Given the relatively lower socioeconomic status of Northern families, it is not surprising, but still disappointing, that there is a lag in reading, writing, and mathematics skills. Table 7.3 shows that Northern Ontario students in English School Boards consistently lagged behind their provincial counterparts in reading and mathematics for both grades three and six. Females scored consistently higher than males at all ages for both mathematics and reading. In grade ten

Table 7.3: Percentage of Children Achieving Appropriate Levels in Reading and Mathematics, Grade 3 and 6, by Region, 2000–01

	Grade 3 (percent)		Grade 6 (percent)	
	Ontario	Northern Ontario	Ontario	Northern Ontario
Mathematics	62	54	54	50
Reading	50	44	55	50

Source: NHIP (2003) from Education Quality and Accountability Office, Grade 3 and 6 Assessments of Reading, Writing, and Mathematics, 2000 to 2001.

literacy tests, the results are better, but still below the provincial average and Ministry of Education standards. For example, only 61 percent of young men in Northern Ontario high schools are passing the standard literacy test. For young women, the results are better but still disappointing, with 74 percent achieving appropriate literacy levels. Further research is needed into the dynamics of rural and Northern school cultures. The research should shift the focus of investigation away from familial and student blame toward the socio-political and cultural aspects of schooling. How can it continually be that Northern Ontario schools do not do a better job of educating marginalized and disadvantaged children and youth?

Aboriginal Children and Youth

There is much evidence that the health of the Aboriginal population in general is significantly worse than that of other Canadians. MacMillan et al. (1996) write:

> Canadian Aboriginal people die earlier than their fellow Canadians, on average, and sustain a disproportionate share of the burden of physical disease and mental illness. This burden is associated with unfavourable economic and social conditions that are inextricably linked to native people's history of oppression.

It is not surprising, though very unfortunate, that Aboriginal children have a significantly worse health status than other Canadian children. It is very difficult to measure the extent of this health disparity because Aboriginal people are not identified in most administrative data sets. While data on health surveys for Aboriginal people on reserve are reliable, they often exclude Aboriginal people living off reserves, or samples are so small as to be unreliable.

According to Indian and Northern Affairs Canada's Northern Ontario data, 37.5 percent of First Nations males and 34.5 percent of females are under the age of twenty, compared to 27.2 percent of males and 25.1 percent of females in the general population. In the North, 18,707 Aboriginal children aged nineteen or less (60 percent) live on reserves and 12,614 (40 percent) live off reserve. About 65 percent of Aboriginal children living on reserves live with two parents. This compares with only 50 percent in Census Metropolitan Areas. In contrast, almost 83 percent of non-Aboriginal children live with two parents. Conversely, twice the proportion of Aboriginal children lived with a lone parent in 2001, as did non-Aboriginal children. On reserves, 32 percent of Aboriginal children lived with a lone parent. This percentage jumped to 46 percent for those in Census Metropolitan Areas. Only 17 percent of non-Aboriginal children lived with a lone parent.

In 2001, according to the Canadian Community Health Survey, the off-reserve Aboriginal population had lower levels of household income and educational attainment, and was less likely to have worked the entire year than the non-Aboriginal population (Tjepkema 2002). For example, 44 percent of Aboriginal persons aged twenty-five and over in Canada — 48 percent in rural areas — did not graduate from secondary school. The percentage for the non-Aboriginal population was 23 percent, 32 percent in rural areas. In terms of poverty, 27 percent of Aboriginal households had a low household income, compared to 10 percent for non-Aboriginal households. Thirty-eight percent of Aboriginal persons aged fifteen to seventy-five worked the entire year, compared to 53 percent for the non-Aboriginal population.

The majority of young Aboriginal children live in low-income families (Hull 2001). In 1996, 58 percent of Aboriginal children from birth to age five lived in low-income families (based on the Statistics Canada definition of "low-income"). Diabetes, infant mortality, and suicide remain as key child and youth health issues in Aboriginal communities. For instance, between January 1 and July 30, 2001, sixteen youth suicides were recorded on the forty-nine Northern Ontario reserves belonging to the Nishnawbe Aski Nation. In the previous year, 2000, there were twenty-six such deaths (Adlaf and Paglia 2001). A Royal Commission report on suicide among Aboriginal people suggests that as many as 25 percent of accidental deaths among Aboriginal people are really unreported suicides (Chenier 1995).

Data are not yet available for the off-reserve population for the years 2000 and 2001. However, it is estimated that there are approximately 15,000 youth in the Nishnawbe Aski Nation in Northern Ontario. If we apply the 1999 youth suicide rate for Ontario of 6.2 per 100,000, we would expect one suicide death to occur each year, but, as noted above, there were twenty-six such deaths in 2000. Those off-reserve people who identified themselves as Aboriginal in the Community Health Survey were three times more likely to have seriously considered committing suicide compared to their non-Aboriginal counterparts. The hopelessness faced by many Aboriginal youth is summed up by Heather Childs (1990), a Native youth who said: "The biggest problem for Native youth today is that they feel hopeless. They can't get a job. They want to get married. And, when they look to the future, they are not educated, how are they going to support a family?"

Conclusions

In the preceding sections, I have presented literature and data to show the numerous ways in which child health is failing. I conclude that child and youth health is failing in Sudbury and Northern Ontario relative to other areas of the province (regionally), failing by social class (class polarization), failing absolutely (declining over time), and failing in relation to the needs and rights of all children (by gender, ethnicity, and age). In short, the trends are looking grim.

It is worth stating that many children and youth live happy and healthy lives while transitioning toward adulthood. However, this resilient state of being a child is progressively threatened as we see trends in poor health arising at local and trans-local levels. In fact, the WHO suggests that children and adolescents continue to bear an undue share of the global burden of disease:

> In 2001, almost 11 million children died before reaching the age of five.... Most of the unfinished health agenda at the doorstep of the 21st century is due to inadequate efforts to address childhood illness. (WHO 2003: 5)

While this is increasingly the case for most children and youth, we have seen that it is especially true for children marginalized by the poverty, rural location, and cultural difference endured by so many Aboriginal children in Northern Ontario. Mental health, chronic illness, faltering literacy, and social isolation are core problems in the North. Youth aged fourteen to nineteen suffer further burdens of ill health and failing transition through secondary school.

Children have differing needs, but basic rights to provision, protection, and participation have been set out in the United Nations Convention on the Rights of the Child and ratified by Canada. It would be difficult to conclude that all children living in Sudbury and Northern Ontario enjoy these basic rights. The Convention attempts to make nations accountable for child policies, but gaps in practices exist and we must move beyond a straight "rights" solution (Volpe et al. 1998; Boyden 1997). The challenge to local health care providers, politicians, policy-makers, parents, teachers, academics, and community members is to work together to track and eliminate these health outcomes across the traditional silos of education, health, child welfare, and mental health. Several initial attempts are in place in Ontario, such as the Institute for Child and Youth Success (Ferguson 2006b). In Sudbury, we have seen the Mayor and Council's Roundtable Child Report Card 2006. A small group of local politicians, practitioners, and research-ers are attempting to put together baseline data that will allow for tracking of trends over time. However, the research has gaps, and is not enough in and of itself to culminate in progressive local outcomes. More needs to be done.

Solutions will not be found by blaming individuals. Boyden (1997) illus-trates how penalizing of the poor takes place when legislation and policy fails to recognize the structural nature of poverty and resorts to individual blame of children, parents, and families for systemic issues that perpetuate failing child health. Other research (Tilleczek 2006; Tilleczek and Hine 2006) illustrates how simple "public health" solutions to cultural issues are inadequate to solve health problems. For example, while youth deaths are most numerous in traffic accidents, graduated licencing has not remediated the problem nor addressed the issues necessary to an understanding of contemporary youth culture and its struggles (Tilleczek 2004). Blaming youth is short-sighted, inadequate, and negligent. Instead, youth culture in modern society needs to be fully explored to uncover labour market, political, economic, and larger social trends that impinge upon daily lives.

Clearly, existing inequalities are indefensible. While we are aware that this chapter itself constitutes a particularly negative and limited view of childhood based on available statistical data, the information presented can be used as an invitation to dialogue and action. Three main principles are offered, as adapted from the WHO (2003), for local consideration and action against child and youth poverty and for better health and well-being for all young people:

1. address inequities and facilitate the protection and fulfillment of child rights, as stipulated in the UN Convention on the Rights of the Child;
2. use a sociological approach to child and youth data that recognizes the variability of childhood by region, social class, ethnicity, and age on the continuum from birth through childhood, adolescence, and adulthood. Policies and action for children can no longer be "one size fits all";
3. implement approaches to intervention and care that focus on major health issues for local populations. Ensure the availability and accessibility of standards of income, health care, workplaces, communities, and schools and the relevant data required to assess them.

How will we address, at the community level, issues of secure employment for parents, youth out-migration, a culture of literacy, and meaningful participation of our children and youth in the life of school and community? To start, we need at least to concentrate on meaningful participation in the everyday worlds of youth at school and families at work.

Notes

The author wishes to acknowledge and thank the staff at the Northern Health Information Partnership (NHIP) for heading up the *Northern Ontario Child and Youth Health Report* and for inviting me to co-chair the committee. I would like to thank especially Vic Sahai, Robert Barnett, Jen Fern, and Mary Ward from NHIP.

1. From 2001–2003, I had the privilege of co-chairing a steering committee of academics, community agency workers, and researchers in producing the NHIP report. The goal of the NHIP report was to accumulate statistical information on the developmental health of children and youth aged seven to nineteen in Northern Ontario, a task not previously undertaken. The data in this chapter were originally analyzed and reported in the *Northern Ontario Child and Youth Health Report* (see <www.nhip. org>).

2. *The Northern Ontario Child and Youth Health Report* (NHIP 2003) purposely sought to attend to this age range, as no such report had yet been produced, and the recent

bulk of Canadian child health policy has focussed on the under-seven age group.

3.   Twelve large-scale provincial and federal data sets were analyzed in the report. Please contact the author at <ktilleczek@laurentian.ca> for the full listing of databases used in this chapter.

4.   Females head most single-parent families. Statistics tend to be provided in both "single-mother" and "single-parent" format and I have here referred to "single-parent" households, knowing that the vast majority are headed by females. It should be noted that current data on single parenthood requires further unpacking and that the numbers are likely underestimates. For example, many children now live in two homes, each of which is single-parent in character, yet they do indeed have two parents. Such detail needs to be collected and taken into consideration in order to understand the complexities of family and child lives.

Chapter 8

Hunger and Food Insecurity in Greater Sudbury

Carole Suschnigg

The term "food security" means that all individuals have access to sufficient, safe, nutritious, and culturally acceptable food at all times, and that all individuals are able to acquire the food they need in a way that maintains their dignity. Thus defined, food security does not exist in the City of Greater Sudbury: estimates for 2002 and 2003 indicate that about 5.6 percent of the population — over 9,000 people each month — are dependent on local food banks for survival (Suschnigg et al. 2003). This chapter examines the limitations of food banks in response to food insecurity in our community, the failure of government policies to eliminate food insecurity, and the contradictory aspects of corporate participation in the Canadian Association of Food Bank's National Food Sharing System.

The problem of food insecurity, of course, is not confined to the City of Greater Sudbury. It is a province-wide and nation-wide problem. Moreover, it is a problem that has been growing since the early 1980s. For reasons of space, this chapter focusses on food banks. However, these are not the only type of emergency food service in our community. Other services include, for example, food pantries (much smaller operations than food banks, but they too collect donated groceries and distribute them to people in need), meals-on-wheels delivered to people whose illness or disability renders them house-bound, three soup kitchens that serve daily meals to people on low incomes, school breakfast programs, and a community kitchen where volunteers come together for special occasions like Christmas to prepare and serve meals for people on low incomes.

The first food bank in Canada emerged in 1981 (Riches 1997: 49). Ten years later the number had sky rocketed to 292. By 2002 there were an estimated 620 food banks and 2,201 affiliated agencies providing emergency food services nation-wide. During March of that year these organizations fed almost 750,000 people across the country (Wilson and Toas 2002: 3–4). By March 2003 the number had swelled again to 777,869 people — more than the entire population of New Brunswick (CAFB 2003).

Ontario's first four food banks emerged in 1984 (Riches 1997: 49). By 1990, the number had expanded to 33, and by 1997 to an astounding 174 (Singh Bolaria 2002: 135). By 2002, the number had increased yet again. In March alone that year over 500 emergency food programs — including 203 food banks — gave help to nearly 300,000 hungry people across the province (DBFB 2002: 1).

Despite the startling proliferation of food banks over the past two decades, the basic food needs of many people remain unmet. These emergency food services are dependent almost entirely on private donations, and limited supplies mean that many food banks are obliged to ration the amount of food they hand out. For instance, interviews with workers at eleven of the sixteen food banks operating in Greater Sudbury in 2002 found that most agencies had to limit households' number of monthly visits and to limit provisions to about three days' worth of emergency food per visit. As well, limited on-site storage space was making it difficult for local food banks to provide fresh produce such as vegetables, fruit, milk, and eggs on a regular basis: most of what they could offer were non-perishables such as pasta, rice, canned goods, and peanut butter (Suschnigg et al. 2002).

Interviews with food recipients help illustrate the difficulties they face. Results for a non-random sample of ninety-two people using food banks in Greater Sudbury found that, on average, respondents had run out of money to buy food on five and a half days during the previous four weeks.[1] A third of research participants had visited their local food bank once during the past three months, another third had visited twice and the other third had visited three times — the maximum allowed in most cases. Access to a food bank, however, was no guarantee that respondents' dietary needs were being met. For instance, 41 percent of respondents said they rarely had access to fresh or frozen vegetables and 54 percent said they rarely had access to fresh fruit. Seventy-six percent of parents had gone without food in order to feed their children (Suschnigg et al. 2003).

Two Major Perspectives on Food Insecurity

So why is hunger on the increase in a country as rich as our own? Literature on the subject can be divided into two major perspectives. The first points to poverty as the root cause of hunger: Canada has more than enough food to feed all its inhabitants, but some people simply cannot afford to buy it. From this "anti-poverty" perspective, the most expedient solution would be to introduce policies that ensure a living income for all, that is, enough money for people to purchase the essentials they need to survive. "Anti-poverty" advocates argue, in particular, that welfare payments and the minimum wage should be raised substantially.

The second perspective, in contrast, focusses on corporate monopoly of the food system itself — not just in Canada, but world-wide. Proponents of this "food-sovereignty" perspective are concerned about the disappearance of the family farm and the loss of local control over food production and distribution. They stress that food is no longer being produced for its immediate "use" value: instead, food is increasingly being produced and traded for its "exchange" value on the world market, that is, as a means to maximize profit. From this perspective, food security can best be achieved by respecting indigenous agricultural practices — especially women's traditional role in food production — providing support for family farms, eschewing "factory" farms, promoting environmentally sustainable methods of food production and distribution, and prioritizing people's right to food over export-oriented trading policies designed to maximize corporate profit.

From the "food-sovereignty" perspective, then, food insecurity is a threat to all humanity, not just to people who are poor. For this reason "anti-poverty" initiatives alone will never be able to eliminate the fundamental cause of food insecurity. At best, they will only be able to treat the immediate *symptoms* of food insecurity — hunger and malnutrition.

Regardless, these immediate symptoms of food insecurity cannot be ignored while the battle over food sovereignty is being waged: hunger and malnutrition, especially among children and pregnant women, undermine the physical, mental, and social well-being of both current and future generations. The immediate and long-term social costs to us all are enormous (NCW 2004). For this reason, in the section that follows I elaborate on the "anti-poverty" approach to the elimination of hunger. I begin by showing how federal and provincial policies have contributed to food insecurity among people on low incomes in Ontario. Then, through simple budget analysis, I demonstrate why people on low incomes in my home community of Greater Sudbury find it difficult to purchase the food they need to maintain their health.

Government Failure to Eliminate Poverty

It is worth noting that people's right of access to medical care in Canada, regardless of their ability to pay, is enshrined in law through the 1984 Canada Health Act. People's right of access to food, however — a far more fundamental determinant of health — has no such guarantee. Yet, along with 186 other countries participating in the 1996 World Food Summit in Rome, the federal government acknowledged that food security is a fundamental human right, that emergency food programs address only the symptoms of widespread hunger, and that poverty is the root cause of food insecurity at home and abroad (Canada 1998: 6). It is disappointing, then, that hunger in Canada is on the rise largely because, despite rhetoric to the contrary, federal, provincial, and municipal governments have failed to come up with effective policies to reduce poverty. It is disappointing, then, that the federal government's performance here at home has failed to eradicate hunger.

In 2001 in Canada, there were just over four million people — 13.3 percent of the population — living below the poverty line (Statistics Canada 2001b).[2] In Ontario, the poverty rate was 14.4 percent, and in Sudbury it was even higher at 14.9 percent. Across Canada, the poverty rate is particularly high for female-headed, single-parent families — 44.9 percent in 2001. For unattached individuals, it was 34.7 percent. Of particular concern, the poverty rate for children in Canada is approximately 16 percent (CSPCT 2004).

A main reason Canada has a disappointingly high poverty rate is the inadequacy of social assistance, or welfare, payments. Almost half of Canada's poor are dependent on some form of welfare for survival (Table 8.1). In turn, a

Table 8.1: Low-Income People on Welfare, Canada and Ontario, 2001

Area	Estimated population in 2001	Number of people below poverty line	Percent of people below poverty line	Number of people on welfare	Percent of people in poverty on welfare
Canada	31,110,565	4,063,000	13.3	1,910,900	47
Ontario	11,894,863	1,611,505	14.4	709,200	44

Sources: Population: Statistics Canada (2001a; 2003). Figures are for July 1, 2001. People below poverty line: Statistics Canada (2001b). Figures are based on incomes for 2000. People on welfare: National Council of Welfare (2002). Figures are for March 31, 2001.

major reason for inadequate welfare benefits has been the federal government's decision to cut its own costs by reducing transfer payments to the provinces. For thirty years a federal-provincial agreement, the Canada Assistance Plan, had obligated the government to pay fifty percent of a province's social assistance costs so long as that province upheld certain standards: that people in need be given financial assistance regardless of the cause of their need, that financial assistance be based on a person's basic cost of living, and that no one be compelled to work in order to qualify for social assistance (Riches 1997: 67). In 1996, however, the federal government replaced this agreement with the Canada Health and Social Transfer (CHST), a system of block funding designed to reduce federal transfer payments to the provinces. Introduced by then-Finance Minister Paul Martin, the CHST resulted in "cutbacks of $7 billion (15 per cent over three years) to the provinces for health, education, and welfare" (Riches 1997: 67).

The CHST, according to critics, proved to be a "significant precursor to emerging food insecurity and hunger in Canada" (Wilson and Toas October 2002: 15). The federal government, purportedly in order to give the provinces more autonomy and flexibility, eliminated its former eligibility criteria for receipt of federal funds: provinces were no longer required to ensure that welfare payments reflected people's basic cost of living. As well, provinces now were permitted to require welfare recipients to work for the financial assistance they received (Oliphant and Slosser 2003: 5–6). The Ontario government took this opportunity to reduce welfare payments and introduce a work-for-welfare program.

The Ontario Government Makes Poverty Worse

Since the mid-1990s, the cost of living in Ontario has risen dramatically. From just 1997 to 2001, for instance, shelter expenditures rose 10 percent, food expenditures rose 14 percent, clothing expenditures rose 15 percent, transportation expenditures rose 23 percent, and education expenditures rose an astonishing 47 percent (Statistics Canada 2002). Minimum wage rates and social assistance payments, however, did not keep pace with these rising costs. At the start of the new millennium, just over 13 percent of the province's population lived below the poverty line, as Table 8.1 shows.

While shelter costs in Ontario rose *in general* by 10 percent, the average *rent* increased by 17.4 percent between 1998 and 2002 (Oliphant and Slosser 2003: 9). Since a one percent increase in the cost of shelter tends to have a relatively large impact on a household's budget, and since people on low incomes are more likely to rent than to own their homes, rent increases are particularly difficult for people on low incomes. Lack of affordable shelter, in turn, means people must decide whether to "pay the rent or feed the kids" (Ontario Non-Profit Housing Association 2004).

The dramatic increase in the cost of rental accommodation occurred after the elimination of rent controls in 1998, when Ontario's Progressive Conservative government replaced the Landlord and Tenant Act with the so-called "Tenant Protection Act." This new Act precipitated a housing crisis across the province: many young adults found themselves unable to afford to leave home, people who tried to reduce costs by "doubling-up" found themselves living in overcrowded and stressful conditions, tenants who could not pay their rent found themselves evicted, and increasing numbers of people found themselves homeless (Ontario Tenant Toronto Tenants 2003).

Despite the escalating cost of living in Ontario, social assistance payments have not kept pace. Back in 1993 the Progressive Conservatives chastised the New Democratic government for increasing welfare benefits by a mere one per-cent (Oliphant and Slosser 2003: 3). Once elected, however, the Conservatives chose to *reduce* those same benefits by about 22 percent. They also introduced the Ontario Works Act, a law that requires "employable" recipients to work for their welfare benefits.

By now, it has become crystal clear that, in most instances, Ontario's welfare payments are not enough to cover basic living expenses (Riches 1997; Wilson with Tsoa 2002; Sistering 2000; Gam 2003; Oliphant and Slosser 2003; Income Security Advocacy Centre 2003). Indeed, as Table 8.2 illustrates, social assistance for a single parent with one child was 59 percent of the low-income cut-off in 2001. For a couple with two children it was 52 percent, for a person with a disability it was 62 percent, and for a single "employable" person it was a mere 36 percent of the low-income cut-off (NCW 2002: 43).

In May 2004, Ontario's new Liberal government finally announced a rise

Table 8.2: Adequacy of Welfare Benefits, Ontario, 2001

Household type	Total welfare income as percent of poverty line
Single employable adult	36
Person with a disability	62
Sole-support parent with 1 child	59
Couple with 2 children	52

Source: National Council of Welfare (2002).

in social assistance payments. This increase, however, was only 3 percent and it did not take effect until early 2005 (Ontario 2004a). For a single parent with one child the increase has provided a maximum of $29.91 more per month, and for a single adult on welfare it has provided a maximum of $15.60 more. In order to close the gap between welfare income and the poverty line, however, payments to single parents would have to almost double, and payments to single adults would have to almost triple.

Ontario's social safety net for people with disabilities is also looking tattered. Ostensibly, a person whose disability prevents him or her from finding employment is eligible for social assistance under the Ontario Disability Support Plan (ODSP). A single person with a disability, for example, is eligible to receive up to $930 per month under this plan — very little when one considers the many additional costs such a person may incur when it comes to support for independent living. Unfortunately, however, compared to the Family Benefits Act it replaced in 1998, the ODSP Act has made it much more difficult for individuals to apply for, let alone receive, disability payments (Hyland 2001; DBFB 2001; Fraser et al. 2003). If a person's application for a disability benefit proves unsuccessful, he or she is left to survive on the much lower Ontario Works benefit. It is of particular concern that research shows that "many people are refused [the ODSP] through the inaccessible and confusing application process and through strict ODSP eligibility requirements" (DBFB 2001). The government, in the meantime, "saves almost $5,000 per person denied ODSP each year." The 3 percent increase in ODSP benefits, starting February 28, 2005, does little to solve these problems.

Like its welfare benefits, Ontario's minimum-wage rates remained frozen for nearly a decade. In the year 2000 there were over 220,000 minimum-wage workers in the province, with 40 percent of them employed full-time, most of them adults (Battle 2003). For people employed at $6.85 per hour, their pay was worth 18.5 percent less than it had been eight years earlier. And while $6.85 per hour had represented 43 percent of average earnings in the province back in 1995, it had dropped to 38.5 percent of average earnings by 2001.

On February 1, 2004, the Ontario government raised the general minimum wage from $6.85 to $7.15 per hour. This increase, however, generated only about $10.50 extra per week, before taxes, for full-time workers. Further increases were promised each year for the following three years until $8.00 per hour was reached in February 2007 (Ontario 2004b). Unfortunately these increases and a further increase to $8.75 on March 31, 2008, are too little too late to have any impact on the poverty rate in Ontario. They will not reduce the need for food banks.

Finally, another policy factor contributing to poverty in Ontario has been the provincial government's claw-back of the National Child Benefit. This was introduced by the federal government in 1998 and was intended as a financial supplement for low-income families with children. Unfortunately, however, provincial governments were allowed to claw back and redirect these funds into programs designed to help parents get and maintain jobs (Bailey 2002). Ontario was one of the provinces that opted to do just that: in 2001 alone, more than

$180 million was clawed back from welfare recipients. It is true that the money was spent on beneficial programs such as the Child Income Supplement for low-income parents with jobs, but "funding a program for poor working families on the backs of the poorest families (welfare recipients) is about the least logical use of money imaginable" (Oliphant and Slosser 2003: 4).

To summarize: despite the increased cost of living in Ontario, the provincial government has eliminated rent control, legislated minimum-wage rates that continue to keep even full-time workers in poverty, maintained social assistance payments at a fraction of the poverty line, and made it increasingly difficult for people with disabilities to obtain adequate financial support. These policies have contributed to harsh economic circumstances that, in turn, have left many thousands of people unable to purchase the food they need.

Poverty and Food Insecurity in the City of Greater Sudbury

In 2001, 22,895 people in Sudbury — almost 15 percent of the population of 155,219 — were living below the poverty line (Statistics Canada 2001a, 2001b). Inadequate incomes coupled with a lack of affordable accommodation have been the main reasons why people have had to turn to food banks.

Perhaps because of the relatively high vacancy rate for rental properties in Greater Sudbury (5.7 percent in 2001), rents here have been somewhat lower than in other cities in the province (CMHC 2002). Nevertheless, just as in other cities in the province, many people in Greater Sudbury are paying what Statistics Canada considers an unacceptably high amount for accommodation: using 30 percent of household income as the "benchmark" for affordability, 38.7 percent of renters in Sudbury paid 30 percent or more of their household income on shelter in 2001 (CMHC 2003). Indeed, the proportion of Sudbury renters who fall beyond the 30-percent "benchmark" for affordability is greater than the proportion for Ontario (37.2 percent) and for Canada (34.6 percent). Lack of affordable housing, in turn, has left many of our neighbours with little or no money to buy the food they need.

Consider what it costs to meet a household's basic food needs in Greater Sudbury. According to research conducted by the Sudbury and District Health Unit (2001), in 2001 a household consisting of one male adult aged nineteen to twenty-four would have needed an average of $36.13 per week to purchase a sufficient amount of nutritious food. A household consisting of a man and a woman aged twenty-five to forty-nine would have needed an average of $67.12 per week. One adult female aged twenty-five to forty-nine with a daughter aged ten to twelve would have needed $56.63 per week. And, a male and a female, both aged twenty-five to forty-nine with a daughter aged thirteen to fifteen and a son aged ten to twelve would have needed $116.33 per week.

These food costs seem quite reasonable until one examines the cost of accommodation in relation to income. A survey conducted by the Canada Mortgage and Housing Corporation in 2001 found that the average rent for a studio apartment in Sudbury was $387 per month, a one-bedroom apartment cost an average of $500 a month, a two-bedroom apartment cost an average of $620 a month, and an apartment with three or more bedrooms cost an average of $694 a month (Committee to Remember Kimberly Rogers 2002). As we will see, these shelter costs gobble up far too much of what people on low incomes receive each month.

Food Insecurity among Welfare Recipients in Greater Sudbury

Take the case of a single adult unable to find a job. In 2001 this person would have been entitled to a maximum of $520 per month under the Ontario Works program. Assuming he or she paid the average rent for a studio apartment ($387 per month in 2001) shelter costs would consume 74 percent of his or her monthly income. The money left over ($133) would not be enough to cover basic food needs ($178), let alone any other essentials.

Put another way, if a single person on welfare paid the average rent for a studio apartment in Sudbury he or she would be left with about $4.43 per day to cover the cost of all other essentials, including food. An adult couple on welfare that paid the average rent for a one-bedroom apartment would be left with $6.68 per person per day. A single parent and child who paid the average rent for a two-bedroom apartment would be left with $6.28 per person per day (Suschnigg et al. 2003: 39–41).

Clearly, these after-rent amounts are not enough to cover the costs of all non-shelter essentials. It is not surprising, then, that most people who use food banks in Sudbury are welfare recipients: the Ontario Works program actually *ensures* that poverty is perpetuated in our province. Seen from this perspective, the program is a flagrant contravention of the government's responsibility to uphold a basic human right — the right to food security.

Food Insecurity among Low-Income Employees in Greater Sudbury

In 2003 in Sudbury, if a person worked thirty-five hours per week at the minimum wage of $6.85 per hour, he or she would have earned about $959 gross per month. Average rent for a studio apartment would have consumed about 40 percent of his or her pre-tax income, while average rent for a one-bedroom apartment would have consumed about 52 percent, and average rent for a two-bedroom apartment would have consumed about 65 percent. These percentages would be higher, of course, if people's post-tax income were used in the equation instead of their pre-tax income.

While a single person working full-time on minimum wage would have been marginally better off compared to a single person on welfare, this would not have been true for a couple with only one wage-earner in the household, nor would it have been true for a single parent employed full-time at minimum wage. Full-time work at minimum wage, in other words, has offered little protection against food insecurity and hunger in our community. And, as mentioned earlier, increases to the minimum wage have done little to improve the situation.

Food Insecurity among People with Disabilities in Greater Sudbury

People receiving ODSP make up a sizeable proportion of the people who use food banks in Greater Sudbury. The amount they receive each month is similar to the pre-tax incomes of people working full-time for the minimum wage. People with disabilities, however, often have additional costs not faced by others — payments for medical equipment and attendant care, for example. All the more evidence, then, that the ODSP is no guarantee of food security.

Contradictory Aspects of Food Banks

Food banks have become an essential means of survival for an increasing number of people in Sudbury and across Canada. For this reason it is vital to investigate and assess the contradictory character of these organizations.[3]

First, the proliferation of food banks does far more than let politicians "off the hook" for the well-being of their constituents. As food banks settle in for the long haul, one observes increased surveillance and regulation of food recipients via registration records, eligibility criteria, and documentation of visits. This development has been prompted by concerns about people visiting more than one food bank per month — so-called "double-dipping" — concerns about people lying in regard to their number of dependents, and concerns about people selling emergency food to maintain an addiction.

But increased record-keeping also has been prompted by concerns about people with "multiple needs" who might benefit from referrals to other support services. Most important — in their effort to eliminate the very need for food banks — many workers are determined to document the size and severity of the hunger crisis in our country. Hard evidence, they argue, is an essential tool when it comes to educating the public and lobbying politicians.

Unfortunately, the combined effect of all these concerns means that food recipients must increasingly demonstrate that they are among the "deserving poor." Their personal records, in the meantime, are vulnerable to unauthorized access, to theft, and even to court subpoena.

Running parallel to the increased regulation of food recipients has been the emergence of a now quite complex system of food collection and distribution that operates across the whole of Canada. Small-scale systems still exist — food donated by parishioners to other members of their church, for example. But food collection and distribution is also occurring on an ever more massive scale. Every year, many millions of kilograms of food and drink are donated by the food industry itself. In 2001, for example, food companies donated 11 million pounds of food and drink. Contributors included corporate giants such as Kraft, Proctor and Gamble, Kellogs, General Mills, Sobeys, Cadbury, Hershey, and Nestlé (CAFB no date b). To manage these donations the Canadian Association of Food Banks (CAFB) has established an infrastructure called the National Food Sharing System. If a food industry donation fills ten pallets or more it is shipped by train, truck, or boat to the Toronto headquarters of the CAFB. There, the items enter an enormous warehouse, are divided into smaller portions, and subsequently are shipped back out to regional "hubs" across the country.

The Sudbury Food Bank is one such hub. It is the umbrella organization to which most food banks in the community belong. The Sudbury Food Bank does not provide direct service to individuals. Rather, it works locally to help raise donations of money and food. As well, it oversees a local warehouse, located in the basement of one of the largest food banks in the city (run by the Salvation Army), to which food from the CAFB is shipped and then redistributed to member food banks in the region.

If one contemplates the ratio of calorie-input to calorie-output associated with the National Food Sharing System, its overall inefficiency is colossal: the energy it takes to produce, process, package, and distribute donations is far greater than the number of calories eventually made available to food recipients. Staff members at the Canadian and Ontario Associations of Food Banks are well aware of this contradiction. Nevertheless, they feel they have no option but to encourage and distribute industry donations when so many people are going hungry.[4]

Another issue to consider is the benefits that accrue to the food industry through its participation in the National Food Sharing System. First, dumping fees are saved when food that otherwise would end up in landfill sites can be redirected to food banks. And, as it turns out, most of the industry-donated food falls into this category. The goods donated may be close to, or past, the due date for safe consumption, they might be surplus product created through over-production, their containers may be dented or lack labels, or they may contain "formula errors" (DBFB no date). Food banks, to put it bluntly, have become a relatively cheap way to dispose of industrial waste.

Then there is the fact that food companies gain a great deal of free advertising by donating food, most of which they would not be able to sell anyway. Moreover, being seen to help "feed the poor" is particularly good for a company's marketing image. Kraft, for example, donates 1.5 million pounds of food to the CAFB each year. For the past five years it has funded the CAFB's annual HungerCount survey, and it has helped raise money (CAFB no date c). The CAFB acknowledges this support with website details on Kraft's and other companies' good works. As well, Kraft's logo is clearly displayed on CAFB posters and on paper bags distributed during local food drives.

To continue with the example of Kraft, one should not forget that this company is a major subsidiary of the biggest cigarette producer on the planet — a corporation whose profits reached $10.6 billion in the year 2000 (CTFK 2001: 7). The Philip Morris Corporation (now known as Altria) has been found guilty of lying about the health impacts of cigarettes and accused of smuggling cigarettes across national borders to avoid paying import taxes. Like other Big Tobacco corporations, Philip Morris has been promoting the sale of its cigarettes abroad to increase profits. In so doing, the corporation has contributed to preventable illness and premature death in underdeveloped countries where health services are vastly under-funded.

Of even greater concern, Big Tobacco corporations like Philip Morris have been shifting tobacco production to these same underdeveloped countries because production costs are lower there. Small farmers in these countries have often been compelled to focus on tobacco at the expense of food production for local consumption. A subsequent glut of tobacco on the world market, however, has reduced the commodity's selling price. Consequently, many tobacco farmers in both developed and underdeveloped countries have been driven to bankruptcy. In short, Philip Morris has contributed, albeit indirectly, to food insecurity both at home and abroad in its pursuit of profit. According to the Washington-based Campaign for Tobacco Free Kids:

> Many tobacco farmers are now stuck producing a crop that is labour and input intensive and brings with it a host of health and environmental dangers. Meanwhile, the cigarette companies continue to downplay or ignore the many serious economic and environmental costs associated with tobacco cultivation, such as chronic indebtedness among tobacco farmers (usually to the companies themselves), serious environmental destruction caused by tobacco farming, and pesticide-related health problems for farmers and their families. (CTFK 2001: 2)

As a major subsidiary of Philip Morris, Kraft is now being hailed as one of Canada's most generous food donors and as a "partner" in the struggle to end hunger. According to the CAFB (no date a), Kraft and other contributors to the National Food Sharing System are helping feed "700,000 [people] through hamper programs and 2 million meals each month." Furthermore, the CAFB says, these companies are helping raise public awareness about food insecurity: food industry donors "help us educate our members, government, the media and the general public about the hunger issue in Canada."

Along the same vein, one of the CAFB's "in-kind" supporters is the Food and Consumer Products Manufacturers of Canada (FCPMC) (CAFB no date d). Affiliate members of this organization include such major biotechnology companies as Bayer Cropscience Canada, Dow AgroSciences Canada, Monsanto Canada, and Pioneer Hi-Bred — A Dupont Company (FCPMC no date a). A visit to the FCPMC website (no date b) reveals a glowing endorsement of genetically modified foods. There is mounting evidence, however, that production of these crops is putting our health, our environment, and our entire food system in jeopardy (Crouch 2001; Heller 2001; Kneen 1999; Shand 2001; Teitel and Wilson 2001; Tokar, 2001).

One final point on the contradictions associated with food banks: during local food drives, food banks are dependent on widespread media coverage if their initiatives are to be successful. But as Riches (1997: 63) has pointed out, even when agencies broadcast a strong political message along with a request for donations, the media tend to highlight the symptoms rather than the root causes of hunger. For this reason, food drives are more likely to encourage individual acts of charity — small sacrifices that make people "feel good" about themselves — than to stimulate public demonstrations against government policy and corporate greed.

Conclusion

Hunger in Canada is entirely preventable. What is lacking is the political will to eliminate this major social problem. In Ontario, advocates of the "anti-poverty" perspective demand that the government reinstate rent controls and increase investments in low-cost social housing, raise the general minimum wage from $7.15 to at least $10.00 per hour, raise welfare benefits and make it easier for people with disabilities to apply for — and to receive — adequate social assistance, invest in publicly funded day-care, eliminate claw-backs to the National Child Benefit, and reduce tuition costs for post-secondary education. Perhaps most important of all, advocates of the "anti-poverty" perspective insist that the Ontario government replace its Ontario Works program with a non-coercive welfare program that guarantees an adequate income for everyone dependent on social assistance.

On the face of it, these recommendations pose little or no threat to capital. Indeed, if instituted, they would help ameliorate the worst impacts of neo-liberal economic policies and leave an increasingly exploitative economic system intact. But even if there were the political will to implement these "anti-poverty" recommendations, the structural constraints on our government would be considerable. In a world where multinational corporations have more wealth and wield more power than many nations do, "welfare states" such as Canada's are becoming an anachronism (Teeple 1995). Canadian jobs are being exported to countries where labour is cheap, work conditions are inhumane, environmental standards are lax, and human rights are violated. There is corporate pressure on all levels of government to reduce social spending and to privatize publicly owned enterprises, and so-called "free trade" policies are being implemented despite public resistance. The proportion of the Canadian labour force that is unionized is declining, and organized labour is losing the ground it fought so hard to win in the past.

Unlike the "anti-poverty" perspective, the "food-sovereignty" perspective poses a direct challenge to capital. Clearly, this means that the Canadian government would face even more formidable constraints if it ever tried to implement the anti-corporate agenda put forward by these advocates: to do so would be to acknowledge, to expose, and to undermine the class-based origins on which the state's own survival depends.[5]

If it is unrealistic to expect the government to come up with solutions to hunger and food insecurity in Canada — let alone in the rest of the world — what other hope is there? Instead of top-down solutions, perhaps bottom-up solutions offer the most promise. In particular, there are historical lessons to be learned from the successes and failures of Canada's cooperative movements, particularly among prairie farmers. More recently, the rise of cooperatives in South America — in Uruguay and Argentina, for example — is helping improve people's standard of living while ushering in governments that are unwilling to submit to externally imposed conditions of neo-liberal "structural adjustment" in order to receive development loans.

Democracy cannot survive without social justice. The planet cannot survive without sustainability. The future looks bleak unless we find ways to achieve both (Power 1999).

Notes

1. Face-to-face interviews were conducted in early 2003. The household composition of respondents was as follows: 33 percent of households contained a single adult, 20 percent contained two or more adults, 24 percent contained a single parent with one or more children, and 19 percent contained two adults with one or more children. Nearly a quarter of respondents had some form of post-secondary education. Sixty percent were on welfare/Ontario Works, and 26 percent were receiving a disability benefit (Suschnigg et al. 2003).

2. These figures are based on a quantitative measure of poverty, that is, on a set of 35 low-income cut-offs (LICOs) produced by Statistics Canada: LICOs are calculated for seven different family sizes and five different community sizes, and they are adjusted each year to reflect changes in the cost of living. While Statistics Canada avoids using the term "poverty line," the National Council of Welfare and many other organizations deem any household falling below its respective LICO to be living in poverty. In 2002, the pre-tax LICO for a one-person household in Sudbury was $16,521, for a two-person household it was $20,651, for a three-person household it was $25,684, and for a four-person household it was $31,090 (NCW 2003).

3. In no way is this section intended to minimize, dismiss, or denigrate the work done by the thousands of food bank workers across this country, most of whom are volunteers. On the contrary, in the face of government inaction, their contributions are essential to the survival of hundreds of thousands of their fellow human beings, especially children.

4. Personal communication, Tanja Kraft, Ontario Association of Food Banks, 2003.

5. See Renaud's (1975) account of the structural constraints on the state when it comes to reforming the mainstream health system.

Chapter 9

"Sometimes I Wonder..."

Language, Racism, and the Language of Racism in Sudbury

Roger Spielmann

Introduction

I would like to reflect on language, racism, and the language of racism currently on display in the Sudbury region. I want to probe what many non-Aboriginal people in the Sudbury region consider the "strange" world of Aboriginal people.

As personal context, it may be helpful to say that, prior to coming to Laurentian University, I had the wonderful opportunity of living in the Algonquin community of Pikogan in Northern Québec for eleven years as a linguistic consultant. After joining Laurentian's faculty in the Department of Aboriginal Studies in 1990, I began to make friends and hang out with Anishnaabe (Ojibwe) people here in the Sudbury-Manitoulin region. Teaching in Native Studies and living in an Aboriginal community has been a transformative experience for me and, over the years, I have observed great similarities between the Pikogan community and the Aboriginal community in the Sudbury-Manitoulin region. Two particular aspects of the communities have been quite noticeably and inexorably related: language and racism.

One key issue about language and terminology needs mention at the outset. Much has been written over the years about what sociolinguists commonly refer to as "in-group" language and "out-group" language (Crystal 1987; Hymes 1981). A specific term of reference used by a people who share a common cultural heritage may be considered derogatory when used by a cultural outsider but is acceptable when used by cultural members themselves. In many First Nations communities, for example, it is common to hear community members refer to themselves as "Indians" or even as "savages" or "redskins." Such terms are commonly used for joking, teasing, and, perhaps most importantly, for expressing in-group solidarity. When I worked with African-American youth one summer in Dallas, Texas, the use of the term "nigger" was commonplace among the youth themselves, as in: "Hey, he's one bad nigger" (a compliment!), or, "Hey, nigger, what it is?" But if a white person were to refer to an African-American person by calling him a "nigger," that person risked being seriously challenged, even assaulted. It is the same with *maudit sauvage* (god-damned savage) in French or even "Indian" in English. Such terms can be, and are, used among Aboriginal people in interaction together, but when used by non-Aboriginal people to refer to an Aboriginal person, it most often results in hostility.

Recently, I did an informal survey of my Aboriginal friends asking what term they prefer and what term they use among themselves to refer to themselves. It was unanimous that they preferred cultural outsiders (non-Aboriginal people) to refer to them as "Aboriginal people," "Native people," or "First Nations people." But most with whom I spoke self-designate almost exclusively as Anishnaabe (First People).[1] We can begin to grasp how "in-group" terms of reference usually spring from unique and culturally specific understandings of the collectivity. For me, it is important to keep in mind this "in-group-out-group" distinction when thinking about how people refer to themselves and how they wish to be referred to by outsiders. At the very least, it is a sign of respect to use terms for a people that the people themselves prefer to be used. The terms "Aboriginal people," "First Nations people" and "Anishnaabe people," then, are the terms I will use to refer to Aboriginal people in the rest of this chapter.

Sudbury is touted as a wonderfully progressive community that embraces diversity. For example, a publication by Laurentian University (2004: 4–5), *Skills for Success*, effuses:

> Sudbury has become a dynamic and diverse regional capital that functions as the service hub for all of north-eastern Ontario.... Success in re-greening land and rehabilitating lakes has earned Sudbury worldwide recognition for its environmental efforts. The City of Greater Sudbury was one of the first municipalities to establish an advanced telecommunications infrastructure.... It seems clear that harnessing the power of local institutions, businesses, and community groups is quickly becoming the next phase of transformation for the City of Greater Sudbury.

But the reality for Anishnaabe people is quite different. In this chapter, I attempt to show how attitudes toward Aboriginal language initiatives and racist attitudes are intricately related to what I refer to as the "language of racism." It has been tough for me to write this chapter, in large part because the issue of racism is one we tend to avoid. My hope is that this chapter will encourage both non-Aboriginal and Aboriginal people in the Sudbury region to take off our blinders and stare the beast of racism squarely in the eye. Only then, I believe, will true reconciliation and healing begin to take place between Aboriginal peoples and Canadians.

"You People...": Is Sudbury a Racist Community?

Aboriginal couple at the door of the landlord of an apartment building:

> *Aboriginal couple:* Hi, we called earlier about the apartment you have for rent.
> *Landlord:* Sorry, it's not available.
> *Aboriginal couple:* Oh, but we just called twenty minutes ago.
> *Landlord:* Sorry, but I don't rent to you people. I've had too many bad experiences in the past.

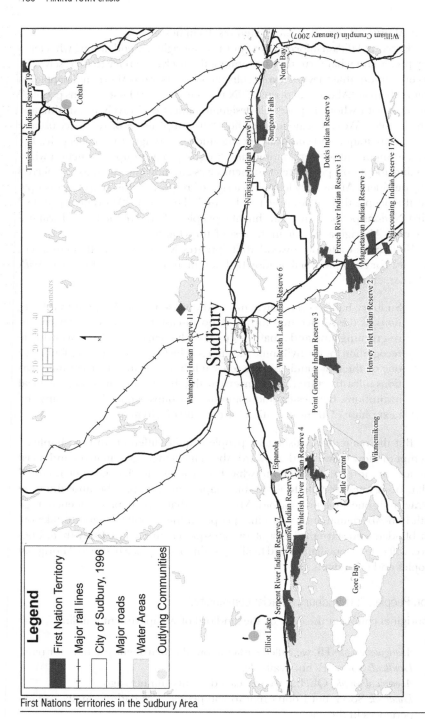

First Nations Territories in the Sudbury Area

Some will think the above conversation is a blast from the past and remark how things have changed and that *this* could never happen today. Sadly, this conversation took place in September 2003, in Sudbury.

In my own research over the past two decades I have encountered some "truths" most Aboriginal people hold about themselves that need to be understood by Canadians if there is ever to be an authentic coming together in understanding one another. First, it is extremely important for Canadians to understand that the vast majority of Aboriginal people in the Sudbury region and across Canada do not consider themselves to be primarily Canadian. When asked about one's citizenship, virtually every Aboriginal person I know personally responds with the name of their respective First Nation. (For example, "I belong to the Sagamok First Nation," and so on.) True, there seems to be some sense that they are "Canadian" to some vague degree, but their *primary* identity is *not* Canadian, but First Nation. Until Canadians understand this basic fact, the wall of ignorance and misunderstanding will continue to exist.

The second thing I believe is important to understand is that Aboriginal people in the Sudbury-Manitoulin region face racist insults, stereotypical attitudes, and discriminatory attitudes as common occurrences. Every Aboriginal person I know personally who lives in the Sudbury-Manitoulin region has experienced overt acts of racism in the past year — *every* one.

The Ontario Council of Agencies Serving Immigrants (OCASI) has a twenty-five-year history of working with Aboriginal people as well as with immigrants in the Sudbury region. One of its key activities is combating racism and discrimination through education. According to a recent survey conducted by OCASI (2003), 35 percent of visible minorities living in the City of Greater Sudbury say they have been discriminated against or treated unfairly in the past five years. Among Aboriginal people, the number who say they are sometimes or often the target of racial discrimination rises to 72 percent.

Debwewin, an Aboriginal anti-racist organization in northeastern Ontario, has conducted surveys in key Northern Ontario cities in order to determine if racism is still prevalent there. The surveys, reported on by Anna Piekarski in the August 20, 2004, edition of *The Sudbury Star*, show that, beyond the shadow of a doubt, discrimination against Aboriginal people is still rampant. According to Project Director Don Curry: "Seventy percent of all Aboriginals [who responded] have seen discrimination in the past twelve months." The questionnaire was prepared by The Union of Ontario Indians in conjunction with Communitas Canada.

In a related article, the Social Planning Council of Sudbury studied more than 5,050 Sudburians and determined that, "About… half of local residents had views consistent with modern racism thinking." Sudburian John Moore, who attended a press conference held in Sudbury in September, 2004, said that he experiences discrimination daily. He gave example after example of how racist attitudes affect him as an Aboriginal man each and every day. The research, which was conducted from mid-December 2003 to late March 2004, consisted of two parts — a neighbourhood survey and a cultural groups survey. The information from these studies is not a surprise. What is new is that, for the first time, we have clear numbers indicating that racism is a reality in Sudbury and that many people experience it.

Statistics Canada census data for 2001 tell us that over 7,000 Aboriginal people reside in the City of Greater Sudbury, and 43.7 percent are under the age of twenty-five. The census also revealed that the unemployment rate for Aboriginal people was 20 percent, while "only" 9.1 percent of Sudburians as a whole were unemployed. Few would doubt that unemployment breeds a climate of suspicion and frustration in which racism thrives. Since the Aboriginal population in the Sudbury region is growing, unemployment, racism, and related problems can only get worse unless some meaningful action is taken.

After hanging out with Anishnaabe people for almost thirty years, I am convinced that it is not easy being an Aboriginal person in Sudbury or in this country now known as Canada. I have talked with too many Canadians in the Sudbury region who seem to think that "real Indians" died off years ago — or should have — and I have seen too many restaurant servers who seem to drag their feet when waiting on a table occupied by "Indians." By contrast, most traditional Aboriginal lands are open for business to multinational corporations, but not open to Aboriginal people.

Worst of all, most Aboriginal people have to put up with all sorts of stupid questions — they are stupid to most Aboriginal people, anyway — that most non-Aboriginal people have about "Indians." These are questions such as: "Why do you Indians get everything free?" and "Why can't you Indians quit your bitching and just learn to be good Canadians?" Another classic goes something like: "Why don't Indians get off their asses and get jobs?" Yet rarely is it asked if there *are* jobs in number — let alone in quality — available to Aboriginal people. While Greater Sudbury itself has an Aboriginal unemployment rate at least double the overall average, many Northern Aboriginal communities have unemployment rates of 80 percent and higher. Recently, with yet another stupid question, one non-Aboriginal asked me, "Why don't those Indians just go back to where they came from?" Now *that* is an interesting idea!

Since I claim that racism is alive and well in the Sudbury region, it is important to have a shared understanding of what is meant by the word "racism." Racism is basically a set of ideas or practices that view or treat one group of people defined by "race" as inherently inferior or subordinate. "Race," an unscientific concept, is typically identified by a person's features, such as skin colour or facial features — how they "look." Even some easily accessible dictionary definitions often capture the sense of racism as a false belief or "pre-judgment" — prejudice — about inherent inferiority, as in the following (Webster 2002: 897):

> prejudice or discrimination based on the belief that race is the primary factor determining human traits and abilities. Racism includes the belief that genetic or inherited differences produce the inherent superiority or inferiority of one race over another. In the name of protecting their race from "contamination," some racists justify the domination and destruc-

tion of races they consider to be either superior or inferior. Institutional racism is racial prejudice supported by institutional power and authority used to the advantage of one race over others.

Racism is increasingly subject to legal sanction. The *International Convention on the Elimination of All Forms of Racial Discrimination* (United Nations 1965) defines racial discrimination as follows:

> Any distinction, exclusion, restriction, or preference based on race, colour, descent, or national or ethnic origin which has the purpose or effect of nullifying or impairing the recognition, enjoyment, or exercise, on equal footing, of human rights and fundamental freedoms in the political, economic, social, cultural, or any other field of public life.

Racism may be less overt or brazen in character today than in times past — though not always — but it still very much exists. As reported by The International Council on Human Rights Policy (2000):

> old and explicit forms of racism are still alive. Nevertheless, those who face discrimination increasingly confront forms of racism that are covert or more complex or are linked to wider issues, such as changes in the nature of the state, gender discrimination, or marginalisation due to developments in the global economy.

Perhaps the saddest part of these numbers and definitions is that most communities in Northern Ontario have very few resources with which to counter racism and discrimination, particularly in the schools. To begin to address this shameful situation, a Multiculturalism Program has contributed $250,000 toward the fight against racism in Sudbury and Espanola. This funding was for the Community Builders Youth Leadership Initiative to run a program at eleven schools that will allow 350 students in grades five through eight to take part in leadership workshops on the impact of racism and how to make sustainable changes to their school culture. Considering how widespread and serious is the experience of racism, this federal grant is a small amount, less than two dollars per person for the entire Sudbury region.

Some Initial Questions

I would like to introduce a few questions that may help to provide some insight on this relationship between First Nations people and Canadians in the Sudbury region. For instance, why is it that most Canadians were disturbed and even outraged by the system of apartheid in South Africa before it was dismantled in 1989, but were — and still are — indifferent to or ignorant of the system of apartheid that exists in Canada? (That system would be, of course, the Indian Act, where we find a different set of laws governing a certain group of people based on race). And why is it that Aboriginal people are expected to be "good

Canadians" when they were not allowed to vote in this country until 1960 and, for decades, were not allowed to gather in groups off their reserves, could not leave their reserves without a pass, could not openly observe their own ways of praying and worshipping without being tossed in jail, and could not attend university or enter professional careers without losing their status as First Nations people?

How about this? Why is it that two immigrant languages, English and French, are considered to be "official" languages in this country now known as Canada while the languages of the original people remain unrecognized and virtually unsupported? Why is it that most Canadians expect Aboriginal people to be knowledgeable about *Canadian* history, languages, traditions, institutions, the justice system, and system of governance while most Canadians remain ignorant about Aboriginal languages, traditions, histories, institutions, justice systems, and systems of governance? Finally, why is it that the European guests who came to this continent imposed — and *still* impose — *their* systems of thinking and governing on their hosts rather than accepting and adapting to existing Aboriginal systems of thinking and governing?

Before continuing to reflect on the relationship between First Nations people and Canadians, though, I should clarify an important issue. A lot of the Aboriginal people I know personally claim that their ancestors lived in an ideal world, a kind of utopia, until the white man came and screwed everything up. Actually, that is just not true. Human beings are human beings, and there is no such thing as a perfect culture. Aboriginal legends and myths in every tradition talk about all sorts of injustices and taboo behaviours taking place well before the coming of the Europeans. Aboriginal cultures were not *a priori* perfect before contact — *better*, yes, but not perfect.

Time to Listen

In many Aboriginal communities it is common to hear the Elders express the following concerns when approached by non-Aboriginal people: "Why do your people keep trying to tell us who we are?" "Why can't you accept us for who we are?" At the same time, it is also true that non-Aboriginal people too often write off Aboriginal people as "assimilated" or "just like white people." One can easily fall into the trap of failing to really *listen* to what one is being taught and thus miss the wealth and richness of Aboriginal cultures, languages, and traditions (Rhodes 1988).

In my experience living in Pikogan, I had many opportunities to observe non-Aboriginal people entering the community in order to "work together" with community members on one project or another. More often than not, the project would be undermined by underlying tension between the Aboriginal and non-Aboriginal researchers. I think one key reason for this is that non-Aboriginal people were not willing to relinquish *control* of a project. I remember working on a community survey with another non-Aboriginal researcher. Since I had been involved with the community for a number of years, community members would invariably bring their complaints about other non-Aboriginal researchers to me, the white guy. It was sometimes awkward to hear Aboriginal people talking about how white people always want to be the "bosses" of these projects and how they're so "pushy." Suffice it to say, they were usually right. On the other hand, I have had more than a few opportunities to listen to non-Aboriginal people involved in teaching and research in the Aboriginal community express frustration about how difficult it is to work with Aboriginal people, comments like: "These people are so rude. They're never on time and they're always laughing at me."

I usually begin any response by saying something along these lines: in any cross-cultural situation, it is important to learn how to interact appropriately, because what is considered to be rude behaviour in one's own culture is often conventionally polite in another, and what is polite behaviour in one's own culture is often considered to be very rude in another. So it is important to pay attention to appropriate ways of interacting and the values underlying these culture-specific ways of doing things.

The value of maintaining the harmony of the moment in face-to-face interaction is very difficult for many non-Aboriginal people to understand. Aboriginal students in a non-Aboriginal school system, such as is the case in the Sudbury-Manitoulin region, for example, will often be seen as "apathetic" or "lazy" because they are not as willing to raise their hand or blurt out the answer to a teacher's question as many non-Aboriginal students are. In Aboriginal culture, to do so might be interpreted as putting yourself in a superior position to your friends and it may bring on the risk of teasing or ostracism. These kinds of cultural differences often lead non-Aboriginal people to the mistaken conclusion that Aboriginal people are dishonest or unreliable. What we non-Aboriginal people often do not understand is the strong cultural values at play in everyday life. In these particular instances, most non-Aboriginal people do not understand the profound importance of maintaining *harmony* in the moment rather than allowing any kind of tension to develop by having to refuse a request or engage in face-to-face confrontation.

Closely related to the cultural value of maintaining harmony in all social relations is that of *sharing*. Certainly, every culture has some sense that it is good to share things. In fact, before entering the community of Pikogan, I felt that I was a very generous person and one who was quite willing to share. Very quickly, though, I realized that I was really quite a stingy person by Aboriginal standards. It took me a long time to come to the place where I was willing to share freely with those around me, especially with my car and my money. Giving gifts, money, possessions, and time are an important part of Ojibwe life. Generosity is an important value in the Ojibwe ethos, and it seems to be rooted in two basic principles. The first is the recognition that all possessions, successes, and honours are from the Creator. Many times, I have observed people receiving such things respond in gratitude and thanksgiving by sharing with those near them. The sender's generosity is rooted, I believe, in the philosophy that giving to another furthers the development of relationships. A consequence of this is that, by giving to another, one is creating a kind of social security for oneself against possible future need, which is the second principle underlying the cultural importance of generosity in the Ojibwe ethos. As one person told me: "Sharing things and giving things away keeps our community going."

Important, too, is how the introduction of technology into many Aboriginal communities has been changing some of these important cultural values — such as sharing — more often than not for the worse. Before electricity came into one Atikamekw community, when somebody killed a moose he would bring it back to the village and distribute the meat according to the culturally proper means of distribution in the community. Nobody would dare think of hoarding the meat for themselves. What would happen to those without meat? And, how would the meat be preserved, anyway? After electricity came into the community, one of the first pieces of technology to follow was the freezer. Before long, the new technology began to undermine the traditional values of sharing. Today, when somebody kills a moose, he or she can just throw all the meat in the freezer and it will feed them all winter. The whole value of sharing meat is changing and, with it, the cultural strength of sharing. It is interesting, too, to think about the term coined to call that piece of technology in the Atikamekw language. They call it a "stingy box," because, now, you don't have to share the meat.

Another strong Aboriginal value, which underlies the importance of not forcing your thinking on others, is respect for individual autonomy. This kind of respect certainly helps promote positive interpersonal relationships in the setting of a small community or extended family. After I began to catch on to this value, I started noticing it at work almost every day in face-to-face community interactions. You simply did not see people going around telling others what to do. The same principle could be seen in how people raised their children in the community. When I first moved to Pikogan with my wife, we observed that the kids on the reserve appeared to "run around" with no supervision. The parents seemed to take a "hands-off" approach to child-rearing, to say the least! After a while, though, we began to catch on to the fact that the kids in the community were being looked after very carefully. All adults in the community shared a sense of guardianship for the kids. In time, we too began to feel more at ease letting our own kids "run free" in the community. We knew they were being watched by others, and we began to take on the same responsibility when there were kids playing in our "space." From a cultural outsider's perspective, it appeared that the kids were running around "wild," to use an expression we heard more than once. This is no small matter, because there are non-Aboriginal people in positions of authority over Aboriginal families and communities, and judgments based on ignorance have had, and continue to have, devastating affects on many of those families and communities.

Of my personal, Western-based values, it was the value related to *respect* that changed most drastically. Living in Pikogan, I found that my friends there had a deeper sense of what respect means. For them, there is a very strong feeling that one's life and experience is, in a very real sense, meant to be just the way it is. The way it was expressed to me many times and in many different ways over the years is that the Great Spirit has a purpose for each individual, each creature, each natural phenomenon, and each event, and nothing happens apart from that design.

It is in respect for other cultures that Canadians so often seem to fail. This is not because we are necessarily racists — although overt racism is certainly seen on a daily basis in Sudbury — but simply because many Canadians remain ignorant of how Aboriginal people think, do things, and view the world. A lot of Canadians simply do not understand Aboriginal people — and what a shame that is! We miss knowing about the richness of a culture, one that has no unwanted children and where old people are not put away in institutions but have a valuable role to play in the community.

Most Aboriginal people already *know* which non-Aboriginal ways are worth learning and which ones are not, and they will quickly take advantage of that knowledge. But this is generally not a two-way street. Most Aboriginal people I know are quite knowledgeable about non-Aboriginal ways of thinking and doing things. Most are conversant in a "foreign" language: English or French. Most Aboriginal people have gone through the Canadian educational system and know about Canadian history from a distinctly non-Aboriginal perspective. In contrast, it is rare to meet a non-Aboriginal person in Canada who is knowledgeable about Aboriginal ways of thinking and doing things, or who speaks an Aboriginal language, or who is knowledgeable about Canadian history from an Aboriginal perspective. When you think about it, which of the different cultural ways of thinking about and doing things — those of Aboriginal people or non-Aboriginal people — has more to offer in terms of coping with life in the twenty-first century?

I was often invited to go into the bush to hunt and trap with some of the Elders in Pikogan. One Elder in particular, Okinawe, taught me many things over the years about his language, his people, and his way of life. He was always patient with me. One night, as we waited quietly in a cool breeze listening for the sound of the moose, he reached down and put his hand on the ground beneath us. He spoke in his Aboriginal language and said, "The earth is our Mother. I can feel her in my very being. We depend on the earth and on each other. So we share what we have with one another." I was struck with the irony of how Aboriginal people in Canada seem to be the very ones possessing the central insights into the land and the environment. The Elder I sat with in the bush that night told me how the land is essential to his way of life. Without it, he said, his people could not survive. His observation was strikingly revealed during the Oka Crisis in 1990. The contrast between this Elder and the Prime Minister of Canada at that time could not have been more stark. One, an Aboriginal Elder, speaks of our harmony with the earth, the community, and one another — the other commits human life and tanks against First Nations peoples in their own country. I believe that the vision each represents is *fundamental* in determining the kind of future we will have in this country we call Canada.

Over the years, I have had many non-Aboriginal students and friends say to me — I paraphrase here — "I'm sorry that Aboriginal people in Canada have been so poorly treated by the Canadian government, but it's not *my* fault. Like, I didn't do anything wrong, so why should I feel guilty about what happened?" I usually respond to that question with the following: "You're right, you shouldn't feel guilty, at least not yet. On the other hand, if you sit back and do nothing for the next ten years, especially by failing to educate yourself about Canadian history and the history of First Nations people, then you will, in fact, be part of the problem."

Toward Linguistic Justice

Now I would like to return directly to the theme of the inter-relatedness of language and racism. Why is it that Aboriginal languages are not recognized as "official" languages in this country now known as Canada? Aboriginal languages have been willfully and systematically destroyed as part of the official Canadian policy of dealing with the "Indian problem." At the core of the Canadian government's self-perceived mandate to "civilize and Christianize" Aboriginal peoples was a strategy to force them to abandon their languages and thus their traditional, millennia-old ways of thinking, relating, and perceiving the world at large. It should be noted that this was not a covert policy, nor is this an issue Aboriginal peoples are inventing to create sympathy for human rights violations. Rather, it is a policy well documented in the books and papers written by non-Aboriginal government officials, missionaries, educators, and other "interested" people (Brizinski 1993; Mawhiney 1993; Aboriginal Languages and Literacy Conference 1991).

In 1993, the Assembly of First Nations (AFN) considered that the right to be able to speak one's Aboriginal language had been so marginalized that it drafted a *Declaration on Aboriginal Languages*. The following comments represent the core of its perspective:

> We believe that our Aboriginal languages were given to us by the Creator as an Integral part of life. Embodied in our languages is our unique relationship to the Creator, our attitudes, beliefs, values, and the fundamental notion of what is truth.
>
> We believe that knowing one's Aboriginal language is an asset to one's own education, formal and informal. Knowing one's Aboriginal language contributes to a greater pride in the history and culture of one's home community, greater involvement and interest of parents in the education of their children, and greater respect for the Elders.
>
> We believe that language is the principal means by which culture is accumulated, shared, and transmitted from generation to generation.
>
> The key to identity and retention of culture is one's ancestral language. (Assembly of First Nations 1993)

Today, most Aboriginal leaders, educators, Elders, and community people see the renewal and strengthening of their languages as the foundation for self-determination and a prerequisite for re-establishing a healthy relationship with the government and people of Canada. In its *Declaration*, the AFN demanded that Aboriginal languages be given equal treatment in the Canadian Constitution with the current "official" languages, English and French. Another AFN recommendation calls for the implementation of an *Aboriginal Language Revitalization Strategy* that would work toward preserving, retaining, and promoting Aboriginal national languages. The AFN proposes that this strategy start at the community level, with First Nations language instruction that begins with daycare and kindergarten and continues through to grade twelve. Hand-in-hand with this proposal is the founding of an Aboriginal Languages Foundation designed to perpetuate, revitalize, and protect First Nations languages. To date, no such foundation has been established.

The question remains: how does Aboriginal language renewal interact with racism and the language of racism, particularly in the Sudbury region?

The responsibility for campaigning against and ultimately eradicating inequality, at least with regard to First Nations languages, rests with First Nations' initiatives backed by federal government funding and the support of Canadians. Keep in mind that these recommendations are not intended to irritate the Canadian public but to rectify an injustice based on prejudice. Language-renewal and support issues are not merely "Aboriginal rights" issues, but matters pertaining to *human* rights.

It is indeed odd that, while the country of Canada has prided itself as a defender of human rights in the international community, its own Human Rights Commission has condemned Canada for its treatment of Aboriginal peoples. Why is it that Aboriginal languages and cultures were freely vandalized and human rights trampled in a country that sees itself as a defender of human rights on the international scene? Why is it that Canadian service providers routinely translate educational and health-related materials into the languages of people they are sent to serve in other parts of the world, but educational and health-related information is not translated into Aboriginal languages in this very country? It is no wonder that most Aboriginal peoples consider that the Canadian government operates by a double standard! These and other questions are at the heart of the issue of decolonization in general, and of the liberation of Aboriginal languages in particular.

Decisions about revitalizing and preserving Aboriginal languages cannot be made solely on economic factors (Is it worth it? How much will it cost? What contributions do these languages make to the economy?). It is a moral as well as a political issue, an issue of respecting human dignity. Aboriginal peoples did not willingly abandon their languages. They were beaten and threatened, and legislation was passed to destroy their languages, and it was often a violent process. What began in residential schools continues through the generations, almost like an inheritance. The history has long been known and documented, but so also have solutions been proposed, in report after report. As noted by Mary Joy Elijah (2002):

The many reports put forward by First Nations communities clamour for the control and the self-determination of their own education systems. Without fail, every proposed educational reform recommends the inclusion of the language and culture of their community to some degree. Government reports have given voice to the same recommendations which are beginning to advance First Nations jurisdiction and control over education. But many other reports criticize the slow pace and question the commitment and will of the Canadian government to act with substance in carrying out the many recommendations repeatedly put forward. Such reports have spanned decades.

In the City of Greater Sudbury, only recently — since 1999 — have elementary and secondary schools been financially able and morally willing to "make room" for the teaching of Ojibwe in particular. According to Sara Gonawabi, a fluent speaker of the Ojibwe language who teaches the language at the secondary level in Sudbury, the opportunity to teach the language in the school system did not exist until new Ontario curriculum guidelines were put into place in 1999. So, it has not so much been that Sudbury educators were against the teaching of Aboriginal languages in the schools, but that they were not able or willing to support such an initiative until the province demanded it of them.

I must also mention the remarkable achievements that have been made in the past five years, mainly due to the expertise, enthusiasm, and hard work of Aboriginal language teachers in the Sudbury Region. Martina Osawamick of the Wabnode Institute at Cambrian College and Mary Ann Corbiere, Professor of Native Studies at the University of Sudbury, have produced a clever and concise introduction to Ojibwe on CD-ROM. Professor Corbiere is also instrumental in the ongoing Nishnaabemwin Dictionary Project, which will soon bear fruit and will update and complement existing Ojibwe dictionaries produced over the years by non-Aboriginal linguists and by Ms Corbiere herself. The aforementioned CD-ROM gives a comprehensive introduction to the Nishnaabemwin language that focusses on building communicative competence in learners with no previous knowledge of the language.

There is perhaps no greater need in any Aboriginal community than to keep the Aboriginal language strong. I believe that language is the soul of a people, and many Elders from a variety of First Nations traditions maintain that a nation that respects itself speaks, preserves, cultivates, and develops its language. Language is at the heart of Aboriginal identity, and language revitalization and preservation are among the most burning issues facing First Nations communities. Virtually everyone agrees that maintaining strong language viability, including the ability to read and write in the language, is essential to developing healthy communities and nations.

Aboriginal Languages and Racism Today

The guiding premise of this chapter is that the importance of revitalizing and preserving Aboriginal languages must be understood as more than something that merely feeds into an individual's or a community's sense of identity. Granted, being able to speak, read, and write in one's language *is* important to one's sense of identity as an Aboriginal person, and many First Nations Elders, scholars, and community people have spoken and written with great passion about the importance of language to one's identity as an Aboriginal person (Bunge 1987; Kirkness 1989; Johnston 1990; Leavitt 1992; Royal Commission on Aboriginal Peoples 1996). But some might ask: is it really that important for Aboriginal languages to remain strong in relation to the practicalities of everyday life? How is language preservation important to issues of community life such as economic development, land claims, band administration, resource development, health-care services, and social services? These are tough questions, but answers are possible if we attempt to approach the question as openly and honestly as possible of what linkages may or may not exist between language and community well-being. Such an approach, I believe, should also ensure that whatever future ideas and recommendations come out of language research be of practical benefit to First Nations communities.

Few would doubt that there continues to be a growing dependence on, and assimilation into, English and French in First Nations communities across Canada. It is also true that fewer and fewer First Nations people are mother-tongue speakers of their respective Aboriginal languages, as many mother-tongue speakers use English and French more and more as the language of home and community. In many communities, children are not learning the language un-less there is a grandparent, aunt, or uncle living in the house. Even then, many still do not learn to *speak* the language. They can understand it, but still respond only in English or French.

That said, according to noted Anishnaabe scholar Basil Johnston (1990), one generation can lose its language without seriously endangering its future. He makes this claim based on the fact that normal language transmission patterns flow from grandparents to grandchildren. However, his observation is offered as a warning: after two successive generations fail to produce a critical mass of mother-tongue speakers, the language will, for all practical purposes, be lost.

Community and individual commitment to the revitalization and preserva-tion of Aboriginal languages is quite strong and widespread, but often the com-mitment is symbolic rather than practical. Another complicating factor is that there are many common causes among First Nations, but English (or French) is the only shared language among diverse First Nations. Even when people speak or write with great passion about the need for language revitalization and preservation, most of the dialogue takes place in English (or French). Further, the interaction of First Nations people with what is commonly called mainstream Canadian society means that First Nations people must necessarily use English (or French) to speak with non-Aboriginal people.

The issue of maintaining Aboriginal languages in the face of extremely strong societal pressures (particularly the need for English or French) is one of the greatest dilemmas facing First Nations people today. Whether it is between Aboriginal persons, between communities, or between First Nations, the basis of understanding in the fullest, culturally specific sense is a question that touches a number of issues relevant to First Nations' concerns today, from treaty interpretation and renegotiation to Aboriginal education, land claims, cultural identity, and beyond. While great strides have been made in the past fifteen years by First Nations peoples striving to reclaim their linguistic identity and heritage — and while we acknowledge all that this implies in terms of distinct ways of thinking and doing things — the crux of the matter is that all negotiations, all dialogue, all arrangements, all agreements, and all misunderstandings are still grounded in English or French.

More often than not, the revitalization and maintenance of Aboriginal languages in Canada is almost an afterthought in the quest for self-determination and self-government. Research on Aboriginal language revitalization explores how it came to be an afterthought and examines whether communities feel that it needs to hold a more prominent place (Valentine 2001; Johnston 1990). The conditions that have supported linguistic hegemony in the past, such as contact with colonial societies in Canada, media penetration into communities, and change in traditional methods of language and culture transference in Aboriginal communities, have just begun to be recognized and are on the verge of being addressed. There is also a growing awareness of the state of Aboriginal languages in relation to the current conditions of language learning and literacy, and to the policies needed for serious change (Faries et al. 2002).

Aboriginal languages have a unique status in this land. They are the only languages originating here. Aboriginal languages contain knowledge and concepts no other language can express, and there is no other sanctuary from which they can be retrieved. When Aboriginal languages in Canada are lost, they are lost to the world and the knowledge and insights they contain are lost with them. What a statement the Greater City of Sudbury could make to the rest of Ontario, even to the rest of Canada, were it to pass a by-law recognizing the Ojibwe language as an official language in this region! True, it might be mere token recognition, but it would make a statement of respect for First Nations languages, and it would most certainly bring the issue to public awareness — a necessary first step if racism is to be seriously addressed in this city.

But I do not wish the discussion to sound like mere political rhetoric. In a 1994 conversation, a member of the James Bay Cree First Nation talked to me about a key concept in the liberation of language for his people. He told me:

> The next time we enter into treaty negotiations with the government, or if we ever renegotiate an existing treaty, we will insist that the treaty document be in the Cree language. Then *we* will be the ones in charge of the primary task of interpreting the contents of the treaty.

Here he presented a position that is integral to the whole concept of respecting Aboriginal languages. The issues of treaty language, language of instruction in educating Aboriginal youth, and the language of preference among First Nations peoples need to be brought to the forefront in the battle to dismantle racism and stereotyping in the Sudbury region.

The current focus on Aboriginal languages and all that linguistic liberation implies cannot be meaningfully discussed outside the context of those social, political, cultural, and spiritual forces that have made it both an issue demanding the attention of First Nations peoples in Canada and a problem to be resolved. Some Elders I have listened to say language revitalization and protection must be ensured before any significant progress can be made in the areas of land claims, self-determination, and the reclaiming of distinctively Aboriginal ways of life (Fox 1991).

Conclusion

When they do not understand the history and cultures of Aboriginal people, it is very easy for non-Aboriginal Canadians to become upset, to throw up their arms and ask, "What do these people want?" or "Why can't they just accept the fact that they live in Canada and be like us?" The result is often confusion, misunderstanding, and reinforced stereotypes, all of which feed into racism. Perhaps as important, we miss the fascinating adventure of discovering a different way of life and way of looking at the world. A whole new world can open up if one is willing to take the time to get to know Aboriginal people and ways of thinking and doing things.

It is not my purpose to paint a bleak picture of a racist or uncaring Sudbury: rather, it is to get us all, Aboriginal people and Canadians alike, thinking about our relationship and what practical steps can be taken to deal with racism — which will be necessary if we wish to achieve genuine reconciliation and healing. One key step is to recognize the value of Aboriginal languages — particularly, in the Sudbury region, Ojibwe — through official declarations by municipal, provincial, and federal governments, all agreeing on the importance of support for Aboriginal language education and cultural programs at all educational levels, and including sufficient funding for Aboriginal language research. Despite enormous difficulties, my point is that things are, indeed, beginning to happen with Aboriginal language renewal initiatives, although much more needs to be done if one is to take the task seriously.

As individuals and as groups, we can choose to make Sudbury a shining example of what it means to live in a culturally rich and respectful Canadian mosaic, not in some pie-in-the-sky distant future, but in our own lifetimes.

Note

1. The term Anishnaabe, originally limited to members of the Algonquian language family, has gained over the years a life of its own to the extent than even Aboriginal people outside the Algonquian language family self-identify as Anishnaabe. The Algonquian language family includes Ojibwe, Algonquin (as distinct from the Algonquian language family), Atikamekh, Odawa, among other linguistic groupings.

Excerpt from an Untitled Poem

(pour Marcel Aymar et Neil Young)

Patrice Desbiens

Treize heures d'autobus entre Hearst et Sudbury.
Je traverse le pays adoptif de mes ancêtres.
Je traverse le pays de l'amour secret.
Je traverse le pays du silence concret.
Chaque ville chaque village chaque visage imprimés
pour toujours dans les fenêtres teintées de cet
Americruiser.
Chaque arrêt marqué par des gangs de jeunes flânant
sous un ciel bleu comme leurs jeans.
Un ciel bleu comme leurs fantaisies.
Un ciel bleu-gris comme le chemin qui se déroule
sous cet autobus.
Cet autobus qui me met hors de moi-même en
m'amenant
plus près de moi-même.
Cet autobus qui me rapproche de mon peuple en le
laissant derrière lui.

From Patrice Desbiens, 2000, Sudbury (Textes 1981–1983), *Prise de Parole, Sudbury, used with permission.*

Chapter 10

French Ontario
Two Realities

Donald Dennie

In the thirty years I have been observing and analyzing Franco-Ontarian society, first as a journalist and then as an academic, I have been struck by the gulf that exists between the official discourse of governmental and political leaders and some underlying realities. This observation is borne out often in the daily political scene in Sudbury, and in Ontario. However, the situation I wish to analyze pertains to French Ontario. On one hand, it is difficult not to see the reality of social classes, of francophone workers: on the other hand, there is an official discourse about Ontario francophones that is at odds with this reality.

The majority of Franco-Ontarians are working class, preoccupied with the daily task of ensuring their survival. However, the official Franco-Ontarian discourse, as conveyed by academics and others, very seldom refers to social classes, and even less to a francophone working class. This discourse refers incessantly to the concept of "minority" to explain the Franco-Ontarian situation and its relationship to the anglophone majority. It goes without saying that, in this official discourse, the francophone minority is on a lower rung of the socioeconomic scale. But discussion of this relationship in terms of social classes is as a whole absent.

As I was preparing this chapter, there occurred two important events that serve to illustrate this argument. The first was the City of Greater Sudbury Council's refusal to hoist the Franco-Ontarian flag on the flagpole at Tom Davies Square in front of City Hall. The second was the memorial service, held every year at the local Mine Mill Hall, to commemorate workers killed at their place of work. The regional French-language media, be they print or electronic, devoted their headlines or lead stories to the first event, and spokespersons for l'Association canadienne-française de l'Ontario (ACFO) interpreted Council's decision as an insult to the regional francophone population. The same media, however, has largely ignored the second event, even though many of the deceased workers were francophones.[1]

In my perspective, these two realities are contradictory. The daily lives and deaths of ordinary working-class Franco-Ontarians are never mirrored in the official discourse by and about them. Rather, the official discourse is always dominated by a nationalist ideology defined and transmitted mostly by ACFO since its establishment in 1912 (then called l'Association d'éducation canadienne-française de l'Ontario). In the following pages I will attempt to summarize the principal elements of this nationalist discourse.

First, I wish to propose the following hypothesis: the gap between the reality of the francophone working class and the official discourse transmitted by the Franco-Ontarian elite has had — and still has — two consequences:

* a growing number of francophones do not identify themselves with the official discourse because it essentially does not reflect their daily lives;
* this lack of identification to the official discourse, which privileges notions of culture, language, education, and minority rights instead of realities related to the daily lives of workers, is partly responsible for the increasing assimilation rates of Ontario francophones.

This hypothesis does not relate solely to Franco-Ontarians of the Sudbury region, but also to those of other regions of Ontario. Circumstances may vary from one region to another, but the assumptions underlying the hypothesis are valid for French Ontario as a whole.

The structural problems that ACFO has attempted to address by renaming itself l'Assemblée de la francophonie de l'Ontario (AFO) are related, in my opinion, to the fact that a large majority of the francophone population does not recognize its legitimacy as their spokesperson. For the last thirty years, that legitimacy has rested on grants handed out by various levels of government, mostly federal.

Structure of Social Classes

In order to give a basis to my hypothesis, I wish to begin with an historical description of the Franco-Ontarian social class structure in the Sudbury region since European settlement. This history can be divided into two periods, from 1890 to 1950 and from 1950 to the present. The year 1950 marks a fundamental change that occurred in Franco-Ontarian society between two different modes of production. Until 1950, an independent small-scale mode of production was dominant in French Ontario. Starting around 1950, Ontario francophones were massively integrated into the capitalist mode of production (Dennie 2001).

When French Canadians (they were not called and did not call themselves "Franco-Ontarians" until the 1960s) emigrated to the Sudbury region following the construction of the Canadian Pacific Railway in the 1880s, most became either farmers or workers, depending on the availability of agricultural land or jobs. From 1890 to 1950, the main group of these French Canadians, emigrating mostly from the Ottawa region (in both Ontario and Québec), settled in the part of the region called the Valley, comprised of the following municipalities: Chelmsford, Azilda, Boninville, Blezard Valley, Val Caron, Val Thérèse, and Hanmer. There, they reproduced what can be called an independent small-scale mode of production. Francophones were in the majority in these municipalities from the end of the nineteenth century to the early 1960s.[2]

French Canadians established and occupied farms in order to survive. They would sell the surplus of their annual crops, when there was any, to the surrounding lumber camps — lumber was the dominant industry until the 1930s — and to residents of mining villages and Sudbury merchants. As the road network extended throughout the region, they would also sell products door to door. Many French Canadian males left their homes during the winter months to work in the lumber camps to earn the money necessary to feed their families and to buy the products needed for farming. Some also worked part-time in the region's mines. During this period, there was a lot of going back and forth between the farms and the mines: they would work in the mines for a month or so, go back to the farm, and then return to the mines six months later.

Besides the agricultural population in rural areas, another part of the French Canadian population lived in mining villages or in Sudbury (see Table 10.1), particularly in the Flour Mill (called Moulin-à-fleur). This urban francophone population was mostly working class. Many worked in the mines, others for the railway companies — particularly the Canadian Pacific and the Canadian

Table 10.1: Population of French Ethnic Origin, City and Region of Sudbury, 1901–2001

Year	Total population		Francophone population		Percent francophone	
	City of Sudbury	Region of Sudbury	City of Sudbury	Region of Sudbury	City of Sudbury	Region of Sudbury
1901	2,207		702		35	
1911	4,150		1,518		36	
1921	8,621		3,091		36	
1931	18,518		6,649		36	
1941	32,203		10,772		33	
1951	42,410		16,060		38	
1961	80,120	110,614	27,340		34	36
1971	90,520	155,465	28,935		32	37
1981	91,829	149,923	25,025		27	34
1991	92,884	157,613	21,365		23	29
2001	85,354	155,601		59,600		38

Note: Statistics Canada has adopted different methods over the various census years to define and therefore count French ethnic origins. This makes comparisons between years difficult. Starting in 1991, Statistics Canada has two definitions for ethnic origin: single origin (when respondents indicate only one ethnic origin) and multiple origin (when respondents indicate more than one, for example, French and British). The table must therefore be read by taking into account these varying definitions. In 1991, the census contains only single origin, whereas in 2001 it has the multiple origins category. This explains the apparent increase in the number of respondents of French ethnic origin in 2001 compared to 1991. Moreover, since the creation of the City of Greater Sudbury it is difficult to obtain data for the old City of Sudbury. The Region of Sudbury includes the City of Sudbury. *Source:* Census of Canada, 1901–2001.

National. Some were employed in the forest industry or were day labourers in small industries. Finally, some had jobs in the service sector: transport, retail, restaurants, and hotels.

I estimate that 90 percent of this francophone population was working class (Dennie 1986). The rest were part of the petite bourgeoisie, that is, merchants and business owners, lawyers and doctors, as well as members of religious communities.[3] The French Canadian elite came from this class. In the rural communities, as well, the elite was also composed of merchants and members of religious organizations.

In summary, from 1890 to 1950, the French Canadian social class structure was comprised of farmer-workers from the Valley, urban workers, and the petite bourgeoisie living mostly in the City of Sudbury.

The great majority of the overall population of the Sudbury region — which was mostly of British origin, but also included East Europeans — was also working class, with people employed in the mines, forestry, rail transport, retail, and the like. Some were farmers who had occupied land to the south and east of the city. The petite bourgeoisie, which controlled city and regional politics, was largely of British origin. There was also what could be called an haute bourgeoisie, which owned large forest companies and other related businesses. (Suffice it to mention the names of W. J. Bell, Ben Merwin, D. H. Haight, W. B. Plaunt, Frank Cochrane, William McVittie, and William Laforest.)

Starting in1950, this social class structure was transformed: most farmers, whether of French Canadian or other origin, left their farms to seek jobs in the mining industry. The land, which had been divided and sub-divided among the members of the pioneers' families, was no longer sufficient to support families. It had never been a very fertile land in any case and, to make matters worse, crops were continuously damaged by sulfur emanating from the mining operations (Dennie 2001). Mining employment became a way of ensuring a regular paycheque, as well as some security and stability. A large number of farmers' sons and daughters also obtained jobs in retail or other businesses, which were expanding in the city in the post-war period.

In the late 1920s, when mining companies considerably expanded their operations, some national firms such as Loblaws, Eatons, A&P, Dominion, Woolworths, and Kresge's opened stores in the city, thus creating employment for the local French Canadian population. The arrival of these national chain stores also created greater competition for local businesses, and led to many going out of business.

To summarize my analysis of the French Canadian social class structure since 1950: 80 percent of the population is in the working class; approximately 15 percent is in the petite bourgeoisie, and the rest is of the middle and upper bourgeoisie. The middle and upper bourgeoisie is mostly anglophone, but there are also a few francophones.

In terms of gender, the Sudbury region is not that different from other areas of Northern Ontario. Until 1950, women — be they of French Canadian or other origins — lived and worked mostly in the home doing housework and taking care of children and gardens. They started to obtain work outside the home during World War II, some in the mines but mostly in the service sector. In the 1960s, more and more women integrated into the workforce, mainly as workers in offices and stores. This integration parallels that of most Canadian and Ontario women (Cardinal *et* Coderre 1990; Guindon 1986).

Franco-Ontarian Nationalist Ideology

I will next analyze the Franco-Ontarian nationalist ideology, which has been articulated since the early 1960s. This ideology resembles in many of its essential elements the traditional French Canadian nationalist ideology as defined and transmitted, before the 1960s, by the clergy and the petite bourgeoisie.

On the basis of certain documents, mostly published in *Revue du Nouvel-Ontario*,[4] I consider that this ideology is made up of four elements: (i) the notion of a people (or community); (ii) notions of language, culture, and religion; (iii) education; and (iv) notions of rights and equality.

The principal element, the notion of a people, has always seemed to me to be very abstract. The typical Franco-Ontarian — usually a male until the 1980s — is a mythical being defined as being born in Ontario and whose mother tongue is French. His only interests are the French language, his Catholic religion, and his culture. Nothing more. He has never had material interests such as working, eating, or reproducing. I am obviously exaggerating, but not by much. Can francophones from other countries and continents, such as Africa, ever be considered Franco-Ontarians, since they were not born here? This has been a subject of debate for the last few years, given the influx of French-language immigrants to certain parts of Ontario. The fact that Franco-Ontarian culture was defined in terms of place of origin (French Canada) prohibited recognition of French speakers from different cultures.

It also took many years to recognize that women were members of the Franco-Ontarian community or people. The movement C'est l'temps had to force the issue in the late 1970s before women became accepted and recognized in the official discourse. Before the 1980s, the typical Franco-Ontarian was a *Franco-Ontarien* (male), then afterwards one added *Franco-Ontarienne* (female). This welcome change has led, thankfully, to more and more francophone women being recognized, in the last twenty years, as legitimate leaders of Franco-Ontarian organizations and associations. But the notion of the Franco-Ontarian community has always been homogeneous: it knows no internal differences. I am aware that political realities partly dictated this definition, but diversity within a people, such as social classes, needs to be recognized.[5]

The notions of language, religion, and culture are also essential categories in this ideology. In my view, these notions have led to the erection of barriers, to the exclusion of persons and groups of other origins, of other religions. What exactly is the Franco-Ontarian culture? It is never well-defined and is always static. Language refers to the one taught in school, the one that is obviously well-spoken and well-written. Consequently, dialects and *joual* are not accepted: they are even prohibited in the context of this ideology. This exclusion of dialects and *joual*, an exclusion of those who do not speak "correct" French, has resulted in the marginalization of a large majority of the Franco-Ontarian population and may even have contributed to assimilation. The fact that Franco-Ontarians' social and cultural experiences have been so controlled historically by the Catholic Church has led, I believe, to excluding persons and groups of other languages, cultures, and religions. It has also resulted in marginalizing French-speaking Ontarians who do not partake of the Church's beliefs and teachings.

The Franco-Ontarian educational system, based for most of the twentieth century on the teachings of the Catholic Church and on well-spoken French, has also been a dominant institution in the daily lives of Franco-Ontarians. In general, the education system has always transmitted a view of the world that privileges an elitist and hierarchical perception of society. This has meant that Franco-Ontarian education has minimized and marginalized more democratic, and even socialist, notions of social organization.

Lastly, let me focus briefly on the notions of rights and equality. According to the Franco-Ontarian nationalist ideology, the Franco-Ontarian, or French Canadian, people has rights, due to its being one of the two founding peoples of Canadian society. These rights are mainly those relating to the preservation of its language and culture, and in the recognition of French as equal to English in most Canadian institutions.

I have no qualms about this last element, because it represents the aspirations of many other ethno-cultural groups in Canada and elsewhere. However, I do find it frustrating that the nationalist ideology does not lead to the recognition of the realties of social classes and of diversity in the daily lives of Franco-Ontarians. By focussing on homogeneity, the nationalist ideology often inhibits discussion of differences and other more general concerns, such as gender equality.

The time has probably come to bury ACFO because it has not been able to modify its discourse and actions for the last ninety years. Deprived of a base of popular support that gave it legitimacy for several decades, since the late 1960s it has been on life support, beholden to both federal and provincial funding. Its status as a client of the state inhibits its actions and its functions as critic. The fact is that it has lost any legitimacy in the eyes of most Franco-Ontarians.

In my opinion, it is time (*c'est l'temps*) to create citizens' committees in order to attempt to organize Franco-Ontarians around their daily perceptions and preoccupations. Based on the principle of direct democracy, these committees could reflect the diversity of Franco-Ontarian needs and voices. They could develop strategies and modes of thinking that are more progressive, that are freed from the inhibitions of the nationalist ideology embraced by ACFO.[6]

Conclusion

The gap between, on the one hand, the realities of social classes in Franco-Ontarian society and, on the other, the official discourse of this society as a homogeneous entity, means that the vast majority of francophones are unable to identify themselves with either this discourse or with their own origins. Moreover, francophones who wish to develop a progressive political program are forced to do it elsewhere, either in unions or social movements, which are excluded from the official Franco-Ontarian discourse. This exclusion of more progressive voices and actors from the Franco-Ontarian community has been a fact of daily life for many francophones, such as the telling example of those involved in Mine Mill in the 1950s and 1960s who had to suffer the wraths of the Catholic Church and the French Canadian elite. Many francophone union militants and leaders were in fact stigmatized in their own linguistic community as communists and radicals.

The establishment of citizens' committees could, in my opinion, bring a new life, new voices and actions that could benefit the francophone population in its aspirations for better equality and rights in Canadian society.

Notes

Une copie du manuscrit dans son français original est disponible en contactant l'auteur à <ddennie@laurentienne.ca>.

1. These two events occurred in the spring of 2003, again in 2004, and continue to date.
2. In 1991, 40.2 percent of francophones in the Sudbury region lived in the Valley. In general, they tended to live in the north and northeast sections of the city and region. See Martin-Guillerm (1991).
3. I have included the last group in this class, as it is very difficult to classify them more precisely.
4. The *Revue du Nouvel-Ontario* has been published since 1978 by the Institut franco-ontarien, the first research institute established at Laurentian University.
5. See the manifesto, "Se prendre en main," in the *Revue du Nouvel-Ontario*, No. 3, 1981, 110–12.
6. Since the writing of this article, ACFO has in effect been declared dead and buried. It has been resuscitated in another form, l'Assemblée de la francophonie de l'Ontario, which, one hopes, will recognize the diversity of opinions and actions found in today's Franco-Ontarian society. I doubt, however, that it will have any more legitimacy, as it still is more a client of the state than a representative of francophone society.

Chapter 11

Traditional Elites and the Democratic Deficit

Some Challenges for Education in French-Speaking Ontario

François Boudreau
Translated by Kate Leadbeater

The objective of this chapter is to analyze certain elements of the school system in French-speaking Ontario. Based on my limited experience as a school trustee,[1] I underline a number of problems tied to the elected representatives on the school board, to the management of the school system, and to the manner of addressing these problems. The chapter also allows me to reflect on how these problems have consequences for the education of our children and for the cultural identity of French-speaking Ontario. The central idea of the chapter can be expressed in the following hypothesis: the dominant ideology motivating elites serving at various school boards does not seem to have allowed the Franco-Ontarian school system to attain its full potential, which its presumed adherence to modernity was supposed to have achieved. The dominant ideological influence in Franco-Ontarian education is at once paradoxical and contradictory. Traditional ideas remain ever-present and take many forms.

I argue that the secularization of some education in French-speaking Ontario did not allow the development of modern French education institutions: the education system is not completely traditional, but neither is it completely modern. We could contrast the situation of education with that of Franco-Ontarian culture.[2] One can say that Franco-Ontarian culture[2] has attained, with and since Coopérative des artistes du Nouvel Ontario (CANO, the Cooperative of Artists of New Ontario)[3] and the accomplishments of 1970s counterculture,[4] a level of modernity through a rupture with tradition. Franco-Ontarian culture thus emancipated itself from traditional reference schemas and traditional reflexes. By incorporating as legitimate elements all the currents of thought and social movements proper to modernity (working class, socialist, progressive, nationalist, identity-based, feminist, ecological) into its "cultural industry," Franco-Ontarian culture assumed its modern form. It is this break with tradition that the Franco-Ontarian education system has not yet made.

The Franco-Ontarian education system is not completely or blindly more traditional than school systems elsewhere. Ontario education as a whole adheres, in fact, to ideas of modernity. But the system is not fully modern because the ideas to which it adheres are not those of modern rationality but those of a rationality that is instrumental, technical, and economist. In this way, the dominant ideology mixes postmodern ideas with traditional ideas and ways, somewhat as if the old ways of thought lived in new clothes, but cut from old cloth. In the final analysis, elected school board representatives remain ill-equipped to respond to the contemporary challenges posed by the reproduction of Franco-Ontarian culture in a minority context.

Definitions

In defining our principal concepts, it is necessary to distinguish "modernity," which is a type of society aware of its break with tradition, from "modern times," which refers to an historical period that extends from the fifteenth to the twentieth century. Modernity is a societal way of being founded on the idea of reason, and is in opposition to all other ideological groundings. French-speaking Ontario has long existed in "modern times," but all its institutions are not completely in "modernity."

Traditional society, of course, is one characterized by the omnipotence of tradition. Within it, dominance and law are arbitrary, while the division of labour is strict and social mobility is limited. Generally, traditional society is characterized by the absence of strict boundaries between church and state, because society's ideological grounding situates transcendence in a divine figure external to humans and human will. By extension, a traditional mentality would find it difficult to understand the borders between rational reflection and a reflection where habit dictates decisions. More often than not, a traditional mentality will use as pretext the notion of forces that are external to it — God, fate, fashion — to justify this or that action or to explain inaction.

Modern society understands itself in opposition to traditional society, from which it was emancipated by revolution (the French Revolution, for example) or by radical break (the Quiet Revolution in Québec). Modern society seeks a social order founded not on arbitrariness or on the vagaries of domination, but on a universal norm: reason. On this basis, modern society attempts to view itself as the result of its own production by its political institutions. To arrive at this it proceeds by a strict separation between the business of the beyond, taken up by the churches and relegated to the private sphere, and the business of the here below, taken up by the state and constituting the public sphere. Modern society develops on a territorial base, in the nation-state, and functions on the basis of the sovereignty of individuals, individuals who on the basis of their free will exercise a capacity for political intervention as citizens. It is the citizen who, by his or her political action, acts in order to shape his or her world. Individualism is the basis of modern society.

"Postmodernity" refers to the strong trend of development in contemporary Western society. The prefix "post" in front of the concept "modern" is used to underline what is no longer, that which comes afterwards. Thus, to speak of Western society as being a postmodern society simply means that Western society tends no longer to be modern. Postmodern society is characterized by the devolution or the dissolution of the political sphere to the benefit of the system of production and world markets. This also means the loss of sovereignty of citizens. Technology, technologism (the belief in the omnipotence of technology), and technocratism (the management of society according to "techniques" of management) are the key concepts of a postmodern society.[5] So is the relativism of values, which tends to multiply indefinitely.

The two concepts of the title, "traditional elites" and "democratic deficit," are used to shed light on the situation of French-speaking Ontario, which mixes at the same time traditional and postmodern elements. Still dominated by the Church, Franco-Ontarian culture is nonetheless woven into the capitalist development of Western society where the dominance of finance capital has been established for more than a century. Northern Ontario, because of its mining and forestry industries, is tangled in the web of globalization. The influences of the two ways of being of Northern Ontario society created some distinctive features that make possible the intermingling of a traditional way of doing things together with an instrumentalist ideology dominated by a belief in the omnipotence of technology and scientific knowledge.

The expression "democratic deficit" comes from Europe in the 1990s, when elections there were marked by a significant level of abstention. Commentators began to call this widespread abstention the "democratic deficit," postulating that electoral absenteeism was tied to the loss of individual sovereignty. It was as though the citizens of Europe were asking themselves: "Why go out of my way to elect a parliament that has only limited power, when the real power rests with the big economic units?" Thus, the concept is linked to the will to come closer to the power of citizens. More and more, the proponents of free markets who want to maintain citizen participation in the affairs of the state use the concept. It was taken up again in Canada by former Finance Minister Paul Martin, as part of his campaign for the leadership of the Liberal Party of Canada.

But this concept presents a problem. It is as though democracy was measuring itself with "pluses" and "minuses" in an attempt to attain an equation that would reflect "more or less" an abstract norm of what would truly be a democracy. It is as though there were a balance to attain in terms of some democratic ideal. It is impossible to measure the state of democracy in such terms. We cannot conceive the difficulties experienced by the leaderships of school boards in terms of "deficits." Neither is it possible to speak of deficits to characterize what elected trustees do not understand, nor can one conceive in these terms the needs felt by parents. The opposite of a democratic deficit is not a democratic surplus. Democracy is not subject to the laws of supply and demand, nor to accounting operations. It is thus with derision and as euphemism that I use this concept, in order to draw attention to the whole illusion it hides.

Common use reserves the expression "traditional elites" to refer to what is best in the social ensemble. In the Middle Ages, the elite was defined as a political class with so-called "superior" qualities, in the sense of a capacity to lead, to occupy managerial positions within institutions. In fact, one part of the elite was made up of "lettered" persons, of those who enjoyed an education, in order to learn how society functions and in order thus to be able to participate in its reproduction. Like the military and the aristocracy, this group worked to protect and preserve the *status quo*. From a sociological standpoint, the concept of "elite" normally refers to the status of an individual in his or her community. The concept of elite relates directly to the status, or to the position of influence, of an individual within the cultural group to which he or she belongs. Generally speaking, an individual possesses elite status when he or she comes to embody the ensemble of norms, prescriptions, and obligations of the culture. The elite status of an individual is generally recognized by established elite groups when the individual active within the community personifies the archetype of contemporary values of the culture to which they belong. In his work, C. Wright Mills (1959) posed the question of whether the existence of an elite was compatible with democracy. This certainly remains a pertinent question.

In the context of this chapter, discussion of an elite aims explicitly to characterize a group that corresponds to traditional ways of doing, thinking, and acting. The education context of Northern Ontario is not one, to use a Marxist concept, where a bourgeoisie and proletariat directly confront each other on the ideological playing field of school boards. If transnational corporations exert some influence, it generally takes the form of pressures exerted on the state, not directly on school boards or trustees. These pressures are generally in the form of calls for reductions in taxes and decreases in salaries and environmental and sanitary regulations, but they appear not to be expressed directly in regard to education. In this way, the influence of capitalism on the education milieu of Northern Ontario is more about the form of contracts, particularly around the provision of food and soft drinks, between various school boards and various corporations.[6]

The general situation in Northern Ontario is one where the Church and traditional culture are in opposition to secularity and modern culture. It is within this framework that one can speak of traditional elites, keeping in mind the role of religious institutions and ideology, but not losing sight of the fact that traditional elites are not exclusively religious personnel.[7] The problem of the quality of political personnel relates to the capacity to manage, in an efficient and enlightened way, an organization as complicated as a school board. Given all the information required to do so and the complexity of the task itself, recruitment of qualified personnel is difficult. The world has changed significantly in the last fifteen, twenty, or thirty years, at a speed such that even the "experts" in the field of education are hard-pressed to keep up with the pace of change and, especially, to understand the meaning of these changes.[8] The problem of the democratic deficit, interlocked with the quality of political personnel, is equally rooted in the concept one has of Canadian democracy and its constitutional foundations, of rights in general, and of rights specific to education related to separate schools, as specified in Article 93 of the Constitution Act of 1867.[9]

A Little History and Context

The Conseil scolaire public du Grand Nord de l'Ontario (CSPGNO) is the product of education reform in Ontario which, with the adoption of Bill 104 in 1997, Loi reduisant le nombre de conseils scolaires (Fewer School Boards Act 1997), reorganized the number, distribution, and funding source for the different school boards of the province. The law, which took effect in January 1998, reduced the number of school boards from 129 to 72 by calling certain school boards "districts." Until 2004, the CSPGNO was called the Conseil scolaire de district du Grand Nord de l'Ontario. Today there are twelve francophone school boards within Ontario: four public boards and eight separate (Catholic) boards.

The CSPGNO covers an immense territory extending more than 65,000 square kilometres, from Noëlville in the south, running to Markstay, Sudbury, Hanmer, Azilda, and Chelmsford to the north, and to Elliot Lake, Wawa, Marathon, Manitouwadge, and Longlac in the northwest of the province. The Commission de l'amélioration de l'éducation (Education Improvement Commission) responsible for implementing the 1997 reform also gave to the new board of the district — known as le Grand Nord de l'Ontario (the Great North of Ontario) — responsibility for francophones belonging to French-language sections of existing public boards in Beardmore, Geraldton, Longlac, Chapleau, Espanola, Lake Superior, Michipicoten, Rive-Nord, and Sudbury, as well as for the Comité consultatif de langue française of the Sault Ste. Marie board. In fact, the potential responsibility of the CSPGNO extends all the way to the Manitoba border: the board's territory thus could cover as many as 550,000 square kilometres.

All in all, the CSPGNO was responsible in 2004–05 for ten primary schools and nine secondary schools, with a total of 2,553 students. The total budget of the CSPGNO was $38 million, of which more than $27 million was spent directly in classrooms, for an average of $10,576 per student per year. If one compares these figures with those of the Conseil scolaire catholique du Nouvel-Ontario, the Catholic school board for the same area, the latter was responsible for the education of 7,513 students distributed across twenty-six elementary and ten secondary schools. The total budget of the Catholic board was about $90 million, of which $61 million was spent directly in the classroom, which works out to $8,119 annually per student.

Without revisiting the history of education in Canada and going over all past decisions of the Supreme Court of Canada, perhaps one can reflect on the idea that the current interpretation of the right to religious education no longer responds to the reality of Canadian society, and that the defence and affirmation of that right, particularly in a minority context, in fact harms the quality of education. In this particular case, one notes that both school boards combined have a budget of nearly $128 million, of which $88 million is spent directly in the classroom, while $6.5 million is devoted to administration. Without being simplistic — and considering that $44 million is spent on transportation, the heating and upkeep of buildings, and the purchase of educational materials —

the presence of two school boards leads to the doubling of tasks and personnel. Though democracy, as previously mentioned, is not simply a matter of numbers, it seems clear from an education perspective that such a small number of students does not justify the existence of two school boards.

It seems to me that the religious dimension alone provided by "religious education" does not in itself justify the creation and funding of two autonomous school boards. Setting aside the religious and moral education provided by these boards, the teaching of mathematics, French, geography, and history has very little to do with religious belief. The maintenance of Catholic administrative autonomy, besides fulfilling "historically acquired rights," leads to the maintenance of a traditional elite and, perhaps more importantly, to the maintenance of a way of doing, seeing, and understanding that is no longer capable of responding to the contemporary, modern challenges faced by education. This is particularly evident with respect to scientific education and to the values of tolerance in ethical development — as opposed to religious morality — that corresponds to the needs of contemporary Canadian society.

Not only are there two francophone school boards for the same area but also two anglophone school boards. The Constitutional Act of 1867 guarantees religious education for Ontario Catholics, of which a significant portion is French-speaking, and for Québec Protestants, who are mostly anglophone.[10] Thus, instead of having two school boards — one providing for francophones and one for anglophones — offering courses of religious education for religious students and courses of moral education for others, there are four school boards in the region of Sudbury alone. This arrangement does not seem best suited to assure the quality of education offered to students.

Perhaps it is time to reflect on education in a way other than that envisaged by the Constitution Act of 1867 and its subsequent interpretation by the courts. It seems possible to envisage the right to religious education as meaning something other than the autonomous administration of Catholic school boards. Let us remember that the purpose of modern education is rational ontology, that is to say the possibility of a true knowledge of the world, as opposed to a traditional vision of the world. Education strives for a scientific and rational conception of the world, conceived as a product of evolution, as opposed to a religious conception of the world, conceived as divine creation. The teaching of religious beliefs as an element of the curriculum in a rational academic course might be a desirable option for those who want it. But the legitimacy of a religious belief system must not imply, as a right, that education springs from a religious conception of the world.

This religious way of understanding the world does not seem to respond to the needs of a modern society, one that is growing more and more complex. Offering a separate Catholic system of education parallel to the public system necessarily requires the coexistence of two opposing world views in the same population, and, naturally, other religious denominations would like to have similar privileges, thus maximizing the potential for conflicts between different conceptions of the same world, particularly regarding relations between church and state. One need only recall the context of Canadian immigration since 1967,[11] as the country has become increasingly made up of more and more followers of diverse world religions. As shown in a recent controversy in France, as the wearing of veils and other religious symbols has increased, the very nature of democracy and the separation of church and state become issues. Modern society assumes the separation of the public and private spheres and, within this model of political organization, religion has long been relegated to the private sphere. Why not, then, respect this imperative in our quest for an open, democratic, modern society?

More troubling still, in my opinion, is the fact that the majority of francophones receive a Catholic education, but among the rest of Ontario's population Catholic education is relatively marginal. This has the effect of maintaining the stereotyped identification of francophone Ontarians with Catholicism. A last argument, no less troubling, is that an important portion of students of the Catholic school system finishes by no longer believing in or practising their religion. These individuals have not necessarily acquired the intellectual tools necessary to evolve within a religious "vacuum."[12] This contributes to a crisis of culture that comes about as individuals, having rejected their education and religious practice, must construct for themselves their presence in the world, without enjoying the philosophical foundations they might have otherwise acquired with a secular education. The crisis is deepened by artificially maintaining an elite that is gradually losing its social position. All these are important manifestations of a "democratic deficit."

Traditional Elites and School Boards

After three years as a school board trustee, it became apparent to me that the question of who gravitates around school boards is an important issue. It seems that an individual who has acquired the essentials of his or her political experience in the "militantly traditional" environments of Franco-Ontarian culture (Catholic youth, les Chevaliers de Colomb, les Richelieu, churchwardens, les Filles d'Isabelle, parish recreation) is capable of holding a seat on a school board. But it is questionable whether an individual who is the product of such militantly traditional milieus would be able spontaneously to adopt political positions that reflect the best interests of the citizens they represent, rather than the more narrow interests — whether local or regional — of the fraternities with which they have identified for as long as they can remember. My own experience indicates that the political reflexes of numerous trustees are traditional and conservative, conforming to the traditional practice of Franco-Ontarian history. These reflexes have been long conditioned by the approval of traditional institutions that have, supposedly, always been able to easily distinguish between "good" and "evil."

And here arises a problem: elected members of school boards are often local personalities who are recognized and approved, as much formally as informally, by the fraternity of personalities active in traditional groups and social clubs, as well as within the Catholic Church. Decisions are therefore spontaneously made with the intent of not making waves regarding traditional interests, rather than with having as a priority the modernization of the culture by making education respond to the challenges of contemporary society. A modern culture insists on the development of critical thought, on the autonomy of the individual, and on a rational conception of the world. In fact, most trustees try to grasp all situations from a "modern" perspective, but are often unable to articulate concretely these situations within a modern framework. For many school trustees, understanding the changes required of the system, knowing how to remain critical in the face of those changes, and being aware of how to judge for themselves the meaning and limits of this change — together constitute a fantastic challenge. As such, decisions made by elected school board representatives are not always made in an enlightened manner or in the best interests of the francophone majority. Too often, decisions are made with tradition itself as the main consideration — "This is how we've always done it" — without asking, "Is this a good way to do things, in the current context, even if it is customary?" Without knowing properly how to address the problem, trustees content themselves by following the local tradition, the way traced out by "local experts."

Further, decisions are too often heavily influenced by professional administrators, even if their recommendations seemed questionable: "If they say it's good for the school board, it must be good." It is as if administrators were infallible and it were impossible that their personal interests could diverge from those of the institution. More fundamentally, in these situations it is by reflex that school trustees acquiesce to the will of administrators, because they are not in the habit of questioning authority figures (even if, in the relationship of trustee to administrator, it is technically the trustee who is "boss"). Trustees are not in the habit of thinking for themselves when an authority says what must be. This attitude is traditional and tends to highlight the fact that the "modern revolution" and its catchphrase "use your own head" are not yet dominant in francophone Ontario.

There are numerous examples of this that suggest that the interests that guide school trustees are products of personal relationships woven over the course of years and rooted in a system of beliefs and attitudes that are a microcosm of a larger context of exclusivity and obedience. Unfortunately, this "larger context" does not constitute the whole of society, but rather the social guarantor or overseer that is the Catholic Church, with its profound cultural influences. It is as if there was always a God above who took care of the well-being of secular school boards! This general attitude often resembles what one would see at a social club, where one is more concerned with convenience and appearance, than what one might observe at an institution that puts children at the centre of decisions. Four examples will illustrate this point.

Concrete Problems

The November 2000 election saw the defeat of four of twelve school trustees. A week after the ballot, the pre-election council, at its last regular meeting, sought to renew the contracts of its two senior administrators and extend their contracts for seven years. The four new trustees, elected on a "progressive" political platform, were eager to denounce this gesture, insisting that, though not illegal, the gesture appeared immoral and illegitimate. The argument was that it was not the place of an outgoing elected group at its last regular meeting to bind the hands of an incoming elected group, especially if that meeting is held after an election at which a third of the outgoing trustees were defeated.

Later we learned that the extensions *in extremis* of the contracts of the two administrators were allowed "because the administrators were fearful of seeing themselves turned down by the new school trustees, whose opinions were not known," and also because the departing trustees wanted to reward the administrators they "have known for a long time" and "because they were doing good work." Once again, this type of behaviour, even if it is, strictly speaking, legal, is not moral and has the appearance of an anti-democratic clique. This game, which consists of rewarding friends before leaving their elected posts, represents what is most reprehensible in politics. Fundamentally, it is a type of traditional gesture that modern persons denounce, and that no longer has a place in our society, if it ever did.

A second example puts into context the attitude the CSPGNO adopted toward the anglophone majority. In order to reduce the staggering costs of school transportation for students, the four school boards in the Sudbury region decided to form a transportation consortium whereby the available resources would be pooled. Anglophones and francophones organized a single system of transportation for all students, without regard to language. The two French-language boards (Catholic and public) agreed "because of numbers" not to insist on policies and guidelines with respect to language and to leave the basic direction of the consortium in the hands of the much larger English-language boards.

Thus, "because of the numbers,"[13] it is decided to form a consortium that is responsible for school transportation for all students in the region, without regard to the language they speak. We know that school buses are hotbeds of assimilation: francophone children, who are ordinarily intimidated by the much larger number of anglophone children, gradually lose confidence in their language and culture and quickly learn to become invisible or, more accurately, inaudible, first in the school bus and later in the crowd, as a way not to attract the stigma of belonging to the francophone minority. The "Cherryfication" of the "French guys"[14] has long been at work in the North!

Intimidation is a serious problem in the seats of school buses, and it threatens the cultural affirmation of vulnerable children. But the financial "bottom line" requires the controlling of costs, even when it is to the detriment of the Franco-Ontarian identity. If the issue were only a linguistic one, it would be a scandal. But there is another, more important issue: the security of children in emergency situations. Minority school trustees have long insisted that in an emergency situation, whether an accident or illness, the adult responsible for the school bus had to be capable of communicating with the child in question using the child's language. Minority trustees have argued that the people who drive francophone children in the primary schools of French-language school boards (it is understood that all Franco-Ontarians at the secondary level speak English) must have the linguistic capacity necessary to do so in safety.

At each of the numerous votes on this issue, the motion that aimed to require that bus drivers transporting francophone children to schools of the francophone boards be bilingual was defeated, and always by the same number, always for the same reasons: "Because of the numbers." "We are in the minority." "We mustn't demand too much." "It's too complicated to organize" "It is not in the priorities of the consortium." "There aren't enough francophone or bilingual drivers." In short, the board bowed its head, compromised safety, compromised culture, abdicated to the majority, and justified it all by the high cost of school transportation and by our minority status, even though the rate of assimilation nears 60 percent. The problem is also a political one: we are afraid to express our needs in the face of a majority that has a tradition of intolerance and exclusion toward us. Lastly, the problem is economic: operating costs and not school policies dictate the path to follow in terms of school transportation.

A third example of this traditional attitude in the face of education challenges involves standardized tests administered to students at the third- and sixth-grade levels by l'Office de la qualité et de la responsibilité in éducation (Education Quality and Accountability Office). CSPGNO students do relatively well in these tests: they are among the best groups in the province in mathematics, and a little above the average in reading and writing French. Students of the public system generally do even better than the students of the Catholic board. All the same, the results demonstrate that nearly two-thirds of students do not attain the level of competency required by the Ontario Ministry of Education. Might this be because the standard set by the Ministry is too high? Perhaps. But, according to progressive trustees, who are in a minority position, it seemed evident that instead of mutually congratulating themselves on the ranking of the board's students, it was necessary to have a discussion as to why nearly two-thirds of students did not meet the Ministry's standards. To insist on debating the issue, to insist on searching for reasons to explain the poor test results and perhaps to point to some solutions — this, according to the majority, was equivalent to calling into question the quality of teachers' work. Thus, the debate was closed before it even started: "Our results are good, higher than the provincial average, and to discuss the issue would amount to denigrating our personnel." End of discussion. A vote was held and the result was the same: The discussion would not take place.

In this debate on the quality of the French language of students in francophone schools, we did not even have time to come back to the fact that some school "cultural" activities involved visiting fast-food businesses. These were justified because "the owner is francophone." Perhaps this does not constitute the best type of cultural activity to support the awakening of our students to the validity, legitimacy, and dynamism of our language and culture. Why not more French theatre, shows, and films in our schools? Why not more books in French in the libraries of our schools? Why not more visits to regions with higher concentrations of francophones? Why not a broader reflection on ways to assure quality education in French in a minority context? All these questions are generally rejected backhandedly with cavalier insinuations that it was simply a veiled attempt to criticize teaching personnel.

A fourth question that seems to pose a problem is territorial representation within the board. In the case of the CSPGNO, twelve school board trustees represent 2,553 students (one for every 213 students). Six trustees represent 2,160 students in Greater Sudbury (one for every 360 students), whereas six trustees represent 395 students in Greater Sudbury's surrounding areas (one for every 66 students). In fact, these last six trustees represent a fifth of the board's students, but they have as much political weight as the six trustees representing the much more numerous students from the large urban centre of Sudbury. Practice has shown numerous times that trustees from Sudbury can easily be put in a minority position, even when the question at issue is one particular to them, such as transportation of students within a densely populated area or the board's meeting places.

There are even, in fact, school trustees who do not represent a single student or a single parent, trustees who don't have a school in their designated territory, who are able with impunity to take positions for and against trustees who represent thousands of students and parents. It is as though these trustees were representing spruce needles, with the right to veto. This poses the question of unbalanced representation between rural and urban communities, and also poses the question of the relationship of new elites to traditional ones.

These four examples are presented to underline how school trustees do not act to find the best ways forward with progressive school policies, to find policies that favour the advancement of a quality education for our children in a francophone school system in a minority context. On the contrary, they show that other considerations dictate how problems that face French-language education are addressed. "Don't rock the boat" is the subtext written everywhere. Join Richelieu clubs and participate in Church activities and live your French culture in private. Do not even try to have the legitimacy of your culture publicly recognized. This important problem is tied to what can be characterized as the "democratic deficit."

Democratic Deficit

As I have underlined above, the concept of democratic deficit is not particularly appropriate to a discussion of the weaknesses of democracy in an education context. Still, I will use it here in speaking about broad problems afflicting education in French-speaking Ontario. I want to emphasize the possibility of democratic administration of a school board, the possibility of school trustees taking decisions knowledgeably, basing their decisions on the real needs of the community and taking into account all pertinent information. This would mean that school trustees would have to be capable of handling and mastering the complex sets of information presented to them, always keeping in mind the goal of assuring quality education in French-speaking Ontario.

A school board is a complex organization requiring a broad range of specialized competencies. Democratic fractures can be numerous, and can involve a continuum of attitudes that range from "the person in charge knows what they are doing, so I'll ask two trivial questions for form, and then support the proposed decision" to "the person responsible does not know what they are doing so, no matter what responses I get to my questions, I will never support the proposed decision."

Let's take the example of finances to illustrate this point: apart from the fact that my competency in mathematics allows me to verify that the amounts indicated in lines 1 to 25 add up to $25 million and that the subtraction of lines 26 to 49 brings the total back to zero, what am I able to understand about the school board's budget? How am I able to verify the travel expenses of a one senior administrator or determine that the credit card of another is not being used to obscure purchases for personal use? How can I evaluate whether the frequency of travel corresponds to legitimate work demands and to the needs of regions visited? How can I assure myself that an administrator's planned trip to the far ends of the region does not in reality hide a hunting or fishing trip paid for by tax dollars? And if I was questioning whether certain business expenses were in fact for a fishing trip, and if I suspected that it "had always been done this way" under the cover of "visiting the regions," is there always a democratic deficit?

Apart from my competence as a parent or grandparent and that I have a number of anecdotes to recount on the nice stories my children or grandchildren bring home from primary school, what do I know of the special education student? Do these children need Ritalin, or would it be preferable to transfer them to a "boot camp"? Are these the only two possible solutions? What are my medical qualifications to decide about the usage of Ritalin within my school board? What are my sociological competencies to evaluate whether or not our children are being over-medicated? Are my ideas and opinions on this issue sufficiently informed (Lagacé et Lamarre 2001)? What are my values on how to educate children? When it comes to pedagogy, am I really in a position to understand the serious delay in educational development of boys compared to girls?[15] Am I really able to question the local specialist who asserts that the gap results simply from the fact that "little girls are more serious than little boys"? Am I genuinely able to evaluate the real impact and the relevance of feminist-oriented pedagogical concepts on the education of boys? And what does a feminist pedagogy mean to me? What is my competence to understand what really constitutes a cultural crisis? Do schools aim primarily to prepare students for the "labour market" or do they, rather, educate citizens (Duquet et Audet 1998)? And if I myself have only a minimal education, or if I work in a degrading environment where I have no responsibilities, or if I am too tired to read the hundreds of pages of documents necessary to prepare for the monthly board meeting, am I truly in a position to make important decisions on an administrator's contract? On school transportation? On educational competencies? And if my competencies flow from the fact that I taught "in the system" for twenty years twenty years ago, am I still competent to understand the challenges of education in today's society? How can I understand education in society if I don't understand society?[16]

Conclusion

Some serious reflection is needed on the migration of economic concepts into the education field, and on the fact that the system is now supposed to respond to children (or to citizens) in the same way a business responds to customers, something which, in my opinion, obscures even the possibility of any deep reflection on the type of education a democratic society demands.[17] It is as though the institution of education were aiming not to educate citizens but rather create consumers who pay taxes and who abhor any deficit, either economic or democratic. But at the end of the day it is not the democratic deficit that one must speak about but rather of "anti-democraticism," because the democratic deficit is a euphemism that camouflages the real problem: the immense difficulty of acting in an enlightened and effective way *within* our institutions in working toward the goal of educating French-speaking citizens who will be proud of their language and their culture.

We have to stimulate the development of a debate on the ideological and political conditions of democracy, conditions that make possible — or make impossible — the real exercise of citizen control over one of the central institutions of Western modernity, namely the education system. The quality of political representation involved in the administration of school boards is one problem: another is the concept that one has of democracy as it relates to education. These two questions constitute the bases of the democratic deficit. In fact, they are probably more closely linked to determining the quality of education in Ontario and to determining the quality of Franco-Ontarian culture than is obvious at first glance. There are very major challenges that arise as a society opens up and traditional mindsets are questioned, especially where the Catholic Church remains the guarantor of the language, of the culture, of "maintaining the numbers" through marriage within "the community" to the exclusion of broader alliances. I believe these questions merit much greater reflection than they have had to date. It does not seem to me that the importance of these questions is understood, nor is the threat they pose to Franco-Ontarian culture.

If we start by gathering all the information required for a school system to properly do its work, if we take into account the range of means approved by the state, and if we assess the quality of elected personnel available to accomplish the task, it appears that, all things said, "the system works." In fact, it does: there are school board trustees who oversee the millions spent by school boards, there are schools that welcome children and adolescents, there are students who study and graduate, there are teachers who teach, there are principals who administer the application of education policies, and so on. But toward what outcomes are we headed by continuing to do "as we have before" in a society that is changing so rapidly it bewilders even the experts?

Notes

Une copie du manuscrit dans son français original est disponible en contactant l'auteur à <fboudreau@laurentienne.ca>. Many thanks to Dieter K. Buse for editorial comments.

1. As background, my experience as a school board trustee was between December 2000 and December 2003 with the Conseil scolaire public du Grand Nord de l'Ontario, known prior to 2005 as the Conseil scolaire de district du Grand Nord de l'Ontario. I was elected, along with three other trustees, on what was intended to be a progressive platform. For the length of our mandate, we four trustees came up against a relatively homogenous bloc of eight trustees, six of whom who were elected to represent taxpayers outside Sudbury, and two others from Sudbury. Overall, in important votes taken over the three years the result was constant: always the same eight against the same four. The two groups, clearly marked by their political perspectives, clashed continuously.

2. Here we speak of culture in the narrower sense of "cultural production" (music, theatre, literature, etc.) not in the broader sense of the accumulation of historical experiences that make culture the "instructions of society."

3. To this collective of young Franco-Ontarian artists, based in Sudbury, one can attribute the modernization and the dynamization of Franco-Ontarian culture. From this group were born several important Franco-Ontarian institutions, including the publishing house Prise de Parole, the Théâtre du Nouvel Ontario, the Galerie du Nouvel Ontario and the festival La Nuit sur l'étang.

4. By "counterculture" I mean the movement for a radical break with traditional culture, a movement that took effect in the entire West. Its manifestation in Northern Ontario happened a little later than in most other places.

5. For a deeper discussion of these themes see, in particular, Freitag 1986 and Freitag 2002.

6. The paradox here is that the boards are obliged to accept these money-making contracts because their budgets were cut as a result of pressures from corporations insisting on reducing taxes that were "too heavy."

7. Donald Dennie (2001) is very clear on this question. It is the whole culture and its leadership that are marred by a deep religious and patrimonial influence of traditionalism and of reverence to authority. Note also the work of Gervais (1993), Choquette (1993), Béland (1952), and Jaenen (1993), who all put emphasis on the incredible weight of the Catholic Church in the community and on the determining influence that this institution maintains on local elected officials.

8. As reflected in the works of sociologist Michel Freitag (1995, 2002), the thrust of the main transformation of society in the twentieth century changed and denatured what modern society was. This change seems to have escaped the attention of most analysts.

9. The Constitution Act of 1867 provides for a division of powers between the federal government and the provinces. It stipulates, in Article 93, that education is a provincial responsibility or field of competence. It also stipulates that the federal government protects religious education.

10. If there are so many school boards, it is because of the political compromise between

the French Catholic clergy of Canada and the English colonial leaders after the conquest of 1760. The French preserved their language and religion, for which the Catholic Church assured the loyalty of the population to the British Crown. This compromise has since been ratified by political and legal authorities, especially under the weight of influence of the Church, in the constitutional laws of 1867 and 1982. Although the arrangement functioned very well for 200 years, in the sense that the Church succeeded in controlling and dominating all French Canadian society, this concept of democracy, of francophone participation in the affairs of society as a whole, is today largely outdated.

11. Recall that before this date, Canadian immigration law overtly favoured immigration that was white, European, and either Catholic or Protestant.

12. The poignant work of Arendt (1972) is clearly and particularly relevant to this subject.

13. The use of the euphemism "because of the numbers" is revealing of this traditional attitude of submission to the majority: one never says "because of the small number of francophone students." One invokes only the word "numbers." With the simple use of this catchword, all are to understand that it is necessary to bend over backward to the anglophone majority, and that one should not make waves.

14. We refer here to the anti-francophone discourse of *Hockey Night in Canada* commentator Don Cherry, for whom francophones are poor cowardly cousins who are easily intimidated.

15. See Boudreau (2002), Gurian and Henley (2001), as well as Lamarre et Ouellet (1999).

16. Dagenais (2000) illustrates with wonder the complexity of the transformation of society that occurs "under our eyes" without our understanding anything, by taking the example of the transformation of the family: its composition, its function, its meaning and its modalities, which, taken from a historical perspective, "reveals" another aspect of the crisis of culture.

17. See the work of Gagne (2002), which deals with the meaning we give to education, and to the modern mission of education, which is to educate citizens, and not workers or consumers. See also Freitag (1995), on the same theme, for whom the university and education system as a whole is too centred on immediate results, on applied knowledge, and on the growing dependence of university research on private funding.

Chapter 12

Dispatches of Longing

Progressive Art and Culture in Sudbury

Laurie McGauley

"What's the difference between Sudbury and yogurt?"
"Yogurt has culture."

As this old joke demonstrates, "Sudbury culture" is an oxymoron in the Canadian lexicon. It just wouldn't work without the assumption of snickers at the absurdity of equating Sudbury with any kind of culture at all, even the yogurt kind. In the face of such a scorching reputation, any serious consideration of progressive art and culture in Sudbury first requires an acknowledgment of the truth behind the joke. This rocky landscape is the foundation and inspiration for both the city's reputation as a cultural wasteland and, as I hope to demonstrate, for its rich contributions to progressive art and culture.

In the late nineteenth century, Sudbury was born on Native land as a lumber camp and railroad stop, and later grew up as a copper mine while being force-fed sulphur fumes. High culture has not been its defining characteristic. Sudbury's history has been largely driven by the profit motives of some of the largest multinational lumber and mining companies in the world. The wild Northern Ontario landscape has been blasted and scarred over the years by rapacious capitalism, corporate greed, and reckless environmental destruction. But equally tenacious has been the countervailing labour and community resistance to corporate excess, and the people's commitment to carving out half-decent lives for themselves and their families. Yogurt culture doesn't thrive on burned, black rock and, even in the few pockets where it can be found, its value as a progressive force isn't obvious, which is why Sudbury's experiments with other forms of art and culture are actually interesting and relevant.

This chapter will approach the margins of the constantly shifting debates about what art and culture actually *are*, even as we address the question of whether or not Sudbury has any. In support of the view that culture has a key role to play in progressive movements for social change, I'll look at some examples from Sudbury's rich labour and activist history, and explore the possibility that cultural democracy in particular remains a crucial site of struggle, even for this small Northern Ontario mining town. The basic premise of this discussion is that Sudbury's progressive cultural movements have grown from the same hardscrabble ground that inspires the joke's punch line. Knowing this ground is important to understanding both, so I'll begin with a personal tour of the territory. Five generations of my familial roots are so tangled under the slag heaps that I can't make much of a claim for objectivity.

By the time I was born in the late 1950s, the trees were chopped down, my great-grandparents' farmland was paved over or poisoned, and Sudbury was an established one-industry town, dominated by two giant multinational corporations, Inco and Falconbridge. I remember Inco picnics in Copper Cliff, the company town where both my parents were raised. Highlights included free pop and hotdogs, and the excitement the year I won the potato-sack race. As far as I can recall as a child growing up, that was the extent of Inco's corporate benevolence. But its presence permeated the landscape: red-hot hissing slag heaps that bled into the night skies, stark black rock, the constant plumes of smoke. On a bad day, the sulphur stung your eyes and seized your throat.

In exchange for this bleakness, the mining companies offered the community jobs — lots of jobs, albeit dangerous ones. Most males over the age of eighteen in my extended family and neighbourhood worked for Inco or Falconbridge, and they were union men (they were all men then), belonging to the Mine Mill or Steelworker locals. Mothers raised families around the mine shifts: afternoon meant shushing the kids while dad slept during the day. Many of us knew of someone who had died or was injured at work, and stories of acid spills, danger, and accidents were common. I remember Labour Day picnics at the Mine Mill Camp: free hamburgers and pop, happily drunken men chasing greased pigs, lots of speeches, music, and dancing, and, of course, potato-sack races.

Sudbury wasn't only a mining town: it was a union town. The workers were legendary for their on-the-job toughness and equally proud of their strength at the bargaining table. It was a hardrock mining town, with much of the emphasis on hard work and hard parties, a hardness that barely concealed a desperation for something better. Some were crushed by the weight of their longings, and broken hearts could be found littered throughout the town's many bars. Others escaped to their camps, usually a shack on the shores of one of the many beautiful lakes that surround the city. There was fishing, swimming, and, of course, partying, as far away as possible from the slag heaps, surrounded by water and dancing birch trees, under a clear sky that inevitably featured a grey plume of smoke. The landscape was both curse and redemption.

All of these contradictions shaped the culture: imagine underground blasts that rattle your teeth; class divisions and bitter strikes; overheard conversations in French, Italian, Finnish, Ukrainian, Russian, and Ojibwe; English versus French; Catholic versus Protestant; Steelworkers versus Mine Mill; union halls and greased pigs; macho toughness, solidarity, and irreverence. Although often tainted with racist undercurrents, there was a strong multiculturalism that celebrated and mourned the histories and traditions of the many "old" countries that were represented here. But what brought us all together in this wildly beautiful and devastated place were the mines. Sudbury's identity was rooted in the solidarity, tensions, and pride of a colourful and diverse labour movement, and its culture had more in common with greased pigs than yogurt. But Sudbury definitely did have culture. It was raw, generous, marked by despair and longing, and it knew how to have a good time.

Mine Mill and Labour Culture

According to distinctions outlined by artist Karl Beveridge (1995), there are elements of an "informal" labour culture, the everyday life of a mining town. But in the 1940s and '50s, it was the Mine Mill Union that understood this as the foundation for building a formal, organized labour culture. "From the legacy of the Industrial Workers of the World and the traditions of Joe Hill," Mine Mill was part of the development of an alternative culture (Beveridge 1995: 251). Explains Dieter Buse (1995: 285): "In the tradition of European labour movements, Sudbury's radical union offered large symbolic actions with political overtones. This included Labour Day picnics (with rock-moving or mucking contests), gripping films, and radical folk singers, such as The Travellers and Pete Seeger."

As well, Mine Mill understood the class barriers to education, recreation, and culture, and was committed to developing opportunities for workers and their families in these areas. This was more than an attempt to improve the quality of life of their members: rather, it was a fundamental principle in its developmental approach to the labour movement. Labour unions were not only responsible for negotiating contracts for their members, they were responsible for supporting a culture of resistance to oppression of all kinds and, just as importantly, a culture of possibility and hope. Workers' cultural education was intended to provide them with the critical tools for an understanding of what is — and the imagination to envision what could be. This approach follows such thinkers as Antonio Gramsci. His theory of cultural hegemony and the necessity of the left to develop counter-hegemonic movements was developed in the 1930s, and it remains very influential in cultural politics.

These are familiar issues to anyone involved in the labour movement, but in the 1940s and '50s, these approaches to culture came to represent what distinguished the good capitalists from the bad communists during the red-baiting of the Cold War. Union interest in cultural democracy and community development was seen as subversive and dangerous to the *status quo*.

In retrospect, the activities undertaken by Mine Mill seem innocuous: a summer camp that offered two-week blocks of programming for children between the ages of six and fourteen, which included "arts and crafts, clay modelling, pottery, plaster casting, wood carving, driftwood [collecting and shaping], paper mâché, metal craft, basketry, singing, folk, square, and social dancing, library, story hour, and camp fires." In 1953, the Mine Mill Ballet School was established, and for six years "hundreds of youths received classical and other training" (Buse 1995: 276–277). More than sixty volunteers from the Ladies' Auxiliaries "made costumes, ushered, and organized the events." In 1955, Mine Mill was one of the first unions in Canada to commission an artist to create a mural for their union hall, a work by Henry Orenstein. In these ways the union, and art, had an everyday and meaningful presence in community life.

Weir Reid is still considered a cultural hero in Sudbury for the vision he brought to many of these projects. Employed by Mine Mill to manage the Camp, he soon expanded his territory to all aspects of labour culture. In 1954 he formed the Hayward Players. As Buse (1995: 276) describes this community-based theatre troupe: "They presented socially concerned plays by Barrie Stavis, Dalton Trumbo and Arthur Miller. Reid won the Quonta Drama Festival best director award in 1958 with an Arthur Miller play cast entirely of miners, who demonstrated they could compete and perform well."

This was not revolutionary art or culture: it did not call for dismantling the state or smashing capitalism. Rather, it provided opportunities for miners and their families to demonstrate that "they could compete and perform well." This awareness was not only relevant to the audience: more importantly, it was empowering to the miners themselves. Union cultural programs offered them access to both the means of cultural production itself and two very powerful outlets for their longings: art and the pursuit of social justice. Both foster critical thinking, are unpredictable, and difficult to control. Both were easily character-ized as subversive, and the cultural elements of Mine Mill were important targets during the right-wing takeover of the unions.

The Cold War was very much alive in Sudbury, and red-baiting and union raids succeeded in dividing the labour movement and destroying much of Mine Mill's cultural projects. The White Block, "a group that schemed for years on how to get Sudbury union members out of Mine Mill and into the United Steelworkers," had identified the Camp and Weir's leadership as a target as early as 1955. Rumours and anonymous sources fed newspaper articles and speculation about "socialist indoctrination" of children at the Camp, and there were accusa-tions that Weir was "the head of a Communist cell in Sudbury, [he] controlled a group of thugs...." All these charges were fabrications and were publicly recanted after Weir spent years fighting them in court (Buse 1995: 278). But, by that time, the damage had been done: the theatre troupe, the dance school, the concerts, and the Camp activities were all casualties. Mine Mill lost Inco certification to the Steelworkers, and it took years for the animosity to die down. By the time I was earnestly hopping my way through the potato-sack races in the '60s, the Mine Mill Camp was a shadow of what it had been. But these experiments in cultural democracy, and the violent reaction to them, had left an indelible lesson about the crucial role culture plays in social-justice movements, and about the threat it implies to the dominant class.

Sudbury and High Culture

Although the days of a strong informal labour culture are pretty much gone, traces can still be found throughout Sudbury's people and landscape, dissipated through downsizing, re-greening, and amalgamation. There is no doubt that since the massive mining lay-offs and diversifications of the last decades, the symbols of "power-over" have become diffused. And although Inco's Superstack can be seen spouting smoke for miles, concerted and enlightened re-greening efforts have softened much of the landscape. Without this locus of meaning, local cultural signifiers of resistance and solidarity that used to be part of a regional identity no longer resonate as strongly, which should come as a blessing to those who have been exasperated in their attempts to re-brand Sudbury as a centre for "real" culture, the high culture that is implied in the yogurt joke.

But high culture always had a hard time establishing itself in Sudbury. Here's one theory: for isolated mining towns subject to corporate rule, long before the anti-globalization movement there was an inherent understanding of the unfairness of global capitalism and the vulnerability of dependence on multinational corporations. When art is used as a veneer to mask the injustices of reality, it becomes illusion, meaningful only to the dominant classes that claim art as their own. Throughout history, art has been used in this way as an affirmation of superiority and power. Some cultural theorists refer to this as the "affirmative" function of art and culture. However, in Sudbury, attempts to deny the discrepancies between the ideal and the real were more likely met with cynicism and derision than with awed acquiescence. The key to this resistance was the pragmatic pioneer spirit of a strong labour movement always ready to counter the pretensions of "affirmative idealism." And, because the owners and shareholders of these mining corporations never actually lived in Sudbury, the privileged never had the weight of wealth or of numbers to forge much of a cultural elite in the midst of such stubborn resistance.

But this resistance was directed toward elitism and doesn't mean that high art had no relevance to the people of Sudbury. Despite all the exclusive class and commercial trappings, art can transcend them to connect to longings in all of us for freedom, beauty, and justice. In this way, according to many theories, art is always subversive or, at least, it has the potential to be. It is precisely this subversive element that must be protected behind the walls of museums, theatres, and galleries, themselves testaments to superiority and power. But art manages to slip through these trappings and, of course, could always be found in pockets throughout Sudbury.

During the 1960s and '70s, the state was recognizing the role of culture, largely as a reaction to the growing push of American cultural hegemony and to our increasing obsession with defining a Canadian identity. Cultural democracy became a national issue. As elsewhere in Canada, new institutions were starting to take shape, and Sudbury managed to cobble together a cultural infrastructure. What is now the Art Gallery of Sudbury; The Sudbury Theatre Centre, Laurentian University's music and theatre programs, and Cambrian College's fine-arts programs are a few of the institutions that were born during this time. But, although high culture was finally getting a foothold in Sudbury, its expansion was pretty much stalled after the neo-conservative onslaught on the culture industry and cutbacks in state funding.

Counterculture Resistance

Sudbury has been no different from other Canadian communities in feeling the effects of the mass commodification of culture: early in the latter half of the last century, television easily became the favoured source of information and entertainment, particularly during the long winters. The "affirmative" function of culture culminates in the culture industry, affirming the capitalist consumer society through trite entertainment and continuous exhortations to buy. But then the counterculture of the 1960s caught up to Northern Ontario. This was a deliberate attempt to introduce a "critical" culture that could countenance the affirmative aspects of the culture industry. Theodore Roszak, who coined the phrase "counterculture," explains that it was "an opposition to hegemony by a utopianist idealism, which promoted an egalitarian ethic through the advocacy of participative democracy on a localised level" (Kershaw 1992: 39). According to this definition, elements of the counterculture already had a foundation in Sudbury's working class resistance to hegemonic culture and in the labour movement's history of cultural democracy.

Now, as the counterculture gained steam, women, visible minorities, Aboriginals, gays and lesbians, francophones, the disabled — all groups traditionally excluded from the cultural ideal — were building on this foundation, insisting on telling their versions of history, and claiming the languages of art as their own. Culture was the place to assert their experiences, to express their identities, to explore their truths — all against the stereotypes, standardizations, and ignorance of affirmative culture. Cultural democracy — the reclaiming of the means of cultural production — was again an essential component in the various social-justice movements.

For Sudbury francophones, culture was the obvious site of struggle, both as a defence and a response to anglophone hegemony. Franco-Ontarians were deeply influenced by the counterculture movements in Québec, with the added urgency of threatened assimilation into Ontario's anglophone majority. The politics of identity and recognition were the priority, and Sudbury's francophones led a movement toward what they called le Nouvel Ontario, the New Ontario. In the early '70s, a group of radical theatre students were the first in Sudbury to experiment with collective creation, resulting in the play *Moé, j'viens du nord, s'tie, (Me, I Come From the North, Damn It)*, an irreverent exploration of the actual lives and experiences of Franco-Ontarians that became a rallying cry for their movement.

This successful demonstration of cultural democracy was followed by an explosion of cultural production that included poetry, music, theatre, film, and visual arts. Sudbury's francophone culture was not only exploring and asserting a community's identity, but was legitimizing and clarifying their struggle for recognition, equality, and justice. But this wasn't a yearning for traditional French culture: this was the creation of culture, the development of distinctive Franco-Ontarian voices. Poets Patrice Desbiens and Robert Dickson, theatre artist Hélène Gravelle, and visual artists Paulette Taillefaire and Michel Galipeau were just a few of the artists who emerged from this wave. Enthusiastically supported by their constituents, francophones developed a strong cultural infrastructure: Prise de Parole is a publishing house that has produced at least three Governor-General Award winners; le Théatre du Nouvel Ontario is a professional, creative, theatre company that has gained national and international recognition; la Galerie du Nouvel Ontario is an artist-run art gallery that features the best in Canadian avant-garde conceptual art; la Nuit sur l'Etang is an annual francophone music festival now in its thirty-fifth year. This rich infrastructure is now institutionalized into the fabric of Sudbury and continues to support the further development of francophone culture.

Northern Lights Festival Boréal was also born out of the counterculture. Sudbury's folk festival was unique from its inception, designed as a bilingual event that also celebrated Aboriginal culture. It was part of the original folk-festival circuit that sprang up across Canada in the '70s. As part of the counterculture's reaction against the culture industry, people were consciously taking back the means of self-expression and dissemination. Anyone who knew a few chords on the guitar and had something to say could become a songwriter or singer and could always find an audience at the Festival, if not on a main stage, then on one of the many open stages. A strong anti-corporate philosophy guided the development of these early festivals: booths featured local homemade food and handmade arts and crafts, there was paper mâché and homemade play-dough for the children, and after-hours parties were open to the community, where people could dance and jam all night with the performers. Northern Lights Festival Boréal became a widely supported focal point for the counterculture in Sudbury and now, more than thirty-five years later, it is still a major annual event. Despite its creeping corporatism, the event still manages to carry traces of its utopian beginnings.

At the forefront of this counterculture, the feminist movement took the lead in the deconstruction of affirmative culture in a wide-ranging critical analysis of high art, the culture industry, representation, history, and language itself. Sudbury's feminist movement developed strong cultural currents: Women Helping Women, one of Sudbury's first feminist groups, created powerful videos on women and madness in the late '70s. The Wives Supporting the Strike Committee during the brutal 1979 Inco strike proved to be a formidable force that garnered international attention for its strike support organizing. Theatre and music were part of its arsenal, and its story was turned into an important film *A Wives' Tale*. Also at this time, a series of annual Northeastern Ontario Women's Conferences brought together activists from throughout the North. These were forums for experimenting with popular education, critical analysis, alternative culture, and organizing approaches.

Throughout the 1970s and '80s, art, performance, and popular education were critical elements of larger feminist campaigns to challenge oppressive practices, to implement or improve services to women, and to change laws and policies. Sticks and Stones Feminist Theatre troupe was a group that in many ways epitomized the character of Sudbury's feminist movement: irreverent, experimental, with a strong class as well as gender analysis.

It wasn't only the message or the content of the work: an inclusive creative process was integral to this movement. This meant experiments in collective creative processes and consensus decision-making. In those days, it wasn't unusual for a fledgling group to fall apart because they couldn't reach consensus on the colour of a pamphlet. A total commitment to an inclusive cultural democracy meant learning new ways of working together that were consensual, creative, and effective.

Many of these practices were influenced by Aboriginal politics and culture. De-ba-jeh-mu-jig Theatre was founded in 1984 on Manitoulin Island, two hours south of Sudbury, and is now the longest running Aboriginal theatre in Canada. The name means "First Teller of Tales," and Native storytelling was central to founder Shirley Cheechoo's artistic and cultural vision for the theatre. Over the years, the theatre has produced such award-winning plays as *The Rez Sisters* by Thompson Highway and *The Dreaming Beauty* by Daniel David Moses, and it has played a key role in the development of contemporary Native theatre and culture in the region. But, more importantly, as current Artistic Producer Ron Berti would tell you, the theatre has given voice to Aboriginal people: "It's all about voice" (Berti, personal communication). De-ba-jeh-ma-jig focusses much of its programming on mentoring Aboriginal youth in the art of theatre, and its present Artistic Director, Joe Osawabine, came through this process. But this is more than technical and skills development: this is a deep exploration of the creative process and its meaning to community. Osawabine explains:

> The Four Directions Creation Process, or 4d, is a unique process for creating new works developed by De-ba-jeh-mu-jig Theatre Group. It is a culturally and socially specific process that is holistic in nature. It recognizes the artist as the creation and the performance as the celebration. It recognizes that as humans we create with our entire beings — our physical, our emotional, our intellectual, and our spiritual selves, and therefore it accepts and specifically supports the artist in all four areas. It is adapted to the skills and intuitions of artists who have been strongly influenced by oral tradition. It is a process that nurtures honesty more than accuracy, and a process that consciously uses personal resources and group creation. (Fernandez 2005: 14)

Cultural Democracy and the Neo-Liberal Storm

Cultural democracy inevitably provokes our definitions of art, and these alternative approaches to art-making are presenting challenges and opportunities to our modernist definition of what Irish curator Declan McGonagle calls "signature culture... the idea of artist as individual genius producer and all the support mechanisms that exist to sustain and project this idea." McGonagle echoes other artists and theorists when he calls for the addition of ideas such as "participation, transaction, and negotiation" (McGonagle 2005: 22). This is a fundamental shift toward a notion, and a practice, of an inter-subjective, shared creation of meaning that is so crucial to any idea of a progressive future. This shift also inevitably signals a struggle for access to cultural resources from the state: women, Aboriginal people, visible minorities, and francophones have managed to muscle their way into most state art institutions.

These stories demonstrate that developing a voice in the public sphere cannot only be the first essential step toward the claim for recognition and a place in the social and political discourse, but it can change the shape of that discourse. As Berti says, it is all about voice, because the alternative is silence and invisibility. Cultural democracy is an essential component, maybe even the foundational component, to social-change movements, and it is inherently subversive to certain elements of the dominant culture.

So it's no surprise that during the neo-liberal storm of the 1990s, much of the expansion of issue- and identity-based cultural activism came to a screeching halt. The fragile cultural institutions went into survival mode as they either lost all funding or had to meet new requirements that focussed on economic indicators. Non-profits had to find "private" funding sources that were then matched on a percentage basis with state grants. Those that survived were more established organizations and institutions; those that couldn't move fast enough, or that didn't already have a corporate base, fell through the gaping holes. Particularly vulnerable were marginal groups that had a history of advocating for social change. One of the many casualties was the Canadian Popular Theatre Alliance, a coalition of political theatre artists and troupes from throughout Canada that had organized national biannual conferences throughout the '80s and nurtured criticism and theoretical debate in the evolving explorations of popular theatre. The death of dozens of small troupes throughout the country, including Sudbury's Sticks and Stones, made the Alliance obsolete.

At the height of this free-market, anti-deficit hysteria came the 1995 election in Ontario of Mike Harris, and suddenly everything was under attack. It was difficult to make a case for cultural democracy when people's welfare checks were being slashed by 23 percent. But the neo-liberal cultural strategy goes beyond simply starving dissenting voices: it relies on taking over the airwaves itself, and there was no doubt that neo-liberalism was dominating the public discourse — disguised as "common sense." The poor could be attacked so viciously and so shamelessly only after the Harris Tories actually ran their election campaign on an anti-welfare platform, normalizing poor-bashing and hate-mongering. Media concentration was narrowing the range of voices to a homogenous right-wing bleat about welfare fraud in a successful campaign to blame the unemployed and the poor for the widespread pain of economic restructuring. It must be noted that Sudbury never elected a Tory, but it didn't make any difference. We suffered along with everyone else who didn't have connections to Bay Street.

This is not to say that there was no dissent, of course, and Sudbury was very active in the original Days of Action, the roving days of protest that took place throughout the province. Following their narrow tradition, Sudbury Steelworkers refused to endorse the protest, but opposition against the Harris government went beyond labour infighting, and community groups took on a large part of the organizing. Groups of young people created giant puppets and large beautiful banners that would be used over the next eight years, every time Mike Harris came to town for his annual fund-raising dinner. But, after a while, the constant "crisis" mode that the government deliberately put people in, combined with their bully tactics toward the marginalized and any forms of dissent, were successful at diffusing resistance.

Before Mike Harris came to power, I had been working in the community with people living in poverty, still using theatre to inform and instigate around social-justice issues. Over the years, we had formed groups like Poetic Justice, which performed stories of homelessness, You Won't Believe It's Theatre, which presented forum-plays on the challenges and injustices of being on social assistance, and the Bleeding Hearts Coalition, a group that took up the challenge of a municipal councillor that "only bleeding hearts would be against welfare snitch lines." Loud exuberant street theatre outside City Council meetings, beautiful bleeding heart buttons that hundreds of people were wearing, together with a well-organized letter-writing and lobbying effort forced the city to back down on its public welfare snitch line. But about a year after Mike Harris came to power, people living in poverty had effectively lost their voice: their lives became so disorganized and they were so afraid of repercussions that raising their voices in opposition now seemed out of the question.

Aboriginal people, women, the poor, gays, and lesbians — all groups that had been pushing for, and making, social progress — were either being attacked or contained. But there was still one space that was difficult to scapegoat: the community, particularly a geographic, neighbourhood community. "Community" is a difficult concept for the right wing to dismiss or demonize as a "special interest" group, and since a lot of Sudbury's activist work had been community-based organizing, there was a foundation to build on.

In 1996, I founded Myths and Mirrors Community Arts as a response to the oppressive and deceitful myths of neo-liberal affirmative culture. Supported by two downtown neighbourhoods, we involved residents in art projects that prioritized critical reflection, collective creation, and public recognition. In this way, over the years since, we have created permanent art installations, murals, theatre, video, photography, exhibits, celebrations, demonstrations, and performances with thousands of people on various themes including racism, poverty, utopia, belonging, water, and HIV/AIDS. For the first six years, we found funding for our work from the Bronfman Foundation's Urban Issues Program, one of the few Canadian programs that supported community activism under the rubric of civic engagement. (The program no longer exists.) Although it was just a start, it gave us a base from which to experiment with the best ways to involve people in the collective creation of meaning, for themselves and for the larger community. At the same time, state art funders, through pressure from cultural activists, had started to open up pockets of funding for community arts. As long as we had the Urban Issues base funding, we could strategize on the best ways to access other funding sources for projects without changing our critical focus. But once

Myths and Mirrors no longer had this cushion, this became more difficult and, inevitably, we began to tailor our programming to funding criteria.

The challenges in community-based art stem from the same characteristics that make it safe for funders. Unlike issue or identity-based politics, there is no inherent critical analysis of economic and social power and no attendant movements to work with. So in most location-based communities, without the support of other social-justice or cultural movements, much of the work is focussed on exploring and sharing values, aspirations, and beliefs, toward what can only be called the common good. These projects are powerful community-building processes and models for democratic discourse, and I'm coming to understand that one of their main functions is the stirring of our suppressed utopian longings, in particular the longing for connection, justice, and meaning. Aesthetically, the more participants are connected to these longings, the better the art and the clearer the voices. But without anywhere for those voices to go, without strong social-justice movements to give support and purpose to new inspiration, it sometimes feels like we're singing into the wind. Which is better than not singing at all, but getting those voices into the public sphere is only half the battle: gaining the recognition to participate in public discourse only makes sense if there *is* a public discourse. As long as these voices remain fleeting oddities, they are too easily co-opted or ignored.

Cultural Industry versus Cultural Democracy

Real cultural democracy implies a strong and vigorous public sphere. Unfortunately, like many medium-sized Northern communities, Sudbury's public sphere is shrinking, partly as a result of private media concentration and public media cuts. The results are more standardized regional news and content, very little debate, and fewer public platforms for local artists, activists, and residents.

One response has been alternative venues that are being opened up through the Internet and other independent means of production and democratic forums for dissemination. The younger techno-generations are freeing themselves from the restrictions of privately and publicly controlled platforms — do-it-yourself culture is the new youth counterculture — although, like most good counterculture, it's never above accepting a lucrative record deal.

As well, film, video, and new media technologies are also becoming more technically and financially accessible and are the mediums of choice for young people in particular, giving them a voice in a conversation they want to be part of. Cinéfest, Sudbury's film festival, is providing inspiration and generating creative energy by providing a platform for local filmmakers alongside the best of international cinema and video. Of course, much of Cinéfest's success lies in the glamour associated with the movie industry, and there is the predictable hype to turn Sudbury into "Hollywood North." But hype is what keeps our new economy going, and it is having some effect in the development of a fledgling film and video infrastructure that supports local productions, opening up possibilities for Sudburians to try their hand at these expressive forms.

In many ways, Cinéfest is setting the stage for the direction Sudbury is currently heading in trying to establish its cultural credentials. This seems to be the strategy: lots of hype generates economic support to create the infrastructure needed to live up to the hype. It's not a bad idea, and most activists are familiar with some version of these tactics. Except that the hype, and the resulting expectations, are mainly focussed on the financial benefits of supporting the arts, which risks undermining other, more important benefits of art and culture. Some people think it worth the risk.

The development of Sudbury's cultural infrastructure is due to the dogged determination of individuals and small groups throughout Sudbury's history, and if there is any doubt about the challenges they have and continue to face, we need only consider these numbers: according to Statistics Canada, in 2001 Canadian municipalities allocated on average $13.50 per capita to arts and culture, but only $1.50 per person was allocated in Sudbury (Frick 2005). Nationwide, there has been growing concern about the lack of audience support for arts institutions, and Sudbury has been no different. So, the challenge for arts and culture advocates has been reduced to proving the relevance of art in order to justify public funding. Since the 1990s, there have been two approaches to this challenge.

The first, and the one that gets the most hype, is the complete integration of art and culture into an economic model: advocates have learned to use economic language to make the case that government investments in arts and culture pay off. The Canada Council for the Arts offers this helpful information on its website: "with roughly $7 billion invested in 2001–02, the sector generated an economic impact of $26 billion, creating 740,000 jobs...." Books like Richard Florida's *The Creative Class and Cities* make the case that cities actually need to attract the artists and creative thinkers that are the basis of the new "information" economy. As I heard explained at one workshop, some of these models include an ideal percentage of the "bohemian" population to generate just the right level — because you don't want too much — of the creative energy needed to make a city truly competitive, "world-class" competitive. These economic development strategies are seen as win-win solutions for artists, cultural workers, government funders, and, of course, business, and are driving initiatives such as Municipal Cultural Planning Forums in Ontario and the Creative Cities coalitions and networks throughout Canada. Cultural "capital" is evaluated according to its economic potential.

This economic approach was recently taken in Sudbury, through a concerted effort to prove the economic benefits of the arts, or of "cultural tourism," as it's now called (Frick 2005). According to all accounts, this approach is proving to be wildly successful. The City of Greater Sudbury's new Economic Development Strategic Plan — "Engine No. 2" — promotes Sudbury's growth as "a city for the creative, curious, and adventuresome." Arts and culture was shifted from the Parks and Recreation Department to Economic Development and, soon after, City Council approved a budget that almost doubled arts funding.

And so, under these new and improved conditions, the arts are now expected to perform — economically that is. This is the dilemma of using a purely economic model for art. Art and culture become just another way to generate jobs, tourism, and business. As these priorities become embedded in public policy, economic indicators guide cultural development strategies and arts and culture are officially commodified within the public as well as the private sphere. There is no doubt that arts advocates' goal of increasing public support for the arts is more likely to succeed with this approach. But once it is categorized as just another economic unit, art by definition becomes pure spectacle. The public's role becomes one of dutiful consumers, a willing audience that will travel from far and wide to pay for artistic spectacles. And maybe they will. Many hope that these investments in cultural tourism will result in an infrastructure that will also serve local cultural development, as a sort of by-product or training ground for the profitable stuff. And maybe they're right. However, although this approach is successful at demonstrating the financial relevance of the arts to economic development, it does little to address the other human needs that the arts respond to.

A completely different approach to the problem of the disconnection between art and the public is the promotion of programs that actually bring artists and communities together in collaborative art projects, a process that makes art very relevant to people's lives. The theoretical and practical foundation that shapes this approach comes from the work of activists and artists who have been experimenting since the 1960s with cultural democracy and collaborative creation. It is their dogged persistence, accompanied by very little hype, that has led to the development of small funding programs to support this work, and now most arts councils in Canada, England, and Australia offer various versions of "community arts" grants. The Canada Council for the Arts has a specific fund that supports "artists and community collaborations," defined as "an arts process that actively involves the work of professional artists and non-arts community members in creative and collaborative relationships." The Ontario Arts Council's Artists in the Community/Workplace program was originally a labour-arts program, initiated in response to strong pressure from labour activists and artists such as Karl Beveridge and Carol Condé. But it became necessary to expand the scope of the program in reaction to the powerful work artists were doing with other identity-, issue- or community-based groups. The Ontario Art Council's current definition of "Community Arts" is:

> an arts process that involves the work of artists and community members in a collaborative creative process resulting in collective experience and public expression. It provides a way for communities to express themselves; enables artists, through financial or other supports, to engage in creative activity with communities; and is collaborative — the creative process is equally important as the artistic outcome.

Such language has been carefully developed by social activists — and not by economic strategists — and it is heartening to find it embedded within major arts funding institutions. The impulse to this work comes not from financial gain, but from what artist Suzanne Lacy (1995: 24) calls a "longing for community." Artists, activists, cultural workers, and others are still reacting to a variety of social ills, oppression, alienation, loneliness, and loss of meaning. However, many progressive artists are no longer approaching communities solely as audiences for their own artistic interpretations of problems and solutions: rather they are inviting people to participate in exploring these questions collectively, through art. This work is a mix of postmodern cultural activism, relational aesthetics, cultural democracy, and utopianism in the sense advocated by Rebecca Solnit (2004): that another world is possible, but we are still figuring out what it might look like. Many of these artists are at the forefront of creating spaces, which are themselves utopian, where people can figure it out together.

Across Canada, the art created through these projects has spoken to our histories, our struggles, our values, and our longings, but also to our sense of fun, ritual, and celebration. These approaches to art-making have proven to have many benefits, including increased civic engagement and participation, safer, more beautiful neighbourhoods, happier children, and a reclaiming and redecorating of the public sphere. And, of course, these participation-based art projects have been reconnecting people with art in a meaningful way, encouraging them to explore other art forms, even to visit galleries or attend the theatre. Art funding agencies have been pressuring traditional arts institutions to shift portions of their programming toward more inclusive community projects as part of their "audience development strategies." As well, large urban arts councils such as those in Toronto and Vancouver have had grant programs for community arts for a few years now, with impressive artistic results that are also touching upon all kinds of urban issues. For the past ten years or so, these funding programs at all levels of government have been developing and are continuing to expand. This level of recognition by granting institutions, not known for their openness to anything that threatens the canon, is a significant shift. All this should be enough to make the case that cultural democracy and collaborative art practices are not fads, that these approaches lay the groundwork for further cultural development that has actual roots in the community, and that it is not based totally on hype and spectacle. Of course, this level of institutional support in itself threatens to pacify the practice — or worse, turn it into a tool for domestication. But cultural activists have managed to carve out a small space where creative resistance is possible, and in these times, this space needs to be defended.

Which Future?

The question now is whether or not Sudbury's own rich legacy in cultural democracy will get lost in the hype strategy. If the only goal is economic development, it would be natural to assume that cultural democracy will not be a big priority, in which case we could risk wasting a good portion of our "cultural capital" on empty spectacles that have no real connection to the land or people of Sudbury. However, a strong argument can be made for a balance between both approaches.

Cultural policy and funding programs focussed on the creation and maintenance of cultural infrastructures, the development of cultural tourism, and in support of local artists should be combined with dedicated policies and funding programs for community-based art projects and cultural development. While private and state-supported infrastructure will provide venues and resources for the spectacles of cultural tourism, they should also provide the community with an open public sphere — sites for discourse, expression, and exchange. The rest is then up to the artists, activists, and citizens of Sudbury.

Although state funding is crucial to arts and culture, it does not guarantee *progressive* arts and culture. As long as we wait for culture to be delivered to us, either by the state or by industry, we're missing opportunities for cultural democracy. By remaining spectators, we are relinquishing our voices and leaving ourselves open to all kinds of abuse. The progressive community, including the labour movement, needs to be ready to support initiatives in alternative media before our voices are completely drowned out by the hype and spectacles of the culture industry, or by the distortions and omissions of right-wing politicians and media.

Like many resource-based towns vulnerable to the whims of capital, Sudbury is struggling to find its place in this brave new world. Despite the challenges, new cultural initiatives continue to take root in our shallow topsoil. Your Scrivener Press has recently published its second anthology of short stories by Northern writers. Le Salon du Livre, a francophone book fair, expanded in its second year to include book readings, theatre, and performances that attracted over 20,000 people. A recent decision by Huntington College to disband its music program caused such community uproar that Laurentian University had to revive it. A stronger working relationship between the cultural sector and the City of Greater Sudbury and a newfound solidarity among the major art institutions will probably ensure their survival, at least in the medium term.

But cultural democracy, the nurturing of new voices, of critical and alternative viewpoints, needs to remain a priority as we navigate the troubled waters of this new century. Community-based art does not guarantee progressive art and culture, but it does stake out and protect a rare public space for creative discourse, critical analysis, and empowerment. A successful project becomes testament to the potential of collective action: if we can come together to create a mural or a play, imagine what else we are capable of creating together. If we can go "beyond the spectacle" with a deeper, more critical search for meaning, imagine what we can understand. Reclaiming our rights as cultural producers is a significant act of power that can inspire a deeper engagement with the world. The focus on yogurt culture may give us the illusion that we are part of the global spectacle, but it is the nurturing of the subversive imagination through a commitment to cultural democracy that can lead us to a truly progressive future.

Chapter 13

Lessons from the Little Blue Schoolhouse

Ruth Reyno

Educational workers understand that the field is liable to change with the passage of time. Ideas about public education are subject to the vagaries of public opinion, theoretical debate, and party politics. With the election of the Harris Conservative government in June 1995, however, education in Sudbury, and in Ontario, became a system under siege. The Conservatives planned a massive "restructuring" of Ontario's education policies and curriculum — which American educator Barbara Coloroso had called "the best in the world" — mostly for financial reasons, to facilitate their promise to Ontario taxpayers of eliminating the provincial deficit and cutting personal income taxes by 30 percent.

To oversee educational reform, Harris chose as Minister of Education John Snobelen, a high-school dropout, wealthy businessman, and "the most aggressive, tactless and outspoken minister of education in Ontario's long history" (Gidney 1999: 236). Snobelen was the Minister who was recorded telling senior civil servants how a "crisis" atmosphere had to be invented to win public support for overhauling the system (Hart 1998). There soon followed a series of announcements, retractions, and postponements that eventually resulted in over a billion dollars being removed from provincial educational funding. Snobelen announced in November 1995 that a completely rewritten four-year secondary curriculum would be in place for students entering grade nine in 1997. The first draft of that document was a "muddle of competing models" that provoked "howls of outrage" from teachers' groups and administrators (Gidney 1999: 239). It was quickly withdrawn, the year of implementation changed to 1999, and a new round of consultations were begun in the fall of 1996.

Legislation governing the Conservatives' restructuring of education was tabled between January 1997 and the spring of 1998. The first bill, Bill 104, reduced the number of school boards in the province from 129 to 72 through amalgamation of existing boards. This created mega-boards that, in Northern Ontario, cover thousands of square miles. It also reduced the number of school trustees from 1,900 to 700. Then the Harris Conservatives appointed an Education Improvement Commission to oversee the transition from the old to the new boards, with "far-reaching power to monitor and approve such things as budgets, administrative appointments, and the initial operation of new boards" (Gidney 1999: 247). The Rainbow District School Board, for example, expanded to include Manitoulin Island. The Board can now assign teachers to more distant schools in its 14,000-square-kilometre jurisdiction. Some teachers who live in Sudbury must travel much farther — two or more hours — to access their employment, and teachers who work or live on Manitoulin have much farther to travel to their union office.

Next came Bill 160, the Educational Quality Improvement Act, which actually had nothing to do with improving the quality of education and everything to do with centralizing school financing and attacking teachers and their unions. It transferred control over educational revenue from municipal governments to the province. It also transferred some specific responsibilities from local school boards to the provincial government, most of which related to teachers' conditions of work. It legislated a maximum class size, as well as a formula that set limits on the amount of teachers' preparation time, or release time for administrative duties, and reduced the number of professional development days. As well, it removed principals and vice-principals from the teachers' collective bargaining unit. Through Bill 160, many of the items — such as preparation time — that had been subject to negotiations between local boards and teachers' unions were now dictated by the province.

As well, Bill 160 introduced a new funding model for education, one that attempted to reduce funding to education through targeting "non-classroom" expenditures such as administration, preparation time, teacher consultants, and custodial services.

In order to limit opposition to its plans to restructure the school system, the Harris government began a campaign intended to destroy the public's faith in Ontario's teachers and thereby undermine the strength of their unions, particularly the Ontario Secondary School Teachers' Federation (OSSTF) and the Elementary Teachers' Federation of Ontario, which were the largest organized forces defending public education in Ontario. With the establishment of the College of Teachers, passed into legislation in June 1996 — which eroded the role of the teachers' federations — and Bills 104 and 160, the government enacted legislation that ignored teachers' collective bargaining rights and denigrated their status as professionals. While the College of Teachers had been proposed under the previous NDP government, subsequent Conservative measures ended the NDP's initiative of mandatory junior kindergarten and dropped NDP equity initiatives in the education system, notably by repealing sections of the Education Act meant to increase the number of women in positions of administrative authority (Gidney 1999: 237).

As early as 2000, public concern and parental dissatisfaction with the changes were growing. In response, the Conservative government struck a committee to report on the results of its educational reforms. Named the Education Equality Task Force, it was chaired by Dr. Mordechai Rozanski, President of the University of Guelph. Rozanski's report, delivered in December 2002, criticized many of the Conservatives' policy changes, especially the removal of $2.0 billion from the education budget over the years of their tenure. His report recommended restoring at least $1.8 billion of that funding, as well as restoring funding to programs for special education, both French and English as a second language, early years, students at risk, and Aboriginal students (OPEIU Local 343 2002).

Mike Harris abandoned his party and its "revolution" before his second mandate was completed, turning the premiership over to Ernie Eves in April 2002. In October of 2003, the Liberal Party won the provincial general election, partly as a result of disillusionment and anger over the Harris attacks on public education and partly because the Liberals' promised to implement the recommendations in the Rozanski Report. However, the far-reaching effects of the Conservatives' educational restructuring, largely initiated by Harris himself, are not easily remediated. First, the public would understandably balk at the expense of yet another overhaul of the education system. Second, properly implemented institutional change must be introduced at a pace its stakeholders can cope with, not dropped like a bomb and implemented by fiat.

Designing a New Curriculum for Corporations

According to *The Mike Harris Round Table on Common Sense in Education*, a 1995 Conservative Party pre-election paper, students in Ontario were "graduating without acceptable levels of skill in language and mathematics" (Progressive Conservative Party of Ontario 1995: 25). This became a much-repeated Conservative refrain despite the fact that a Royal Commission on Learning, tabled a year earlier, stated that although there were shortcomings in the education system of Ontario, "there is no serious evidence that our schools are failing our kids any more or less than they ever have" (Royal Commission on Learning 1994: 3). The cornerstones of the Harris government's new curriculum were higher educational standards, proof of success through standardized testing, and greater involvement of the business sector in education, to ensure that students were well-prepared for the demands of the workplace.

The Conservatives, who had declared that Ontario was "open for business," planned their educational policy with the marketplace in mind. In the new curriculum, "emphasis in all subjects seemed to fall on practical, career preparation exercises" (Gidney 1999: 238), while programs for non-academic students (the former "basic" level) were eliminated altogether. In this way, Ontario would provide a workforce schooled in the laws of the marketplace rather than in reflective or critical thinking, while also providing a large contingent of dropouts willing to work for minimum wage.

The Harris education agenda followed in the footsteps of conservative, pro-globalization governments in Great Britain and the United States, which had both implemented similar changes within the past decade. The following observation, made about Great Britain's educational reforms, could equally describe the political environment of the Harris-Eves years:

> there is, within education, a rising tide of bellicose managerialism mani-
> fested in hierarchical lines of command and decision-making, centraliza-

tion of power, massively increased bureaucracy, a management-oriented vocabulary of pedagogy and... a... curriculum dreamed up by politicians and an inspection service run as an enforcement organization. (Parker 1997: 4)

It is well recognized that educational curricula reflect "the interests and agendas of specific people in specific situations" (Brookfield 1995: 40), but never before has the Ontario school curriculum been so clearly subservient to the interests of corporate business. Early drafts of the new curriculum allowed non-certified personnel to teach art, music, technology, and other courses. Up to one-third of the credits necessary to graduate from high school could be obtained through unpaid, part-time jobs where students would, in the words of Education Minister Snobelen, "learn job skills, learn the value of showing up, learn how to work in teams, and learn how to serve people." To ensure the relevance of the curriculum, "the private sector [would] become involved in its content, delivery and evaluation" (Robertson 1998: 56–57).

The Harris government announced its intention to assist in the privatization of education — as had the American and British governments — by allowing charter schools, which are in effect private schools funded by the government through per-student grants. As well, it initiated a large tax credit for parents who enrolled their children in existing private schools. This forced the underfunded public system to compete for students: public schools had to devote much of their time to public relations in order to attract "customers." Under such circumstances, "keeping the consumers happy enough so that they don't buy the product elsewhere is the bottom line for educational institutions" (Brookfield 1995: 21). Interestingly, private schools were not required to submit their students to independent Educational Quality and Accountability Office testing, the tool of standardization and educational equality according to the Harris government.

Although public schools in Ontario must be supported by tax revenue, the Harris and Eves governments demanded that schools become more self-supporting — more like a business. In the eight years of Conservative rule in Ontario, $2 billion was cut from the education budget. It became the job of the consumer — namely, the students and their parents — to raise the money to ensure that schools were well equipped. This, of course, produced inequities: fundraising in a middle-class suburb is a lot more profitable than in a poor inner-city area. Such a policy has a particular bias against Northern Ontario, where unemployment is generally higher and incomes generally lower.

The result is that schools today face desperate shortages of books, sports equipment, musical instruments, and other necessities. Yet parents and neighbours are now accustomed to the sight of pint-sized salespersons selling chocolate bars, cookie dough, fresh fruit from Florida, wrapping paper, and a host of other items door-to-door after school. In 2002, parents' councils in Ontario raised $30 million for their schools, most of which went to pay for pencils, books, computers, paper, and other necessities, rather than "frills." It is important to remember that when children are going door-to-door with chocolate bars they are not playing basketball or street hockey, they are not practising the piano or guitar, they are not making a snow fort or playing on swings at the park. What they are doing is acting as fundraisers for the school system, the same system that their parents are paying for through their taxes.

John Snobelen, at the beginning of his tenure as Education Minister, promised a computer for every child in every classroom, but in the end was unable to fund his promise. He was, however, able to dig up $33 million per year to pay for the standardized tests that have been introduced for grades three, six, nine, and ten, despite the fact that study after study has proven that standardized tests are not accurate predictors of student achievement or ability. Teachers' formal and informal evaluations of student achievement are better predictors. However, "the strongest predictor of student performance is socioeconomic status" (Rogers, cited in Robertson 1998: 72). By underfunding the public school system, the Conservatives ensured that students of low socioeconomic status went to schools with equally low ability to meet their needs.

It is difficult, if not impossible, to serve two masters at once. An original intent of public education, to create a populace with the analytical ability and literacy skills to participate in democratic debate and decision-making, is in a sense antithetical to the primary goal of corporate business, which is to increase profits and to maintain the illusion of consumer choice. As Brookfield (1995: 21) writes: "The most hallowed rule of business — that the customer is always right — is often pedagogically wrong. Equating good teaching with how many students feel you have done what they wanted ignores the dynamics of teaching and prevents significant learning."

The Corporate Curriculum and Its Casualties

Instead of focussing on the development of critical and analytical thinking skills and intellectual curiosity, the Conservatives' new curriculum relentlessly emphasized the importance of employment rather than vocation, making it abundantly clear to students that their primary goal in life is to get and keep a job. In 1996, the Education Minister called for each student's "career file" to be opened in grade one (Abraham 1996). Under the new curriculum, students learn how to write résumés in elementary school, a compulsory half-course called "Careers" is twinned with another on "Citizenship" — as if employment were the primary responsibility of citizenship. In a grade twelve *English* course, a suggested unit topic is "Budgeting."

One critic has said that, as a result of the new curriculum, in Ontario "we do not educate, we train. We do not teach students, we teach curriculum" (Ricci 2004: 7). The needs of students are subsumed to the needs of the corporate sector through three key means: the implementation of standardized testing, the narrowing of educational levels in secondary school, and the diminution of teachers' autonomy in the classroom.

There is enormous pressure on principals and school staff to improve school test scores. Although the government maintains that the scores will not be used to compare one school to another, the Ontario Secondary School Teachers' Federation, reports that:

> the results of the standardized tests in grades 3, 6 and 10 have turned into media reports ranking schools and district school boards. The grades 3 and 6 tests have placed enormous stress on our 8- and 11-year-old children.
> Standards must match student development and readiness and these [test standards] don't. Without textbooks, resources or funds for remedial programs, setting higher standards is meaningless. (OSSTF 2003)

As one critic of the process admonishes, "We have standardized tests, but we have to understand that we do not have standardized students" (Ricci 2004: 7).

To improve students' scores on these all-important standardized tests, time is taken from the regular curriculum for a practice known as "teaching to the test." Students are given practice in the type of questions asked on the test in order to improve their success rates. What these tests really measure is the students' ability to write standardized tests. Brazilian educator Paulo Freire calls this the "banking system of education," in which students are empty receptacles to be filled up with knowledge by the teacher (Freire 1973). The banking system of education regards students as objects, not subjects. The more students are taught in this manner, Freire asserts, "the more completely they accept the passive role imposed on them, the more they tend simply to adapt to the world as it is and to the fragmented view of reality deposited in them" (Freire 1973: 60). The new Ontario curriculum, with its de-emphasis on critical and reflective thinking, aims to produce workers who do not question the *status quo*, who believe that all else must be subsumed to the need to find and keep a job — *any* job.

The shortcomings of the new curriculum quickly became evident. A 1999 study indicated that "the unease among many parents about the welfare of their children [is] palpable" (Gidney 1999: 280). By 2004, 162,000 of the students who started grade nine in 1999, when the new secondary curriculum was implemented, had dropped out. This is a drop-out rate of 30 percent — the highest at any time in the history of public schools in Ontario (Ricci 2004: 7). This has enormous ramifications in terms of the province's workforce. Educational requirements, even in primary industries such as mining, which are so important in Northern Ontario, have risen as more technological advances require strong literacy and numeracy skills. Major employers such as Inco now require a high-school diploma for entry-level jobs. High-school dropouts are left to compete for low-paying "McJobs" with few benefits or prospects for improvement. Who benefits from this?

Despite widespread recognition in the Ontario education system of Gardner's (1993) theory of multiple intelligences, the new curriculum favours courses that emphasize verbal and logical intelligence to the exclusion of other types. It places less value on courses in which non-academic students excel. In fact, there is little time in the new curriculum for any but the core courses such as mathematics, science, and English: "optional" courses such as physical education, music, construction and automotive technologies, family studies, and art are becoming more and more difficult to fit into the school day. Courses in music and art are often offered before school or at lunchtime, if they are offered at all. And, the traditional "liberal arts" courses — history, sociology, geography — are downplayed: students can graduate from the university-bound stream having taken only one history and one geography course in the entire four years. However, as mentioned earlier, time is found for a compulsory course in "Careers," and schools are required to offer optional courses in "Career Exploration and Workplace Preparation," while there is no similar requirement to offer family studies, shop courses, or drama. There is little in the school day to maintain the interest of the non-academic student, as the subjects they excel at are slowly being eliminated from the curriculum.

A study by Queen's University's Dr. Alan King, which came out in August 2002, substantiated that the new curriculum is inappropriate for many students:

> Of the more than 22,000 applied program students in the province, only about 35 percent were able to acquire 16 credits in two years compared to almost 58 percent under the old curriculum. This increase in failure rates of almost 50 percent causes grave concern because the inability to acquire credits in grades 9 and 10 is one of the best predictors of the drop-out rate (OSSTF 2002).

Since its election in October 2003, the McGinty Liberal government has tried desperately to remediate some of the worst effects of the Conservatives' curriculum. A review of the grade nine and ten math courses at the "applied" level resulted in considerable curriculum change. All other courses are under systematic review. The grade ten literacy test has been downsized and altered. A huge new "Student Success Initiative" has poured millions into finding ways to keep potential dropouts in school, and to counteract the exclusionary effects of the new curriculum. The sad fact, however, is that there is no "quick fix." It may be many years before Ontario's education system recovers. In the meantime, according to one Rainbow District administrator, there is a whole secondary school's worth of dropouts on the streets of Sudbury.

The Role of Teachers

Most teachers understood in advance that the Conservatives' new curriculum and its rushed implementation would produce problems and inequities. It was obvious that teachers would be the most vocal opponents of much of the Tory education policy. To counter this, the Conservatives began an anti-teacher campaign early in their mandate. Teachers were characterized as lazy and obstinate, their concerns dismissed as self-interested. The government ran political ads misrepresenting the effects of Bill 160 on teachers' working conditions. At one point, teachers were mandated to teach an extra period each year. The government's ad said, "It's only an extra twenty-five minutes." In fact, it meant an extra seventy-five-minute class with an extra twenty-five to thirty-five students' work to mark during one semester. The government ad was a blatant lie.

In some ways, teachers have tended to be a conservative occupational group. In the past, they have identified more with professionals such as doctors and lawyers than with unionized workers. Even in a relatively union-friendly community like Sudbury, many teachers disapproved of the hard-nosed confrontational tactics used by the mining unions and preferred to refer to teachers' unions as "federations."

Despite this, Sudbury was the site of one of the longest strikes by secondary teachers in Canadian history. On February 6, 1980, 870 secondary teachers in Sudbury, represented by the Ontario Secondary School Teachers Federation and the Association d'Enseignant(e)s Francophones de l'Ontario — the two groups bargained jointly in the 1980s — began a strike that was to last fifty-six school days.

Issues included salaries, cost-of-living allowances, workload provisions, and a proposal by the Sudbury Board of Education to cut 130 teaching jobs — at the time, 17 percent of the teaching force. The strike began after the failure of nineteen bargaining meetings assisted by two different mediators, held over a twelve-month period. In March, a three-person panel consisting of Rick McDowell (later Chair of the Labour Relations Board), James Noonan (representing the Education Board), and Stephen Lewis (representing the teachers) failed to end the dispute. Other teachers across Ontario supported the strike despite pressure for the government to enact back-to-work legislation. At the OSSTF's Annual Assembly that spring, members agreed to threaten a half-day provincial walkout if such legislation was introduced. The strike was finally ended in early May, after a thirteen-hour bargaining session in Education Minister Bette Stephenson's office. Even then, the membership voted only 63 percent to accept the agreement (Albert 2005). The long weeks on strike appeared to toughen, not weaken, the teachers' resolve, and their resistance made clear to the provincial government that teachers were willing to strike if they needed to. This experience carried over into the resistance of Sudbury teachers to the Harris-Eves restructuring, as teachers participated in such actions as the Days of Protest organized by other labour organizations and activist groups throughout Northern Ontario.

In the early days of the Harris government's tenure, teachers realized that a serious attack on their rights was in the offing. Bill 136, designed by the Conservatives to avoid labour problems during the transition period of municipal, health, and education restructuring, eliminated the right to strike during the transition phase. Although it was a temporary measure, and its key clauses did not cover teachers, Minister Snobelen promised similar legislation aimed at teachers. In the spring of 1997, OSSTF members voted to take job action if the government attacked their bargaining rights (Gidney 1999: 255).

In September 1997, Snobelen introduced Bill 160. Among the measures directly affecting teachers were:

- control over class size, instructional hours, preparation time, and the use of non-certified teachers were all to be set by regulation, and therefore would not require approval by the Legislature or be negotiable in collective agreements;
- the number of teaching days in the school year was extended;
- preparation time for secondary teachers was cut by 50 percent. (This act alone, according to the teachers' unions, would eliminate 10,000 teaching jobs.)

While the OSSTF tended to be the most militant of the teachers' unions, the elementary teachers' union — the Ontario Teachers' Federation — now responded to Bill 160 with a statement setting out a list of non-negotiable items. Harris chose this time to replace the unpopular John Snobelen as Minister of Education with Dave Johnson, who nevertheless budged very little from Snobelen's stance. After a series of meetings where nothing was resolved, teachers called for a shutdown of the province's schools on October 27, 1997.

This action by teachers was not a legal strike, but a political protest. At first, most teachers supported it, as did many principals and vice-principals. Not one school board came out in support of the government's position. However, as Johnson and Harris held their ground, three of the five teachers' unions called for their members to return to work in the face of public disapproval of the school shutdown. While the OSSTF and Ontario English Catholic Teachers' Association held out, without solidarity among all the teachers' unions, there was little they could do. On Monday, November 27, teachers went back to work. The break in solidarity was seen as a betrayal, and caused bitterness between elementary and secondary teachers' unions that remains to this day. The Conservatives wasted no time enacting Bill 160 into law.

Having won its battle against teachers over Bill 160, the Harris government assumed that it had popular support for *any* anti-teacher legislation it chose to enact. In 2000 it announced its intent to mandate compulsory participation for teachers in extracurricular activities, which had always been done on a voluntary basis. This came at the same time as teachers were struggling with the loss of half their preparation time and its replacement with an extra class: in other words, more students, more preparation and marking, and less time to do it in. Overwhelmed and angry, teachers instituted a province-wide boycott of all extracurricular activities. This was a difficult choice, as coaches had to abandon teams they had nurtured for years, drama clubs produced no plays, debating teams had no debates — a curtailment of the very activities many teachers will tell you add immeasurably to their job satisfaction, and which are done voluntarily and without financial compensation. After almost a year with few extracurricular activities, public dissatisfaction forced the government to back down on the issue.

The Conservatives tried to implement a further attack on teachers through the College of Teachers. They initiated a "Professional Learning Plan," to be overseen by the College of Teachers. Teachers would have to re-qualify for their teaching certificates every seven years by taking a series of Ministry-approved courses. No other professionals in the province had to re-qualify for their certification on a regular basis. This action would not only diminish the role of teachers' unions, it would remove teachers' control over their own choice of professional upgrading courses. Teachers saw it as a punitive measure to increase their workload. Again, teachers chose to resist, by boycotting the Learning Plan. A large bureaucracy hired by the Conservative government to oversee the program sat idle as teachers refused to submit information regarding any courses they had taken.

In both these cases, Conservative punitive actions toward teachers had finally backfired. The anti-teacher agenda was so transparent that the press and public became more sympathetic to teachers than they had been before. However, this sympathy arrived too late, after the worst aspects of educational restructuring had been implemented. The voices of teachers who correctly predicted its effects went unheard and unheeded when it could have made a difference.

Where Are We Now?

The educational restructuring and new curriculum imposed in eight years of misrule by the Harris-Eves Conservatives have been a major setback for our students, schools, teachers, and communities. These have been the results:

- local control over education has been virtually eliminated, school boards have been made less accessible, and educational funding and decision-making has been centralized in Toronto. This has serious ramifications, particularly in Northern and rural locations where regulations created for urban populations are not appropriate;
- the new funding formula has proven inadequate, and has meant substantial school closures — such as Capreol High School and Northeastern High School — job losses, and program cancellations, all of which the Harris government said would not happen;
- the 30 percent drop-out rate is the highest in Ontario's history;
- the government has imposed educational policies that speak the language and serve the needs of corporate globalization, including an emphasis on standardized testing and evaluation that increases centralized control of the education process;
- the role of school administrators has been altered from that of educators to that of business managers. Administrators have been excluded from the teachers' unions, and a new layer of centralized bureaucracy made up of non-educators has been installed in Toronto through the College of Teachers;

- the level of trust and cooperation between the government and teachers' unions has dramatically eroded, despite the 2003 change in government;
- the government's attempt to save money through a costly early-retirement incentive to senior teachers has resulted in the retirement of over 10,000 experienced teachers across the province. The loss of both their accumulated experience and their mentorship of younger teachers cannot be calculated.

Public disenchantment with the education policies of the Harris and Eves Conservative governments was a major factor leading to the Liberals' majority electoral victory in 2003. However, a change in government does not automatically remediate the problems created by the previous government. Responsible change — unlike that imposed by the Harris-Eves governments — takes a great deal of time and money. Political journalist John Ibbitson, who called the Harris government "the most radical in the democratic world," believes that many of the changes made to the province under the Tories will never be unmade (Robertson 1998: 44).

Certainly, for the 162,000 dropouts in Ontario, nothing can give them back an education appropriate to their skills and needs. They will forever remain what current Education Minister Gerard Kennedy calls "curriculum casualties" (Ricci 2004: 7). Nothing can return to schools the assets lost when veteran teachers retired early rather than submit to the anti-teacher and anti-democratic regulations of Bill 160. Nothing can replace the mentoring these teachers might have given to young teachers struggling with the demands of learning their craft.

R.D. Gidney describes the effects of the loss of morale among teachers during the Conservatives' tenure, as well as the consequences of removing principals and vice-principals from teachers' bargaining units:

> In-school leadership had long had a substantial managerial element; but it also had collegial qualities which made good principals into educational leaders as well. To the extent that changes, it will be a loss, and not a trivial one. High morale and a collegial environment are of crucial importance: after all the rhetoric about the new departures, all the promises of excellence and accountability, all the new curriculum guidelines and testing initiatives, what actually happens in classrooms happens because teachers make it happen. No one can afford to ignore that simple truth. (Gidney 1999: 281)

The people of Sudbury and Ontario continue to face the pressures of an educational system dominated by corporate demands and values. The Harris-Eves experience showed in a harsher form what corporate domination means to students, teachers, and communities. But the actions of the Harris and Eves governments also did a great deal to dislodge teachers from complacency and politicize their actions. Today teachers in Ontario are more cognizant of their position as workers, and less trusting of their government employers. This is good, because they have a greatly diminished ability to negotiate salaries and conditions of work. The boycotts of extracurricular activities and the Professional Learning Plan, both of which were successful, demonstrated that teachers have the means at their disposal to resist the imposition of unfair practices. The solidarity within individual federations is greater: the boycott of extracurricular activities was probably the first of its kind that had near 100 percent compliance across the province.

It is encouraging that the people in charge of educating Ontario's children were willing to fight against anti-democratic legislation and to insist on their right to participate in the processes that govern their workplaces. It is to be hoped that these are the lasting lessons from the Little Blue Schoolhouse.

Chapter 14

The Rise and Decline of Local 6500 United Steelworkers of America

Bruce McKeigan

The Rise

In 1975 a transition took place in the United Steelworkers Local 6500, from traditional suit-and-tie business trade unionism to a progressive, proactive, political force. Local 6500 in Sudbury was the second-largest Steelworker local in Canada, with more than 18,000 members. Many of these were young people still not far removed from the so-called "hippy" generation of the 1960s, who gave rebirth to the notion of questioning authority. In the summer of 1975, collective bargaining was taking place between the employer and our union. Inco was the largest nickel corporation in the world. The contract expiration date was fast approaching and the membership was becoming agitated at the lack of communication from the Bargaining Committee and Local President Mickey Maguire.

The membership had already unofficially adopted a "no contract-no work" policy: if we had no word of a tentative agreement by midnight on the contract's expiration date, picket lines would be up. With negotiations taking place 240 miles away in Toronto, there was much confusion — rumours, calls for patience, radio reports — but no official word from the union. So the minute the contract expired, picket lines went up at all Inco mines, mills, and surface plants across the forty-five-mile radius that Inco's Sudbury operations spread. Finally, there was word from President Maguire and, after only ten days on the picket lines, we ended up with a tentative agreement, membership information meetings, and a vote in favour of accepting the new contract proposal. But the seeds of change had already been planted.

The Executive Board elections for Local 6500 were due shortly after the strike. Dave Patterson, a "long-haired radical," as he came to be labelled by both company bosses and the Steelworker establishment, had forged a name for himself among the membership as a fighter and leader. This was particularly true at one of the largest mines in the region, the Frood Mine where he worked and was a shop steward. Patterson, with the encouragement of rank-and-file members, decided to challenge Mickey Maguire for the presidency of Local 6500. Patterson's election team consisted of a handful of activists — you could count them, literally, on one hand. In the forefront were shop stewards like Joel Dworski, Dick Kerr, and Ray Jones, three of the best and most respected stewards in the entire Local, where the desire for change was tangible. You could feel it in every department and in every conversation. All that was needed was the right leadership.

Dave Patterson's first campaign leaflet set the tone. Its front cover was taken up almost entirely by a picture of Patterson in his underground hardrock miner's clothing, complete with hard hat. This was a drastic, but refreshing, change for much of the young membership used to the traditional suit-and-tie look of union "bosses." Patterson's campaign was simple: it was time to change the old ways and to involve the average member. Dave was an activist and a fighter: he was one of us.

The last point was important. When leadership rises above, rather than with, the membership, it loses contact with the members and you end up with the traditional "representative" democracy that marks most governments. People become apathetic and leave everything up to elected representatives. Rank-and-file members come to see the people at the top as union bosses rather than union leaders. That is what happened in the '75 strike.

Patterson was the right person at the right time to change the situation. He actually finished second to Maguire in the election, with Bob Chartrand placing third. However, the ballots of students working at the Levack Mine were segregated and subsequently not counted, and an appeal was filed on this issue. The question was whether or not student workers had the right to vote. At the Steelworkers' International convention, the final step in the appeal process, the case was put to the floor. Despite heated debate, there was still no clear answer from officials. Jim Hicke, a former Mine Mill member and founding member of Local 6500, refused to leave the microphone until he got a straight answer. He proclaimed adamantly that the integrity of Steelworker elections was at stake, so a clear answer was required. A hastily called meeting took place among on-stage officials. When the huddle broke up, officials announced that because students paid dues, they should be entitled to vote.

A new election took place in Local 6500, with only those candidates who ran in the original election allowed to take part. While Maguire's vote stayed about the same, Patterson took votes from Chartrand and was elected President of Local 6500. Jim Hicke's stance at the International convention was important in more ways than one. Ironically, Hicke was never a Patterson supporter. His argument was based strictly on the integrity of our elections. This points out what many of us have always said — there was a time in Local 6500 when principle came before politics.

More and more rank-and-file members got involved in the Local. Some of us eventually ended up on the Executive in support of Patterson. We actively sought the input and involvement of rank-and-file members. We kept them informed with issue-oriented leaflets that we handed out at plant gates. Many members were surprised: this was the first time local union representatives had gone to plant gates in Sudbury on a regular basis with leaflets that did not involve an election of some sort. Talk about being thrust into the eye of the storm! The

Maguire-Patterson transition consisted of Maguire sniping at Patterson, "You wanted the job, you got it," and then walking out of the office. Patterson's first set of negotiations as head of the bargaining team resulted in what was then the longest strike in Canadian industry.

The 1978 Strike: A Defining Moment

The strike of '78 began September 15 and did not end until May 31, 1979. It was reported to have the largest number of "man-hours" ever lost during a strike in Canada. It was also a defining moment for Local 6500 of the United Steelworkers of America.

Inco had amassed a one-year stockpile of nickel, though not by choice. We were in the middle of one of the worst busts of the nickel market's perpetual boom-and-bust cycles. Although the company could not sell all the nickel it wanted, it saw the strike as an opportunity to break Local 6500 or, at the very least, to leave it totally ineffectual. It hired outside hacks to head up negotiations and put more than twenty demands for concessions on the bargaining table — everything from reducing wages to weakening grievance procedures and the power and influence of shop stewards. The shop stewards are the backbone of any union — ours more than most, because of the large size of our local and the proactive nature of our stewards. Inco's industrial-relations lackey in the negotiations promised that the company was going to "recoup."

Homer Seguin, one of the most knowledgeable and skilled trade unionists I have known, was active in explaining the fight against concessions. He always used to say that when times are good and the companies are hauling in heavy profits, we don't try to negotiate exorbitant settlements. Consequently, in bad times, no matter how bad the economy or losses for the company, we do not accept concessions. We bargain responsibly. Bolstered by a recent Canadian Labour Congress resolution that called for no concessions in contract negotiations, we took on a battle that would influence collective bargaining throughout North America.

One of the first signs of a change from Local 6500's old ways was when Linda George and others organized the Wives Supporting the Strike Committee. This was a key factor in the success of the strike, given what had happened in the '58 strike. During that earlier strike, company and business interests, some politicians, and other conservative groups organized the wives into opposing the strike. After a huge meeting held in the Sudbury Arena, the strike quickly fell apart and resulted in a disastrous contract for the union (then Mine Mill). This time around, the Wives Committee held regular meetings to keep people informed on the issues as they evolved, handed out leaflets, attended and organized rallies, and sent out news releases. More than 200 women were on the group's active list, including a seven-woman steering committee. They organized and prepared various bean suppers held at schools, halls, and for all three shifts of picketers. They organized the first children's Christmas party for the kids of Local 6500 members, with gifts collected from other unions and organizations across the entire country. Other projects included organizing family pickets, printing a comic book called *What's a Strike?*, establishing baby and clothing depots, and researching and informing members and the rest of the community about Inco's operations in Guatemala.

All of this, of course, was not a matter of blind subservience. When the Wives Committee disagreed with things that were going on in the strike, the union heard about it, loud and clear. The Wives Supporting the Strike Committee had a major impact on the success of the strike. Their efforts became the subject of a documentary produced through the National Film Board of Canada entitled *A Wives' Tale*, which emphasized the growing and increasingly important role of women in the labour movement.

Another important aspect of the 1978 strike's organization was the formation of a Citizens' Strike Support Committee, a group of friends of the labour movement that worked to organize community support for Local 6500's strike. Lawyer Richard Pharand as chairperson and community activists such as Joan Kuyek led the way. The Committee produced one of the most impressive newsletters I have ever seen. It was printed on a regular basis throughout the entire strike. It contained stories on the strike, editorial comic strips, reports on upcoming meetings and events, and even the Support Committee's financial statement. Typesetting was by volunteer labour and printing was by Acme Printing, a union shop.

This kind of strike support activity was new to Sudbury. The public stance of committees like these led to unprecedented, open community support. Landlords postponed rents or made other payment arrangements, banks postponed loan payments for the duration of the strike, pharmacies provided certain prescription drugs and over-the-counter necessities, and numerous businesses provided food or cut-rate services. Many rank-and-file members were involved in these actions, including countless volunteers who travelled the entire country for plant-gate collections and tended tables at the Union Hall as a regular stream of members collected strike pay, prescription drugs, or other services.

For the first time, Inco was wholly criticized by a wide cross-section of Canadian society, including some conservative business magazines. Even Sudbury Mayor Jim Gordon, a card-carrying member of the Conservative Party, jumped on the bandwagon. At one rally in our Union Hall he tore up his party card on stage, much to the delight of the audience. He once stated, "We learned that this community is certainly united in support of the working people who create the wealth which keeps Ontario and Canada going. We recognized the needs of the workers." Gordon was subsequently re-elected Mayor with the help of a group of active Steelworkers. Unfortunately, he must have taped his Party card back together, because he ended up running for the anti-union Conservative Party in a later provincial election — to the embarrassment of the Steelworker activists who had helped re-elect him. In short, Inco was painted as the big, bad, "corporate welfare bum" that it is. Faced with all this active solidarity and the tenaciousness of our Bargaining Committee, at one point one company spokespersons threw his hands in the air and said, "I've never seen anything like this."

From the very beginning, this was not a strike about money. It was about fighting concessions and not taking a step backwards. The final exclamation point was put on that statement eight months into the strike when Inco finally made a contract proposal acceptable to the union's Bargaining Committee. Despite this, 57.3 percent of the membership rejected the offer. The pensions and wages, among other things, were not good enough, considering what we had been through. The membership did not blame the Bargaining Committee, instead focussing our sentiments toward Inco. The headline in *Northern Life* newspaper said it best, "Sudbury, May 12, 1979 — a quiet night full of hate."

Within two weeks the company put forward another "final" offer, and this one was accepted by the membership. It resulted in a significant wage increase, a cost-of-living clause that included roll-ins to the base rate, no concessions, long-term disability, and the first thirty-and-out pension in the industry, just to name a few highlights. The Inco hacks left town, never to be seen in our parts again. From unions all across Canada there was an outpouring of congratulations and appreciation. As the President of Local 222 of the United Auto Workers wrote, "You have won the total respect of our entire membership and every union in the country." For years to come we heard from unions all across North America about how important our victory was to the fight against concessions and making gains in collective bargaining. Once again, this showed that contract negotiations and any subsequent strikes must not be measured by immediate dollars alone.

However, there was an even more valuable lesson learned. Arja Lane, the Wives Supporting the Strike liaison with the union said, "Until this strike, none of us knew what power we had to work with. Now we do." As long-time Steelworker and negotiator Gib Gilchrist tried constantly to remind union leaders, less than 10 percent of a union's time is spent on collective bargaining — the other 90 percent of our time is spent on representing the membership and fighting the issues of the day. Gib wrote: "Unions are an economic force in our society, free to speak out on all issues of the day, free to fight for better laws, free to strive for better wages, benefits and working conditions." As a result of this strike and our numerous travels, many rank-and-file members and union leaders had met with everyone from striking British coal miners to representatives discussing the Palestinian struggle to average South Africans spreading the word in the battle against apartheid. We came to empathize, rather than just sympathize, with the struggles of others. It did not matter to us whether it was a small union on the other side of town, another union 2,000 thousand miles to the south, or an entire people being repressed on the other side of the world — we now saw the big picture. It became clear: the struggle continues.

Patterson versus Steelworker Business Unionism

Dave Patterson's popularity grew immensely during the '78 strike. He became the first President of Local 6500 ever to be re-elected following a strike. His opponent was one of two members of the sixteen-member 1978 Bargaining

Committee who voted against the strike from the beginning. Patterson won the 1979 election for President by a landslide.

The Steelworkers' International Union elections were now just around the corner. This involved the election of all International executives in North America, including the District 6 Director for Ontario. Much of our local membership had been disappointed with District 6 Director Stu Cooke during our strike, and there was a groundswell of support for Patterson to run against him. After meetings with other Steelworkers across the province, Patterson decided to take up the challenge.

We were still naive to the massive power of the International Union, although we knew that most of Steelworker locals were small and dominated by "staff representatives" appointed by the International Union. At the time, elections for higher positions in our union were a formality. Usually, these positions were filled by acclamation. We knew ours was going to have to be a grassroots campaign.

Organizational meetings were held all over the province. Ontario is massive, so we had to travel a lot to attend numerous meetings. Using many of the contacts established during the '78 strike, we planned meetings in the north, south, southwest, and eastern parts of Ontario. With local organizations in place, we booked vacation time and hit the road. We jumped in our cars and travelled to one city after another. We took our leaflets to every plant gate we could find, most of which had been laid out for us. As we were told time after time, it was unusual to see anyone at the plant gates, particularly for an election for a high position in the union — unusual and refreshing. Most rank-and-file members had heard of our strike, and of Dave Patterson. Many expressed overall dissatisfaction with the Steelworker leadership, or the lack thereof, and were looking for a change. For most members, this was the first time they had been presented with any alternative, let alone a viable alternative.

Never having been faced with this kind of challenge before, most of the appointed Steelworker staff representatives in the province didn't seem to take it seriously. Some local officers who were under the thumb of staff reps, however, were starting to feel the winds of change. Two of them came to plant gates where we were campaigning and actually started grabbing our leaflets out of their members' hands and throwing them on the ground. They were definitely scared. Unlike the staff reps, these guys worked on the job and could feel the desire for change, which was evident everywhere we went.

To the shock of many, Dave Patterson was elected Steelworkers District Director for Ontario. The swearing-in ceremony took place September 1, 1981, at Linden Hall in Pittsburgh, Pennsylvania, where the Steelworkers' International head office is located. Actually, there was no Linden "Hall" at the time: it was just an open field. The experience was surreal. We watched International officers from all over America pull up in one Cadillac or other gas-guzzler after another. We watched the parade of three-piece, gun-bulging suits and horseshoe-diamond pinky rings. At the reception later that day, a table full of these guys ended up comparing weapons. By contrast, we pulled up in a bus. Patterson was still wearing his tattered, good-luck cowboy hat.

In a sign of things to come, a customs agent at the border stepped onto our bus when we crossed the border heading toward Pittsburgh. With approximately fifty people on the bus, he walked down the aisle, eye-balling each and every passenger. He only talked to one person. Patterson was about three-quarters of the way down the aisle. The agent pointed right at him and said abruptly, "You sir, please show me some identification." Everyone burst out laughing. Naively, people were thinking, "Of all the people on the bus, isn't it funny that Patterson was the one they randomly chose?" It was an omen.

From day one it appeared the job of the more than fifty International-appointed staff reps in Ontario was to battle Patterson until the next election. It seemed that, as far as they were concerned, the next District Director election campaign was going to be four years long. Staff reps are the chief spokespersons for each local's bargaining teams. Patterson would have to go into these locals and veto concessionary contracts that had been negotiated by the staff reps. And, there was a "whisper" campaign that included red-baiting and talk of Patterson "not being a team player." When the International union elections came up again, with virtually every major position throughout North America being acclaimed in the traditional manner, the entire weight of the International's awesome election machine came down on Patterson. They ran Leo Gerard, a staff rep originally from Local 6500 in Sudbury, which was also Patterson's home local. In fact, Gerard had been acclaimed to the 1978 Bargaining Committee but left shortly thereafter to take a staff rep job with the International union.

The power of the Pittsburgh-paid staff reps in a Steelworker election is something to behold. They control most of the small local executives and are the "go to" authorities on how elections are to be conducted and ballots counted. As you would expect, Gerard won the next District 6 Director's election. It seemed little consolation that, in their shared home local, where the membership knew both candidates best, Patterson won the vote by an almost three-to-one margin. The International union added insult to injury. It was common practice for presidents or others in high positions who had finished their term of office to be given union leave to take either appointed staff-rep jobs or union-related jobs with the government. Along with other Steelworkers, Patterson was offered a job as a union representative at the Ontario Labour Relations Board. But he was told his leave had been denied. Inco was naturally never a fan of Patterson's. He phoned them immediately, expecting to have another battle with his long-time nemesis to get his leave. The Inco representative told him that, despite their history, the company did not deny him leave — it was his own union that had denied it. Dave would never collect the thirty-and-out pension he had negotiated for everyone else.

Back to Business as Usual in Local 6500

Things were also changing for the worse at Local 6500. When Patterson was still Local President, Ron Macdonald was considering running against Patterson in the executive election that took place after the '78 strike. We made the tactical error of repeatedly telling Macdonald he should not bother running because Patterson was unbeatable in Local 6500. Macdonald eventually dropped out of the race. He was Vice-President at the time and a conservative, long time, anti-Patterson foe. It would have been better that he run openly as a right-winger against Patterson and lose. He would then have had to go back into the plant to work. Unlike small unions, Local 6500's top five table officers worked full-time at the Union Hall. As it turned out, Macdonald, as Vice-President, automatically took over as President when Patterson won the District Director's job and moved to Toronto in 1981.

The troubles got worse. Dave Campbell, a Macdonald supporter, ran against Keith Lovely, a Patterson supporter, for Recording Secretary in the Local's executive elections. Lovely won by a wide margin, but Campbell appealed, as is the right of any member under the International constitution of the United Steelworkers of America. There were two slates of candidates in the election. Lovely had a teeshirt with the name of his slate printed on the front. Local 6500's voting polls are set up in the mines, mills, and plants where we work. There was also a hospital poll and a poll at the Union Hall for members on their days off who preferred to stop into the Union Hall to vote than to travel all the way to their work sites. Next to the hospital poll, the Union Hall is the smallest poll. Campbell's grounds for appeal were that when Lovely voted at the Union Hall he wore this teeshirt! Campbell's appeal seemed ridiculous, given the margin of victory and the fact that there needed to be more than a violation of the constitution: the violation must also be shown to have affected the outcome of the election.

The first step in the appeal process was to take it to the membership meeting. Some of us told Lovely that we should get people out to the meeting because the other slate was going to "stack" the meeting. Lovely, having just fallen off the turnip truck, said, "They wouldn't do that," and that if they did, members would see through it. However, the membership meeting was indeed stacked, and eighty people overturned the results of the thousands of members who voted in the election. Lovely appealed to the International union. After a few backroom dealings, it agreed to sanction a new election for Recording Secretary of Local 6500, which Lovely won by an even larger margin.

While some Local 6500 officers couldn't be found during the day, Lovely was always in his office in the Union Hall. He had the reputation of being a tireless worker. Despite this, only Lovely had his job cut down to three days a week. Despite Lovely winning the two-out-of-three battle for his job, the political precedent had been set. The anti-Patterson slate now knew complete control of the Local 6500 could be achieved within the confines of the Union Hall. This clique could now do whatever it wanted, despite what the thousands of members on the job felt. As one right-wing Local 6500 official pointed out, "We look after the people who come down here," referring to the Union Hall.

Most of us wanted Lovely to run for President. He was one of the most popular, dedicated members of Local 6500, and was also strongly associated with Dave Patterson. Lovely not only chose not to run but to quit Inco altogether, even though he was more than halfway to his pension. He said he could handle anything Inco threw at him, but the backstabbing inflicted by his so-called "brothers" was more than he could stomach. Another union was later fortunate to count Keith Lovely among its ranks.

Undermining Elections

To many members, it might seem as if Local 6500 is having elections all the time. Its executive elections are held every three years. In between these, we also hold Bargaining Committee elections. Following the success of Campbell's "stacked" meeting in 1979, the anti-Patterson group did it again at a membership meeting to elect the Election Committee for the 1982 Bargaining Committee. The Election Committee is a three-person committee made up of a Chief Teller and two others. They are in charge of all aspects of the election, including the appointment of the approximately thirty-five to forty paid tellers at the numerous, individual polls located in Inco plants, mines, and mills. Prior to this time, the Election Committee was always made up of the same apolitical members, but from this time forward, there would be no more independents on the Election Committee — now there was partisan control that would lead to one suspect election after another.

In two subsequent, separate Bargaining Committee elections, my observers caught election tellers giving my votes to my opponent and his votes to me. Both times my observers were told not to interfere, but they persisted. If not for observers Sam Enver and Norris Valiquette, who refused to be intimidated, I would have lost those elections instead of winning them, and I would have been none the wiser. All this happened after meetings were stacked to elect partisan Election Committees.

Unfortunately, the internal situation in Local 6500 continued to deteriorate. In two separate elections, a number of us filed appeals alleging a total of twenty-six violations of the union's constitution and its elections manual. Just a few of our alleged violations of the constitution included:

- a disappeared ballot box;
- two separate sets of ballots being ordered, not just extra ballots, while observers were not permitted to see the unused ballots;
- the selection of Election Committees that were not acceptable to all candidates (as required);
- Election Committee members openly campaigned for incumbent candidates and had their names on endorsement leaflets, but this did not constitute "fair and impartial" behaviour;
- observers were told they would have to leave the count if they continued to use their tally sheets to mark the votes at individual polls, despite this being the practice taught at Steelworker classes for observers at provincial and

federal elections;

- observers were told during the counting of votes to stand at a location where they could not see how the ballots were marked, despite written Steelworker instructions to observers at provincial and federal elections that read in bold capital letters, "Make Sure You See the Ballots";
- observers were denied their right to observe all aspects of the count, including the final tabulation that took place on a stage observers were prevented from entering.

These were violations that could affect and, as seen in two previous occasions, *had* affected the outcome of elections.

The people at International headquarters scheduled our first appeal during Inco's summer shutdown. They were well aware that the shutdown was an annual event when members were on vacation, but they chose deliberately to go ahead at that time anyway. I returned home from an out-of-town vacation to find a letter in my mailbox stating the International's Appeals Committee had come and gone and the appeal was heard and dismissed. Still, we persisted and proceeded to push our appeal through the "proper channels" in the International union. The final answer, which dismissed our appeal, came approximately two-and-a-half years after the election — or, just six months before the next scheduled election.

A second appeal, following another election, was heard by a so-called "independent" staff representative from another area. Naturally, most of us believed that if these appointed staff reps wanted to keep their jobs, they would toe the International's line. To us, "independent staff representative" was an oxymoron. I felt like a guy appealing a decision of the Mafia, with the Godfather sending one of his lowly lieutenants to "independently" hear the claim. The "lieutenant" did not seem to have a clue what I meant when I said, "Justice must not only be done, but must be *seen* to be done." Despite lengthy testimony and evidence, much of it uncontested, supporting our long list of alleged violations, our appeal was dismissed. These dismissed appeals, of course, came from the same International union that *supported* their friend Dave Campbell's appeal. In our case, twenty-six violations, backed up with unrefuted testimony and evidence, were not grounds enough to get a new election. Apparently, for the International union, what constituted an egregious constitutional violation was one opponent, like Keith Lovely, wearing the wrong teeshirt in one poll for one minute!

We have even heard admissions from some low-level people who took part in the vote rigging. I was told directly by someone whose colleague had finally confessed to him that in a past election he had stuffed the ballot box, possibly costing my confidant elected office. This was followed by Local 6500 presidential candidate Norris Valiquette, who walked right up to a certain election teller days after an election and called him a "lying, cheating son-of-a-bitch." Now, you would expect most people to deny it, or dismiss the allegation, or at the very least, pass it off as sour grapes. Instead, this election teller looked over both shoulders, ensuring there was no one within earshot, leaned over to Valiquette and said, "Norris, you know how it is around here — I just do what I'm told." Another teller accused of cheating had told Valiquette earlier, "You'd do the same thing."

"Total Control" at Local 6500

With Patterson in the District 6 office in Toronto during the 1980s, we were now the opposition in Local 6500. Some people began to jump ship, to back the incumbent right-wing slate, offering pathetic excuses such as: "Well, I have to look out for number one," "I want a steady day job instead of shift work, and they promised me they could get me one," or "I want to go to conventions too." Of the turncoats who left us, not a single one ever said they were leaving because they disagreed with our principles, policies, or actions. In fact, many of them kept telling us privately, "I hope you win the next election" or "I voted for you."

As well, jobs at Inco were being drastically cut. There had been next to no new hires for many years, so there were no young people in the Local 6500 to energize the grassroots. With only a handful of us left in opposition, the business-unionist takeover was complete. We went full circle, back to "representative" democracy, where obstacles to, and lack of, involvement allows staff reps to do as they please.

Though we kept trying to get people out to membership meetings, even our faithful supporters were getting fed up. We repeatedly heard things like, "They're going to do whatever they want anyway," "We don't have a union anymore," and "We're tired of being ruled out of order or shouted down every time we try to speak." It was even worse for those of us who remained active out of principle. Although open red-baiting had finally subsided in the political atmosphere of the 1990s, blacklisting was still in full bloom. Many of us were summarily removed from committees. Certain stewards, including myself, were sometimes not even informed of arbitration dates for grievances we had initiated, despite my previous involvement as a case steward in precedent-setting arbitration and Ontario Labour Relations Board cases. Despite his being a former "Steward of the Year," a Local 6500 Vice-President, a Chairperson of the Grievance Committee, and a contract language expert, Norris Valiquette was also denied the right to present arbitrations. Some of the presenters Local 6500 chose instead were people who still went to Valiquette for advice on how to conduct themselves.

I volunteered to teach at the Union Hall on my own time for free. I was continually bypassed, though the incumbent slate had no problem allowing a Designated Individual to teach at the Union Hall for full pay. Designated Individuals are supervisors in training on their way out of the Union and into Inco management, though under our collective agreement they are technically still Union members. Perhaps the slate was afraid I might put in a mileage claim. I was once told by a Local 6500 trustee, "You're not claiming enough mileage, and it's making the other guys look bad." I thought it would be more appropriate for the trustee to talk to the guy down the hall who was laughing and bragging that he made almost as much in mileage as he did in wages, because he put his out-of-town cottage address on his mileage sheets.

The incumbent slate would be satisfied with nothing less than absolute control. One of its leaders was known to have said, "Either buy off or eliminate your opposition." Union involvement declined and self-service increased. It was like living the quote, "Power corrupts — absolute power corrupts absolutely." There came a period where I was one of only two or three people running against Local 6500's entire incumbent slate. As a result of the dismissed appeals mentioned earlier, a number of long-time activists, including founding members of Local 6500 Norris Valiquette and Ernie St. Jean, boycotted the elections. They did so because they said they could not get an honest election in Local 6500. And they said so openly, to Union Hall people and to anyone who asked why they were not running.

The right-wing, business-unionist leaders had the power of office but they did not have deep support in the community. After Ron Macdonald retired as President of Local 6500 and entered municipal politics, he eventually ran for Regional Chairman of the Region of Sudbury. In an election where those involved in its running were fair and impartial and observers were allowed to see all aspects of the count, including the final tabulation, he finished a distant sixth. When Macdonald retired from Local 6500 in mid-term, Vice-President Dave Campbell, who initiated the frivolous appeal against Keith Lovely's teeshirt, inherited the President's job. This mid-term automatic succession process became so common that some members started to refer to it as a "divine right of passage."

With Campbell at the helm, one of his friends on the Election Committee charged me under the union constitution, claiming falsely that I had said publicly that you could not get an honest election in Local 6500. Campbell denied putting his friend up to it, but he was nonetheless chief witness for the prosecution at my trial. As I mentioned, the founding members had gone to the right-wing leaders and told them to their faces what they had been telling everyone else. One of them, my trial counsel Norris Valiquette, said to my accuser and Campbell that they knew full well that it was he — Valiquette rather than myself — who had made the statement about the impossibility of an honest election in Local 6500, so, he asked, "Why wasn't *I* charged?" Valiquette's question went unanswered.

We knew the answer. I was the only one left who would run in Local 6500 elections. Besides being elected to a number of Bargaining Committees, I took 42 percent of the vote in a Presidential election running against Campbell and his entire slate — at least that's what I was told. The three-person Election Committee, which was openly campaigning and/or endorsing the incumbent Campbell, never let my observers keep their own tally, see the marked ballots, see the unused ballots from the two separate sets that were ordered, or see the final tabulation. We had no way of verifying if, *once again*, they had given my votes to my opponent and his votes to me.

Getting back to the question of why I was charged, if I were to be found guilty in their kangaroo court I would be deemed to be a union member "not in good standing." According to the union constitution, only members in good standing are allowed to run for office. The incumbent slate had run this charade successfully once already in a previous presidential election. This time around, I was able to get enough members out to the membership meeting to defeat a preliminary report, which — no surprise — had found me guilty. As much as these members hated going to the Union Hall, they thought trying to throw a twenty-five-year steward and activist out of the union on trumped-up charges was going a little too far.

So with the right wing in almost total control, what kind of people did we end up with at the Union Hall? Well, there was the one Chief Steward who said, "I wish I had a pair of breasts so I could get the good jobs." How about another Chief Steward who thought it was funny to make a comment about "a nigger"? And there was the member of the Human Rights Committee, which, among other things, hears harassment complaints, who wore Playboy paraphernalia. Then there was the now retired President, the one who was chief witness for the persecution at my "trial," matter-of-factly discussing his being a consultant for a contractor — one of the biggest at Inco — now that he was retired. We had filed hundreds of grievances against this and other contractors and had tried constantly to negotiate tougher contract language to protect our jobs from them. Of course, our task was made all the more difficult when a few stewards kept showing up at contracting-out grievance hearings wearing free ball caps with the contractors' names and logos on them.

The Grave Consequences of Business Unionism

A small but all-powerful group that accepts, or even tolerates, these sorts of politics and attitudes has devastating effects on a union. The active, dedicated trade unionists that make up the majority working so hard in Local 6500, in the plants, and in the Union Hall end up fighting a demoralizing uphill battle.

Where do you suppose the aforementioned "leadership" stood on affirmative action, globalization, or mobilization against job cuts and layoffs? Actually, it has not usually been a matter of this clique being so right wing that they openly took reactionary positions on the issues. Usually they simply did not have a policy or position one way or the other on the issues of the day, or they simply put up roadblocks to debate and action. During the 1980s and 1990s it became standard practice to accept job cuts as long as there were no layoffs. Many thousands of jobs were given away at great cost to the union and to Sudbury. During the same period, contracting out continued to grow. Local 6500's membership dropped from more than 18,000 to fewer than 4,000. Then there has been the issue of the working week. Despite a Canadian Labour Congress resolution calling for a thirty-two-hour workweek — and success in Europe toward achieving this goal — the right-wing leadership actually encouraged members to sign onto twelve-hour shifts. Their reasoning was that "the company told them" that the only other option was an even worse seven-day schedule.

One of the most startling examples of non-leadership by Local 6500's "leadership" came during negotiations in 1997. Just as union and company representatives were settling into the room for the latest exchange of proposals, there came a knock at the door. Someone came in, announced that he was from the Steelworkers National Office and informed us that he had an entourage of representatives of Russian nickel workers with him. He then asked if anyone had questions for our Russian brothers. There were a couple of mundane questions such as, "Did you bring any vodka?" and "Is it as cold as they say over there?" I piped up and said that, even though our employers were in competition, did they not believe that coordinated international bargaining would be a great benefit to both our unions? Company heads immediately snapped around to our discussions. My Local 6500 brothers looked at me as if to say, "There he goes again, getting serious." The Russian representative's face lit up, his head enthusiastically nodding up and down as he said "Yes, yes." As he stepped toward me, though, the Steelworker National Office's tour guide put his arm out and quickly guided the group out of the room, saying they had to keep on schedule. I was astounded that no one had even told our Bargaining Committee that these Russian representatives were coming and that no meeting with them would take place. Despite the fact that Inco's market share had dropped from 90 to 29 percent over the years, it was still the largest nickel producer in the Western Hemisphere. Most of the production numbers from Russia were not public knowledge, but it was now purported to be the largest nickel producer in the world. While some people were looking for vodka, some of us could imagine the enormous benefits of coordinated bargaining between the unions of the two largest nickel producers in the world.

Inco now has a reported million-dollar public relations budget. As well, its hiring practices have changed significantly. In the years when we were hired, there was a five-person-a-day turnover, but now hirings are few and far between, as the workforce has gone from 18,000 to less than 4,000, though nickel production has remained steady. When Inco does hire, a post-secondary education is now mandatory. Part of the testing procedure it uses for potential new recruits has an insidious anti-union slant. Some people have reported that, despite getting better test results than other candidates, children of union activists have been screened out. Repeated requests for the results of this testing have been denied by the company on the grounds of confidentiality: the union has been denied access to the tests. New employees are told, in a roundabout way, that someday they themselves might be bosses, so it's best not to "make waves." Inco's actions, however, such as during the 2003 strike over concessions, are opening the eyes of younger workers.

Inco now openly brags about "collaboration" with its unions in newsletters and meetings with employees. The union *should* be involved in cooperation with our employers, but we must never forget that our needs are different than theirs. There was a time when Inco would never dare use the word "collaboration," knowing it would never be tolerated by Local 6500 members. In the labour movement, "collaboration" is still a dirty word.

In April 2003, in the first election after my retirement and for the first time in our history, all eleven Executive Board members and three Chief Stewards were acclaimed. The election posters in the plants were simply stamped over with the word "cancelled." The subversion of union elections is one of the main ways a clique keeps the membership quiet and themselves comfortably in power. Over time, intimidation leads to cynicism, which in turn leads to apathy. And apathy is exactly what any group concerned first and foremost with its own power wants in its membership. A union membership kept in the dark does not challenge business unionism.

On one hand, for the business-unionist establishment, almost anything goes in clinging to power — might is right. (In truth, right is might.) On the other hand, having an undying belief in the fact that you are right and that you are part of a larger movement for social justice is all the power we need to keep going, whatever the odds. The majority of Steelworkers are good, dedicated trade unionists who just want to do their job. Most of them prefer to avoid the petty self-interested "politics" of the Union Hall. Unfortunately, in Local 6500, avoiding politics means never, ever running in a democratic election against an incumbent member of the right-wing slate, or even endorsing such a challenger. If you do, you risk ending up on the blacklist. However, a member does not have to hold an official "position" to be an activist or to make progress. If fat-cat "union bosses" are content to sit on their asses, any activist still has access to their District or National office. It also needs to be said that, while most union bosses are politically connected to one another, their support staff are part of the majority that just wants to do their job. A friend of mine in Sudbury recently contacted our District 6 office in Toronto regarding a particular issue. It was like they were hearing from a long lost friend: "It's really good to hear from someone up there."

Locally, some of the new hires are starting to see through Inco and are signing up as shop stewards or Health-and-Safety Committee members. As well, there have also been some victories in Bargaining Committee elections and negotiations. In 1988 there were only three of us as non-slate members on the Bargaining Committee. While certain union leaders had to be kept "hidden" from the proverbial backroom meetings for fear of caving in, the company was always desperate to know our position, knowing that we could influence the members for or against ratification. Norris Valiquette knew this, and asked me, "Have you noticed that whenever the company is trying to settle an important issue, they're looking directly at us?" According to the union, the 1997 contract turned out to be the "best contract we have ever negotiated." Of course, this did not happen just because we were present at the bargaining table. It happened because there was a cross-section — not just a clique — of workers on our Bargaining Committee.

Over time, with no one to fight except each other, some of the slate began to divide and turn on one another. Two high-profile Executive Board members quietly paid for much of one of my two Presidential campaigns. They were a day away from openly endorsing me at a press conference, when they caved in to the right-wing leadership. They told me that if I did not win, the slate would "crucify" them. They would lose their long-standing jobs at the Union Hall and be sent back to the plant or mine, and their aging bodies just could not take that. Maybe the devil had possessed their souls too long for them to take that final vocal step, but they still had enough left in them to know the membership deserved better leadership than they were getting and were willing to do something about it, even if only with cash rather than voice. Other slate supporters were more forthcoming. Jim Gosselin and some of his friends decided to switch to our side.

The difference between the people we lost to the slate and the ones who left the slate to join us was one of principle. The people coming our way said they disagreed with what the slate was doing, or not doing, for the membership. They turned their backs on the promise of being "looked after." We had no payola to offer these people, just the promise to fight for what was right. Jim Gosselin ended up running with us and being elected Vice-President. Unexpectedly, he ended up becoming President a few months later when the then-President, Dan O'Reilly, took a staff-rep job. Unfortunately, Jim completed only one term. He chose not to run for re-election, citing the same sorts of reasons for leaving as Keith Lovely had. Like Lovely, Gosselin could take anything the company threw at him, but health and sanity suffer greatly when your own "brothers" constantly use your back for target practice. Fortunately, he had already achieved enough service for his thirty-and-out pension.

For our union and community to survive and progress we need to establish a left presence on a large scale. As a *New York Times* correspondent observed on the front page of its February 16, 2003, edition, just over a month before the Iraq war and after a weekend of huge anti-war protests across the globe, there are now only two superpowers in the world — the Unites States and public opinion. The left is the conscience of the world and the source of progressive social change. It is up to us to continue to rouse this conscience from the grassroots up. Whether it be by trying to keep a union honest and democratic, by pointing out the injustice of a Conservative government's attack on a welfare mom trying to better herself, or by gaining world-wide support in opposition to the illegal and unjust American invasion of Iraq, we on the left have a history of fighting and winning against huge odds. We can change things for the better in our city, our country, and our world. There is no finish line in the fight for social justice.

The Struggle Continues — Solidarity Forever!

Chapter 15

My View from the Blackened Rocks

Cathy Mulroy

I am sitting atop the blackened rock hills overlooking the Superstack, Inco's 1,200-foot chimney. It pours hundreds of tons of sulphur dioxide out over our fair city and beyond. I am thinking. "What an appealing sunset it presents — purples, oranges, and other colours I can't figure out." I shake my head in disgust and look down at the flyer in my hand. It reads: "2003 Local 6500 Union Election Cancelled — All Positions Acclaimed." It's April 1, April Fools Day. I had called the Union Hall, and asked the President of Local 6500, "Is this an April Fools joke?" He replied, "No, this is no joke... well, yes, it's a joke all right, but it's not funny." I hung up the phone. This is the first time in my thirty years as a member of Steelworkers Local 6500 that union elections have been cancelled. Saddened, I wonder how we got to this point. My head floods with memories.

In June 1974 a nineteen-year-old Sudbury girl applied for a job at Inco, one of the largest mining companies in the world. At the time, there were more than 18,000 men working in Inco's Sudbury operations. The only women there were in clerical jobs, working in offices. There were *no* women in the smelters, refineries, mills, or underground — no unionized hourly rated women. On June 10, Inco hires this girl — me, Cathy Mulroy.

Many people asked me why I wanted to work at Inco. I replied, "It's because of the money and the benefits." I think the pay was $7.25 per hour to start, which compared to the $1.65 I was making as a sales clerk. Most other girls my age were still in school, dreaming of getting married and having children. If they were working, it was as a waitress, a clerk in a retail store, or a bank teller. I was already married at sixteen and had a child. This is what happens when you know nothing about unprotected sex, are brought up Roman Catholic, and don't say "no." It wasn't a happy marriage. I felt that if I had a job with good pay, I could change my life.

My mother was a stay-at-home mom. She looked after Dad, her five children, and one foster child, cooked, cleaned, made pies, and liked to knit. We were lucky because she was interested in us, her children. She always went to Parent-Teacher Association meetings and was involved with Brownies, Girl Guides, and Boy Scouts. Her children and husband were her main focus. My Mom, Rita Kennedy, was in the Women's Army Corps, but she was in the Navy when she met Dad. Dad was a paratrooper during World War II and fought on the front lines. He was working for Inco and didn't have to go to war, but he volunteered. After the war was over, he went back as a miner at Inco, where he worked for forty-three years. Dad was proud but never boastful, quiet and introverted, a self-taught man who read all the time, and I was very close to him. My destiny was not to follow the "normal" life, like other girls or like my Mom: I was going to follow in Dad's footsteps.

Inco and Women

Mining had long been perceived as a man's domain, largely due to its past requirement for heavy manual labour. But I have seen women on farms who could put a lot of men to shame when it came to baling hay. Prior to World War II, legislation stated it was too dangerous for women to do this work — but it's not dangerous for men? During World War II, our men were needed to fight the war, so then it was okay for women to work at Inco. On August 13, 1942, the federal government issued a special Order-in-Council on the "Employment of Female Persons by International Nickel Company of Canada Limited in the vicinity of Sudbury." Inco hired more than 1,400 women to work in its surface operations.

After the war was over the women on these jobs were laid off. The Mining Act of Ontario made it no longer legal to employ women in mining operations. I guess they thought it was too dangerous again! Little changed for a long time. Even Ontario's Human Rights Code, passed in 1962, read that discrimination was based on colour, race, national origin, or religion — there was nothing about sex or gender. It wasn't until 1970 that human-rights legislation included sex as grounds for discrimination. This right was not handed out to women: it was fought for by the women's movement.

But Inco did not start to hire women even in 1970. It didn't happen until after January 1974 when a journalist asked Inco why it had no women on hourly rated jobs. Its answer was, "Women did not apply for those jobs." Within days after that comment, the company was flooded with applications. And so we were hired — during 1974, just ten women at the Copper refinery, three at the nickel refinery, and a few at the smelter or mills. Women were still not allowed, by law, to work underground. At the time, the historical myth was that the presence of women in the mine was "unlucky" — it led to the collapse of mines and the death of miners. Yet, in 1959, Queen Elizabeth II and Prince Philip could visit Inco's Frood Mine in Sudbury during their Royal Tour and, in 1939, Her Majesty's mother and father had also been underground to view operations in the same mine — and no employee was hurt or died.

We knew that being the first women was going to be rough. In fact, sometimes it was nasty and downright cruel. The company didn't want women there, the men didn't want us there, and their wives didn't want us there. The wives would call my house and ask me why I was taking a job away from a man — what was wrong with me? In my opinion, the only reason Inco hired women was because 1975 was going to be International Women's Year. I think Inco feared that, if it did not have any women working in these high-paying jobs, the government would force it to do it by a quota, a minimum number of women per hundred men, or something similar. Inco has always denied this.

On the Job — and Injured

In 1974 Inco did not do much training before a new employee went on the job — not for men or for women. What I remember was two or three days of training and a few horror stories. One story Inco told us was about a man who had his foot amputated after a train ran over it. They showed us his boot. It was cut in half. Another story was about a guy with long hair. His hair got caught in a machine and ripped off the top of his scalp. I was glad they didn't have a training aid for that. After the training, all the new employees pushed broom for a few days. I guess this was so our bodies could get used to the noise, dust, gas, and heat of our surroundings.

I was a thorn in the company's side right from the start. They had to make a special order for my work boots. At five-foot-one and 105 pounds, I wore a size four work boot. The boots were so small they came without metatarsal guards. The company ordered a pair of metatarsal guards that were as large as the top of my boots. They had to be laced to my boots to stay on. This made going up and down ladders very dangerous. The guard would lift and get caught on a rung of the ladder. I would have to wiggle and pull to get free while hanging onto the ladder. Today, the laws would not accept this as safe practice.

My first job was working in the Copper refinery's Anode Department, around the copper furnaces and on a casting wheel. This is where we cast molten copper into large moulds. The product is called an "anode" and each one weighs 700 pounds. There are thirty-two moulds on the wheel. The moulds are about twelve to fifteen inches thick and also made of copper. The molten copper comes out of the furnaces down a cement chute called a "launder." The launder has large burners above it that are fed by natural gas. We turn the gas on, light a paper towel, and put it under a nozzle. The gas ignites and blows on the launder to keep it hot, to maintain the heat of the molten metal so it won't freeze. It flows down the launder like a small river into pots called "ladles." The ladles also have gas-burning nozzles blowing into them. Chains hooked to the back of each ladle lift the ladles.

This lifting is controlled by a wheel operator, a job I have done many times. The operator pours the molten metal into moulds, then turns the wheel to line up each mould to be filled. As the wheel turns, it passes under water taps suspended above the freshly poured anode. This helps solidify the copper. You can put water on molten metal but you can't put molten metal on water or it will explode. I have seen that happen many times. We would run to get under the wheel stand for safety, but sometimes we didn't make it. Our instinct would be to protect our heads, leaving the backs of our necks exposed. The molten copper would be airborne and look like gigantic fireworks. Somehow, the copper would find that exposed neck. It would burn as it went down your back, leaving a trickle of burn marks. You learned to jump and fan the back of your shirt so the copper would fall out. You didn't want the copper to stay in there! Copper takes a long time to cool down, and if it stayed, it would keep burning down deep into your skin.

As the wheel turned about halfway around, the anodes were lifted off the mould with a manual air hoist and put into a tank of water. The tank would fill up. The crane would then bring a rack over to the tank. The rack would be lowered and the anodes picked up, about thirty-two or thirty-eight of them, depending on what rack was used. The crane follower, or bailer, would guide the rack of anodes into a narrow-gauge train car. The car was then weighed and pushed into another department, the Tank House, where it sat in an acid bath for twenty-eight days. The precious metals would fall to the bottom of the tank in the form of sludge. The copper anodes were then sent to another part of the plant, Fine Casting, to be melted again. It was all hard, hot, and dangerous work.

After only three months on the job at the Copper refinery I was injured. It was during the graveyard shift, 11:30 p.m. to 7:30 a.m., though casting was done at any time no matter the shift, whenever the furnaces were ready to go. I was picking up an anode to put in the tank using the manual air hoist, which weighs about 1,200 pounds. Something happened. Either the hoist or one of the lugs of the anode broke. The 700-pound anode fell off the hooks of the hoist, causing the handle of the hoist to come at me. It hit me on my right side just above my ovary. I flew backwards off the stand and fell four feet to the floor. The pain was excruciating. I knew I was hurt.

I didn't want anyone to see me cry. I got up, ran away, and hid among the trains. A fellow employee found me and took me to the first-aid room. From there I was transferred to hospital. After blood work, the doctor came back and told me I was pregnant and so they couldn't take X-rays, but the bruising showed there could be some damage. He would follow my pregnancy. Then I was told by a union representative to go down to the Union Hall on Frood Road.

I was still innocent, naïve, and inexperienced about worldly issues. One day, I noticed money was coming off my pay cheque: the deduction read "union dues." I thought the money was going into a saving account at the Credit Union — I had no idea what a "union" was. Now my eyes were going to be opened. I was going to be introduced to a whole new world: the world of union and company politics.

Suits at the Union Hall

When I arrived at the Steelworkers Hall a man in a suit ushered me into a room where there were other men. They too were in suits and gave me cold glares. The man who ushered me in said, "Sit over here," and pointed to a chair between two men I didn't know. They began to talk about me as if I wasn't there, something about keeping my pregnancy quiet. They didn't want to set a precedent over this incident. "Set a what?" I thought to myself, "What are they talking about?" They talked and talked. I had no idea what was going on. My mind started to wonder, and I looked around the room. There were portraits of past union presidents hanging on the wall, all these men also in suits. The Vice-President of the local sat behind a large oak desk in a black leather chair. He shuffled papers as the conversation continued. Behind him was a massive bookshelf that went from ceiling to floor. It was filled with hard-covered books with gold type on their spines.

The men began to wrap up the meeting, and the Vice-President looked at me: "Cathy, you can go home now. There is no need to tell anyone about your pregnancy. After the baby is born, you will be sent for X-rays." A balding man scowled at me and shook his head. "What's his problem?" I thought to myself. "Okay," I responded to the Vice-President, and I left the Union Hall muttering to myself. I couldn't understand what all the commotion was about. After all, I was married — what difference did it make to others that I was pregnant. Little did I know at the time that this could cause all kinds of problems with the company and the union.

I was put on something called "compensation." I had to see the doctor regularly and fill out forms. The pregnancy was not easy. The baby was sideways, and that's the way she grew. (I don't know if this was because of the way the hoist had hit me.) A few days after the baby was born, I had the X-rays, and in six weeks I was back casting anodes. This was very hard on my body.

My co-workers and the company men seemed to be really mad at me. I couldn't comprehend what I had done to make everyone so upset. My shift boss didn't like me, and talked down to me all the time. Once I was sitting outside on the railroad tracks with a co-worker — a man, of course, since there were no other women on my shift of forty men. We were eating our lunch when I was called into the foreman's office. The foreman was a short, skinny man who wore a blue work shirt and pants, and the pocket in his shirt bulged from the twenty pens shoved into his pocket protector. No one knew why he carried so many pens. Maybe he thought it made him look important. He was the brunt of jokes in the workers' lunchroom.

"Don't you value your reputation?" he shouted.

"What are you talking about?" I asked, a little annoyed.

"I saw you," he continued to yell, "you and Denis out on the tracks — what were you doing out there?" There was the sound of accusation in his voice.

For me, this was the last straw of staying quiet. I could feel my temper rise, and I have a bad temper. I yelled back, "What do you think I was doing out there — screwing the guy on the railroad track?"

He didn't know what to say: "Well... well," he stammered, "you should be eating in the lunchroom — it's for your own good."

I screeched back, "I don't need you to look after my reputation! I can do that just fine!" I left his office, slamming the door. From that day forth, my life at Inco took a turn. I was going to follow this road for the next thirty years.

As punishment for my outburst, Inco gave me a "Step One" for insubordination. A Step One — the first level of disciplinary measures in the collective bargaining agreement — was about the same as a counselling slip. The severity of a Step is determined by the severity of your behaviour or infraction. Step One is for mild infractions. Step Two stays on your record for two years. This can be added to if the same kind of infraction is done again, so it could become a Step Three or a Step Four. After a Step Four, you are sent home for the day to think about your actions. You can then be fired. You can fight through the grievance procedures to have a Step reduced or taken off of your record, if it is unjustly given and falls under our collective bargaining agreement.

When the foreman handed me the Step he also told me that I had a bad attitude. I rolled my eyes. "I want to talk to a steward," I said. A steward is a union member who is like a lawyer. The steward can issue the grievance and fight for you. This is how I met my long-time friend, Bruce McKeigan. Bruce had just become a steward in Local 6500. This was my first grievance and it was Bruce's first as well. He was sitting at the lunchroom table in the Wire Bar part of the plant. The foreman introduced us and left. I explained to Bruce what had happened and watched as he wrote out the grievance: "I, Cathy Mulroy, have a grievance under the collective bargaining agreement..." I would watch Bruce write out this line for me many times in the future. I don't remember what the outcome was on that first grievance, but I was going to be Bruce's number-one client for the next thirty years.

The Right to Refuse Unsafe Work

In the 1970s, workplace health-and-safety laws were changing, especially following the Ham Commission Report in 1975. In 1976, workers in Ontario won the right to refuse unsafe work with the passage of Bill 139. This was one of the biggest wins for the labour movement. The right to refuse meant that if workers felt a job was unsafe we could refuse to do it without penalty. Of course, there was more to it than that, but that was the bottom line of the law. Bruce McKeigan and I were among the first to exercise this right.

I had been working in Fine Casting for a few years. This is where the pure (99.9 percent) copper that comes from the Tank House is melted down. Years before, Inco used to cast all kinds of shapes — I think about twenty-three — for different clients. But by the time I started, they were only casting wire bar — 300-pound bars. We also cast very large ingots, maybe two stories high, and smaller ones eight inches thick and about ten to twelve feet long. One of the jobs on the twelve-foot ingot was called "the doors." I was on the Number Two casting furnace, an old casting system. It wasn't used much, maybe every three or four months.

The moulds on Number Two were vertical. Copper was poured into them from the top by hand-held ladles. There are two workers under the wheel. The first worker was placed just before the moulds reached the pouring and had to close them before the molten metal was poured into the mould. The second was on the far side of the wheel and had to open the doors so the ingots could fall into a bosh tank filled with water, about fifteen to twenty feet deep. The doors were on swinging hinges at the bottom of the moulds and had to be swung upward to close. The doors were made of thick copper and were very heavy. If they were not closed right, copper would come through and a worker could get burned or the copper would leak out and freeze — the ingot would get stuck and not slide out on the other side of the wheel.

The first worker had to close the doors using their feet. To do this we used a brown metal chair that was tied by copper wire to a pole leaning against a cement wall. The chair was tilted so that when you are sitting on it you are lying on your back with your feet in the air. There was no support at all. I was too short to reach the doors with my feet, so I was almost on my shoulders. After a good push on the doors, the wire would loosen on the chair, the chair would twist, and I would fall off. When I did get the door closed, I would have to get off the chair, insert a copper pin, which is shaped like a large wedge, into a latch attached to the door, then take a hand-held sledgehammer and hammer the pin in to keep the door closed. Then I would get back on the chair, put my feet in the air and get the next mould. If you missed a door, or if it didn't close it properly, it could cause all kinds of problems. You would have to tell the ladle tender — the person pouring the copper. But the only way to get the ladle tender's attention was to hit a steel pipe with a crow bar, and hope he heard you over the roar of the furnace, gas blowers, cranes, and the moving of the wheels.

I brought the problems of this job to my first-line supervisor. I told him I was too short for the job and that I was not the only one. My complaint went to the joint Occupational Health and Safety Act (OHSA) Committee. The five union and five company representatives decided that a proper chair would be put in, one that could be adjusted up and down for tall or short people, so that everyone could close the doors more easily. A work order was written up.

Months went by. One day I looked on the board for the job line-up and saw I was scheduled to work on the doors. I thought this was strange, because I wasn't even in that department anymore. I had bid out and was working in Wire Bar, a different department. I went into the office to confront the foreman. This boss was known to be vicious. He never talked nicely to any worker. I asked him "What's going on here? Why am I on doors?"

He sat at his desk, his greasy black hair glistening under the fluorescent light. "You have to do it," he snickered. "You're the only one qualified."

"What do you mean?" I asked. "I don't work for you. And besides, the OHSA Committee said the chair was not fit for me to work on. It hasn't been changed yet."

He laughed, "Well, I guess you're only half qualified."

"It's been two months," I protested. "That chair should have been here by now."

In a Hitler-type command, he ordered, "Cathy, go down on the doors."

"What about the chair?" I continued my protest.

"I don't know anything about a f—ing chair. Just go down there," he yelled, "and you will stay on one side all night."

"What do you mean, stay on one side? Past practice is that doors change every half hour. A grievance has been won that the worker changes every half hour because of the heat."

"So," he said smugly, "I am telling you to go on one side only."

I went down to examine the workplace. There was the same old steel chair.

Nothing had been done. I came back up. The foreman was now standing by the furnace.

"There's no new chair," I told him. "I'm not going to work down there. It's not safe for me."

"Like hell!" he said. "Grab your lunch pail and go home!"

"I want to see a steward," I demanded.

"No!" he yelled. "You're not seeing a steward until you come back tomorrow."

"You are refusing me a steward," I yelled back. "You don't leave me any choice. I'm using Bill 139."

"Go f— your Bill," he yelled.

"Okay, you want to be like that, fine I want to see the safety engineer," I demanded. Again he refused. "No. You're not seeing anybody."

"Okay, call in a mining inspector." I started to calm down now. I knew I had rights. I was going through proper procedures.

Again he said: "No."

"So, what you are saying is that you are refusing me a steward, a safety engineer or committee person, and a mining inspector? And you are sending me home?" I reiterated.

He turned to me, his eyes burning with hate. "You just f— off!" he yelled and walked away.

I went to the chairperson of the OHSA Committee and told him what had happened. He told me that I should grab my lunch pail and go home. I didn't even have to grieve to get paid for the shift. The company knew I was in the right.

The next morning, I went to the Union Hall and told them what had happened. I was informed I should press charges. It's a criminal offence for the foreman to refuse to investigate the dispute, refuse to notify a Health and Safety representative or committee member, or to refuse to notify a government inspector. That is how the Bill reads.

My steward, Bruce McKeigan, union representatives, and I all went to a meeting in the Superintendent's office. The foreman looked scared, nothing like that madman of the night before. He apologized to the company for not going by the Bill. He admitted: "Well, I didn't know the rules of the Bill. It's not my fault."

I laughed at his ignorance, and said, "Well, if I was to be driving down the highway twenty kilometres over the speed limit, then all I would have to say to the police officer is, 'Well, I didn't know the rules of this highway?' What do you think he or she would say to me?"

Nobody answered. The foreman never apologized to me for his actions.

After the investigation, the Ministry of Labour wouldn't lay charges against the foreman. The government inspector who checked the case said he would have to look at the job description. If the two employees on the doors were supposed to alternate, then he would have to rule in favour of the employee (me). If each employee stayed on one side for eight hours, he would have to rule in favour of the company. He checked it out and found we were supposed to alternate sides, yet the Ministry still dropped the case. Even though all the other information about the chair, the OHSA Committee, and the unsafe practice were in order, no charges were ever laid. But I never had to work the doors again, and a month later the new chair was installed.

The 1978–79 Strike

Although Bill 139 gave us some protection against unsafe working conditions, there were no laws to protect us from layoffs, cutbacks, plant closures, and work-force "adjustments." In 1977 and 1978 Inco had massive layoffs: up to 3,000 people lost their jobs.

Then Inco set us up for a strike. Having a large stockpile of nickel, it was offering us only a four-cent raise and also wanted to take away parts of our grievance procedure. We knew that if we went out on strike it was going to be long and hard, and winter was coming. I think the vote was 83 percent in favour of a strike. The members were ready to fight, to put our nickel back to work for us. We were about to embark on something we had never seen before and may never see again.

The strike began on September 15, 1978. There were 11,700 members out on strike, to which should be added a spouse or partner to each and, say, 2.7 children — but that was only the tip of the iceberg. This kind of action would cripple the city. We began to organize. Workers were in the kitchen at the Union Hall making sandwiches for people on the picket lines. Committees were set up for vouchers to pay 11,700 people, and this was before computers — all the work was done by hand on hard copy. There were committees for housing and gas, committees for collecting donations, and committees for bus rides so people could get to plant gates all over Ontario to ask for donations.

The wives of the workers organized the Wives Supporting the Strike Committee. The women came from their homes, set up clothing depots, and organized bean suppers and Christmas parties for the children. As the strike continued, the wives became more political. They wanted to know what was going on and what we were fighting for. It was wonderful to watch them grow. I was asked to join their group, which was an honour. My teeshirt read, "I Support Wives Supporting the Strike." They gave that to me as an honorary member. I could not vote at their meetings, which was only fair, because they could not vote at my membership meetings. A documentary film called *A Wives' Tale* was made during the strike that is still used in university and college courses.

All of this together was what I would refer to as a real class struggle. Let me remind you that we were very young. I was twenty-three and our President, David Patterson, was thirty. In my opinion, Dave was a true leader. He wasn't very tall, maybe five-foot-five, with long blond hair. He had his heart into everything he did. He stood for the people, for the union, and for the community. I remember once when Dave called me and another woman into his office. He said, "So you want to get involved with the union. Tell me what you think unions are?"

I, of course, went rambling on about how I thought unions were to represent the workers, and about all the good things unions could and should do for the people — boy, was I naive! Dave then made a statement. "I am not going to say you're right or wrong. But unions are big politics, and you may be disappointed." On that note he left his office and left us with our thoughts.

Dave Patterson spent most of the strike in Toronto with the union's Bargaining Committee. They were getting pretty weary. Most of their days were spent waiting for Inco's negotiating team to show up, and most days they never showed up. The message our Bargaining Committee was getting from Sudbury was, "Reach an agreement. The members want to get back to work." Our Bargaining Committee had little or no idea how everything was actually coming together in Sudbury. They were not told that unions from across the country and into the United States, and even from across the ocean, were giving us support. We were very busy in Sudbury and were under the impression the Bargaining Committee knew what was happening. I didn't know until years later that they were not getting the real story.

As the strike wore on and people were really hurting, a split started to appear among union members, and among the wives. Some thought we were getting too radical, while others thought we weren't doing enough. Some wanted to hold more rallies and plays to get the people out, to communicate what was happening. Some wanted to block all the oil trucks going through Inco's gates. Others thought we should let some of the oil trucks through: there were threats of an injunction if we blocked the trucks.

After eight months out on strike, there was a tentative agreement. The Bargaining Committee recommended we accept it. The Union Hall was packed at every meeting held to discuss the tentative agreement. But the members stood strong and said it wasn't enough. They demanded the Bargaining Committee go back to get thirty-and-out (pensions after thirty years of service, no matter your age.) And we wanted part of the pie, some kind of profit-sharing, a "nickel bonus." The Bargaining Committee was surprised to see members so unified and so strong that they went back to Toronto to re-negotiate. In my opinion, this was the true victory — workers standing together. Even though we were poor, families had split up (mine being one of them), and people were suffering, our attitude was, "We will not be defeated."

In two weeks, we got what we demanded. The strike was over. I remember a bunch of us standing in the parking lot of the Union Hall. It was like we were in a void — no smiles, no cheers. One of the wives commented, in a subdued voice, "What, no fireworks?" We all just stood there looking at each other.

Losing Democracy

Our members went back into the mines, the smelters, the refineries, and the mills. Some of the wives went back to home life, while others went out and found other jobs. One of the wives opened up her own business, doing income taxes. I went back to casting copper. We were not the same people we had been nine months before: we had knowledge and life experiences that you could never learn from a book. We were smarter and tougher.

As I sit on my blackened rock hills looking at the Superstack, I find myself smiling at the memories. I feel very fortunate to have had the experience and gratification of being part of that strike. I feel proud that we had done a great job. Then I remember how a pompous attitude went to our heads. Gloominess fills my heart as I remember what happened next. The way things went in the union, I doubt I will ever again feel the kind of togetherness or power we shared in 1978 and '79.

Our group behind Dave Patterson thought that if we could win against a big multinational company, we could take on the conservative establishment of the United Steelworkers of America. We could run Dave Patterson for the position of District 6 Director of the Steelworkers. (District 6 covered Ontario.) We thought we could do so much for the union workers. But, as Mom would say, "We got too big for our britches."

We worked hard on Dave's campaign. We campaigned all over Ontario. We even found small locals down south whose members didn't know they were unionized. Dave won the election — or so we thought. Dave became District Director, but we lost him as *our* leader. The Steelworker establishment and staffers didn't seem to share our happiness. Dave was "buried," isolated in his new position, with no backup. In my opinion, running Dave for District Director was not the right thing to do. We were naive. We didn't understand the power structure of the union. We thought that if we could win among 11,700 workers, we could do it for all Ontario. We bit off more than we could chew.

Back at Local 6500, there were a lot of changes that grew out of the split I mentioned earlier. The other side was now back in charge. Over the next few years a lot of our group quit Inco and went to work in other places. I just assumed they had had enough. After an eight-and-half-month strike, then in 1982–83 another strike, a ten-month shutdown, and more layoffs, they must have felt it was best for them to leave. But some of us stayed, though I was no longer welcome in my own Union Hall. If I got up to the microphone to make a comment or question, I would get catcalls, called names like "f—ing slut" and other derogatory remarks so I couldn't be heard. It was impossible for me to get on the OHSA Committee. Even though money came off my cheque every week for union education, I never got to take any courses at the Union Hall. Neither did Bruce McKeigan.

As I watched over the years, my view of our union changed. Bruce and I tried to bring in some changes. In 1997, for the first time, I ran in the union Executive elections, along with Bruce. Bruce ran for President and I ran for Vice-President. We wanted to get back the solidarity that had been lost. We wanted to clean house, to get the deadwood out of the Hall, and get people in there who would do more for the members. I wanted to educate the members on issues and not on collaboration with the company.

I wasn't about to spend a lot of money on my campaign. My husband took my picture in our living room. I made my own flyers using an old Gestetner machine (the kind you have to add ink to and turn the handle). It was good that I used the Gestetner, because my boss called me into his office.

"Cathy, we got a call from your Union Hall today, telling us that you were using Inco paper and an Inco Xerox machine to make up your leaflets."

"Oh, really?" I said. "Was it the guy I'm running against?"

"I can't tell you that," the boss said.

"Well, you just sit right there," I smiled at him, "I'll be right back." I went to my car, got my leaflets, walked around his desk and stood beside him.

"See?" I said as I threw the leaflets on his desk, where they fanned out. He could see multiple pictures of me.

"What am I looking at?" he asked.

"I made these on a Gestetner machine — not a Xerox machine. Does Inco even own a Gestetner machine?" I could see my boss was uncomfortable about all this. "You can call you-know-who and let him know his informant is wrong," I laughed. I could see my boss was happy about that. He was a good boss, and we got along well. I am glad I didn't cheat in making up my leaflets — I would have been fired.

During the campaign, I went to every gate at the plants and mines throughout Inco, passing out my leaflets. We were allowed to have scrutineers for the voting, so I asked four of my friends to go to the Union Hall during the count and watch for my votes. They were given paper and pencil to mark down my votes. I told them what polls I wanted them to be at and to stay at that poll, not to move to another. I would wait for them at a restaurant.

The day of the election, it wasn't long before my scrutineers showed up at the restaurant. They looked very despondent. "That didn't take long," I said.

"We were kicked out of the hall," one of them said.

"What do you mean you were kicked out of the hall — what happened?" I was so surprised.

Sam, a good friend, was fuming. "We were told to move to other polls and, when we refused, they told us we were intimidating the counters and to get out."

I was staggered. "Can they do that?"

"No," Bruce confirmed, "but they did."

One scrutineer said, "Cathy, you had one-third of the vote before this happened." I was very angry. How could these men intimidate my scrutineers? They were all injured workers on modified work. One was so full of arthritis he could hardly stand up.

"Isn't this against the law?" I questioned again in my naive way. "What can we do?"

"We can put in a complaint and have a hearing with the International. We can ask for another election," Bruce replied.

"Yeah, like that's going to do any good," I said in a cynical way. I felt defeated in more ways than one.

While Bruce and I were preparing our case, we found out that there had been 8,000 ballots printed for the election, though there were only 4,700 members eligible to vote. We asked to see the unused ballots. We were offered a recount, but we wanted to see the unused ballots. We have never seen them to this day.

The hearing was a kangaroo court. The people who came down from District 6 to preside over the hearing joked with the other side and carried on conversations about their camping trips together. I gave Bruce a look and shrugged my shoulders. This was the same group Dave Patterson had been up against.

I believe my scrutineers were denied their basic democratic rights under Local 6500's Union Election Manual: "The tellers shall afford observers/scrutineers a reasonable opportunity to observe the conduct of the election on Election Day, including observation of the ballots and tally sheets during the tabulation conducted by the tellers." Our scrutineers were not given this right. Scrutineers are an essential part of the election machinery, no less important than the deputy returning officer and the poll clerk. Our membership was trained by our union to work on elections for the NDP. One of the sheets given to volunteer scrutineers read: "Make sure you see each ballot" and "Check your count."

As soon as the hearing started, I knew our complaint wasn't going to go far. But it was the principle, the lost democracy and standing up again for what is right — even if you are going to lose. I am not the only person who feels this way about the union. I am not the only person to get ridiculed at membership meetings, or never to get picked for conferences or educational courses. In talking to workers on the job, they too felt like giving up and walking away, saying, "F— it." That's the attitude that has developed.

Bruce and I ran again three years later. The membership was not interested in union politics. Participation was declining. Things were getting worse.

In my opinion, most of the people who are now in union positions like stewards, committee people, executive officers, and so on are there chiefly for themselves — "What's in it for me?" For example, the American-based Steelworkers have their yearly conventions in places like Las Vegas — you can imagine how much union business for workers gets done there! It seems they care supremely for themselves, regarding their own comfort and advantage in union positions, and they have a disregard for union principles and for others not in their camp. They judge others according to their own private appetites and selfish passions. They recruit new activists only if they walk their walk. When they bring people in, it's because they have accepted the conservative, male ways of doing things, ways that I think are killing the true meaning of what a union is.

It's not only in our internal politics and elections that you can see the decline. Safety is down: stress and incidents are up. Overtime is very high. Contractors are working twelve-hour shifts seven days a week. Laws are being broken. Training is at a minimum, and often the people who do go on courses are ready to retire. More contractors are doing our jobs and their workers are getting paid half of what we make. Workers are retiring and then getting called back to do the same job with high pay but no benefits.

Local 6500 does nothing about what's happening in the broader world. Take the Days of Action that began in 1995 against the Conservative Harris government. Our local did nothing, never spoke out or took action about the Conservatives allowing scab labour during strikes. If they did, it was only mentioned at a membership meeting — and that's how far it went. They did nothing about cutbacks to our health care or against Conservative policies to make it illegal for teachers to strike. When the war in Iraq broke out, there was not a word from our local, even though other Steelworkers spoke out against the war.

Then, on June 1, 2003, we went out on strike. I believe Inco had set this up as a maintenance shutdown. Inco threatened a take-away of pensioners' health benefits, benefits that had already been negotiated and agreed upon. Members had already given up things over the years and had been out on strikes in order to win this benefit. How could Inco take away things from pensioners, people who are not even in the bargaining unit and who could not vote? Inco also wanted to take away the right from hourly rated employees to transfer throughout the plants and mines in the Sudbury area. Yet, Inco transfers management staff throughout the world to operations in Voisey's Bay, Indonesia, Manitoba, Wales, and Australia. This was just another way of keeping control of working people. Of course, provoked by such company take-aways, the workers would walk off the job. And how many people would really complain if they got the whole summer off? More than one-third would have most of the strike covered by vacation pay anyway.

Local 6500's leadership ran a pathetic strike. Some of Inco's plant and mine gates didn't have picketers on the line. There were no rallies, no membership meetings for information, only a community picnic near the beginning of the strike. Even our $100 per-week strike pay was paid through Inco's payroll. Some of us were lucky to have scheduled our vacations during the strike, but these were only people like me who had seniority. As a result of the strike, most of us lost $12,000 to $15,000. Our younger workers lost more, much more.

When Inco had finished its maintenance work, we got a contract offer and our Bargaining Committee unanimously recommended we accept it. One of the things it negotiated for us was that on Workers' Memorial Day — April 28, a day already set aside in remembrance of workers who lost their lives on the job — Inco agreed to fly its flags at half-mast and employees would be *allowed* to have one minute of silence! Well, thank you very much, Inco. I would think that should be a given.

Real Unionism Never Completely Dies

Now for the cherry. On October 7, 2003, there was a worldwide protest against Inco. The protest was about how much pollution Inco is putting out globally, from Indonesia, to New Caledonia, to Australia, to Manitoba, to Newfoundland, to Port Colborne, to Guatemala, to Sudbury. Our union was asked to participate in this day. It refused.

So some of us decided to sing with The Raging Grannies of Sudbury. We had a small demonstration, a vigil of around twenty to thirty people at Inco's main Copper Cliff smelter gate, just below the 1200-foot Superstack putting out all those hundreds of tons of sulphur dioxide. It was another effort where the union had failed to bring to the attention of people the pollution in the Greater Sudbury area. But the media workers were great and we had good coverage. Even though we were small, the message got out and people noticed. It says a lot that the people who were there were mostly people who had been involved in the 1978–79 strike.

The sun is almost down now. The smoke coming out of the Superstack takes on its true colours — blacks, grays, and browns. The sun whitens the smoke. People don't seem to complain about white smoke. I watch as it spews out, making its long trail across the sky — it's known as the "Inco Milky Way." It comes down about forty to fifty kilometres and more from Sudbury, sharing our pollution with others.

My thirty years at Inco are now at an end. I feel I have made my mark, made a difference in my time. I can walk away with my head up and my heart full of pride. I've stood up and spoken up for what I believe in. Maybe that's why I was "buried," like Dave Patterson. I didn't work alongside other Local 6500 members anymore. Three years before retiring, I was assigned, without a job description, to an office with mostly managerial staff — isolated from my union flock. There is power in numbers and weakness in division.

Right to the end, Inco continued its unethical behaviour, by covering up a false report to the Workplace Safety and Insurance Board. When I challenged this lie, I was ordered not to socialize with anyone in the building — not even non-unionized staff — during working hours. I challenged this, too, with a grievance: it is against the Human Rights Code to isolate workers from other workers. In the end, finally, the union came through. They were there to help me win. Unionism demonstrated its power and gave me some hope in the true meaning of solidarity.

I will leave behind some advice for our young workers. Get off of your ass — make changes. Learn the laws and how to apply them. Remember that leadership *does* matter. Bad leadership creates bad followers. Run in union elections. Organize the troops. Don't be fooled by buzzwords like "collaboration." Companies and workers have different agendas when it comes to work.

To the women: hold your ground — you can do it. Try to put differences aside and work as a team. Take some time and learn the history of the women who have paved the way before you. Remember that a paved road doesn't stay paved without some patchwork. Fill in the potholes before they get too big. A wise woman learns from others' mistakes and wins. After thirty years, I am sorry to say, washrooms are still an issue — Inco still can't admit that we to have to go!

To all workers: lots of forces make up a union — it's not homogeneous. So have a voice and make sure you are heard. If you don't heed this advice, there will be stormier weather ahead.

Sudbury Saturday Night

Stompin' Tom Connors

The girls are out to Bingo and the boys are gettin' stinko,
And we think no more of Inco on a Sudbury Saturday night.
The glasses they will tinkle when our eyes begin to twinkle,
And we'll think no more of Inco on a Sudbury Saturday night.

With Irish Jim O'Connel there and Scotty Jack MacDonald,
There's honky Fredrick Hurchell gettin' tight, but that's alright,
There's happy German Fritzy there with Frenchy getting tipsy,
And even Joe the Gypsy knows it's Saturday tonight.

Now when Mary Ann and Mabel come to join us at the table,
And tell us how the Bingo went tonight, we'll look a fright.
But if they won the money, we'll be lappin' up the honey, boys,
'Cause everything is funny, for it's Saturday tonight.

The girls are out to Bingo and the boys are gettin' stinko,
And we think no more of Inco on a Sudbury Saturday night.
The glasses they will tinkle when our eyes begin to twinkle,
And we'll think no more of Inco on a Sudbury Saturday night.

We'll drink the loot we borrowed and recuperate tomorrow,
'Cause everything is wonderful tonight, we had a good fight,
We ate the Dilly Pickle and we forgot about the Nickel,
And everybody's tickled, for it's Saturday tonight.

The songs that we'll be singing, they might be wrong but they'll be ringing,
When the lights of town are shining bright, and we're all tight,
We'll get to work on Monday, but tomorrow's only Sunday,
And we're out to have a fun day for it's Saturday tonight. Yeah.

The girls are out to Bingo and the boys are gettin' stinko,
And we think no more of Inco on a Sudbury Saturday night.
The glasses they will tinkle when our eyes begin to twinkle,
And we'll think no more of Inco on a Sudbury Saturday night.

We'll think no more of Inco on a Sudbury Saturday night.

Words and music by Tom C. Connors, © Crown Vetch Music, used by permission. First LP release, 1967.

Bibliography

Aboriginal Languages and Literacy Conference. 1991. *Towards Linguistic Justice for First Nations: The Challenge.* Ottawa: Assembly of First Nations.

Abraham, Carolyn. 1996. "Ontario Sets Out Vision for High Schools." *Ottawa Citizen* September 20.

ACMS District Health Council 2002. *Health System Report 2001.* Sudbury: Algoma, Cochrane, Manitoulin, and Sudbury District Health Council.

Adlaf, E.M., and A. Paglia. 2001. *Drug Use Among Ontario Students 1977–2001: Findings from the OSDUS.* Toronto: Centre for Addiction and Mental Health.

Albert, Rod. 2005. "Je me souviens." *The Rock:* OSSTF District 56 Newsletter, February.

Allaire, Gratien. 1999. *La francophonie canadienne: portraits.* Sudbury: Prise de parole.

Altmeyer, Chris A. et al. 2003. "Geographic Disparity in Premature Mortality in Ontario, 1992–1996." *International Journal of Health Geographics* 2, 7. Retrieved from <http://www.ij-healthgeographics.com/content/2/1/7>. (Accessed July 28, 2006).

APA. 2000. *Diagnostic and Statistical Manual of Mental Disorders: DSM-IV,* fourth edition, text revision. Washington, DC: American Psychiatric Association.

APMMR. 2008. *A Refined Argument: Report of the Advisory Panel on Municipal Mining Revenues.* Sudbury: City of Greater Sudbury.

Arendt, H. 1972. *La crise de la culture.* Translation of *Between Past and Future.* Paris: Gallimard.

Arnopoulos, Sheila McLeod. 1982. *Voices from French Ontario.* Montréal: McGill-Queen's University Press.

Assembly of First Nations. 1993. *Declaration on Aboriginal Languages.* Ottawa: AFN Press.

Bailey, S. 2002. "Flagship to Ease Child Poverty Missing Those Most in Need, Critics Say." *Canadian Press,* October 26. Retrieved July 17, 2003, from <http://www.child-carecanada.org/ccin/2002/ccin10_26_02.html>. (Accessed July 17, 2003.)

Barlow, Maude 2002. *Profit Is Not the Cure.* Toronto: McClelland and Stewart.

Barnett, R., and J. Fearn. 2003. "Children's Mental Health Profile: Implications for Services in Northeastern Ontario." Ministry of Community, Family, and Children's Services. Northeast Regional Forum presentation, Sudbury.

Battle, K. 2003. "Ontario's Shrinking Minimum Wage." Ottawa: The Caledon Institute of Social Policy. Retrieved from <http://www.caledoninst>. (Accessed July 9, 2003.)

Beamish, R.J., and H.H. Harvey. 1972. "Acidification of the LaCloche Mountain Lakes, Ontario, and Resulting Fish Mortalities." *Journal of the Fisheries Research Board of Canada* 29: 1131–43.

Beck, Kaili et al. 2005. *Mine Mill Fights Back: Mine Mill/CAW Local 598 Strike 2000–2001, Sudbury.* Sudbury: Mine Mill/CAW Local 598.

Beck, U. 1992. *Risk Society: Towards a New Modernity.* London, UK: Sage.

Béland, C. 1952. "La vie religieuse à Blind River." In *Blind River, centre industriel: Blezard Valley, paroisse agricole.* Document historique No. 24. Sudbury: Société historique du Nouvel-Ontario.

Belzile, N. et al. 1997. "Acid Mine Drainage in the Sudbury Area, Ontario." In N. Eyles (ed.), *Environmental Geology of Urban Areas,* Geotext 3. St. John's, NF: Geological Association of Canada.

Beveridge, Karl. 1995. "Working Partners: The Arts and the Labour Movement." In Mercedes Steedman et al. (eds.), *Hard Lessons: The Mine Mill Union in the Canadian Labour Movement.* Toronto: Dundurn Press.

Bird, E.C.F. et al. 1984. *The Impacts of Opencast Mining on the Rivers and Coasts of New Caledonia.* Tokyo: United Nations University.

Blackmar, Elizabeth. 2005. "Of REITS and Rights: Absentee Ownership in the Periphery." In Diefendorf and Dorsey (eds.), *City, Country, Empire: Landscapes in Environmental History.* Pittsburgh: University of Pittsburgh Press.

Blais, J.M. et al. 1999. "Regional Contamination in Lakes from the Norilsk Region in Siberia, Russia." *Water, Air, and Soil Pollution* 110: 389–404.

Bollman, Ray D. 1999. "Factors Associated with Local Economic Growth." *Rural and Small Town Canada Analysis Bulletin* 1, 6: 1–10.

Bostrom, Loretta. 2004. Personal communication, August 16, 2004. Sudbury: Communications Office, Sudbury Regional Hospital.

Boudreau, F. 2002. *Garçons et filles: Deux sexes, deux genres. Les implications sociales et pédagogiques de la différence.* Rapport du comité Ad Hoc sur les difficultés scolaires des garçons. Sudbury: Conseil scolaire de district du Grand Nord de l'Ontario.

Boydell, K. et al. 2004. *Pathways and Barriers to Care for Rural Children's Mental Health.* Report to the Canadian Health Services Research Foundation, Ottawa.

Boyden, J. 1997. "Childhood and the Policy Makers: A Comparative Perspective on the Globalization of Childhood." In James and Prout (eds.), *Constructing and Reconstructing Childhood,* second edition. London, UK: Falmer.

Bradford, Neil. 2000. "The Policy Influence of Economic Ideas: Interests, Institutions and Innovation in Canada." In Burke et al. (eds.), *Restructuring and Resistance: Canadian Public Policy in an Age of Global Capitalism.* Halifax: Fernwood.

Bradley, Bill. 2008a. "Our Soils Are Safe, Study Says." *Northern Life* May 14.

———. 2008b. "A Primer on the Study, the Process and the Players Involved." *Northern Life* May 29.

———. 2008c. "Soil Study Terms of Reference Flawed, Expert Says." *Northern Life* May 15.

Brasch, Hans. 1997. *A Miner's Chronicle: Inco Ltd. and the Unions, 1944–1997.* Dowling: Hans Brasch.

Bray, Matt. 1993. "1910–1920." In Wallace and Thomson (eds.), *Sudbury: Rail Town to Regional Capital.* Toronto: Dundurn Press.

Brizinski, Peggy. 1993. *Knots in a String: An Introduction to Native Studies in Canada.* Saskatoon: University Extension Press, Extension Division, University of Saskatchewan.

Bronfenbrenner, U. 1979. *The Ecology of Human Development: Experiments by Nature and Design.* Cambridge, MA: Harvard University Press.

Brookfield, Stephen. 1995. *Becoming a Critically Reflective Teacher.* San Francisco: Jossey-Bass.

Bunge, Robert. 1987. "Language: The Psyche of a People." Reprinted in Crawford (ed.), *Language Loyalties: A Source Book on the Official English Controversy.* Chicago: University of Chicago Press.

Burris, Anne, and Bob Puhala. 1987. "The Thomson Machine: Small Papers, Big Profits." *Columbia Journalism Review* May: 12–13.

Buse, Dieter. 1993. "The 1970s." In Wallace and Thomson (eds.), *Sudbury: Rail Town to Regional Capital.* Toronto: Dundurn Press.

———. 1995. "Weir Reid and Mine Mill: An Alternative Union's Cultural Endeavours." In Steedman et al. (eds.). *Hard Lessons: The Mine Mill Union in the Canadian Labour Movement.* Toronto: Dundurn Press.

CAFB. No date a. "Supporters." Retrieved from <http://www.cafb-acba.ca/supporters_e. cfm>. (Accessed July 12, 2003.)

_____. No date b. "Food Supporters." Retrieved from <http://www.cafb-acba.ca/supporters_food_e.cfm>. (Accessed July 12, 2003.)

_____. No date c. "Financial Supporters." Retrieved from <http://www.cafb-acba.ca/supporters_financial_e.cfm>. (Accessed July 12, 2003.)

_____. No date d. "In-Kind Supporters." Retrieved from <http://www.cafb-acba.ca/supporters_inkind_e.cfm>. (Accessed July 12, 2003.)

_____. 2003. *HungerCount 2003.* "Something Has to Give": Food Banks Filling the Policy Gap in Canada." Toronto: Canadian Association of Food Banks.

Camfield, David. 2000. "Assessing Resistance in Harris's Ontario, 1995–1999." In Burke et al. (eds.), *Restructuring and Resistance: Canadian Public Policy in an Age of Global Capitalism.* Halifax: Fernwood.

Canada. 1998. "Canada's Action Plan for Food Security: A Response to the World Food Summit." Ottawa: Agriculture and Agri-Food Canada.

Canadian Family. 2005. "Top 10 Family-Friendly Canadian Cities." Retrieved from <http://www.canadianfamily.ca>. (Accessed May 2007.)

Cardinal, Linda, *et* Cécile Coderre. 1990. "Les francophones telles qu'elles sont: les Ontaroises et l'Économie," *Revue de Nouvel-Ontario,* No. 12: 151–82.

Carmichael, Harold. 2000. "The New Way Report to be Released Today." *The Sudbury Star* October 11.

_____. 2004. "Labour Leaders Target City Council." *The Sudbury Star* September 23.

Case, R. 1991. *The Mind's Staircase: Exploring the Conceptual Underpinnings of Children's Thought and Knowledge.* Hillsdale, NJ: Erlbaum.

Case, R. et al. 1999. "Socioeconomic Gradients in Mathematical Ability and their Responsiveness to Intervention During Early Childhood." In Keating and Hertzman (eds.), *Developmental Health and the Wealth of Nations.* New York: Guildford.

Catalano, Ralph A. 1991. "Health effects of economic insecurity." *American Journal of Public Health* 81, 9: 1148–52.

CAW. 2006. "Two Sides of the Coin: The Opportunities, and Risks, of Creating the World's Largest Nickel Producer." Booklet. Toronto: Canadian Auto Workers Union

Chan, W.H. et al. 1984. "Impact of Inco Smelter Emissions on Wet and Dry Deposition in the Sudbury Area." *Atmospheric Environment* 18: 1001–1008.

Chenier, N.M. 1995. *Suicide Among Aboriginal People: Royal Commission Report.* Political and Social Affairs Division, Parliamentary Research Branch, Library of Parliament, Catalogue MR-131E. Ottawa: Library of Parliament.

Childs, H. 1990. "Community Response to Suicide: A Model for Caring and Sharing for our Young." Nishnawbe-Aski Nations Suicide Prevention Workshop, April 3–5.

Choquette, R. 1993. "L'Église de l'Ontario français." In C. Jaenen (ed.), *Les Franco-Ontariens.* Ottawa: Presses de l'Université d'Ottawa.

CIHI (Canadian Institute for Health Information). 2004. *Improving the Health of Canadians.* Ottawa: Canadian Institute for Health Information.

Clarke, Meghan. 2003. "Lord Sifton of Fleet?" *Ryerson Review of Journalism* Summer. Retrieved from <http://www.rrj.ca/issue/2003/summer>. (Accessed 2006.)

CLC (Canadian Labour Congress). 2005. "Left Out in the Cold: The End of UI for Canadian Workers." Ottawa: Canadian Labour Congress.

Clement, Wallace. 1981. *Hardrock Mining: Industrial Relations and Technological Changes at Inco.* Toronto: McClelland and Stewart.

CMHC (Canada Mortgage and Housing Corporation). 2002. "Average Rental Vacancy Rates Rise to 1.7 Per Cent." Ottawa: Canada Mortgage and Housing Corporation. Retrieved from <http://www.cmhc-sch1.gc.ca/en/News/nere/2002/2002-11-26-

0815.cfm>. (Accessed August 20, 2004.)

———. 2003. "Housing Affordability Improves." *2001 Census Housing Series,* Issue 1. Ottawa: Canada Mortgage and Housing Corporation.

Coates, Ken, and William Morrison. 1992. *The Forgotten North: A History of Canada's Provincial Norths.* Toronto: Lorimer.

Coburn, David. 1999. "Phases of Capitalism, Welfare States, Medical Dominance, and Health Care in Ontario." *International Journal of Health Services* 29, 4: 833–51.

———. 2000. "Income Inequality, Social Cohesion and the Health Status of Populations: The Role of Neoliberalism." *Social Science and Medicine* 51, 1: 135–46.

———. 2004. "Beyond the Income Inequality Hypothesis: Class, Neo-Liberalism, and Health Inequalities." *Social Science and Medicine* 58: 41–56.

Coish, David. 2004. *Census Metropolitan Areas as Culture Clusters.* Ottawa: Statistics Canada. Retrieved from <http://www.statcan.ca>. (Accessed May 2007.)

Committee to Remember Kimberly Rogers. 2002. "Ontario Works Statistics: Some Useful Statistics Related to the Inquest into the Death of Kimberly Rogers." Retrieved from <http://dawn.thot.net/Kimberly_Rogers/ow_stats.html>. (Accessed July 5, 2003.)

Crouch, M. 2001. "From Golden Rice to Terminator Technology: Agricultural Biotechnology Will Not Feed the World or Save the Environment." In Tokar (ed.), *Redesigning Life? The Worldwide Challenge to Genetic Engineering.* London, UK: Zed Books.

Crystal, David (ed.). 1987. *The Cambridge Encyclopedia of Language.* Cambridge, UK: Cambridge University Press.

CSPCT (Community Social Planning Council of Toronto). 2004. "Poverty Statistics: What's Available and Where to Find It." Toronto: Community Social Planning Council of Toronto. Retrieved from <http://www.socialplanningtoronto.org>. (Accessed August 25, 2004.)

CSTF (Community Stakeholders' Task Force). 2006. "Claiming Our Stake! Building a Sustainable Community." Sudbury: The Community Stakeholders' Task Force on the Future of the Local Mining Industry.

CTFK (Campaign for Tobacco Free Kids). 2001. *Golden Leaf, Barren Harvest: The Costs of Tobacco Farming.* Washington, DC: Campaign for Tobacco Free Kids.

Dagenais, D. 2000. *La fin de la famille moderne: la signification des transformations contemporaines de la famille.* Québec: Presses de l'Université Laval.

Davies, Tom. 1988. "Response of the Private Sector: A Challenge Toward Economic Expansion and Diversification." In *Toward Economic Diversification: Economic Expansion and Diversification: A Challenge to the Private Sector.* Sudbury: Regional Municipality of Sudbury.

Davis, John. 1957. *Mining and Mineral Processing in Canada.* Ottawa: Royal Commission on Canada's Economic Prospects.

DBFB (Daily Bread Food Bank). No date. "Corporate Food Donation." Toronto: Daily Bread Food Bank. Retrieved from <http://www.dailybread.ca/donate/donate_corp.html>. (Accessed July 12, 2003.)

———. 2001. *Disabled Benefits.* Report prepared for the Ontario Association of Food Banks. Toronto: Daily Bread Food Bank.

———. 2002. *The Food Bank Report: Food Bank Assistance in Ontario, 2002.* Report prepared for the Ontario Association of Food Banks. Toronto: Daily Bread Food Bank.

Dearden, P., and B. Mitchell. 2002. *Environmental Challenge and Change: A Canadian Perspective,* second edition. Toronto: Oxford University Press.

Dennie, Donald. 1986. *La paroisse Sainte-Anne-des-Pins de Sudbury, 1883–1940: étude de démographie historique,* Documents historiques de Société historique du Nouvel-Ontario, No. 84. Sudbury: Société historique du Nouvel-Ontario.

_____. 2001. *À l'ombre de l'Inco: étude de la transition d'une communauté canadienne-française de la région de Sudbury (1890–1972).* Ottawa: Les Presses de l'Université d'Ottawa.

DesMeules, M. et al. 2003. *Canada's Rural Communities: Understanding Rural Health and Its Determinants.* Research in progress funded by the Canadian Population Health Initiative, Canadian Institute for Health Information.

Deverell, John. 1975. *Falconbridge: Portrait of a Canadian Mining Multinational.* Toronto: Lorimer.

Dewees, D.N., with Michael Halewood. 1992. "The Efficiency of the Common Law: Sulphur Dioxide Emissions in Sudbury." *University of Toronto Law Journal* 42, 1: 1–21.

Dixit, A.S. et al. 1992. "Assessment of Changes in Lake Water Chemistry in Sudbury Area Lakes Since Pre-industrial Times." *Canadian Journal of Fisheries Aquatic Sciences* 49 (Supplement 1): 8–16.

Dooley, David et al. 1996. "Health and Unemployment." *Annual Review of Public Health* 17: 449–64.

Dukelow, Daphne A. 2004. *Dictionary of Canadian Law,* third edition. Scarborough: Thomson Carswell.

Dungan, D. Peter. 1997. *Rock Solid: The Impact of the Mining and Primary Metals Industries on the Canadian Economy.* Toronto: Institute for Policy Analysis, University of Toronto.

Dunning, John H. 1997. *Alliance Capitalism and Global Business.* London, UK: Routledge.

Duquet, D., *et* C. Audet. 1998. *Éduquer à la citoyenneté.* Avis au Ministre de l'éducation. Québec: Conseil supérieur de l'éducation du Québec.

EDC (Environmental Defence Canada). 2003. Press release, July 24. Retrieved from <http://www.incowatch.ca>.

Edinger, E.N., and M.M.R. Best. 2001. "Environmental Impacts of Nickel Mining in Soroako, Sulawesi, Indonesia." *Report to Miningwatch Canada.* Ottawa: Miningwatch Canada..

Elijah, Mary Joy. 2002. *Literature Review — Language and Culture.* Ottawa: The Minister's National Working Group on Education. Retrieved from <http://www.ainc-inac. gc.ca/pr/pub/krw/com_e.pdf>.

Enright, R.D. et al. 1987. "Do Economic Conditions Influence how Theorists View Adolescents?" *Journal of Youth and Adolescence* 16: 541–59.

Epp, Jake. 1986. *Achieving Health for All: A Framework for Health Promotion.* Report No. H39-102/1986E. Ottawa: Minister of Supplies and Services.

EPS (Environmental Protection Service). 1982. "Environmental Aspects of the Extraction and Production of Nickel." *Environmental Protection Service Report* series EPS 3-AP-82-5.

Evans, Robert G. et al. (eds.). 1994. *Why Are some People Healthy and Others Are Not?: The Determinants of Health of Populations.* New York: Aldine DeGruyter.

Falconbridge Limited v. Sudbury Mine Mill et al. 2000. Court file No. A9020/00 (Ontario Supreme Court) September 15, 2000.

Faries, Emily et al. 2002. *"Beyond Rhetoric": Exploring the Linkages Between Language, Literacy, and First Nation Social Security Programming.* Ottawa: AFN Press.

Federal/Provincial/Territorial Ministers of Health. 1994. *Strategies for Population Health.* Ottawa: Health Canada.

Ferguson, B. 2006a. "Making Our Kids Successful." Keynote address delivered to the

Ontario Ministry of Education, Toronto. February.

———. 2006b. "The Institute for Child and Youth Success: Conceptual Overview." Working Paper, Hospital for Sick Children, Toronto.

Ferguson, B., et al. 2005. *Early School Leavers: Understanding the Lived Reality of Student Disengagement from Secondary School.* Final Report to the Ontario Ministry of Education, May 31. Retrieved from <http://www.edu.gov.on.ca/eng/parents/schoolleavers. pdf>.

Fernandez, Melanie. 2005. "Reflections of a Former Community Arts Officer." *Fuse Magazine* 28, 3: 9–14.

FCPMC (Food and Consumer Products Manufacturers of Canada). No date a. "Affiliate Members." Retrieved from <http://www.fcpmc.com/about/affiliates/index.html>. (Accessed July 12, 2003.)

———. No date b. "Myth vs Reality: The Truth about Foods from Biotechnology." Retrieved from <http://www.fcpmc.com/government/bioltechnology/reality. html>. (Accessed July 12, 2003.)

Forestell, Nancy. 1999. "The Miner's Wife: Working-Class Femininity in a Masculine Context, 1920–1950." In McPherson et al. (eds.), *Gendered Pasts: Historical Essays in Femininity and Masculinity in Canada.* Don Mills, ON: Oxford University Press.

Fox, Mary Lou. 1991. MCTV News Report. Sudbury, Ontario.

Fraser, J.C. et al. 2003. "Denial by Design… the Ontario Disability Support Program." Toronto: Income Security Advocacy Centre. Retrieved from <http://www.incomesecurity.org/paytherent/resources/pdf_R/ISAC.pdf>. (Accessed June 2008.)

Freire, Paulo. 1973. *Pedagogy of the Oppressed.* New York: Seabury Press.

Freitag, M. 1986. *Dialectique et société:* Tome 1, *Introduction à une théorie générale du symbolique* et Tome 2, *Culture, pouvoir et contrôle: les modes de reproduction formels de la société.* Montréal: Éditions St-Martin et L'Âge d'homme.

———. 1995. *Le naufrage de l'université et autres essais d'épistémologie politique.* Québec: Nuit blanche.

———. 2002. *L'oubli de la société: pour une théorie critique de la postmodernité.* Québec: Presses de l'Université Laval.

Freudenburg, William R. 1992. "Addictive Economies: Extractive Industries and Vulnerable Localities in a Changing World." *Rural Sociology* 57, 3: 305–32.

Freudenburg, William R., and Lisa J. Wilson. 2002. "Mining the Data: Analyzing the Economic Implications of Mining for Non-metropolitan Regions." *Sociological Inquiry* 72, 4: 549–75.

Frick, Tammy. 2005. "City Council Pondering Investing in the Arts." *Northern Life* December 9.

Gagné, G. 2002. *Main basse sur l'éducation.* Québec: Nota bene.

Gam, E. 2003. "Ontario Works Benefit Rates: Loss of Purchasing Power Since 1995." Report to the Community Services Committee from Toronto's Commissioner of Community and Neighbourhood Services, Social Services Division.

Gardner, Howard. 1993. *Frames of Mind: the Theory of Multiple Intelligences.* San Francisco: Jossey-Bass.

Gaudreau, Guy. 2003. *L'histoire des mineurs du nord ontarien et québécois, 1886–1945.* Sillery, PQ: Septentrion.

Gedicks, Al. 2001. *Resource Rebels: Native Challenges to Mining and Oil Corporations.* Cambridge, MA: South End Press.

Gervais, G. 1993. "L'Ontario français (1821–1910)." In C. Jaenen (ed.) *Les Franco-Ontariens.* Ottawa: Presses de l'Université d'Ottawa.

Gidney, R.D. 1999. *From Hope to Harris: The Reshaping of Ontario's Schools*. Toronto: University of Toronto Press.

Gilbert, Craig. 2004. "Bonin Says Claims of 500 Federal Jobs Leaving City Simply Not True." *Northern Life* June 23.

Gilchrist, Gib. 1999. *As Strong as Steel*. Sudbury: Journal Printing

Gilmore, Jason. 2004. "Health of Canadians Living in Census Metropolitan Areas." Analytical paper. Ottawa: Health Statistics Division, Health Canada.

Glynn, T.A. 2006. "Community-Based Research on the Environmental and Human Health Impacts of a Laterite Nickel Mine and Smelter in Sorowako, Indonesia." M.Sc. thesis, Memorial University of Newfoundland.

Goldsack et al. (eds.). 1999. *Sudbury '99: Mining and the Environment II*. Sudbury: Laurentian University.

Goltz, Eileen. 1992. "The Image and Reality of Life in a Northern Ontario Company-owned Town." In Bray and Thompson (eds.), *At the End of the Shift: Mines and Single-Industry Towns in Northern Ontario*. Toronto: Dundurn Press.

Goudie, R.I. 1998. "Review of Voisey's Bay Environmental Impact Statement, Avifauna." *Report to Innu Nation*. Sheshatshiu, NL: Innu Nation.

Government of Canada. 1998. "Fetal and Infant Mortality Study." *Canadian Perinatal Surveillance System, Progress Report 1997–1998*. Ottawa: Public Health Agency of Canada.

Grylls, Rick. 2008. "Sudbury Soil Study 2008." Press release, June 9. Retrieved from <http://www.minemill598.com/PDF%20Files/RICK-GRYLLS-Sudbury-Soils-Study-2008.pdf>. (Accessed June 14, 2008.)

GSDC (Greater Sudbury Development Corporation). 2003. *Coming of Age in the 21st Century: An Economic Development Strategic Plan for Greater Sudbury*. Sudbury: Greater Sudbury Development Corporation and Pickard and Laws Consulting Group Inc.

Guindon, René. 1986. *Les francophones tels qu'ils sont*. Ottawa: ACFO.

Gunn, J. M. (ed.). 1995. *Restoration and Recovery of an Industrial Region*. New York: Springer-Verlag.

Gurian, M., and P. Henley. 2001. *Boys and Girls Learn Differently: A Guide for Teachers and Parents*. San Francisco: Jossey-Bass.

Haddow, Rodney, and Thomas Klassen. 2006. *Partisanship, Globalization, and Canadian Labour Market Policy: Four Provinces in Comparative Perspective*. Toronto: University of Toronto Press.

Haffner, G.D. et al. 2001. "The Biology and Physical Processes of Large Lakes of Indonesia: Lakes Matano and Towuti." In Munawar and Hecky (eds.), *The Great Lakes of the World (GLOW): Food-Web, Health and Integrity*. Leiden, Netherlands: Backhuys.

Halifax Initiative. 2003. "Seven Deadly Secrets: What Export Development Canada Does not Want You to Know." Ottawa: NGO Working Group on the EDC, Halifax Initiative.

Hall, David. 2003. *Public Services Work! Information, Insights and Ideas for Our Future*. Ferney-Voltaire, France: Public Services International. Retrieved from <http://www.psiru.org/reports/2003-09-U-PSW.pdf>.

Hardman, C. 1973. "Can There Be an Anthropology of Children?" *Journal of the Anthropological Society of Oxford* 4: 85–99.

Hart, Doug. 1998. "Crisis, What Crisis?" *Research in Ontario Secondary Schools* 5, 1. Retrieved from <http://www.oise.utoronto.ca/field-centres/TVC/RossReports/vol5no1.htm>. (Accessed June 2008.)

Hayes, Michael V., and James R. Dunn. 1998. *Population Health in Canada: A Systematic*

Review. CPRN Study No. H-01. Ottawa: Canadian Policy Research Network.

Health Canada. 1999. *Towards a Healthy Future: Second Report on the Health of Canadians.* Ottawa: Health Canada.

———. 2002. *A Report on Mental Illnesses in Canada.* Catalogue H39-643/2002E. Ottawa: Health Canada.

———. 2003. *A Statistical Profile on the Health of First Nations in Canada.* Ottawa: Health Canada.

Heller, C. 2001. "McDonald's, MTV and Monsanto: Resisting Biotechnology in the Age of Informational Capital." In Tokar (ed.), *Redesigning Life? The Worldwide Challenge to Genetic Engineering.* London, UK: Zed Books.

Hendrick, H. 1997. "Constructions and Reconstructions of British Childhood: An Interpretive Survey, 1800 to the Present." In James and Prout (eds.), *Constructing and Reconstructing Childhood,* second edition. London, UK: Falmer.

Hertzman, C. 1999. "Population Health and Human Development." In Keating and Hertzman (eds.), *Developmental Health and the Wealth of Nations.* New York: Guildford.

Holcroft, Chris. 2001. "Ontario Teachers Need Better Leadership." *Pundit Magazine,* June 5.

Hull, J. 2001. *Aboriginal Single Mothers in Canada, 1996: A Statistical Profile.* Ottawa: Indian and Northern Affairs Canada, Research and Analysis Directorate.

Humphreys, David. 2005. "Corporate Strategies in the Global Mining Industry." In Bastida et al. (eds.), *International and Comparative Mineral Law and Policy: Trends and Prospects.* The Hague, Netherlands: Kluwer Law International.

Hyland, T. 2001. "A Critical Analysis of the ODSP Act and Social Citizenship Rights in Ontario." Masters research paper. Ottawa: Faculty of Graduate Studies and Research, Institute of Political Economy, Carleton University.

Hymes, Dell. 1981. *"In Vain I Tried to Tell You": Essays in Native American Ethnopoetics.* Philadelphia: University of Pennsylvania Press.

Hynes, T.P., and M.C. Blanchette (eds.). 1995. *Sudbury '95: Mining and the Environment.* Sudbury: Laurentian University.

Ibbitson, John. 1997. *Promised Land: Inside the Mike Harris Revolution.* Scarborough: Prentice-Hall Canada.

Income Security Advocacy Centre. 2003. "Submission to the Provincial Standing Committee on Finance and Economic Affairs, January 29, 2003." Retrieved from <www.incomesecurity.org>. (Accessed July 8, 2003.)

International Council on Human Rights Policy. 2000. *The Persistance and Mutation of Racism.* Versoix, Switzerland: International Council on Human Rights Policy. Retrieved from <http://www.ichrp.org/paper_files/112_p_01.pdf>.

Jaenen, Cornélius (ed.). 1993. *Les Franco-Ontariens.* Ottawa. Press de l'Université d'Ottawa.

Jambor, J.L. et al. (eds.). 2003. *Environmental Aspects of Mine Wastes,* Mineralogical Association of Canada, Short Course Notes #31.

Jankowski, W.B., and B. Moazzami. 1993. *Northern Ontario's Economy in Transition: National and International Perspectives.* Thunder Bay: Department of Economics, Lakehead University.

Jenks, C. 1996. *Childhood.* London, UK: Routledge.

Johnston, Basil. 1990. "One Generation from Extinction." In New (ed.), *Native Writers and Canadian Writing (Canadian Literature* Special Issue). Vancouver: UBC Press.

Judge Epstein. 2001. *Rogers v. Administrator of Ontario Works for the City of Greater Sudbury* et al. (2001) 57 O.R. (3d) 460 at paragraphs 18–20.

Kauppi, Carol. 1999. "Child Poverty in the Regional Municipality of Sudbury: 1981 to 1996." In van de Sande (ed.), *Child and Youth Poverty in Sudbury*. Sudbury: Laurentian University.

_____. 2002. "Report on Homelessness in Sudbury: Comparison of Findings July 2000 to July 2002." Sudbury: Social Planning Council of Sudbury.

Keating, D. 1996. "Families, Schools and Communities: Social Resources for a Learning Society." In Ross (ed.), *Family Security in Insecure Times: New Foundations* (Volumes 2–3). Ottawa: Canadian Council on Social Development.

Keating, D., and C. Hertzman. 1999. "Modernity's Paradox." In Keating and Hertzman (eds.), *Developmental Health and the Wealth of Nations*. New York: Guildford.

Keating, D., and J.F. Mustard. 1993. "Social Economic Factors and Human Development." In Ross (ed.), *Family Security in Insecure Times* (Volume 1). Ottawa: National Forum on Family Security.

Kechnie, Margaret, and Marge Reitsma-Street (eds.). 1996. *Changing Lives: Women in Northern Ontario*. Toronto: Dundurn Press.

Keck, Jennifer, and Mary Powell. 2006. "Women into Mining Jobs at Inco: Challenging the Gender Division of Labour." In Gier and Mercier (eds.), *Mining Women: Gender in the Development of a Global Industry, 1670 to 2005*. New York: Palgrave Macmillan.

Keller, W. et al. 1999a. "Acid Rain — Perspectives on Lake Recovery." *Journal of Aquatic Ecosystem Stress and Recovery* 6: 207–16.

_____. 1999b. "Effects of Emission Reductions from the Sudbury Smelters on the Recovery of Acid- and Metal-damaged Lakes." *Journal of Aquatic Ecosystem Stress and Recovery* 6: 189–98.

_____. 2001. "Sulphate in Sudbury, Ontario, Canada, Lakes: Recent Trends and Status." *Water Air and Soil Pollution* 130: 793–98.

Kelly, P. 2000. "The Dangerousness of Youth-at-Risk: The Possibilities of Surveillance and Intervention in Uncertain Times." *Journal of Adolescence* 23: 463–76.

Kershaw, Baz. 1992. *The Politics of Performance: Radical Theatre as Cultural Intervention*. London, UK: Routledge.

Kidder, K. et al. 2000. *The Health of Canada's children: A CICH Profile*, third edition. Ottawa: Canadian Institute of Child Health.

Kiecolt-Glaser, J. et al. 1995. "Slowing of Wound Healing by Psychological Stress." *Lancet* 346: 1194–96.

King, A. 2004. *Double Cohort Study: Phase 3 Report*. Toronto: Ontario Ministry of Education.

Kirby, M., and W. Keon. 2006. *Out of the Shadows at Last: Transforming Mental Health, Mental Illness and Addiction Services in Canada*. Ottawa: The Senate Of Canada.

Kirkness, Verna J. 1989. "Aboriginal Languages in Canada: From Confusion to Certainty." *The Journal of Indigenous Studies*, 1, 2: 97–103.

Klubock, Thomas. 1996. "Working-Class Masculinity, Middle-Class Morality, and Labor Politics in the Chilean Copper Mines." *Journal of Social History*, 30, 2: 435–63.

Kneen, B. 1999. *Farmageddon: Food and the Culture of Biotechnology*. Gabriola Island: New Society Publishers.

Kuyek, Joan. 2008. "An Open Letter to the SARA Group." *Northern Life*, May 29.

Kuyek, Joan, and Catherine Coumans. 2003. *No Rock Unturned: Revitalizing the Economies of Mining Dependent Communities*. Ottawa: MiningWatch Canada. Retrieved from <http://www.miningwatch.ca/index.php?/Impact_on_Communitie/No_Rock_Unturned>. (Accessed June 2008.)

Labrosse, P. et al. 2000. "New Caledonia." In Sheppard (ed.), *Seas at the Millennium: An Environmental Evaluation*. Amsterdam, Netherlands: Pergamon.

Lacy, Suzanne (ed.). 1995. *Mapping the Terrain: New Genre Public Art*. Seattle, Washington: Bay Press.

Lagacé, L., and J. Lamarre. 2001. *Les élèves en difficulté de comportement à l'école primaire: comprendre, prévenir, intervenir*. Avis au Ministre de l'éducation. Québec: Conseil supérieur de l'éducation du Québec.

Laite, Julian. 1985. "Capitalist Development and Labour Organisation: Hard-Rock Miners in Ontario." In Greaves and Culver (eds.), *Miners and Mining in the Americas*. Manchester, UK: Manchester University Press.

Lalonde, Marc. 1974. *A New Perspective on the Health of Canadians*. Ottawa: Health and Welfare Canada.

Lamarre, J., and M. Ouellet. 1999. *Pour une meilleure réussite scolaire des garçons et des filles*. Avis au Ministre de l'éducation. Québec: Conseil supérieur de l'éducation du Québec.

Lang, John. 1970. "A Lion in the Den of Daniels: A History of the International Union of Mine Mill and Smelter Workers in Sudbury, Ontario, 1942–1962." MA thesis, University of Guelph.

Latham, R. 2002. *Consuming Youth: Vampires, Cyborgs and the Culture of Consumption*. Chicago: University of Chicago Press.

Laurentian University. 2004. *Skills for Success: Welcome to Laurentian University*. Sudbury: Laurentian University Press.

Lautenbach, W.E. 1987. "The Greening of Sudbury." *Journal of Soil and Water Conservation* July–August: 228–31.

Leacy, F.H. (ed.). 1983. *Historical Statistics of Canada*, second edition. Ottawa: Statistics Canada.

Leadbeater, David. 1992. *Setting Minimum Living Standards in Canada: A Review*. Working Paper No. 38. Ottawa: Economic Council of Canada.

_____. 1998. "Single-Industry Resource Communities and the New Crisis of Economic Development: Lessons of Elliot Lake." Sudbury: Laurentian University, Elliot Lake Tracking and Adjustment Study.

Leavitt, Robert M. 1992. "Confronting Language Ambivalence and Language Death." In Miller et al. (eds.), *The First Ones: Readings in Indian/Native Studies*. Craven, Saskatchewan: Saskatchewan Indian Federated College Press.

Lee, Kevin K. 2000. *Urban Poverty in Canada: A Statistical Profile*. Ottawa: Canadian Council on Social Development.

Letourneur, Y., P. Labrosse, and M. Kulbicki. 1999. "Commercial Fish Assemblages of New Caledonian Fringing Reefs Subjected to Different Levels of Ground Erosion." *Oceanologica Acta* 22, 6: 609–21.

Lowe, Mick. 1998. *Premature Bonanza: Standoff at Voisey's Bay*. Toronto: Between the Lines.

_____. 2001. "Solidarity? Whatever…" *Straight Goods* March 5. Retrieved from <http://www.straightgoods.com>.

Macdonald, Brian, and Norm Chammus. 2001. "Falconbridge Strike Analysis: A Union Perspective." *Mine Mill/CAW Local 598 Newsletter* March 25.

MacMillan, H.L. et al. 1996. "Aboriginal Health." *Canadian Medical Association Journal* 155, 11: 1569–78.

Maddison, Angus. 1991. *Dynamic Forces in Capitalist Development: A Long-Run Comparative View*. Oxford: Oxford University Press.

March of Dimes. 2002. *International Comparisons of Infant Mortality Rates, 1998*. White

Plains, New York: March of Dimes. Retrieved from <http://www.marchofdimes.com/perstats>.

Martin-Guillerm, Marguerite. 1991. "Portrait statistique des Franco-Ontariens de la région métropolitaine de Sudbury (1991)." *Revue du Nouvel-Ontario*, No. 21: 9–38.

Mathers, Colin D., and Deborah J. Schofield. 1998. "The Health Consequences of Unemployment: The Evidence." *Medical Journal of Australia* 168, 4: 178–82.

Mawhiney, Anne-Marie, (ed.). 1993. *Rebirth: Political, Economic and Social Development in First Nations.* Toronto: Dundurn Press.

McCain, M.N., and J.F. Mustard. 1999. *Reversing the Real Brain Drain: Early Years Study, Final Report.* Toronto: Ontario Children's Secretariat.

McGonagle, Declan. 2005. "The Temple and the Forum Together: Re-Configuring Community Arts." *Fuse Magazine* 28, 2: 19–27.

McLeod, Christopher et al. 2003. "Income Inequality, Household Income, and Health Status in Canada: A Prospective Cohort Study." *American Journal of Public Health* 93, 8: 1287–93.

McNally, D. 2002. *Another World Is Possible: Globalization and Anti-Capitalism.* Winnipeg: Arbeiter Ring.

McNish, Jacquie. 2006. "The Great Canadian Mining Disaster." *Globe and Mail* Nov. 24.

Mercier, Laurie. 1999. "'Instead of Fighting the Common Enemy': Mine Mill Versus the Steeworkers in Montana, 1950–1967." *Labour History* November.

Messing, Karen. 1995. "Chicken or Egg: Biological Differences and the Sexual Division of Labour." In Messing et al. (eds.), *Invisible: Issues in Women's Occupational Health.* Charlottetown: Gynergy Books.

Mills, C. Wright. 1959. *The Power Elite.* New York: Oxford University Press.

Myers, N. et al. 2000. "Biodiversity Hotspots for Conservation Priorities." *Nature* 403: 853–58.

National Forum on Health. 1997. *Canada Health Action: Building on the Legacy.* Ottawa: National Forum on Health.

Navarro, Vincente (ed.). 2002. *The Political Economy of Social Inequalities.* Amityville, NY: Baywood Publishing.

NCW (National Council of Welfare). No date. *Fact Sheet: Welfare Recipients (Estimated Number of People on Welfare, by Province and Territory, March 1993–March 1999).* Ottawa: National Council of Welfare.

_____. 2002. *Welfare Incomes, 2000 and 2001.* Ottawa: National Council of Welfare.

_____. 2003. *Fact Sheet: Poverty Lines 2002.* Ottawa: National Council of Welfare.

_____. 2004. *The Cost of Poverty.* Ottawa: National Council of Welfare.

Nelles, H.V. 1974. *The Politics of Development: Forests, Mines and Hydro-Electric Power in Ontario, 1849–1941.* Hamden, CT: Archon.

NHIP (Northern Health Information Partnership). 2003. *The Northern Ontario Child and Youth Health Report.* Sudbury: Northern Health Information Partnership.

NHISSC (Northern Health Issues Strategy Steering Committee). 2003. "Background Information on the Health Status and Health Care System in Northern Ontario." Sudbury: Northern Health Issues Strategy Steering Committee.

Nissen, Bruce. 2003. "Alternative Strategic Directions for the U.S. labor Movement: Recent Scholarship." *Labor Studies* 28, 1: 133–55.

NOLUM (Northern Ontario Large Urban Mayors). 2007. "Northern Lights: Strategic Investments in Ontario's Greatest Asset." Northern Ontario Large Urban Mayors. Retrieved from <www.greatersudbury.ca/content/div_mayor/documents/NOLUM-

Report_April18_2007.pdf>. (Accessed June 2008)

NRC (Natural Resources Canada). 2006a. *Mineral and Mining Statistics On-Line*. Ottawa: Natural Resources Canada. Retrieved from <http://mmsd1.mms.nrcan.gc.ca>. (Accessed May 2007.)

_____. 2006b. *Resource-reliant Communities, 2001*. Ottawa: Natural Resources Canada. Retrieved from <http://atlas.nrcan.gc.ca>. (Accessed April 2007.)

NUPGE (National Union of Provincial Government Employees). 1998. *Easy Targets: A Critical Review of the Campaign to Destroy the Value of Public Services*. Ottawa: National Union of Provincial Government Employees.

OCASI (Ontario Council of Agencies Serving Immigrants) Survey. 2004. Retrieved from <http://www.settlement.org/site/OUTREACH/Outreach_Survey.asp>. Conducted in The Greater City of Sudbury, Spring, 2003.

Offord, D.R. et al. 1992. "Outcome, Prognosis and Risk in a Longitudinal Follow-Up Study." *Journal of the American Academy of Child and Adolescent Psychiatry* 31, 5: 916–23.

O'Flanagan, Rob. 2004. "It's a Union Town: Sudburians Mark Labour Day in the Shadow of Another Labour Dispute." *The Sudbury Star* September 7.

Oliphant, M., and C. Slosser. 2003. *Ontario Alternative Budget 2003. Targeting the Most Vulnerable: A Decade of Desperation for Ontario's Welfare Recipients*. Ottawa: Canadian Centre for Policy Alternatives. Retrieved from <http://www.policyalternatives.ca>. (Accessed July 8, 2003.)

OMHLTC (Ontario Ministry of Health and Long-Term Care). 2001. *Mandatory Health Programs and Services Guidelines*. Toronto: Queen's Printer.

_____. 2002. *Ontario's Health Systems Performance Report: 14 Common Indicator Areas of Health and Health System Performance*. Toronto: Ontario Ministry of Health and Long-Term Care.

Ontario. 2004a. "Ontario Social Assistance Rate Increase and Special Payments." June 30. Toronto: Ministry of Community and Social Services. Retrieved from <http://www.cfcs.gov.on.ca/CFCS/en/newsRoom/factSheets/040630.htm>. (Accessed July 21, 2004.)

_____. 2004b. "McGuinty Government Raises Minimum Wage." February 1. Toronto: Ministry of Labour. Retrieved from <http://www.gov.on.ca/LAB/english/news/2004/04-09.html>. (Accessed July 21, 2004.)

Ontario Ministry of the Environment. 2001. *Metals in Soil and Vegetation in the Sudbury Area (Survey 2000 and Additional Historic Data)*. Toronto: Queen's Printer for Ontario. Executive summary retrieved from <http://www.ene.gov.on.ca/ envision/sudbury/metals/ esummary.htm>. (Accessed July 24, 2006.)

Ontario Ministry of Public Safety and Security, Office of the Chief Coroner. 2002. *Verdict of the Coroner's Jury Into the Death of Kimberly Ann Rogers*, December 19.

Ontario Non-Profit Housing Association. 2004. "What's Wrong with this Picture?" *Newsroom*, July 21. Retrieved from <http://www.onpha.on.ca>. (Accessed July 21, 2004.)

Ontario Progressive Conservative Party. 1994. *The Common Sense Revolution*. Election platform leaflet. Fifth printing.

Ontario Tenant Toronto Tenants. 2003. *New Ontario Rental Housing Statistics and Their Meaning*. Retrieved from <http://www.geocities.com/torontotenants/reports/rent2002.html>. (Accessed July 7, 2003.)

OPEIU (Office and Professional Employees International Union) Local 343. 2002. *Response to the Rozanski Report on the Ontario Education Funding Formula*. Toronto: Office and

Professional Employees International Union Local 343 (now Canadian Office and Professional Employees Union).

OPSEU (Ontario Public Service Employees Union). 2000. "Sudbury Kicks Off Privatization Fight." *Lock Talk: A Publication of the OPSEU Corrections Campaign,* January 21.

_____. 2001. "Fighting for Jobs, Rights." *Lights and Sirens: A Publication of the OPSEU Ambulance Division* February 12.

_____. 2002. *Reality: Ontario's Mental Health Care System Isn't Working.* Toronto: Ontario Public Service Employees Union.

OSSTF (Ontario Secondary School Teachers' Federation). 2002. *Update* 30, 3, November 5.

_____. 2003. Retrieved from <www.osstf.on.ca/issues/studentesting/rhetoric.html >.

Panitch, Leo, and Donald Swartz. 2003. *From Consent to Coercion: The Assault on Trade Union Freedoms.* Aurora, ON: Garamond.

Parker, Stuart. 1997. *Reflective Teaching in the Postmodern World.* Buckingham, UK: Open University Press.

Peat, Marwick and Partners. 1975. *Sudbury Region Economic Base Study.* Toronto: Peat, Marwick and Partners.

Peck, Gunther. 1993. "Manly Gambles: The Politics of Risk on the Comstock Lode, 1860–1880." *Journal of Social History* 26, 4: 701–23.

Pitblado, R. et al. 1999. *Assessing Rural Health: Toward Developing Health Indicators for Rural Canada.* Report submitted to the National Health and Research Development Program, Health Canada. Sudbury: Centre for Rural and Northern Health Research, Laurentian University.

Pitblado, R., and R. Pong. 1999. *Geographic Distribution of Physicians in Canada.* Sudbury: Centre for Rural and Northern Health Research.

Polèse, Mario, and Richard Shearmur. 2006. "Why Some Regions Will Decline: A Canadian Case Study with Thoughts on Local Development Strategies." *Papers in Regional Science* 85, 1: 23–46.

Pong, R. 2001. *Health Transition Fund Rural Health/Telehealth Synthesis Report.* Report prepared for the Health Transition Fund, Health Canada.

Pong, R. et al. 1999. *Rural Health Research in the Canadian Institutes of Health Research.* Report submitted to the Canadian Health Services Research Foundation and the Social Sciences and Humanities Research Council. Sudbury: Centre for Rural and Northern Health Research, Laurentian University.

Power, E.M. 1999. "Combining Social Justice and Sustainability for Food Security." In Koc et al. (eds.), *For Hunger-Proof Cities: Sustainable Urban Food Systems.* Ottawa: International Development Research Centre.

Progressive Conservative Party of Ontario. 1995. *The Mike Harris Round Table on Common Sense in Education.* Toronto: Progressive Conservative Party of Ontario.

Project Group on Urban Economic Development. 1985. *Case Study Report: Sudbury, Ontario Canada.* Toronto: Community Planning Programs Division, Ontario Ministry of Municipal Affairs and Housing.

Qvortrup, J. 1997. "A Voice for Children in Statistical and Social Accounting: A Plea for Children's Right to be Heard." In James and Prout (eds.), *Constructing and Reconstructing Childhood,* second edition. London, UK: Falmer.

Rae, Bob. 1997. *From Protest to Power: Personal Reflections on a Life in Politics.* Toronto: Penguin Books.

Rapaport, David. 1999. *No Justice, No Peace: The 1996 OPSEU Strike Against the Harris Government in Ontario.* Montréal: McGill-Queen's University Press.

Reguly, Eric. 2006. "Osprey Media Should Fear an Empty Nest of Buyers." *Globe and Mail* February 4.

Renaud, M. 1975. "On the Structural Constraints to State Intervention in Health." *International Journal of Health Services* 5, 4: 559–73.

Reshef, Yonaton, and Sandra Rastin. 2003. *Unions in the Time of Revolution: Government Restructuring in Alberta and Ontario.* Toronto: University of Toronto.

Rhodes, A.E. et al. 2002. "Do Hospital E-Codes Consistently Capture Suicidal Behaviour?" *Chronic Diseases in Canada* 23, 4: 139–45.

Rhodes, Richard. 1988. "Ojibwe Politeness and Social Structure." In Cowan and Mailhot (eds.), *Papers of the Nineteenth Algonquian Conference.* Ottawa: Carleton University Press.

Ricci, Carlo. 2004. "From Invention to Reality: Our Educational Crisis and a Call for Action." *Nipissing University Review* 10, 2. North Bay: Nipissing University.

Riches, G. 1997. "Hunger in Canada: Abandoning the Right to Food." In Riches (ed.), *First World Hunger: Food Security and Welfare Politics.* London, UK: Macmillan Press.

Riegel, K. 1972. "Influence of Economic and Political Ideologies on the Development of Developmental Psychology." *Psychological Bulletin* 78: 129–41.

Robertson, Heather-Jane. 1998. *No More Teachers, No More Books: The Commercialization of Canada's Schools.* Toronto: McClelland and Stewart.

Robinson, David. 2003. "21 Measures: A Statistical Review of Sudbury's Socio-Economic Performance." Institute for Northern Ontario Research and Development Background Paper. Sudbury: Laurentian University.

Robinson, K.M. 1986. *Stepchildren of Progress: the Political Economy of Development in an Indonesian Mining Town.* Albany: State University of New York Press.

Romanow, Roy J. 2002. *Building on Values: The Future of Health Care in Canada.* Saskatoon: Commission on the Future of Health Care in Canada.

Rosenblum, Jonathan D. 1998. *Copper Crucible: How the Arizona Miners' Strike of 1983 Recast Labor-Management Relations in America.* Ithaca, NY: ILR Press.

Ross, C.E., and C. Wu. 1995. "The Links Between Education and Health." *American Sociological Review* 60: 719–45.

Ross, N., M. Grandmaison, and D. Johnson. 2001. *Healing the Landscape: Celebrating Sudbury's Reclamation Success/Un paysage en renaissance: Sudbury, inspiration d'un succès ècologique.* Sudbury: City of Greater Sudbury.

Ross, Nancy A. et al. 2000. "Relation Between Income Inequality and Mortality in Canada and the United States: Cross Sectional Assessment Using Census Data and Vital Statistics." *British Medical Journal* 320, April 1: 898–902.

Ross, Nancy A., and Michael C. Wolfson. 1999. "Income Inequality and Mortality in Canada and the United States: An Analysis of Provinces/States." *Annals of the New York Academy of Sciences* 896: 338–40.

Ross, Val. 1979. "The Arrogance of Inco." *Canadian Business* 52, 5: 44–55, 116–142.

Rousell, D.H. et al. 2002. "Bedrock Geology and Mineral Deposits." In Rousell and Jansons (eds.), *The Physical Environment of the City of Greater Sudbury.* Sudbury: Ontario Geological Survey.

Royal Commission on Aboriginal Peoples. 1966. *Report of the Royal Commission on Aboriginal Peoples.* Ottawa: The Commission.

Royal Commission on Learning. 1994. *For the Love of Learning: Report of the Royal Commission on Learning.* Toronto: Royal Commission on Learning.

Royal Commission on Newspapers. 1981. *Royal Commission on Newspapers: Report,* "The Kent Report." Hull: Supply and Services Canada.

Russell, Bob. 2000. "From Workhouse to Workfare: The Welfare State and Shifting Policy Terrains." In Burke et al. (eds.), *Restructuring and Resistance: Canadian Public Policy in an Age of Global Capitalism*. Halifax: Fernwood.

Saarinen, Oiva. 1992. "Creating a Sustainable Community: The Sudbury Case Study." In Bray and Thomson (eds.), *At the End of the Shift: Mines and Single-Industry Towns in Northern Ontario*. Toronto: Dundurn Press.

Sampat, Payal. 2003. "Scrapping Mining Dependence." In Worldwatch Institute (ed.), *State of the World 2003*. New York: Norton.

Sancton, Andrew. 2000. *Merger Mania: The Assault on Local Government*. Montréal: McGill-Queen's University Press.

SARA Group 2008. *Sudbury Soil Study, Volume II*. Retrieved from <http://www.sudburysoilstudy.com> (Accessed June 14, 2008.)

Schatz, Laura, and Laura Johnson. 2007. "Smart City North: Economic and Labour Force Impacts of Call Centres in Sudbury, Ontario." *Work Organisation, Labour and Globalization* 1, 2: 116–30.

Schindler, D. 1999. "From Acid Rain to Toxic Snow." *Ambio* 28, 4: 350–55.

Schmitz, Christopher. 1986. "The Rise of Big Business in the World Copper Industry, 1870–1930." *Economic History Review* 39, 3: 392–410.

Schor, J. 2004. *Born to Buy: The Commercialized Child and the New Consumer Culture*. New York: Scribner.

Seager, Allen, and Adele Perry. 1997. "Mining the Connections: Class, Community, Ethnicity and Gender in Nanaimo, BC, 1891." *Social History/Histoire Sociale* 30, 59: 55–76.

Séréni, Jean-Pierre. 2007. *"Les États s'emparent de l'arme pétrolière." Le Monde diplomatique* 54, 636: 1, 18–19.

Shand, H. 2001. "Gene Giants: Understanding the 'Life Industry.'" In Tokar (ed.), *Redesigning Life? The Worldwide Challenge to Genetic Engineering*. London, UK: Zed Books.

Siegel, Arthur. 1983. *Politics and the Media in Canada*. Toronto: McGraw-Hill Ryerson.

Singh Bolaria, B. 2002. "Income Inequality, Poverty, Food Banks, and Health." In Singh Bolaria and Dickinson (eds.), *Health, Illness and Health Care in Canada*. Scarborough: Thomson Nelson.

Sistering. 2000. "Workfare." Retrieved from <http://www.sistering.org/workfare.html>. (Accessed June 2008.)

Smith, Patricia. 1992. *The Next Ten Years: A Conference Discussion Paper*. Sudbury: The Next Ten Years Committee.

Smol, J. P. 2002. *Pollution of Lakes and Rivers: A Palaeoenvironmental Perspective*. London, UK: Arnold.

Snucins, E. et al. 2001. "Effects of Regional Reductions in Sulphur Deposition on the Chemical and Biological Recovery of Lakes within Killarney Park, Ontario, Canada." *Environmental Monitoring and Assessment* 67: 179–94.

Solnit, Rebecca. 2004. *Hope in the Dark: Untold Histories, Wild Possibilities*. New York: Nation Books.

Solski, Mike, and John Smaller. 1985. *Mine Mill: The History of the International Union of Mine, Mill and Smelter Workers in Canada Since 1895*. Ottawa: Steel Rail.

Southern, Frank. 1982. *The Sudbury Incident*. Toronto: York Publishing and Printing.

Sperling, Bert, and Peter Sander. 2007. *Cities Ranked and Rated*, second edition. Hoboken, NJ: Wiley.

Statistics Canada. 1983. *1981 Census of Canada: Census Tracts: Population, Occupied Dwellings,*

Private Households and Census and Economic Families in Private Households, Selected Social and Economic Characteristics, Sudbury. Ottawa: Minister of Supply and Services Canada.

———. 1994. *1991 Census of Canada: Profile of Census Tracts in North Bay, Sault Ste. Marie, Sudbury and Thunder Bay, Part B.* Ottawa: Industry, Science and Technology Canada.

———. 2000/01. *Canadian Community Health Survey.* Ottawa: Statistics Canada.

———. 2001a. *Community Profiles.* Retrieved from <http://www.statcan.ca/bsolc/english/bsolc?catno=93F0053X>. (Accessed June 2008.)

———. 2001b. *Canadian Statistics: Families, households and housing.* Retrieved from <http://www.statcan.ca/english/Pgbd/famili.htm#inc>.

———. 2002. *Survey of Household Spending – 3508. Table 203-0001: Household spending, summary-level categories by province and territory, computed annual total.* Retrieved from <http://cansim2.statcan.ca/cgi-win/CNSMCGI.EXE. (Accessed July 7, 2003.)

———. 2003. *2001 Aboriginal Peoples Survey: Community Profiles (Wikwemikong Unceded 26).* Ottawa: Statistics Canada. Retrieved from <http://www12.statcan.ca/english/profil01aps/statistics.cfm?component=1&community=RES_014&theme=4&lang=E>. (Accessed July 24, 2006.)

———. 2004. *2001 Census of Canada: Profile of Census Divisions and Subdivisions.* Ottawa: Industry Canada.

Stedman, Richard C. et al. 2004. "Resource Dependence and Community Well-Being in Rural Canada." *Rural Sociology* 69, 2: 213–14.

Steedman, Mercedes. 2006. "Godless Communists and Faithful Wives, Gender Relations and the Cold War: Mine Mill and the 1958 Strike Against the International Nickel Company." In Gier and Mercier (eds.), *Mining Women.* New York: Palgrave Macmillan.

Steedman, Mercedes et al. (eds.). 1995. *Hard Lessons: The Mine Mill Union in the Canadian Labour Movement.* Toronto: Dundurn Press.

Stevenson, Ray. 1993. "Acting Justly, and Fearing Not... United We Possess Strength." In *100th Anniversary: The Western Federation of Miners and Canadian Mine, Mill and Smelter Workers.* Sudbury: Mine Mill Local 598.

Stewart, Walter. 1975. "Mister Stewart goes to Washington." *Maclean's* September 4.

Storey, K. 2001. "Fly-in/Fly-out and Fly-over: Mining and Regional Development in Western Australia." *Australian Geographer* 32, 2: 133–48.

Sudbury and District Health Unit. 2001. *The Cost of Eating Well in the Greater City of Sudbury.* Sudbury: Health Promotion Division – Nutrition.

Sudol, Stan. 2004. "Sudbury Dumped on the Slag Heap of History." *The Sudbury Star* February 6: A9.

Suomi, S. 1999. "Developmental Trajectories, Early Experiences, and Community Consequences: Lessons from Studies with Rhesus Monkeys." In Keating and Hertzman (eds.), *Developmental Health and the Wealth of Nations.* New York: Guildford.

Suschnigg, C. et al. 2002. *Survey on Food Bank Use, Sudbury and Region, 2002.* Sudbury: Department of Sociology, Laurentian University.

———. *Dependence on Food Banks, Greater Sudbury, 2003.* Sudbury: Department of Sociology, Laurentian University.

Swift, Jamie. 1977. *The Big Nickel: Inco at Home and Abroad.* Kitchener: Between the Lines.

———. 1991. "New Democrats in Power." *The Whig-Standard* March 2.

Tallichet, Suzanne E. 1995. "Gendered Relations in the Mines and the Division of Labour Underground." *Gender and Society* 9, 6: 697–711

Tanzer, Michael. 1980. *The Race for Resources: Continuing Struggles over Minerals and Fuels.* New York: Monthly Review Press.

Teeple, G. 1995. *Globalization and the Decline of Social Reform.* Toronto: Garamond.

Teitel, M., and K. Wilson. 2001. *Genetically Engineered Food: Changing the Nature of Nature.* South Paris, ME: Park Street Press.

Tester, Jim. 1980. *The Shaping of Sudbury: A Labour View.* Sudbury: Mine, Mill and Smelter Workers Union.

_____. 1994. *Son of a Working Man.* Edited by Mick Lowe and Carol Mulligan. Sudbury: Laurentian Publishing.

Tilleczek, K. 2003. "Terrors of Omission: Schooling and Youth Culture in Canada." Paper presented at the International Sociological Association Mid-term Conference: Critical Education and Utopia, Lisbon, Portugal, September 18–20.

_____. 2004. " The Illogic of Youth Driving Culture." *Journal of Youth Studies* 7, 4: 473–99.

_____. 2006. "Igniting Student Success: Cautious Optimism from the Margins." Invited keynote address, Toronto District School Board. Toronto, February 10.

Tilleczek, K. et al. 2006. "Why Youth Leave School? Ask Those Who Do." *Education Canada* 46, 4: 19–25.

Tilleczek, K., and D.W. Hine. 2006. "The Personal Meaning of Smoking as Health and Social Risk in Adolescence." *Journal of Adolescence* 29, 2: 273–87.

Tilleczek, K., and J.H. Lewko. 2001. "Factors Influencing the Pursuit of Health and Science Career Pathways for Canadian Adolescents in Transition from School to Work." *Journal of Youth Studies* 4, 4: 415–28.

Tjepkema, M. 2002. "The Health of the Off-Reserve Aboriginal Population." Supplement to *Health Reports.* Catalogue 82-003-SIE. Ottawa: Statistics Canada.

Tokar, B. (ed.). 2001. *Redesigning Life? The Worldwide Challenge to Genetic Engineering.* London: Zed Books.

Trembley, R. 1999. "When Children's Social Development Fails." In Keating and Hertzman (eds.), *Developmental Health and the Wealth of Nations.* New York: Guildford.

United Nations. 1965. *The International Convention on the Elimination of All Forms of Racial Discrimination.* Geneva, Switzerland: Office of the High Commissioner for Human Rights. Retrieved from <http://www.unhchr.ch/html/menu3/b/d_icerd.htm>. (Accessed June 2008.)

Valentine, J. Randolph. 2001. *Nishnaabemwin Reference Grammar.* Toronto: University of Toronto Press.

Veinott, G. et al. 2001. "Baseline Metal Concentrations in Coastal Labrador Sediments." *Marine Pollution Bulletin* 42, 3: 187–92.

Vilchek, G.E. et al. 1996. "The Environment in the Russian Arctic: Status Report." *Polar Geography* 20, 1: 20–43.

Volpe, R. et al. 1998. "Images of Children's Rights: A Review of Canadian Policies." In Richardson (ed.), *Children and Youth: An International Odyssey.* Edmonton: Kanata.

VON (Victorian Order of Nurses). 2004. "VON Sudbury Closes its Doors." News release, June 16.

Walkom, Thomas. 1993. "NDP Talks Language it Once Scorned." *Toronto Star* April 10.

_____. 1994. *Rae Days.* Toronto: Key Porter.

Wallace, C. M. 1993. "The 1930s." In Wallace and Thompson (eds.), *Sudbury: Rail Town to Regional Capital.* Toronto: Dundurn Press.

Wallerstein, Immanual 1979. *The Capitalist World Economy.* Cambridge, UK: Cambridge University Press.

Webster's Third New International Dictionary of the English Language. 2002. Edited by Philip Gove et al. Springfield, MA: Merriam-Webster, Inc.

Werner, E., and R. Smith. 1992. *Overcoming the Odds: High-Risk Children from Birth to Adulthood.* Ithaca, NY: Cornell University Press.

WHO (World Health Organization). 1946. *Preamble to the Constitution of the World Health Organization,* as adopted by the International Health Conference, New York, June 19–22. (Official Records of the World Health Organization, No. 2: 100).

_____. 1986. *The Ottawa Charter for Health Promotion.* Geneva, Switzerland: World Health Organization.

_____. 2003. *Strategic Directions for Improving the Health and Development of Children and Adolescents.* Geneva, Switzerland: World Health Organization.

Whynott, Cheryl. 2003. "Industry and Workers: A Report on the Labour Force in Sudbury and the Industrial Composition of the Area." Unpublished placement report in the Labour and Trade Union Studies Program, Laurentian University. Sudbury: Sudbury and District Labour Council.

Wilkinson, Richard G. 1992. "Income Distribution and Life Expectancy." *British Medical Journal* 304, January 18: 165–68.

Willms, D. 1999. "Quality and Inequality in Children's Literacy: The Effects of Families, Schools and Communities." In Keating and Hertzman (eds.), *Developmental Health and the Wealth of Nations.* New York: Guildford.

Wilson, B., with E. Tsoa. 2002. *HungerCount 2002. Eating Their Words: Government Failure on Food Security.* Toronto: Canadian Association of Food Banks.

Winfield, Mark et al. 2002. *Looking Beneath the Surface: As Assessment of the Value of Public Support for the Metal Mining Industry in Canada.* Ottawa: MiningWatch Canada.

Wolfe, David A., and M.S. Gertler. 2003. "Clusters Old and New: Lessons from the ISRN Study of Cluster Development." In Wolfe (ed.), *Clusters Old and New: The Transition to a Knowledge Economy in Canada's Regions.* Montréal: McGill-Queens University Press for Queen's School of Policy Studies.

Wolfson, Michael et al. 1999. "Relation between Income Inequality and Mortality: Empirical Demonstration." *British Medical Journal* 319, October 9: 953–56.

Wong, Chee H. 2003. "The Gini Coefficient of Income Disparity of Ontario by Census Division in 1996 and 2001." *Public Health and Epidemiology Report* 14, 8, September 30: 130–35.

Yount, Kristen. 2005. "Sexualization of Work Roles Among Men Miners: Structural and Gender-Based Origins of 'Harazzment'." In Gruber and Morgan (eds.), *In the Company of Men: Male Dominance and Sexual Harassment.* Boston, MA: Northeastern University Press.

Contributors

François Boudreau has taught at the École de Service social (School of Social Work) at Laurentian University since 1991 and been active in social causes since the 1970s. In 2000 and 2006 François was elected as a Sudbury school trustee to the Conseil scolaire public de Grand Nord de l'Ontario, the French-language public school board. He is an international cooperant in educational development in West Africa. François has a doctorate in Sociology from the University of Québec at Montréal, where he worked with Michel Freitag.

John Closs was born and raised in Sudbury. He has taught carpentry since 1986 at Cambrian College, where he has been active as President of OPSEU Local 655 and on the provincial Executive for OPSEU's college sector. Currently, he is President of the Sudbury and District Labour Council and a representative to Laurentian's Labour and Trade Union Studies Committee. In the early 1980s, John was Artistic Director for Northern Lights Festival Boréal. He is a graduate of Laurentian University, with both a BA and MA in History.

Donald Dennie is a native of Blezard Valley and a graduate of Laurentian University (BA, MA) and Carleton University (MA, PhD). Once a journalist at the daily *Le Droit*, he is a Full Professor at Laurentian University, where he taught in the Department of Sociology from 1974 and was Dean of the Faculties of Humanities and Social Sciences from 1999 until his retirement in 2006. He is the husband of Lucille Pharand and father of Jean, Joëlle, and Danielle, as well as grandfather of Alexie, Anik, and Bennett.

Evan Edinger is Assistant Professor of Geography and Biology at Memorial University of Newfoundland at St John's. After completing his doctorate in Geology at McMaster University, he lived in Sudbury, working as a post-doctoral fellow in Palaeontology at Laurentian University. His current research activities include the environmental impact of tropical mining and the biogeography of deep-sea corals. Evan lives with this wife, Jennifer Rendell, and two children in Torbay, Newfoundland.

Rick Grylls was born in Saskatoon and raised in Garson. He began work as a labourer at Falconbridge in 1972 before he apprenticed in the mines, mill, and smelter as an electrician. He was elected as a steward in 1973, then to other offices, including union Vice-President and Strike Coordinator for the 2000–01 strike, before becoming President of Mine Mill Local 598/CAW in 2001. Rick and Linda have celebrated thirty-three years of marriage and raised two daughters in the town of Falconbridge. Rick was a founder of Workers' Memorial Day, held annually since 1985 on June 20.

Don Kuyek has been a lawyer in private practice in Sudbury for thirty-five years. He grew up in Bankend, Saskatchewan, studied Political Science at the University of Saskatchewan (BA Hons.), and Law at Queen's University (LLB), before coming to Sudbury in 1970. Don has co-authored articles in the *University of Toronto Law Journal* and the *Queen's Law Journal*. He was counsel for Mine Mill during the strike of 2000–01 and counsel for the Sudbury Social Planning Council at the Kimberly Rogers coroner's inquest in 2001.

David Leadbeater was raised in British Columbia and Alberta. He has taught in the Department of Economics at Laurentian University since 1989 and has been a coordinator of the Labour and Trade Union Studies program. He has been active in Laurentian's faculty union and the local labour movement, including as a delegate to and board member of the Sudbury and District Labour Council. He is Dad to two daughters, Kate and Jane. David holds degrees from the University of Alberta, Oxford University, and the University of Toronto.

Laurie McGauley lives and works under the shadow of Inco's Superstack in Sudbury, where her family has been mucking around in the copper dust and sulphur for five generations. Laurie helped found the Sudbury Women's Centre, Sticks and Stones Theatre, and the community anti-poverty organization Better Beginnings Better Futures. In 1996, she started Myths and Mirrors Community Arts, which remains her artistic base. Laurie has worked nationally on cultural policy and has studied cultural theory at Laurentian University, where she is completing an MA.

Bruce McKeigan came to Sudbury from his Ottawa home in 1971 to work for Inco. Soon after starting at the Copper Refinery, where he worked for thirty years as labourer, anode operator, and trainer, Bruce was petitioned on as a steward in Local 6500 USWA. He also served as a health-and-safety representative, member of the Executive Board and of several Bargaining Committees, and delegate to the Sudbury and District Labour Council. After retiring from Inco in 2002, Bruce went on to work as a health-and-safety officer with the federal government.

Cathy Mulroy was born and raised in Sudbury. She has been an hourly rated employee at Inco for the last thirty years. Cathy is a union activist and a member of USWA Local 6500. She is involved in women's issues and was among the women who founded the Sudbury Women's Centre. Cathy is a graduate of the Cambrian College Teacher of Adults Course. She has helped raise six children with her wonderful husband Merv.

K. V. Nagarajan is an Associate Professor at Laurentian University, where he joined the faculty in 1988. He received his education in India, Canada, and the United States, obtaining his doctorate from the State University of New York at Buffalo. His doctoral work involved developing forecasting models of fertility in the United States. K. V. teaches in the Department of Economics as well as the Faculty of Management, and is affiliated to the Centre for Rural and Northern Health Research. His main research interest is in the area of health economics.

Ruth Reyno came to Northern Ontario to teach, first to Elliot Lake in 1976 then to Sudbury in 1980. She has taught for three school boards, one college, and two universities over the last thirty years. Her ongoing concern has been the delivery of education to working-class and rural students. Ruth has been active in the Sudbury Women's Centre, the YWCA, and the Sudbury Community Legal Clinic. Ruth has received a BA in English, a BEd from Queen's University, and an MEd from Acadia University.

Denis St. Pierre was born and raised in Sudbury and Valley East, where he attended École Secondaire Hanmer. After studying Journalism at Cambrian College he began working as a reporter for *The Sudbury Star*. Denis has been active in the Northern Ontario Newspaper Guild (Local 30232) of TNG Canada/ Communication Workers of America for over twenty years and has served as its President since 1997. Denis and his wife, Laura, live in Valley East, where they have raised their blended family of six children.

Roger Spielmann teaches in the Department of Native Studies at Laurentian University. For eleven years prior to joining the Department in 1990, Roger lived with his family in the Algonquin community of Pikogan in north-western Québec, where he was involved in research, teaching, and curriculum projects. Roger has published in academic journals, Native community-based publications, and the book, *"You're So Fat!": Exploring Ojibwe Discourse* (University of Toronto Press 1998). He holds a PhD in Anthropology from the University of British Columbia.

Carole Suschnigg is a sociologist who teaches statistics, research methods and international health issues at Laurentian University. Her past work experience includes community-development projects in New Zealand, Vanuatu, and Northern Ontario. Her current research compares public responses to food insecurity in Uruguay and Canada. Carole studied at the University of Western Ontario and Massey University in New Zealand, and received her doctorate in Sociology from York University.

Kate Tilleczek grew up in Toronto and Barrie and spent summers on Manitoulin Island before moving to Sudbury in 1989. A former school teacher, she is currently Associate Professor in the Department of Sociology at Laurentian University, where she teaches social science research methods, the sociology of childhood and youth, and pursues research on education and child health. Kate is raising two sons, William and Elliott, and tries to find time to paint and write poetry. She received her PhD from the University of Toronto at the Institute of Child Study.